Rough Places Smooth

Moments In A Journey Through Blindness

ANITA PEDEN SHERER

Written and published by Anita Peden Sherer
hello@faithbeyondsight.com
www.faithbeyondsight.com

ISBN: 979-8-9860386-0-5 (paperback)
ISBN: 979-8-9860386-1-2 (Kindle eBook)

Printed in the United States of America

To my son, Jonathan,

You don't remember that terrifying day in 1993. You didn't hear the doctor's words, the four little words that turned our world upside down. You didn't understand what happened, but you felt the hurt, and you fostered the healing.

In the dark and difficult days that followed, you became my sunshine, my reason to get up in the morning. Even when I felt like giving up, my love for you gave me the will to go on. This is my story, but it is also yours, for your life was forever changed on that fateful day.

As you read these words, may you feel my love and be encouraged by my faith. Know that you are never alone. God walks the hard roads of this life with you. Trust Him with your hard things. God can, and He will, make your rough places smooth.

My love forever,

Mom

TABLE OF CONTENTS

INTRODUCTION

Five little letters. One single word. Yet, when the word was first spoken, my heart was crushed. My whole world changed. Fear spiraled. Dreams crashed. Hope vanished.

It was years before I could even say the word myself without panicking. Imagine, all that angst over one single word.

"B-L-I-N-D."

I can still hear the doctor's words ringing in my ears. The room was dark, almost oppressive. He sat in the corner, head bent, staring at a computer screen. He looked up from reviewing the images and uttered four words I will never forget.

"You are legally blind."

"What? How can that be?" I stammered. My heart felt like it would leap out of my chest. "That can't be right!"

But it was right. I was losing my vision to a disease called Retinitis Pigmentosa. I was going blind.

I was 33 years old, a cardiology nurse, and the mother of a toddler. In that one moment, my life was forever changed.

That moment marked a beginning, the beginning of my journey through blindness. In the years that followed, by the grace of God, I found hope beyond hurt, and life beyond loss. Throughout this journey, I have learned several timeless truths:

- Everybody has something.
- Grief is a process, not a one-and-done deal.
- Chronic disease doesn't have to be crippling.
- Love triumphs over tragedy.
- Beauty can come from brokenness.

Hard things happen in this life. How we choose to handle them makes all the difference. When suffering strikes, we can let despair defeat us, or forge on in faith. Choosing to accept the hardships of this life opens the pathway to peace.

INTRODUCTION

In the hands of God, all things are possible. God can take our hard things and work them together for good. When we place our trust in Him, God can, and He will, make our rough places smooth.

This is a story of how dreams are lost and then reborn. This is a story of how God takes a very bad thing and works it for good. This is a story of how faith, hope, and love triumph over adversity. This is a story of grace.

Anita Peden Sherer
December 31, 2021

Part 1
The Journey Begins

OCTOBER 1993

You will seek me and find me when you
seek me with all your heart.

—Jeremiah 29:13 *NIV*

Part 1
The Journey Begins

CHAPTER 1
Something's Not Right

Paper Clips

It all started with a paper clip. Actually, it was about lots of paper clips. The year was 1993, and my 33rd birthday was just around the corner.

Believe it or not, I didn't have a computer to use at work. Everything was handwritten. If something needed to be typed, I paper clipped a note to the handwritten document and sent it to the secretary for typing.

I'm a tidy sort. I like things organized. A place for everything, and everything in its place. I'm also a big fan of notes. There were notes about meetings, lists of ideas for future projects, and to-do lists for next week. Of course, all those lists must be organized, so I kept all the notes in order with my paper clips. I had a preference for the large kind of clips. They simply worked the best.

To my great annoyance, I had a bad habit of knocking those paper clips off my desk. There I'd be, busily working away on my notes when a sweep of my hand would send one of those clips sailing.

One morning, in the midst of my usual paper shuffle, I sent one of those paper clips flying. Pushing back and turning in my rolling office chair, I scanned the floor to retrieve the wayward paper clip, but I couldn't find it. I swiveled around, turning back and forth to no avail. Slightly annoyed but unconcerned, I grabbed another paper clip and went on with my work.

A half hour later, I crossed the room to retrieve a file from the filing cabinet. Returning to my chair, I glanced casually at the floor, and there, staring up at me, was the missing paper clip. It was lying exactly where I had searched for it only minutes before. It was weird, but I didn't give it much thought. It was just a paper clip. I just assumed I was in a hurry and simply missed it.

CHAPTER 1
Something's Not Right

But then it happened again, and again, and again. It was certainly odd, annoying even, but I kept shrugging it off until stranger things started happening.

I could ignore the paper clips. They were small, after all. Still, when my pen began to vanish, it was hard not to notice.

I remember the afternoon when I knocked my pen off the desk while answering the phone. No big deal. Yet, for the life of me, I couldn't find that black pen. I swiveled back and forth in my chair, scanning the white tile floor. No luck, no pen. I frowned, grabbed another pen, and went on with my work.

An hour or so later, I rose and walked across the room to the filing cabinet. As I returned to my desk, I glanced at the floor, and there right beside my chair, lay the black pen. It was lying right where I had searched so diligently the hour before. It was exactly where I thought I had dropped it. "Now that is weird! What is wrong with me? Slow down, Anita, you're going too fast. Take your time."

That was not the last time I would say those words to myself. In fact, the frequency of that mantra would increase dramatically in the months to come.

These odd things kept happening, and I kept brushing them off. I was a new mother managing a busy two-year-old boy at home. I was working part-time as a Cardiology Clinical Nurse Specialist. My work days were hectic, with lots of varied responsibilities. The job could be quite stressful and demanding. I was juggling a lot, trying to balance life in the world of work with that of home.

"I'm just easily distracted. I have too much on my mind." Those were the things I would say to myself, but the reality was that I had been having some difficulty with my vision ever since my son Jonathan was born. I had noticed little things at home, but didn't pay them much attention. When Jonathan was only 3 months old, my husband Eric started a playtime routine after supper. Spreading a play blanket on the carpet of our sun porch, Eric would pull out a few toys to entertain Jonathan while I finished the dishes. By the time I joined them to sit cross-legged on the floor, the sun was setting, the light beginning to fade. I kept noticing how the light seemed to flicker. The room around me seemed a bit distorted, almost moving like someone had turned on a tiny strobe light. I hadn't noticed this in the daytime. Perhaps it was just the way the light was fading at sunset. Still, I was puzzled because I didn't remember it doing that before.

I kept noticing the flickering light until I finally asked Eric about it one evening. "Does the light seem jumpy out here?" The quizzical look he gave me told me he wasn't seeing the same thing I was. So, what was I seeing?

By the time Jonathan was nine months old, I had really started noticing a difference in my vision. I decided that my contacts needed an adjustment and made an appointment with my optometrist. Over the next year or so, we must have changed my contacts four or five times. I had high hopes for each adjustment, but things remained fuzzy and distorted no matter what we tried. My doctor was incredibly patient with me, trying diligently to adjust the prescription, but somehow, it just wasn't right.

I particularly noticed the difference at night. Really, anything I did at night seemed different. When working evening or night shift, I seemed to need more light in the patient rooms. In order to do a task, I had to turn on a light. This seemed strange because I used to be able to do such tasks with only the illumination of a flashlight.

Daytime tasks were not as difficult, but I still noticed weird things. It seemed to take me forever to dispense medications. When several nurses were all using the med cart at the same time, I was easily befuddled. It was hard to check the medications against the patient's record. It seemed to take me longer to make sure I had the right drug.

Untangling IV lines was another task that seemed harder, taking longer than it should. Given that I was teaching and doing project work for the bulk of my time, I mostly shrugged it off as being out of practice. Things were starting to mount up though. Something just didn't seem right. "It must be my prescription. These contacts just aren't right."

Driving home at night was tricky. I was driving down roads I knew by heart, but I was struggling to see where to turn, particularly left-hand turns. The headlights from the other cars almost blinded me. If it was dark and raining, I became really nervous.

The truth was that I had never liked driving at night. My grandfather had put me behind the wheel at age 12, teaching me to drive in the pasture of his farm. One of the happiest days of my life was the day I got my driver's license. I adored driving, yet from the outset, I never felt comfortable driving in the dark. I remember that even in high school, I would always let someone else drive at night if I could. Once again, I didn't think much about all this.

Then came the fender benders. I had never had an accident in all the years of driving. Yet, in the course of 18 months, I had two fender benders. Both times, I knew I was not following too closely. Both times, I saw the person's tail lights come on and immediately started braking. However, both times, I could not get stopped in time.

"I have too much on my mind. I need to pay better attention. I need to not follow so closely." These were the words I said in my head, but I knew I was not following too closely. No one was hurt, and neither accident was a big deal.

Next came the battle with the little red rocking chair. It was my chair from childhood. We had given it a fresh coat of red paint, and Jonathan loved it. As soon as he was able to walk, he started flopping himself into that little red rocking chair. I brought it into the kitchen, placing it next to a cabinet near the sitting area where we have two recliners. It was fun for Jonathan to have his own little chair near ours. Not that he sat that often, mind you, but it was still cute to see him sitting there near us.

The problem was that as I was working in the kitchen and traveling back and forth to the bedrooms or sunporch, I would run into that rocker. Over and over again, it happened. I had bruises on my shins. It didn't make sense. "I know that thing is there. Why do I keep running into it? Slow down, Anita, take your time. You are rushing again."

Finally, there was the accident that I never told my husband Eric about. I was just too embarrassed. I also thought that he would think I was losing my mind. Perhaps I was. I certainly seemed to be making a mess of things.

I was late for work with Jonathan tucked in his car seat behind me. Headed to the babysitter, I was driving down a road not too far from our home. Suddenly, I realized that I had an 8:30 AM meeting. There was no way I was going to be able to drop Jonathan off at the babysitter and get to Greensboro in time for that meeting. I needed to let someone know I would be late. Those were the days without cell phones, if you can imagine that.

I was passing by the local grocery store, and I knew there was a payphone outside the store. I swung left quickly, headed straight for that payphone. The sun was just over the horizon, shining brightly across the parking lot. The sun blinded me for a moment as I raced toward the store. I knew I was going too fast, but I wasn't worried since hardly anyone else was around. Suddenly, I heard a crash. I had hit the storage rack for the shopping carts, plowing right into one of the railings. I slammed on the brakes and jumped out of the car. There was no damage to my car, but I had bent the frame of the storage rack. I guess it was just a little tap, but I stood there in the parking lot, shaking my head. Here came the mantra in my head once more.

I remember running in the store and handing the manager a $20 bill because I felt so bad about damaging the storage rack. He laughed and said it was not necessary, but I told him to take it anyway. I made my phone call and got back in the car. Even though I would be late, I slowed down. It just wasn't worth it.

That was the last straw. Something just wasn't right. For more than a year, I had been noticing these odd things. I kept shrugging them off, blaming the busyness of motherhood and work for leaving me tired and distracted. But the oddities were piling up, and I couldn't ignore them anymore. By this point, I was seeing a pattern that bothered me. I still wasn't sure what to do, but I made an eye appointment anyway.

The Little Light

I sat in the exam chair in the optometrist's office. Dr. Woodard was studying my chart. He began the exam, patiently flipping the lenses back and forth as I studied the eye chart.

In a soft, calm voice, he instructed, "Tell me which one is better. This one or this one?"

We went through the usual lenses and then, he paused. "So, tell me again what you're having problems with."

"Well, I just don't know what's wrong with me," I began uncertainly. My odd story came tumbling out. I started with the paper clips, progressed to the driving issues, and then followed up with my night shift struggles. Almost as an aside, I mentioned running into the little red rocking chair.

I was watching the doctor closely as I told my strange story. When I described my bruised shins brought on by the bumps into the little red rocker, I saw Dr. Woodard frown. He paused for a long moment, lost in thought, his brow furrowed in concentration. Without a word, he turned and began flipping back-and-forth through my chart studying it carefully. Then, he started asking more questions.

The more I said, the more concerned he seemed to be. I felt my anxiety ramping up. It was one thing to notice these things individually. It was another thing to link all the odd things together. After all, as a nurse, I was trained to assess symptoms and look for patterns that would signal a potential diagnosis. As I answered the doctor's questions, I began to see a pattern emerging. That pattern worried me.

"Anita, I want to do a visual field test on you."

I nodded hesitantly. That didn't sound good.

Dr. Woodard showed me the machine in the far corner of the room, a round white dome mounted on a pedestal. He ushered me over to the machine, offering me a seat in a rolling office chair. He instructed me to place my chin on the chin rest situated in front of the large white dome.

"Do you see the little black dot in the center of the dome? I want you to stare at that dot. Once the test starts, don't move your head or your eyes. Just stare at the dot." Dr. Woodard applied an eye patch over my right eye and handed me a black cord with a small buzzer on the end.

"The machine will begin flashing a small light on the back of the white dome. The lights will move around across the dome. Whenever you see the little light, just press the buzzer. The machine will record your responses. OK?"

"OK, I think I can handle this." I smiled at him to hide the sick feeling that was stirring in my gut. I recalled a bit of what I knew about visual field testing. I understood that as the test progresses, the computer records a notation of each time the buzzer is pressed. These notations identify where each of the small lights are seen, offering something akin to a topographical map of the different areas of the visual field.

Staring at the big black dot, I held the buzzer tightly, poised to press when ready. "When is it going to start?"

I felt Dr. Woodard come closer to me, His tall frame bending low to peer over my shoulder. "Are you seeing any little lights?"

"No, not so far." I could feel him standing right behind my chair, but he said nothing. After a minute or two, I started seeing a few lights and began pressing the buzzer.

"Anita, are you seeing more of the lights now?"

"I'm seeing some now, yeah."

Dr. Woodard made no comment, but continued to stand right behind me. There was something in his silence that did not feel right. I could sense his concern. Warning bells were ringing in my head. It did not seem like there were enough flashes of light. I thought to myself, "I'm not seeing these lights like I should. What in the world is wrong with me?"

Stopping the test, the doctor removed the eye patch and then used it to cover the left eye. We repeated the test on the right eye without further conversation.

Once the test on the right eye was complete, Dr. Woodard asked me to have a seat in the exam chair while he studied the computer printout.

Finishing his review of the report, he sat down in front of me and began asking more questions. "I would like to take a look at the back of your eye, at the retina. I am going to need to dilate your eyes, if that's OK?"

I consented, and he reached for the eye drops, putting a couple of drops in each of my eyes. "It will take a little while for your eyes to dilate. I will be back in a few minutes to take a look."

As he stepped out of the room, I slumped back in the chair and let out a big sigh. "I have a bad feeling about this," I said out loud.

When Dr. Woodard returned, he spent a long time staring through the lens into the back of my eyes. I was quiet, giving him time to concentrate. Finally, he rolled back in his chair and looked at me.

"Dr. Woodard, is there something wrong?"

"Yes, Anita, I think there is," he said quietly.

I pressed him for information. He explained that I had visual field changes. He was not quite sure what was going on, but thought we needed to do further testing. Being the nurse, I pushed for more specifics. "Tell me what are the likely possibilities."

He explained that it could just be an inflammation in the eye that could be easily treated or perhaps some other conditions.

"Like what?"

The good doctor reluctantly explained that it could be one of several possibilities such as a pituitary tumor, multiple sclerosis, another neurological condition I had never heard of, or perhaps a retinal problem.

"This doesn't sound good," I blurted out.

"I am not quite sure what is going on, but I think we need some more tests before we jump to any conclusions. I'd like to schedule an MRI of the brain."

I swallowed hard. He wanted to schedule the MRI as quickly as possible. I agreed and he said he would have his office work on arranging the test.

His eyes were full of kindness as I stood to leave. "Now Anita, don't worry too much. We will get this figured out. It is probably just a little infection or inflammation in your eyes. But just to be safe, we need to rule out the other things."

He reached for my hand and gave it a squeeze. I nodded and let out a deep sigh.

I understood his message. "Let's get the tests first and see what they show. Don't jump to conclusions." I knew he was right. My clinical background told me you rule out the worst first. I just hoped it was not the worst.

Waiting

I left the doctor's office feeling a bit shaky. My eyes were still dilated, and it was tricky to see. I drove myself home mostly because there was not another choice.

Later that afternoon, I told Eric about my visit, but I minimized the situation. "It's probably just a little inflammation in the eye, but it's a good idea to get it checked out."

My husband is a man of few words, preferring to think about something for a while before commenting. I, on the other hand, am a verbal processor. I usually shower him with way too many words, but there was something holding me back from giving him a lot of detail about my visit to Dr. Woodard. It was as if I didn't want to say it out loud, so that maybe it wouldn't be real.

Eric concurred with the idea that I needed to follow up on the findings of the visual field test. I noted the question in his eyes

CHAPTER 1
Something's Not Right

when I mentioned an MRI, but his stoic expression hid his true feelings on the subject.

My little two-year-old tolerated our serious discussion for a little while, but soon grew impatient. Jonathan was used to being the center of attention and decided it was time to adjust our focus. With his short blonde hair and huge brown eyes, he had his mother wrapped around his finger; his father too, for that matter. "Mama, come play. Daddy, see my car." We really didn't mind the interruption. Neither of us knew what else to say on the matter.

I had seen Dr. Woodard late on a Friday afternoon. The date was October 1, 1993. There was no way to schedule the MRI until Monday morning. I had to wait the entire weekend before I even knew when the test would be scheduled.

I tried not to worry, but I had this knot in the pit of my stomach that wouldn't go away. Eric said nothing more on the topic, but I think he was worried too.

I vacillated between fretting and praying. "Lord, please don't let this be something serious!" I kept replaying the symptoms in my mind. I couldn't stop thinking about that little light. "What in the world is wrong with me?"

I decided not to mention the tests to anyone else. I didn't even call my parents. "Better not to worry anyone until I have more information." At least that's what I told myself.

Things changed though when I caught up with my across-the-street neighbor Tami. One look at her kind face, and the whole story came gushing out.

Over the preceding months, Tami and I had grown quite close, forging a strong friendship while our children played on the swings or in the sandbox together. Like me, Tami is a way-out-there extrovert. She loves to talk and has never met a stranger. It was wonderful to have another young mother in the neighborhood, and I found our conversations easy and quite therapeutic.

Tami listened carefully as she always does. While she was obviously concerned, she agreed we needed to just wait and see. I knew she would start praying, and I surely needed those prayers.

On Monday morning, I got a call that the test could not be scheduled until Tuesday evening. The doctor also suggested that I call and make an appointment with a neurologist. That way, once we had the test results, I would have an appointment already scheduled if we needed it. I made the call. There were no available appointments for two weeks. More waiting. More worrying.

Suffocating

I had never had a panic attack before, but I did on that Tuesday evening when I found myself trapped inside an MRI machine. Between the anguish of an uncertain diagnosis and the pounding noises reverberating all around my head, I practically came unglued.

The MRI appointment was scheduled for 8PM on that Tuesday evening. Eric and I had left Jonathan with Tami. Jonathan and her daughter Linsey had become best buddies, and we knew he would be well entertained at their house.

As we headed for Greensboro, I started feeling queasy. I was really nervous. I tried so hard to think that this was routine, repeating to myself over and over that this test would prove that the problem was nothing serious. Dr. Woodard was just ruling out the worst case scenario first. "I'm sure that's all this is. We just need to rule out the big stuff. It'll be fine."

Call it nursing intuition, but I did not like the way things were going. I could see a pattern and that grouping of symptoms made me cringe inside. Deep down in my gut, I knew something was terribly wrong.

On the drive over, Eric was very quiet. I don't think he knew what to say. Neither did I, so we rode in silence.

When we arrived at the imaging center, I went and checked in. Eric took a seat in the waiting room and pulled out his book. Settling

CHAPTER 1
Something's Not Right

into the seat beside him, I felt him squeeze my hand, but he remained mute.

I certainly knew what an MRI was all about, having taken lots of patients to radiology over the years, monitoring them through all types of procedures. I had seen an MRI machine up close. I had taught patients about what to expect. I had told my patients not to worry. "It's not a big deal. It doesn't last long."

Yet, when the technician called me back to the procedure room and began prepping me for the test, it sure did feel like a big deal. The technician helped me up onto the hard table and positioned my head before sliding me head first into the MRI machine. Lying there, surrounded by that white circular dome, I thought I would suffocate.

"Now Ms. Sherer, please lie still and don't move your head." The machine began with its pounding, pulsating noises, and my heart began to race. I couldn't catch my breath. The walls were closing in on me. I was about to jump out of my skin. "I'm going to smother. I can't do this."

I knew how important it was to finish the test. I knew I had to be still. The technicians were talking to me, reassuring me, but their reassurances couldn't reach inside my panicked brain. The anxiety kept rising, and my chest felt like it would explode. "I've got to calm down. I need to finish this."

It is amazing how you finally turn to God when all your options are lost. They say there are no atheists on the battlefield. I can understand that. It is one thing to doubt God exists when everything is going your way. However, when the chips are down, and your world is falling apart, you really want God to be there. You want some help.

I have always had a strong faith. I come from a long line of staunch Scotch-Irish Presbyterians. I was brought up in church. While I had slacked off of regular attendance during college and my early 20s, I was now active in a local Methodist church. I prayed often, read my Bible occasionally, and attended church regularly.

Yet, as I lay there panicking, feeling like the air was being sucked out of my chest, I began to pray with a fervor I had not experienced in a long time. I needed God, and I so wanted Him to be there. "Help me, Lord! I can't do this. Please let this be OK."

As if to answer this plea, the words of Psalm 23 popped into my head. Now I had learned lots of Bible verses over the years. Yet, as I lay there trying to be still, Psalm 23 was the only scripture I could remember. I had learned that passage as a little girl, and the words flowed back to me in that desperate moment. "The Lord is my Shepherd. I shall not want" (Psalm 23:1 *KJV*).

"Oh Lord, I can't do this!"

"Yea, though I walk through the valley of the shadow of death, I will fear no evil, for Thou art with me, Thy rod and Thy staff, they comfort me" (Psalm 23:4 *KJV*).

"O Lord, help me!"

I repeated the Psalm over and over, focusing on the words, trying hard to stop the panic bubbling up inside me. Then the words of the Lord's Prayer popped in my brain. "Our Father which art in heaven, Hallowed be Thy Name. Thy Kingdom come, Thy will be done" (Luke 11:2 *KJV*).

"O Lord, why is this happening to me?... The Lord is my Shepherd, I shall not want..."

When the technicians wheeled me out of that long, narrow tube, I felt like I was being released from a deep, dark tomb. I could breathe again.

The test was complete, but the waiting was not. Eric and I drove home with little conversation. I don't know why, but I couldn't even bring myself to share the panic attack I had endured while lying in that coffin-like machine. I was out of words, a true rarity for me.

As we neared our home, I asked Eric to drop me off at our house before picking Jonathan up from Tami's. I knew my talkative friend would want the details of the procedure from me, and I just didn't have the words to offer. When Eric returned with Jonathan, we began the nightly routines despite the late hour.

CHAPTER 1
Something's Not Right

It was Thursday morning before Dr. Woodard called with the test results. The MRI was negative. That was a relief. There was nothing seriously wrong in the brain.

"Well, if the MRI is negative, then what else can it be?"

"Perhaps it is something with the eye, with the retina. I think we need to check it out further. I would like for you to see a specialist." Dr. Woodard was matter-of-fact in his tone, but I could sense his concern.

His office called back later in the day. The appointment with the ophthalmologist was made for the following Tuesday, October 12.

I tried not to worry. It had been almost a week since that first office visit. Now I had to wait another five days for the specialist appointment. That much time makes you think all kinds of thoughts that you ought not to think. I kept telling myself that it would be okay, that it would be easy to fix, and of course, I kept on praying.

CHAPTER 2
The Diagnosis

Four Little Words

Tuesday finally arrived. I was scheduled for a late morning appointment at an eye clinic in Greensboro. Since my eyes would be dilated as part of the evaluation, we thought it best that I not drive myself to the appointment. Eric had offered to accompany me, but he had a lot going on at work. I reassured him that I was fine to go by myself.

While I was still quite concerned, more than anything, I just wanted to get this over with. I wanted to know what was wrong and start fixing it.

We asked an old friend if he would take me to the clinic and drop me off. That way, Eric could just swing by after work and pick me up. We thought it was a workable plan.

Our friend dropped me off at the front entrance, and I checked in with the registration desk staff. After a short wait, I was ushered into an exam room where the technician asked the typical questions. Everything seemed pretty routine. The technician put me through some preliminary testing, and then the doctor came in.

The ophthalmologist was a short, stocky man who briskly strode into the room without a pause for introductions. His body language conveyed that he was a busy man with little time for small talk. There was an air of impatience in the way he moved or asked questions.

He reviewed the papers that I had brought with me from my optometrist and then began his questions. I tried to answer as best I could, but his rapid-fire manner kept me to short responses. I felt rushed to tell my story. He clearly was not interested in a lot of detail.

Reviewing my visual field test results from Dr. Woodard, he stated that the results did not make sense. "This can't be accurate."

CHAPTER 2
The Diagnosis

With a wave of his hand, he directed me to take a seat at the machine across the room. It was the white circular dome again. He was going to repeat the visual field test.

I settled into the chair, buzzer in my hand, chin on the chin rest. The test began.

In a few moments, I heard him sigh. "Are you seeing the lights? Press the buzzer when you see them!"

He repeated his question several times, his tone growing more and more impatient. "You have to be seeing more of these lights. Keep your eye straight ahead and press the buzzer when you see them. You should be able to see them now," he snapped haughtily.

"I don't know. I'm having trouble seeing them." I knew I should be seeing the lights, and once again, they weren't there. I felt his impatience, and sweat began to trickle down the middle of my back. My heart was thumping in my chest, my brain spinning so fast I almost felt dizzy.

We repeated the test in the other eye with the same set of difficulties. Abruptly, he stood up and told me to sit back. He jerked the paper from the printer and reviewed the test results. "If this is all you can see, you must have Stargardt's disease." He threw the comment out there flippantly, like it was no big deal.

"What is that? What does it mean?"

"It's a retinal disease. We need a retinal angiogram to confirm it." Without another word of explanation, he turned to the technician and instructed her to get me set up for the angiogram.

As he stepped through the office doorway, he muttered, "I'll talk to you after the angiogram."

I sat there staring at the empty doorframe, stunned and confused. "What just happened? What does all this mean?"

I had no clue what Stargardt's disease was, but I did know about the retina. A retinal disease did not sound good. This was not a simple inflammation or infection to be treated with a few eye drops. This sounded serious, and my stomach churned in response.

The technician ushered me to a busy waiting room. I was to wait there until they called me for the test. I sank into the chair vaguely aware of the constant stream of people passing back and forth just inches from my feet. My mind was racing, trying to put the pieces of the puzzle together. The whole thing seemed surreal.

One thing was clear. I did not like this doctor. I was really annoyed at his abrupt and flippant manner. I vacillated between indignant frustration and unbridled panic. "I have to calm down. I have to do this test. Just get through the test and see what happens." I kept the self-talk going, trying to hold it together.

After about an hour wait, I heard the technician calling my name. I entered a dimly lit room and took a seat in the exam chair. The technician was polite as he explained what was involved in a retinal angiogram.

He put the drops in my eyes to dilate them and then started an IV, explaining that the test would require dye to be injected. The dye would allow the retina to be illuminated, and therefore, highlight what, if any, problems existed. Once everything was ready, the doctor would join him to view the images of my retina.

The technician injected the dye and had me place my chin on a chin rest with my eyes against a lens apparatus. Once I was in position, I heard the doctor enter the room. He and the technician talked back and forth as the images were collected. Neither of them spoke to me during this process. I tried to hold still as instructed, but it was all I could do to not scream in anxious frustration.

When the test was over, the technician instructed me to sit back and relax. The doctor sat in the corner staring at the images on the computer screen. He finally stood and turned to face me from across the room.

"You do have Stargardt's disease. Your retinas are badly deteriorated." His tone was matter-of-fact, like he was placing a fast-food order.

I felt like I had been punched in the gut. "What? What do you mean?"

CHAPTER 2
The Diagnosis

"You have Stargardt's disease. There is significant damage to both of your retinas."

"What? I still don't understand."

"You are legally blind."

"What? How can that be?"

He had turned away from me and was making some comments to the technician in a low voice, not even listening to my question.

"This can't be right," I blurted out. My mind was reeling, trying to grasp what all this meant. It made no sense.

"So... can I drive with this?" Obviously, I was still very confused about what all this meant.

He turned to look at me again. "What? No, you shouldn't be driving."

"How can that be? But...but...I'm a nurse!"

That stopped him in his tracks. He looked at me intently. "You're a nurse?" There was a tone of incredulousness in his voice.

"Yes. I'm a nurse. I need to be able to drive."

He paused, staring at me for a long moment. "Well, maybe we need to get a second opinion."

At this point, I got mad. "You bet we're going to get a second opinion." My voice was louder than it should have been, and my face was no doubt flushed with anger. I could not believe this man's attitude.

He stood, crossed the room, and opened the door. Calling out to the group of staff at the nurses' station immediately across from the doorway, he bellowed out, "I need an appointment with Dr. Machemer at Duke for a second opinion." Then, he turned as if to leave the room.

"Wait! But can I drive? What about going back to work?"

"The staff will go over all the paperwork with you. We'll see what Dr. Machemer says."

He turned abruptly and walked out of the room. That was the last I saw of him.

I thought the walls were going to cave in around me. I wasn't sure if I could get up out of that chair. The technician was kind enough as he ushered me out the other door. He explained that another staff member would come and get me to review my discharge instructions. He nodded and walked away, leaving me standing beside an empty chair.

"What just happened? How can this be?" I thought to myself, my head spinning, my hands shaking. I took a seat before I passed out on the floor. No one seemed to notice. Everyone just passed me by like it was the most routine of days.

For me, this day was anything but routine. I felt dazed, almost disoriented. I had no one with me, no one to cling to, no one to lean on for support, and clearly, no one there cared. I have never felt more alone in my whole life.

I stared at the wall across from me, trying to make sense of what had just happened. My nurse brain was beginning to put the pieces together, analyzing the symptoms and test results.

Snippets of the doctor's words floated in and out of my mind. But the words that wouldn't leave, the four words that kept resurfacing were, "You are legally blind."

After about twenty minutes, the discharging nurse called me to her office. In a brisk, efficient tone, she spelled out my instructions which were nothing more than listing my appointment date for the second opinion, and that I could return to work at my discretion. She skipped over any instructions about driving.

I could hardly focus on anything she said. I just wanted out of there. I wanted to be left alone. I wanted Eric to get there and get me out of this awful place.

Finding a seat in the waiting area near the front entrance, I watched for Eric to arrive. People passed by to and fro. I observed these passing figures as if I was in some other dimension.

My thoughts were swirling. I wanted to scream at the passersby. "Do you know what just happened to me? How can you all be so calm?"

CHAPTER 2
The Diagnosis

I started admonishing myself, "Hold it together, Anita, you can't fall apart right here. Not here, not now."

I was never so glad to see Eric's little black truck in all my days. As he pulled into the parking lot, I jumped up from my seat, headed for the door. It was pouring down rain as I ran out to the truck. I pulled open the door, jumped in, and slammed the door shut behind me like some goblin was chasing me across the parking lot.

Eric looked up and asked calmly, "How did it go?" I burst into tears, mumbling almost incoherently.

Placing a gentle hand on my arm, he said, "Tell me what happened."

The rain was pounding on the roof of the truck as the wipers scraped back and forth across the wet windshield. I took a deep breath, and the whole story started tumbling out.

I finished the story, tears still streaming down my cheeks. I sniffed as we sat in silence. Eric just sat there, staring at the windshield wipers moving back and forth. He was stunned. He had no idea what to say. Neither did I.

After a long moment of quiet, he put the truck in gear, and we started for home. What else was there to say?

I stared out the window as the raindrops ran down the glass. As the shock began to pass, I grew more and more angry.

I could not believe how poorly I had been treated by that doctor. I was stunned that he had been totally oblivious to how difficult that news was for me. His approach in giving that terrible news to a patient was despicable. I could not believe his callous arrogance. "How could he care so little when he just ruined my life?"

I was thankful for the second opinion because I doubted whether his diagnosis was even correct. "Does he even know what he is talking about? Can I even believe this diagnosis?"

Still, as much as I tried to talk myself into doubting his diagnosis, I knew something was terribly wrong. I felt it in my gut. This was not good.

"And Thursday is my birthday. Thirty-three years old, and my life is falling apart. What a birthday present..."

More Waiting

It felt like I was living in a dream. Actually, it was more like a nightmare. When I woke up the next morning, I just couldn't go to work. I was too much of a mess. I called my boss Lynn, briefly explained the situation, and went back to bed.

I kept Jonathan home with me that day. He was a good distraction, and I certainly needed one. The hot tears of the day before had dried up, leaving numbness in their wake.

I kept thinking about the phone calls we had made the night before. Our parents were devastated, our friends, shocked. It was all I could do to get through the calls and then collapse.

Dr. Woodard had called in the late evening to check on me. When I conveyed the diagnosis and essential information, there was a long pause on the other end of the line. I could tell he was upset by this news. When I told him about the poor treatment I had received, he was genuinely apologetic. He was relieved to hear I had an appointment at Duke for the second opinion and promised to check on me after that appointment.

During the heart-wrenching phone call with my parents, they had declared that they were coming up to be with me. It was a comfort to know that they were on their way, but I wondered what I would say to them when they arrived. I knew they were as heartbroken as I was.

Jonathan seemed to sense that something wasn't right. Instead of entertaining himself with his toys on the porch, he followed me around the house. He came hunting for me as I made the bed, bringing me a toy in hopes I'd stop and play with him. As I did the dishes, he brought a couple of his little cars into the kitchen and plopped on the floor near me. He wasn't really whining, just more clingy than usual. As I did my household duties, I tried to pay him some attention, but my mind was a thousand miles away.

CHAPTER 2
The Diagnosis

My thoughts were spinning as if stuck on a merry-go-round that I couldn't get off. "How can he be right? This can't be happening. This can't be real."

I vacillated between shock and anger. I had a hard time even contemplating the possibility that I was losing my vision. It just seemed impossible to believe.

My furious anger at the ophthalmologist had not abated. I could not believe his lack of compassion. As a nurse, I had worked with many physicians over the years. While there were always a few who lacked a positive bedside manner, the majority of the physicians I had worked with really cared about their patients. I could not believe the callousness with which that ophthalmologist had delivered the news that I was legally blind.

I could understand being busy. I could comprehend the hectic schedule. I could even understand having limited time available to talk with multiple patients. What I could not fathom was his total unwillingness to sit down, look me in the eye, and explain the diagnosis more clearly. There was no opportunity to ask questions. There was no concern about whether I had someone with me to support me or to take me home. It was simply unbelievable.

I think the fact that I was a nurse made it even more awful. I knew how he should have shared such news with a patient. I knew it could have been handled better. After all, I doubted that he ran across a patient like me every day. "How many times in a day does he tell someone they are going blind?"

Because of his lack of concern and his refusal to explain things adequately, I could not help but doubt his diagnosis. While I replayed the conversations in my head, I kept thinking to myself, "Maybe he's wrong."

Of course, I would look up Stargardt's Disease and read about it. I could go to the medical library at the hospital and see what I could find. I doubted that the information would make me feel any better, but I wanted to know anyway. The nurse in me knew it was best to deal with such things in a straightforward manner. I had to know. "But was he right?"

There was nothing to do but wait. More waiting. The appointment at Duke with Dr. Machemer could not be scheduled until the following Monday. I had to get through the next five days. I reached down and picked up my wiggly little boy. "Let's go find a puzzle, buddy." Denial and distraction was the best plan that I could muster.

Bearing Pansies

I heard the car door slam. I opened the back door and bounded down the steps. As I crossed the carport, I caught sight of Mary headed my way. She came, bearing pansies. A whole flat of the colorful, smiling flowers was nestled in her arms.

My tall, gracious friend was smiling as she greeted me. "I brought you something to do." She held up the flat of happy flowers as if they were a trophy I had won. Her smile was genuine, while her eyes were moist with tears. At nearly 5'11"tall, Mary is one of the women in my life that I literally look up to. She towers above me, but it's more than that. I have always admired her deep, abiding faith. We bonded like sisters the instant we met, and I can always count on her for wise counsel.

My eyes glistened with tears as I returned her smile. She sat the flat of plants on the pavement and bent low to give me a tight hug.

Trailing behind Mary, my friend and supervisor, Lynn, quietly stepped forward. Short in stature and frugal with words, Lynn is one of those friends who will step up to the plate and go to bat for you. In a faltering voice, she stammered out, "We wanted to come check on you." Strongly introverted, Lynn had a habit of guarding her emotions carefully, but I knew from the shakiness of her voice that she was struggling with the seriousness of the situation.

I bent down to hug Lynn, tears welling up in my eyes. "Thank you guys for coming. It means a lot."

CHAPTER 2
The Diagnosis

My feelings were so raw. I had no idea what to say. Imagine that, me who is never at a loss for something to say was almost tongue-tied.

Mary's eyes were wet as she rushed into small talk, trying to defuse the emotion of the moment. I was grateful for the change of focus.

They followed me into the house, and we settled on the sun porch. Since both Mary and Lynn live almost an hour away from me, we rarely got a chance to visit outside of work. It had been several months since either of them had seen Jonathan. They were amazed at how much he had grown.

Mary wasted no time in getting reacquainted with my outgoing little two-year-old. She plopped down on the carpet, and Jonathan began showing her his toys. He was delighted to entertain this tall lady who sat cross legged beside him, and the two of them had a lively chat.

Lynn sat across from me, searching for the right thing to say. Her eyes locked on mine as she asked, "So…what did the doctor say?"

Mary was watching me closely as I took in the question. I knew from the tone of Lynn's voice and the look in Mary's eyes that they expected an honest answer. There was no need for polite subterfuge with these two ladies. They really wanted to know what was going on and how I was doing.

I answered honestly, "It's not good." I relayed the events of my appointment the previous day, and they both shared my fury at the doctor's callous delivery of the diagnosis.

Lynn asked a few more questions, while Mary managed to entertain Jonathan and still keep an ear on the discussion.

I honestly don't recall the substance of the conversation. It was a bit disjointed as Jonathan vied for our attention. It was just as well, because I had no words to express how I was really feeling. They knew that. Intuitively, they understood my dazed emotional state.

These were my friends, real friends, the kind that really know you and accept you for who you are. I had worked side by side with these women day in, day out, dealing with the life and death struggles inherent in managing a busy cardiology nursing unit. We were three members of a five-person leadership team. Donna and Katie were back at the hospital, holding down the fort. We were a tightly knit group, working in tandem, capitalizing on each other's strengths. We were good together, highly respected by our nursing staff. More than that, we were friends. We truly cared about each other, a bond that reached far beyond the hospital walls.

I had worked with Lynn for five years, and she was now the nurse manager of our nursing unit. I had the utmost respect for Lynn. I appreciated her calm, determined leadership style that offered the right mix of caring support with clear accountability. While she was my boss, our interactions were never hierarchical. We were teammates solving problems together, and we were good friends. I could count on Lynn.

Mary had become part of the team two and a half years earlier as I prepared for my maternity leave. She had joined our team to job share with me, both of us desiring part-time work schedules to be home with our young sons. The arrangement had worked beautifully with the added bonus that Mary and I had become the best of friends. She knew me so well that I often joked that she could read my mind. Just being in her presence was soothing to my unsteady nerves.

They did not stay long, but their visit had been just what I needed at that moment. To know that you had real friends who loved you, who cared about your pain, who were praying for you, well, it meant the world to me. They could not fix it, though they would have if they could. All they could do was be there, to reach out with love, and to pray. Oh, how I needed that.

I had told Lynn that I needed a few days off, and she immediately concurred. "Take whatever time you need. We'll take care of things."

As Mary opened the car door to leave, she called out with a smile. "Now you get to work. I expect to see pretty pansies when I come back."

CHAPTER 2
The Diagnosis

I didn't feel much like planting pansies, but I knew why she had brought them. I needed something to do. I needed to keep going. There was still a long, uncertain road ahead and I needed to stay the course.

Heartbroken

I heard the quick knock of announcement followed by the squeak of the back door opening. "Hello!" My mother's voice echoed from the kitchen. With lightning speed, Jonathan dropped his puzzle piece on the coffee table and raced for the back door, calling out, "Grandma!" My parents had arrived.

Taking a deep breath, I rose from the couch wondering how we would all handle this awkward moment. It had been one thing to hear the heartache in my parent's voices on the phone last night. Seeing it in person might just undo me.

My parents and I have always been unusually close, due in part to the constant moves we endured as a military family. Our little nuclear family was tight knit, adopting an "us against the world" attitude that saw us through some trying times. We were facing some trying times again.

Stepping into the kitchen, I heard Jonathan bellow out, "Grandaddy!" Jonathan was babbling away, thrilled to see his grandparents. At the sound of my footsteps, Mom and Dad both looked up, forcing smiles that didn't quite reach their eyes. Our hugs were tight, but we kept the words light, all of us trying to hold it together.

Jonathan was tugging on Grandma's arm, dragging her toward his toys. As Dad went to retrieve their luggage, I followed my mom and my babbling little boy onto the sun porch. Jonathan's chatter prevented much conversation, but I could see the worry lines on my mother's face working overtime.

My mother is a sweet Southern lady with a kind, generous spirit that puts people at ease. She has always been a pretty woman with soft brown curls and big brown eyes that match my own. Those eyes were watching me now, casting quick glances my way as her grandson tugged on her hand, vying for her attention.

I knew she was reading my thoughts. Mom and I have always shared a tight bond that was not lessened with my entry into adulthood. Throughout my life, my mom has been there for me, readily putting my needs above her own. Now retired from teaching secretarial science at the community college level, my mother regularly showed up to help me even though we lived far apart. When Jonathan was born, Mom came for three weeks to shepherd us into parenthood, and that early time with Jonathan sealed a snug bond between them, a bond clearly evident as her grandson offered her his coveted Thomas the Tank engine train to hold.

Having settled their luggage, Dad joined us on the porch. I noticed he was unusually quiet as if searching for the right thing to say. Never at a loss for words, I knew with one look at his expressive face that he was struggling with this unsettling situation. I had always been the center of his universe, and this worrisome news was rocking his world. He tried to put a good face on it, but I knew him too well.

Like me, my father is a gregarious, talkative extrovert who loves a good story and thrives in a room full of people. Short in stature, his small frame might fool you, but he is tough as nails. A career soldier and Vietnam Veteran, my dad served in both the Army and the Army Reserves. A Green Beret, Special Forces type of guy, Dad is not a man to be toyed with, but that military-man exterior simply melts away when it comes to Mama and me.

As Jonathan's excitement waned, we found time to discuss the events of the day before, each of us trying to get our minds around the terrifying diagnosis. They shared my fury at the callous attitude of the doctor. Like me, they questioned his assessment, hoping somehow that he was wrong. They were relieved to have the upcoming second opinion. We soon ran out of steam on the subject, not knowing what else to say. We were all heartbroken, and our only remedy was to immerse ourselves in playtime with the adorable two-year-old that pranced around the room.

Birthday Blues

"Happy Birthday to you," Jonathan did his best to mimic his grandparents as they chimed in on the birthday song. I couldn't help but smile at him as he struggled to sing me a song for my 33rd birthday.

The chocolate cake was sliced and placed before me, but I didn't have much appetite for it. In an effort to cheer me up, my neighbor Tami had brought over one of her signature mocha chocolate pound cakes to celebrate my birthday. I smiled appreciatively, and yet my heart didn't feel like celebrating.

Birthday cards had filled the mailbox, but I didn't feel much like reading them. For my family's sake, I put on a good face and went through the motions. The stoic expression on Eric's face told me that he was not into the festivities either.

Aunt Sandra called with her usual birthday greeting. My parents had already shared the news with my close family members. I could hear Auntie's tears in her voice, although she did her best to cover up her raw emotions.

My friend Susan called from Georgia to wish me a happy birthday. A career Army nurse, Susan had been a lifeline for me during our graduate school days at The Catholic University of America in Washington, D.C. Though we had lived far apart for the last five years, we stayed in touch with frequent phone calls and infrequent visits. She never missed my birthday, and this year was no exception. However, she was not prepared for the shocking news I had to share. The long awkward silence on the other end of the line ripped at my heartstrings. I hated telling people this terrible news. I felt as sorry for them as I did for myself.

Had it not been for Jonathan's cute little cherub face, I don't think we could have gotten through the day. The upcoming appointment at Duke loomed over us like a dense fog. We all kept wondering if the diagnosis would be confirmed or rejected.

My parents stayed only two nights before returning home. Perhaps they sensed that we needed some space to regroup. No doubt, they needed some space of their own to absorb this awful news. They planned to return on Monday and keep Jonathan while I went for the second opinion at Duke.

A Big Deal

We needed a distraction to help us through the next few days. Eric suggested that we call our best friends Ricky and Laura and see if they could come down for the weekend.

I gave them a call and told them what was going on. Of course, they promised to come down late Friday night.

We had been the best of friends for over 10 years at that point. I had met Laura in college during our freshman chemistry class. She cut a striking figure with her long blonde hair that danced down her back as she glided across the floor of the theater style classroom. She was hard to miss.

We were both in the pre-nursing program at James Madison University in Harrisonburg, Virginia. While we had lots of mutual friends, she and I rarely crossed paths. When it was time for nursing school, Laura transferred to the Medical College of Virginia in Richmond, while I stayed at JMU. We lost touch at that point as we both went our separate ways.

After graduation, I had returned home to live with my parents and landed a job at St. Mary's Hospital in Richmond, VA. On the first day of hospital orientation, I was seated in the front row as each new hire stated their name and position. Imagine my surprise when I heard a familiar voice speaking from the back of the room. I remember turning quickly to find Laura's beautiful face smiling back at me.

It turned out that we were the only two nursing interns in that first summer rotation. Laura and I had so much in common. We were both engaged and planning December weddings. Both of us only children, she and I were back living at home until our marriages. Laura and I were interested in critical care nursing, sharing a passion for cardiology. We quickly became inseparable. With our blonde 80's style "Farrah Fawcett" hairdos, people around the hospital had trouble telling us apart.

Within a couple of weeks of working together, we introduced our fiancés to one another over lunch. Ricky's handsome face and tall, slim figure was the perfect match for Laura's striking beauty. They made a handsome couple.

Eric and I had been dating for five years. I had met my big, strong, good looking football player during my last year of high school. He had won me over with that mischievous grin and those gorgeous hazel eyes that seemed to stare straight into my soul. We had both attended JMU together, and Eric was finishing up the last semester of his degree in Computer Science. Our wedding was planned for just a few days after his December graduation.

From the outset, Eric and Ricky hit it off. They were both in computer career paths, and their connection seemed instantaneous.

Although both Laura and I had wanted to work in critical care after completing our summer internship, the hospital pushed us to get some general medical-surgical experience first. Laura took a position on a busy medical-surgical unit while I ended up on a hectic medical unit that specialized in renal, respiratory and oncology. Caring for as many as 21 patients on night shift, I certainly learned a lot. When our anniversary employment date rolled around, Laura and I transferred to the Coronary Care Unit. It was a great move for both of us, offering a wonderful opportunity to expand our nursing skills.

Throughout our time in Richmond, our friendship with Ricky and Laura had grown strong, spending lots of evenings and weekends together. When Eric and I moved to Washington, DC and then later to North Carolina, our relationship continued to be as strong as ever. Over the years, we had traveled lots of places as a foursome. If there was anyone that could make us feel better, it was Ricky and Laura.

They arrived on Friday night with the usual hugs and catch-up conversation. We didn't talk too much about my eyes. It was late, and we skirted the issue.

Being nurses, Laura and I talked more the next day about the diagnosis and the symptoms. Eric and Ricky had gone to play golf. When we were all together and Jonathan was around, it was easy to avoid the subject and just talk about other things. That was fine with me. I really didn't know what to say.

On Sunday, it was time for them to leave. We were standing in the driveway, watching Jonathan scamper back-and-forth as he played with his toys. Ricky walked over to me and put his arm around my shoulders. Turning to Eric and Laura, he announced, "Me and this girl are going for a walk." He gently tugged on my shoulder and steered me toward the backyard.

It was a beautiful fall day with one of those gorgeous October skies. The sun was shining brightly, the light dancing on the autumn leaves.

We walked slowly, Ricky's arm still around my shoulders. When we got to the old maple tree at the side of our backyard, he paused and turned to face me. Quietly, he said, "So, how are you doing?"

In typical Ricky style, his eyes were locked on mine. This was no time for a casual answer. He wanted the truth.

I heard myself say, "I'm OK."

He shook his head and pushed, "No, Anita, how are you really doing?"

I couldn't speak. It was as if all my words had run away, leaving me helpless and mute. I turned away from his gaze, unable to meet his eyes.

After a few long moments, I blurted out, "I don't know. It's been hard. I'm worried about Eric."

Ricky put his hand on my shoulder. "I didn't ask about Eric. I asked about you. How are you?"

35

CHAPTER 2
The Diagnosis

I just stood there, slowly shaking my head, not knowing what to say. I'll never forget what he said as his eyes locked on mine. "Anita, this is a big deal, a really big deal. This is the biggest thing that any of the four of us have ever had to deal with. It's OK to not be OK. You can say how you feel and it's OK to be honest with us."

We were quiet for a bit, just standing there looking out across the yard, taking in the autumn beauty. I know I said a few more things, but I don't remember much about what they were.

What I do remember was the feeling. For two weeks, I had been holding my emotions so tightly, trying to stay in control. Like a dam across a rushing river, I was holding my feelings back, not allowing them to flow out. The emotions were there, swelling up, ready to rush across that dam, to push through the impasse. I could feel all of those rising emotions, but somehow, something inside me would not let them go.

Standing there in the autumn sun, I felt a little bit of that great big dam break open, and a tiny burst of water was released. Just for a moment, I allowed myself to let some of those bottled-up emotions out. I felt the tears cloud my eyes, sensed the inner turmoil surfacing. No words were released, but I allowed myself a good long look at my pain. Ricky remained quiet, recognizing that space, not words, were what I needed. We stood in silence until with a slight shake of the head, I plastered that retaining wall right back up. The moment was over.

It was time for them to go, but our talk had helped. Ricky was the first person who had not only asked how I was doing, but had taken the question further. With his bold and direct manner, he had managed to push through the wall of control I had erected around my heart. Yes, I had shared the story, told people the facts, but not my feelings. Ricky was the first to ascertain my feelings and acknowledge my struggle of emotions. He understood that I was worried about everyone else's reaction, but he was intent on focusing on my reaction, and that's what I needed at that moment.

I knew he and Laura understood how hard this whole situation was for us. I knew that they had no idea how to help, except to let me know how much they cared. They had no idea just how much that meant to me.

As Eric and I watched the two of them drive away, I stood remembering Ricky's words. "This is a big deal, a really big deal."

I thought to myself, "Yeah, it is. It really is. I just don't know if I can do this. How in the world are we going to do this?"

As if to answer the question, Ricky's words flowed into my mind once more. "It's OK to not be OK."

CHAPTER 2
The Diagnosis

CHAPTER 3
Second Opinion

Another Opinion

I was scared to death. Seated in the waiting room, I fidgeted nervously in my chair. Eric sat beside me, quiet, just waiting. He had driven me to the Duke Eye Center for our early morning appointment with Dr. Machemer. We were both on pins and needles, waiting to see what this doctor would say.

From across the bustling waiting room, I heard my name being called. Eric and I stood and crossed the room toward the staff member who acknowledged us and then turned to lead us down the busy corridor. Pausing outside an office doorway, she fumbled with some paperwork in a mail slot. Standing just behind her, I could see into the dimly lit office. An older gentleman was leaning over a large desk, a small lamp illuminating the papers in front of him. As the assistant moved forward and laid a stack of papers on the desk, I paused in the doorway, trying to let my eyes adjust to the change in lighting. The doctor looked up and smiled politely. Pushing back in his office chair, he stood and crossed the room toward me, reaching out to grasp my hand. He greeted me with a kind, welcoming smile as he introduced himself. "Good morning! I am Dr. Machemer. Please come in."

With a broad sweep of his hand, he ushered me into his office and gestured toward the exam chair for me to sit. He then turned to Eric and shook his hand, introducing himself once more. He politely asked Eric to sit down in the extra chair.

He was a tall, handsome man with gray hair, kind eyes and a reassuring smile. He spoke with a bit of an accent, but his speech was slow and deliberate, making him easy to understand. He had a grace about him, a respectful attitude. He was so polite, taking extra effort to make us comfortable. Although the office corridor outside was hustling and bustling with hurried people passing by, inside the office was a sense of peace. That feeling came from him.

CHAPTER 3
Second Opinion

Another doctor came into the room and closed the door behind him. Dr. Machemer introduced him as a resident who would be joining us. He then turned to me and asked me to describe why I was here and the events that brought me to this visit. "Tell me your story."

As I described the events of the past few months, he listened intently, his eyes locked on mine. Occasionally, he would lift his hand, motioning me to pause so he could ask a question. As a follow-up to my answer, he frequently would turn to Eric and ask a similar, but slightly different question. He was very interested in Eric's observations of the events. He listened intently, encouraging us to be as descriptive as possible and never once making us feel rushed.

"Anita, do you see stars?"

I stopped for a moment and thought about this. "Sort of, but not like I used to see them."

He turned to Eric and asked, "Have you noticed this?"

Eric thought for a moment and said, "Yes, I have noticed that she can't see the same things I can. I like to look at the constellations. I have pointed them out to her over the years, but she always struggles to see what I see. Thinking about it, it does seem like she doesn't see them like she used to."

Dr. Machemer nodded, "Ah, this is important. This is an important sign." As he said this, he turned to the resident and gestured that he should pay attention to this point.

"Do you go to the movies, Anita?" I nodded. "Do you have trouble when you are walking into the movie theater?"

At this, Eric sat up straighter in his chair and blurted out, "She always has trouble when we first walk into the movie theater and usually grabs my arm. She's been doing that for a really long time, for years I guess."

Dr. Machemer nodded again and turned to me, "Anita, how is it when you come out of the movie theater?"

40

"Oh, I usually don't have any trouble coming out of the theater. I can see just fine then. It's just a problem when I first go into the theater."

Dr. Machemer nodded again and pointed up in the air with his index finger in an "Aha" gesture. Turning toward the resident, he emphasized, "This is important, this is an important sign."

Several times, other staff members knocked and opened the office door, intent on getting Dr. Machemer's attention. I could tell by their mannerisms that they had an urgent question. Patiently, he turned toward the door, raised his hand, and shook his head in a polite but dismissive gesture. Without missing a beat, he returned to the conversation, giving us his full attention.

As we talked, Dr. Machemer used the conversation to teach the resident, always taking great care to make us comfortable and included in the conversation. In response to my comments, he often asked follow-up questions of the resident. He was so patient with his teaching, and the resident hung on his every word.

After an hour of discussion, he asked if he could examine my eyes. Both he and the resident did a full eye examination. They spent a long time looking at the retina in the back of both eyes. When they had finished the examination, Dr. Machemer sat back quietly in his chair.

"Is it Stargardt's disease?" I asked nervously.

He shook his head slightly and said, "No, Anita, I think it is retinitis pigmentosa."

He went on to explain that this was a similar disease, but one with a different pattern. Both were degenerative retinal diseases, but the pattern of vision loss that I displayed was more consistent with that of retinitis pigmentosa, commonly referred to as "RP." He explained that this was a disease where the light receptors in the retina, also known as photoreceptors, progressively die. As the photoreceptors die in a specific portion of the retina, vision is lost in that area. He explained that it was likely that I had the rod-cone dystrophy form of RP. With this type of RP, peripheral vision is lost

Second Opinion

before losing central vision. He felt that this diagnosis was more consistent with my history as well as my physical exam.

He explained that the disease is genetic and that I have had the disease all my life. The vision loss is usually slow and insidious. It often takes until age 30 to have enough vision loss to begin to notice the symptoms. This is particularly true in someone who has no family history of the disease. He explained that loss of night vision is usually the first sign of the disease. As the disease progresses, the losses in the visual field begin to show up as missing objects in a particular field of view.

Eric and I sat there quietly, just taking it all in. The good doctor paused and asked, "What are your questions?"

"Will it get worse?"

The doctor nodded gently, "Yes, Anita, I am afraid so. I do believe that you have been in a period of rapid vision loss. It is our hope that now, this vision loss will shift to a period of more gradual, slow vision loss. Though I am not sure, it may be that your pregnancy made the vision loss more rapid for a time. Now, we will hope that it will slow down."

"Is there any treatment?"

"No, there is no definitive treatment at this time. But I am excited about some new research that has just been published." He went on to describe a recently published study on the effects of high dose vitamin A in slowing vision loss in retinitis pigmentosa. While this treatment did not cure the disease, it did slow the vision loss down, adding as much as seven years of useable vision to a given patient's prognosis. He was very hopeful about the impact of this therapy.

I sat there thinking about all the questions he had asked. I could see the pattern of my symptoms. I could tell from the questions and the answers that this diagnosis was likely correct. I had hoped that it would be something less severe, more treatable. Sitting there in that dimly lit room, my heart sank.

"Anita, I would like to do a visual field test on you. This will be a different kind than what you have done before. It is a manual version, and we will be able to pick up more information about what you actually are able to see. This will give us some good information. Would you be willing to have that done today?"

I gave my consent. He then explained that there was a series of tests that he would like to perform, but I would need to come back on a different day for those tests. "For now, the most important test is the Goldman visual field test, and we will do that one today."

After pausing once more to ensure we had no more questions, he ushered us out to the waiting room and explained that the technician would come and get me as soon as the test could be scheduled. "Anita, I will see you when the test is done and explain the results," he added as he began to step away. I thanked him, and he turned to retreat down the hall.

We found a seat in the waiting room and settled in. My thoughts were a blur. I finally had a diagnosis that made sense, but it was not the one I wanted. There was a sense of relief at knowing what we were dealing with, and then, a sense of dread at the uncertainty of what this disease would mean to my life.

My intellectual side heard all the clinical information, and I was processing it just like a nurse. My emotional side was in a state of shock, vacillating between panic over what all that information meant and trying to just shut the thoughts down. I didn't want to go there because I didn't know how to deal with it.

I had to hold my emotions tightly. I could not lose it here in the middle of this busy waiting room. I kept telling myself, "Just get through the test and see what it tells us."

Pondering all that had happened in the past week, I was struck by the differences in the two doctors. At both appointments, the news had been bad. Each doctor had proposed a diagnosis and each diagnosis was frightening. The difference was in their approach.

The first doctor was so rushed, never stopping to explain things, never taking time to really ask questions and understand my symptoms. He was in a rush to jump to a conclusion so he could move on with the next patient. There was no caring or compassion in the way he presented the information to me as his patient. To him, it was like solving a mystery, presenting the solution, and then moving on to the next puzzle. The person behind that mystery meant nothing to him.

The experience with Dr. Machemer could not have been more different. He had spent over two hours with us. His demeanor was kind, respectful and deeply caring. He asked the questions and made his assessment, but he was always careful to be sensitive to our feelings and concerns throughout the process. He wanted us to understand the diagnosis and to ask questions. He understood how devastating such a diagnosis would be to a 33-year-old woman in the prime of her career. He took that into account in the way he handled himself, in the manner in which he described his assessment. He was sensitive to Eric and his questions, careful to include him in the discussion. He saw us as a team, and he wanted to make sure that both of us had our questions answered.

The end result of Dr. Machemer's sensitive, caring approach was that it made hearing this devastating diagnosis a little easier. While I had a knot in the pit of my stomach, and it felt like a weight was settling on my shoulders, I was not in a state of panic as I had been the week before. Dr. Machemer's calmness had washed over me for the moment, allowing me to keep it together and get through the next test.

More Little Lights

Hearing my name called, I looked up to see a pleasant looking young man in a white lab coat, holding a paper in his hand. He called my name a second time. I stood and crossed the waiting room, moving toward him. Introducing himself as Tom, he explained that he would be performing the Goldman visual field test.

I followed Tom down the hallway to an exam room housing a small table with a large white dome on top. It looked just like the white dome I had seen in the other doctor's offices. This one was different, however.

Tom explained that while I would be looking for the light inside the large white dome, he would be on the other side of the dome mapping out my responses. Tom would be in control of the position of the lights. He would be noting every time I pressed the buzzer indicating that I could see the light. I was to press the buzzer as soon as the light appeared.

He explained that the test is very similar to the computer-generated version. However, with patients like myself, the computerized test moves too quickly, making it difficult to get accurate results. With this manual version of the test, he could take his time and carefully check my responses for accuracy. "This will be a much more accurate test for you."

He turned off the lights in the room, and I placed my chin on the chin rest. Beginning with a large white light, Tom started mapping the outer area of the dome. This allowed him to check my far peripheral vision, which was still quite good, allowing me to pick up the light very easily. As he moved the light in closer to the center of the dome, I noticed that there were sections where I could not find the light anymore. Tom was on the other side of the dome scratching away with his pencil, marking the paper map that displayed a diagram of my responses.

It was tedious and exhausting. Yet, Tom was so patient, so diligent about recording everything accurately. We went back over the same areas several times to ensure that he was getting my responses noted correctly. I tried my best to pay attention and be as accurate as possible. I knew it was important to be able to tell what I could and could not see.

The test took over two hours. When we were finally finished, I sat back in the chair, thoroughly exhausted. I felt like I had just run a marathon.

CHAPTER 3
Second Opinion

Tom tidied up his drawings while I tried to stretch my neck and shoulders. He instructed me to wait in the exam room, and he would take the drawings to Dr. Machemer to review.

In a few minutes, Tom returned, ushering Eric into the room. Shortly thereafter, Dr. Machemer came through the door. Motioning for us to sit beside him, we pulled our chairs together in a row.

Patiently, the kind doctor explained the drawings to us. Tracing with his fingers, he showed me the areas where I had good vision. Then, he showed me the areas where my vision was limited or completely absent.

He explained that my visual field loss was consistent with what is referred to as a mid-peripheral scotoma. This was the technical term, and it confirmed his diagnosis of retinitis pigmentosa.

He explained that my vision loss was similar to the shape of a donut. I had good vision in the center of the visual field where the donut hole would be. "Here, Anita, in this area that looks like a donut is where you do not see anything. But outside the donut, in the far periphery, you see well."

Eric and I sat there closely scrutinizing the drawings, trying to make sense of the information. Dr. Machemer explained that the size of the donut, the area where I had lost vision, would grow larger with time. He hoped that it would continue to expand out into the peripheral area before turning toward the central field. He explained that the central field is where my vision for focused tasks and reading comes from. He hoped that I would retain the central visual field for a long time to come. He was, however, concerned about the size of my central field, finding it quite small in both eyes. Though small, it seemed to be quite healthy, because my visual acuity was still so good. "We have no way of knowing how it will progress, but it is my hope that you will keep that central visual field for a long time to come."

Then, he said the very thing I had hoped not to hear. "Anita, you cannot drive." His expression was pained as he looked up at me, his eyes brimming with sorrow. Using the diagram, he explained that if a child on a bicycle or a car happened to be in this part of my visual field, I would not see them. "It would be so easy for you to miss something in this area." He went on to explain that it was just too dangerous for me to drive. While he could not take away my driver's license according to the law, he strongly encouraged me to consider giving up driving. "It is for your safety, Anita, for your child, for the other people, the other children you might not see."

I felt like someone who was standing on the edge of a cliff. In one brief moment, a gust of wind had engulfed me, hurling me over the edge. I was tumbling downward, falling with no hope of anything to break my fall, nothing to stop my descent into the great abyss below. I could hear him continuing to say a few additional things, but I couldn't focus on what this kind doctor was saying.

As he prepared to go, he took my hands in both of his and clasped them gently. "Anita, it will work out. You will come back and see me for the other tests, and we will learn more information. I will answer any questions that you have then, when you have had more time to think about things. We will talk more then."

Eric and I both stood and thanked him profusely for his time and kindness. Clasping my hand gently between his own, his eyes held mine for a long moment. With a warm but sad smile, he quietly turned, and walked away.

The Long Way Home

Eric went to get the truck while I waited out in the front of the eye clinic. I suppose I was in shock. My thoughts were swirling, and nothing made sense. Feeling dazed, I thought, "Now what?"

When Eric pulled up to the curb, I opened the truck door and climbed inside. Without a word, Eric pulled away from the curb and headed out of the parking lot. "I'm just not ready to go home yet," I said quietly.

CHAPTER 3
Second Opinion

He knew what I was thinking. My parents were at home taking care of Jonathan. I would have to tell them the news. Eric nodded, then replied, "I'll take the long way home."

We rode in silence, both of us lost in our own thoughts. I replayed the conversation with Dr. Machemer over and over in my mind.

Staring out the window, I gazed at the brilliant October blue sky above me. The sun was shining brightly. The leaves were turning, their gold and orange colors magnificent in the golden sunlight. An overwhelming sense of sadness enveloped me. "One of these days, I won't see this anymore," I thought to myself.

I just couldn't imagine that. I couldn't grasp the concept that this was really happening to me. I was losing my vision. One day, I might not be able to see any of this.

In my mind, I heard Dr. Machemer's words. "Anita, you must not drive."

"How can that be? How in the world am I going to stop driving?" I couldn't imagine it.

I thought about our hometown. When we moved out of the Washington, D.C. area five years before, we were so thrilled to buy our comfortable little home situated several miles from the center of our sleepy Southern town. We loved our large yard and the open spaces around us. I had never given the distance from town a second thought. It was just a quick drive into town to run errands. Now, there was no driving, no way to run errands without help.

"How will I get to work? How will we take Jonathan to the babysitter? What about the doctor? This can't be happening."

The drive home took about 40 minutes. As we got closer to town, I said, "I still don't know what to say. I'm not ready to go home yet."

Eric nodded and quietly said, "Yeah." He turned and headed out to a small park not too far from our house. Parking the truck next to the walking track, we got out and began to slowly walk along the path. I took his hand, needing the comfort of his touch.

Following the path up to the crest of the hill, we wandered over to a picnic table and sat down on the tabletop, our feet resting on the bench. From that vantage point, we could look out over the park into the distance. The rolling hills of the countryside stretched before us, the changing leaves offering a splendid display of color.

We sat there quietly together, both lost in thought, each of us trying to get our heads wrapped around the information we had just received. Eric was motionless, staring straight out across the horizon, his elbows on his knees. Likewise, I stared at the Carolina blue sky, my hands clenched tightly to match the knot in my stomach. Without altering his gaze, Eric said quietly, "How in the world are we going to do this?"

I struggled to respond. After a long moment, I shook my head in bewilderment. "I don't know. I just don't know."

One thing was certain. Neither of us knew the answer to his question.

Telling The Story

As we pulled into the driveway, I spotted Mom and Dad out at the swing set with Jonathan. I swallowed hard as I walked toward them, Eric following closely behind.

Jonathan ran to give us a hug, my parents trailing after him. As Jonathan trotted back to the swingset, Mom asked in a shaky voice, "So what did the doctor say?"

I shook my head and said quietly, "It's not good news."

Together, Eric and I gave them the basics of the information. The conversation was a bit disjointed as Jonathan vied for our attention. I don't know if he sensed there was something wrong. Perhaps in his little two-year-old world, it was just a pretty day to play outside with his family. Could he see the pain in our faces, hear the worry in our voices? He certainly kept trying to get us to come play with him. Was he trying to lighten the mood, sensing somehow that we were sad? Did he have any inkling of just how much the course of his life changed on that fateful day?

CHAPTER 3
Second Opinion

From that moment forward, our family life was radically altered. With a legally blind mother who couldn't drive, Jonathan would grow up with a very different reality than his peers. One day, I would have to explain how this devastating diagnosis changed the course of his life as much as it did my own.

"Grandma, push me!... Grandaddy, watch this!"

We managed to get the essentials explained between Jonathan's playful interruptions. In a way, it was a good distraction to be entertaining Jonathan. The interruptions kept our emotions at bay and allowed the news to be digested gradually.

Over the rest of the evening, Eric and I answered a few more questions from my parents. Then, we had to begin the phone calls. Our family and friends had been waiting anxiously for more information. Everyone had been so concerned and had been praying for us.

We made the call to Eric's parents, Liz and Pete. Together, we stumbled through the essential information from the doctor's assessment. His parents listened intently, but you could almost hear their hearts breaking on the other end of the line. They had known me since I was 16 years old and felt like they had helped raise me, always treating me like their own daughter. This was not the news they wanted to hear. We ended the call with choked voices and stifled tears.

The phone rang several times with friends calling to check on us. Of course, both Mary and Tami called. Ricky and Laura checked in too, as did Susan, my Army nurse friend. Dr. Woodard also called, anxious for an update.

I heard myself repeating the information over and over. I was getting good at delivering the information while keeping my emotions in check. I felt like I had to be brave and keep my feelings under control. I did not want to lose it in front of my parents or Jonathan.

Thankfully, Dad called our extended family for me. Mom's twin sister Tina had been so concerned. She and Uncle Randy had called in their prayer chain on my behalf. Aunt Sandra and Uncle Tom had been checking on us since the first eye appointment and were anxious for the results of the second opinion. I was glad Dad had taken those calls on. The tension of the day was giving way to exhaustion, and I just couldn't keep on repeating the awful news.

The evening progressed with the usual tasks of childrearing. As we were all getting ready for bed, I was tidying up the kitchen. I thought everyone else had gone to bed, but I looked up to see Mom standing there watching me. Slowly, I crossed the room toward her. She held out her arms and I fell into her embrace, my head resting on her shoulder. "Mama, I just don't know how I'm going to do this," I cried out, tears rolling down my cheeks.

She patted my back like she did when I was a little girl. "You can do this. You will figure it out."

"I just want to see him, Mama. I just want to see him grow up."

She pulled me upright then and looked intently into my eyes. "Jonathan will be your eyes. He will help you see. It will all work out, it really will," she murmured, nodding her head. Tears welling in her eyes, she stared deeply into mine, as if willing me to listen. She wanted me to hear her words, to know that it would somehow work out.

In that moment, I just couldn't imagine how.

Running In Circles

My parents offered to stay the rest of the week. From family to friends, everyone was worried about me. We were all trying to come to grips with what the doctor had told us.

There really was something wrong with me, something terribly wrong. I had hoped the initial diagnosis was wrong. It was. The problem was that the initial diagnosis was replaced by an equally devastating disease process. Bottom line, I was going blind, and I was devastated.

Dealing with the diagnosis was made even more difficult because there was no clear prognosis. We had no idea how fast the disease might progress. Dr. Machemer had made that clear. "Everyone is different. The disease progresses differently for each person. There is no way to know what the progression will look like for you."

As far as returning to work, there were no restrictions. Dr. Machemer had encouraged me to do as much as I was comfortable with. "You will learn to limit those things that make you uncomfortable. There will be things you struggle to do because of your vision loss." In other words, it was up to me to decide what I was safe to do and what I needed to avoid.

I thought about taking care of patients. "What if I make a mistake? What if I miss something I should have seen?" The thoughts made me cringe. "How am I going to do my job? How can I be a nurse if I cannot see?"

As if an undetermined prognosis and the professional concerns were not overwhelming enough, the thought of giving up driving was absolutely gut-wrenching. I simply could not fathom how we could do it. I was working three days a week at a hospital that was 30 minutes from our home. Eric had a 45-minute drive to work in the totally opposite direction. On top of that, our wonderful babysitter was 20 minutes away in yet another direction. "How can we live without me being able to drive?"

The list of questions was endless and I had no answers. I got sick on my stomach even contemplating the questions.

Emotionally, I was all over the place. I wanted to crawl under the covers and cry myself to sleep. Yet, I felt like I needed to be doing something. I needed to make a plan. On the one hand, I didn't want to talk about it. On the other hand, I fretted constantly over what to do.

The thought of work gripped me with panic. Not only was there fear over making mistakes, but also over how would I fulfill my job responsibilities. I was providing direct patient care about 20% of my time, with much of those shifts on evenings, nights or weekends. "How would we manage that? How could I get there at those hours? Can I even do the nursing tasks when I do get there, particularly at night?"

Because of my teaching and project work, I was well known throughout the hospital. "What would I say to all those people? How in the world do I explain this?"

I had a deep bond with the nurses on my nursing unit. I was well respected and well loved by the staff. I worried about what to tell them. "How am I going to explain all this to my nurses? What do I say when people ask me how I am doing?"

I knew everyone would be so upset to learn of this devastating news. I had no idea how to handle their emotions, much less my own.

I was scheduled to return to Duke in two weeks for further testing. Dr. Machemer would explain more details to us following those tests. I had no idea what else we would learn at that visit.

Given my part-time schedule, I had only missed a couple days of work thus far. I knew my manager Lynn would support whatever I needed to do. She knew what we were dealing with and had been extremely supportive.

My partner Mary had been holding down the fort as far as our work responsibilities. I knew that she would gladly continue to cover our duties, but how much longer could I let that continue? I knew Mary would do anything I needed, but I felt guilty not doing my share. Besides, I did not want to drop the ball on several projects I was leading. "But how can I go in there and hold it together? How do I do that job when my whole world is falling apart? And even if I decide to go back to work, how do I get there?"

My thoughts ran in circles, round and round on that awful merry-go-round. Try as I might, I could not find a way to get off.

Behind The Mask

I was so overwhelmed that I had no idea what to do next. My parents had the answer. They would stay the rest of the week, drive me back and forth to work and take care of Jonathan. "Go back to work while we are here. You can get stuff caught up. Just get through this week while we are here. You don't have to figure it all out today. This will give you and Eric some time to figure out what you are going to do."

"But what do I tell people? I can't deal with that right now."

Dad offered, "You don't have to tell anyone anything right now. Just wait until you go back to Duke. You'll know more then. You can decide what to say then."

My father has always been a source of wisdom for me. I surely needed his wisdom at that moment. I needed a plan, and I was too overwhelmed to make one. I wasn't sure I was ready, but it seemed to be a sensible plan.

On Wednesday morning, Dad drove me to work. My manager and office mates were the only people at the hospital who knew about my situation. I still wasn't ready to share my story with anyone else. I could not imagine what I would say. I could not bear the thought of others' reactions. It had been hard enough telling my family and close friends. A live broadcast to a large audience was the last thing I wanted to endure.

Hence, I put on the mask, the mask adorned with a bright smile and a sunny disposition. I forced an upbeat tone into my voice and greeted the day. My demeanor was business as usual, plowing directly into work discussions and project updates. No one was the wiser. The mask worked like a charm. I made it through the day without a hitch.

The only time I removed the mask was with Lynn, Mary and our office mates, Donna and Katie. These women were my dearest friends. They had been praying for me throughout the whole ordeal. I had to give them the full description of the visit to Duke. We cried together as we sorted through the information. Surprisingly, I felt better after talking to them. It was good to open up a bit.

Still, when I stepped outside the office, I put on the mask and hid behind it. The rest of the week went smoothly enough, and I was glad when Friday afternoon arrived.

My parents left for home on Saturday morning, but they announced their decision before they departed. They would return on Tuesday afternoon so that Dad could take me to work the next week. Despite the four-hour drive from their home to ours, they insisted on returning. "This will get you through until you go back to Duke and get the final word. Then you can figure out what to do from there."

Eric and I were so grateful for my parents' help, not just for the transportation, but for the support. They helped me process my concerns, yet kept me distracted enough to get through the business at hand. They entertained Jonathan which was a huge help. The reality was that Eric and I had very little to give at that moment. It was all we could do just to get through each day and hold it together.

Final Word

We returned to Duke for further testing on November 1st. The battery of tests was extensive and exhausting, taking most of the day. The technician checked my perception of colors and my light-dark adaptation. They measured pressures and checked visual acuity.

The worst test of the series was the ERG. I was given eye drops to numb my eyes. Specialized contacts were then inserted into each eye. An electrode with a separate cable was placed on my forehead. My eyes were covered with patches so that I could see nothing. I sat in a pitch-black room for thirty minutes to adjust to total darkness.

After thirty minutes, the patches were removed. Tiny electrical cables were attached to each contact. The numbing solution helped, but it still felt like watermelons with ropes sticking out of my eyes. It was quite unpleasant.

CHAPTER 3
Second Opinion

The technician wheeled me over to another white circular dome. I placed my chin on the chin rest and stared at the black dot in the center of the dome. A computer then began generating flashes of bright lights, some varying in color, some with rapid motion like a strobe light. I was required to hold as still as possible and stare straight ahead. It was awful, and it was all I could do to sit there and not scream. The test took well over an hour to complete, not counting the time spent sitting in the dark.

I was absolutely worn out and frazzled by the time we met with Dr. Machemer that afternoon. He had reviewed the data from the testing and confirmed that his initial diagnosis of rod-cone retinitis pigmentosa was correct. He explained the test results in depth. We reviewed much of the same information we had covered in the previous visit. I asked some of the same questions just to ensure I understood the answers correctly. He reiterated several of his points to ensure we had a clear understanding.

Although he was very direct in his advice not to drive, his compassion for the impact of that directive was unmistakable.

"Anita, I know how hard this must be for you, but you must really consider giving up driving. It is what is best for you, for your family, for the others on the road."

Since the last visit, I had done some research on the use of Vitamin A in RP, reviewing the research study that had recently been published. I queried Dr. Machemer on the dosage and how to obtain the medication. We discussed the pros and cons of this therapy. "I do think it is something that you might try, Anita. It is only one study, but a good, well-done study and the results are promising." I told him that I wanted to start the drug. "From the sounds of it, it is the only thing that might help me, since there are no other treatments right now. I may as well give it a shot."

Overall, there was very little new information, but the time spent reviewing matters with Dr. Machemer was very helpful. He explained that he would see me again in one year. I was a bit surprised that I would not be evaluated more frequently. "Anita, the changes with this disease are typically slow and incremental. There is no need to evaluate things more often than that."

On the one hand, that sounded encouraging. The disease will be slow in progressing. On the other hand, I could not help but think that there was no point in coming back any sooner because there was really nothing to do about it anyway. That thought made my stomach tighten.

As we rose to leave, we thanked this kind doctor for his compassion and patience with us. It was all so hard, yet his caring approach made such a difference. He took my hand in his and said, "Anita, you will get through this. You will figure it out, and we will have hope for the future."

With tears in my eyes, I gave him a smile of gratitude and walked away. We had the diagnosis. We had the information. What we would do with all of it, I had no idea.

CHAPTER 3
Second Opinion

Part 2
The Way Forward

NOVEMBER 1993 - AUGUST 1994

He lifted me out of the slimy pit, out of the mud and mire;
He set my feet on a rock and gave me a firm place to stand.

—Psalm 40:2 *NIV*

Part 2
The Way Forward

CHAPTER 4
The Long Climb Out

The Aftermath

The day after we came home from seeing Dr. Machemer at Duke, I could barely crawl out of bed. Jonathan was making noises on the baby monitor, and I knew I could not ignore him for much longer. He was ready for the day. I was not.

I stumbled through the morning routines as if I were adrift in a dense fog. Nothing seemed normal. It was like the earth had slipped off its axis, and someone had forgotten to warn me. I was just plain out of it.

I was enveloped by a bone numbing kind of exhaustion. Unable to focus, my brain waves were adrift in a sea of chaos, the words of the day before on a constant replay.

The thought of going back to work tomorrow simply made me nauseous. I had nothing left to give anyone. All my reserves were spent. I just couldn't go in there. I couldn't put on that mask again and pretend that I was OK. I was not. My world was falling apart, and I could not pretend anymore.

Eric and I had talked about things on the way home from Duke. "I just don't know what to do. I just can't go back to the hospital right now. I can't figure it all out."

He had encouraged me to take some time off. "Then maybe we can figure out what we are going to do." He, too, was weary and overwhelmed. I could see it in his eyes.

I called my manager Lynn later that morning. Lynn and I had worked side by side for over five years. I had first met Lynn when I arrived at the hospital and started my Clinical Nurse Specialist position on our nursing unit. She was working weekends finishing her bachelor's degree, and several months later, Lynn took on the assistant manager role. From the outset, we had shared a mutual respect for each other. Lynn had even nominated me for the Nursing Excellence Award and stood by my side beaming with satisfaction when I won this incredible honor four years earlier. When the nurse manager position had opened up on our unit, I had advocated for Lynn to assume that role. Yes, Lynn and I had supported each other professionally, but it was more than that. Lynn was my friend, a real friend that I could always count on.

I gave Lynn the essence of the information from the eye clinic visit. Then I got honest with her. "Lynn, I'm a mess. I can't come in there. I just can't."

There was a long pause on the other end of the line as Lynn processed my words. "I understand. I know you need some time to sort things out. How much time off do you think you need?"

My voice broke with emotion as I replied, "I don't know. I just don't know. I'm just so overwhelmed. I can't even think straight."

Lynn's voice was soft as she said, "I understand. I know you need some time to process it all. You take the time you need. We'll work things out here."

I knew from the tone of her voice that my heart was not the only one aching. She was hurting for me and concerned about my welfare. "Just take care of yourself right now and we can talk about that when you have had some time to think."

Hanging up the phone, I stood staring out the kitchen window at another day of bright sunshine. Like the fallen leaves tumbling across the backyard, my mind tumbled with a swirl of heavy thoughts. I had the time off. There would be no work for me tomorrow. There was relief in that thought, but also bewilderment because I had no idea what to do next.

I stared at those tumbling leaves and asked aloud, "Now what? Now what do I do?"

"Mama! Mama! Where you at?" I smiled at the sound of my little boy's voice and went to find him. He was standing at the coffee table on the sun porch, puzzle piece in his hand. I plopped down on the couch, and he immediately climbed up into my lap, babbling a mile a minute. Cradling him in my arms, he snuggled in tight against my chest. I had no idea what was ahead for me, but in that moment, this was enough.

Jonathan had the answer after all.

Going Through The Motions

Honestly, the days that followed are a blur in my mind. I recall lots of sunny autumn days that allowed Jonathan and me to play outside in the late mornings or early afternoons before his naps. I remember waking up to the sounds of my little boy on the baby monitor, chatting with the stuffed animals in his crib. I would lie there listening, not able to summon the energy to drag myself out of bed. Eventually, he would call out "Mama!" and my procrastination would come to an end. I would get up and go through the motions, but my mind was in a perpetual fog.

Nothing seemed real. It was like I fell asleep one night and woke up to a totally different world, a world I was struggling to come to grips with.

The only bright spot in those days was Jonathan. He was such a cheerful and active little boy with a smile that would melt your heart. For a two-year-old, he was very congenial and agreeable, content to play with his toys and entertain himself.

Periodically, he liked to check in to see where I was and show me his toy. Then, he would run off to find another game to entertain himself with. He had a wonderful little laugh that never failed to make me smile.

He enjoyed everything. It was all a great adventure to him, something new to figure out, someplace new to explore. His curiosity was insatiable. His zest for life was contagious as he greeted each day with glowing enthusiasm. I could not help but grin when I was around him.

He was busy, oh, so very busy. He kept me hopping. That was good, because he was a daily distraction from the rollercoaster of emotions I found myself stranded on. I honestly don't think I could have gotten through those days without him.

CHAPTER 4
The Long Climb Out

Each morning, Eric trudged off to work. I know he did not feel like going anywhere either, but somebody had to work and pay the bills. When he came home at night, there was little chance for conversation with a chatty two-year-old sitting between us. In truth, I don't think either of us knew what to say anyway. After a long day at a stressful job, Jonathan was a beacon of light for Eric in this dark time. Our evening play time together provided the perfect distraction from the otherwise dreary thoughts that plagued our minds.

Now What?

While Eric and I took refuge in the daily routines of parenting, we both knew we had to make some decisions about my work and our transportation issues. It's just that we had no clue what to do.

We did talk about our options, but at the end of every conversation, there seemed to be no workable solution. We discussed my quitting work to stay home with Jonathan. I kept thinking that if I had a limited time to see, I wanted to spend it seeing my little boy. Eric was certainly supportive of that idea, but we needed to figure out the finances.

We discussed my applying for disability. I even called to inquire about the process, only to learn that I did not qualify. I was told I had too much usable vision. That smarted a bit. I could not see well enough to drive, but at the same time, I had enough vision to not warrant assistance.

Regardless of the financial implications of not working, there was the fact that I loved my job. I am one of those somewhat unusual people who found their calling. I loved being a nurse, and delighted in helping people. Teaching was my passion. I adored teaching nurses new skills, helping them grow to be better nurses. The project work fascinated me, offering a chance to improve patient care. Figuring out better ways of doing things was both interesting and rewarding.

By nature, I have always been an overachiever, always wanting to do my best at anything I pursued. I had worked hard to earn my Master's degree in nursing about 5 years earlier. I had dreamed of being a Clinical Nurse Specialist and had landed the perfect position. I was making a real difference in the lives of my patients and my nurses.

The part-time schedule I had negotiated after Jonathan's birth was perfect. Working three days a week gave me the opportunity to impact patient care in a significant way, while still leaving me ample time to be at home with Jonathan. For four days a week, I got to do "the Mommy thing." He and I could go to the park or play in the backyard. I was able to be there to teach and nurture him, to instill our values into him. Having that focused time with Jonathan had been a priority for Eric and me, and my part-time work schedule had supported that choice beautifully.

We had a fabulous babysitter who adored Jonathan, and he loved her back. He so enjoyed his playmates there. It was a great opportunity to interact with other children. We could not have been more blessed with our daycare arrangements.

While I had worked full-time prior to Jonathan's birth, my priorities shifted with pregnancy. Desiring to keep my job while cutting back my hours, I had negotiated the opportunity to job-share the role. We had searched for someone with a clinical background that matched my own. Amazingly, we found Mary.

From the first moment of the interview, I knew she was the one. In all the world, I could not have found a better partner. Our clinical skill sets were perfectly matched. We made an awesome team, playing off each other's strengths, often reading each other's minds. Not only was Mary a perfect work partner, but this tall, gracious woman had become like a sister to me. We had forged a tight bond of friendship, and the thought of losing this connection made me heartsick.

"Am I ready to give all this up? Am I ready to throw in the towel on my career?"

CHAPTER 4
The Long Climb Out

In truth, my identity was intricately tied to being a nurse. It's who I was, and I couldn't imagine tossing my profession out the door. "But how can I be a nurse if I cannot see? How do I do my job if I am constantly scared to death that I will miss something because of my eyes? What if I hurt a patient?"

On top of all those concerns, there was the issue that my work was 30 minutes away, in the absolute opposite direction from Eric's work. "If I do go back to work, how in the world am I going to get there?"

Watch Me, Mama

"Watch me, Mama!" Jonathan squealed with delight as he scampered up the steps to the big yellow slide. It was a gorgeous, early November day. Jonathan and I were playing together on the swing set in the backyard. The sky was the brilliant blue of a crisp fall day in the Carolinas. The golden rays of sunlight were reflecting off the fallen leaves scattered across the yard. The day was exquisitely beautiful, the kind of day you wish you could bottle up and keep with you forever.

We had come outside to play for a while after lunch. I had high hopes for getting him to take a good nap after wearing him out on the slide. He loved that yellow slide.

At two years old, it was tough for Jonathan to climb up the wooden rungs of the ladder. The slats were fairly far apart and his little legs could just barely make the stretch from one step to another. I stood behind him, ready to catch him if he stumbled as he climbed. As he reached the platform at the top, he turned and grinned at me with delight, "I did it!" In his little two-year-old world, he was all about accomplishing some difficult physical tasks. Every accomplishment would be accompanied by the celebration, "I did it!"

I could not help but smile at his little cherub face grinning at me. In a flash, he turned and faced the direction of the big yellow slide.

As he plopped his little bottom on the edge of the slide, he cried out "Watch me, Mama!"

The words flew through the air and hit me like a stab, placed firmly in the center of my heart. "Watch me, Mama!" I could hear the words ringing in my ears. All I could think about was "What happens when I can't watch you anymore? What happens when I can't see you anymore?"

I didn't want to think these thoughts. I just wanted to enjoy these moments with my little boy, but the thoughts would not stop coming. The questions kept hammering against the walls of my mind.

"What happens when you can't see him grow up? What happens when you can't watch him slide or swim or sing in the church play? How many more days do I have to see him like this? What will I do when the day comes and I can't see him? Will I be able to see him graduate high school? What about college? Will I be able to see him as a young man, to know what he looks like? Will I see him get married? Will I be able to see my grandchildren someday?"

With every unanswered question, I felt my heart breaking just a little bit more.

There were no answers. I had no way of knowing what the future would hold. No one does. Yet, dealing with the thought of eventual blindness was like an anchor around my neck, threatening to sink me into a pit of despair. All I wanted to do was see Jonathan grow up. Silently, I began to pray.

"Lord, just let me see him grow up. Let me be able to see his face as a young man. Let me know what he looks like when he's all grown up. Please let me see him graduate high school. Please, Lord, please give me that time."

Tears welled up in my eyes as I thought, "I just want to remember this moment. I want to remember what he looks like right now. I want to capture this moment and keep it forever."

"Watch me, Mama!" he squealed as he started to sail down the slide. I scurried over to catch him at the bottom. A wide grin lit up his precious face, his soft brown eyes sparkling with joy.

CHAPTER 4
The Long Climb Out

"I did it!" He exclaimed with delight.

"Yes, you did," I said with a smile, "Yes, you did!" With a merry chuckle, he tumbled into my arms for a great big hug. I had no idea what the future would hold, but in that moment, his hug was what I needed most.

The Mailbox

Every day, there was a surprise awaiting me in the mailbox. For the nearly six weeks since the first news of my vision issues, Eric made his nightly trek to the mailbox, and almost every day, there would be a card or letter waiting there for me. These mailbox blessings ranged from a simple "Thinking Of You" card with a short note to a long letter filled with words of encouragement. Each correspondence shared the same message, "I am praying for you."

My friends and family were hurting for me. While they could not change my circumstances, they could surround me with prayer. Their words of encouragement soothed my aching heart.

What surprised me the most were the cards I received from people I didn't know. Upon hearing of my diagnosis, friends and family had placed my name on prayer lists all over the country. Perfect strangers heard of my plight and responded with prayers lifted on my behalf. Furthermore, they took their precious time to send me a note. I was absolutely amazed by that.

While I knew that my friends and family would pray for me, I must admit to being overwhelmed by the sheer outpouring of love shown to us in those difficult weeks. I shouldn't have been surprised. I am blessed by a wealth of strong Christian friends as well as a large and loving family of faithful believers. Of course, they would pray. Yet, I still marveled at the extent of their concern for us. Add to that, the kindness of strangers to pray and communicate with me, I was simply blown away by that. More than once, I held one of those notes in my hand and thought, "Can all this really be for me? Wow…"

One evening after returning from his mailbox duty, Eric handed me an envelope with an unfamiliar return address. Peeling back the flap, I plucked the contents from the envelope. As I opened up the carefully folded note, something wrapped in tissue fell into my hand. Curious, I began to unwrap the little parcel. Nestled in the tissue paper was a tiny cross, its beautiful blue ribbon intricately woven across a miniature frame. I stared at the delicate cross, fingering its smooth, silky ribbon. Who had sent me this?

Returning to the single sheet of paper that lay on the counter, I found a short handwritten note penned in small cursive letters. The note read, "I am praying for you. I hope this tiny cross will remind you of God's love for you in this difficult time." The signature at the bottom of the note was unfamiliar.

Staring at the words on the page, my eyes filled with tears. Someone I didn't even know had sent me this lovely gift, a cross to hold onto, a reminder of God's love for me. I was deeply moved.

I have heard countless people say "I felt your prayers." In that dark and difficult time, I truly understood what others meant by that remark. I could feel these people's prayers. Holding one of those notes in my hand, I could feel God's peace enfolding me. It was palpable.

People cared. Even if they did not know me, they cared about my hardship. They sacrificed their time and energy to send me a greeting of encouragement and to lift up a prayer.

Holding that miniature cross in the palm of my hand, I marveled at the kindness of this woman whom I had never met. I thought of all the little acts of kindness shown to me in the past few weeks. I was overcome by gratitude. While notes and calls could not change my circumstances, these simple actions spoke Christ's love to me in a way I had not fully experienced before. The adage, "Prayer changes things" was proving true. For there even in the midst of my misery, my heart was being comforted by the lovingkindness of friends and strangers. I was being reminded, again and again, that I was not alone.

CHAPTER 4
The Long Climb Out

Checking In

After two weeks, my manager Lynn called to check in. She wanted to know how I was doing. As we talked, I remember thinking that I was stuck. I really had not made any progress since I had talked to her the day after returning from Duke. I had not been driving, yet I had not fully committed to the idea that I would never drive again. I could not seem to let that go, even if it was the safe thing to do.

I was not in a good place at that point. Because of the driving issue, I could not make any decisions about work. I could not go back to work until I figured out how to get there, and I still had no idea how to manage that overwhelming hurdle. Lynn knew me well, and I am sure she could hear the anguish in my voice. I am sure she could hear how shaky I was.

To her great credit, Lynn did not push me to come back to work. She understood the challenges, and as one of my dearest friends, she hurt for me. Still, she had a job to do and a nursing unit to run.

"If you need to take more time, that is OK, but, Anita, what do I tell the staff?" She explained that the nurses had been asking where I was. It was not like me to miss work and the staff had begun to notice.

Out of respect for me, Lynn and my close co-workers were trying to keep my situation private until I was ready to deal with it. Yet, as the days turned into weeks, the questions were increasing, and Lynn was uncertain how to handle this.

I immediately understood the concerns. "I am not ready to come back. Lynn, I just can't right now. But you can start telling the staff what has happened."

We discussed a bit more detail of what should be shared. Lynn seemed relieved. We agreed that I would take another two weeks off, and then I would have to give her a decision about whether I would return to work and when. I thanked her for her support. She had been more than gracious, and I appreciated her kindness and understanding.

The Great Abyss

I was sad beyond belief. All the plans I had for the future seemed to go up in smoke. I was convinced that I would be blind in a couple of years, and my life would be over. I was so afraid that I would never see Jonathan grow up, never know what he looked like as an adult. I would never see him walk across that stage for high school graduation, let alone college.

As the days passed by, I had hoped to feel better. I had hoped to make a plan. Yet, with every passing day, I felt more and more paralyzed by uncertainty. My emotional state seemed constantly in flux.

When I thought about my nursing career, I felt hopeless. I was convinced that my career was over. "What can I possibly do as a nurse with failing vision?"

I knew that the hospital leadership would not make me quit right away. I felt sure they would do their best to work with me. They would no doubt find me some kind of desk job that I could do for a while. "But for how long? How long can I expect to keep a job when I cannot see? What if I hate the desk job they give me to do? "I won't be able to do what I've been doing. I won't be the nurse I have been. It won't be the same."

At that particular moment, all I could see were dreams lost. I could not envision that there would be anything in my future career that would be rewarding and fulfilling. "My career is over. I may as well give it up."

I felt like my heart was being crushed, caught in a vice grip that I couldn't release. It was as if all my hopes and dreams were dashed with the stroke of a hand, or more aptly, with the stroke of four little words. "You are legally blind."

I simply could not believe that my life had changed so radically in such a short span of time. Just over six weeks ago, I had been sitting

CHAPTER 4
The Long Climb Out

at a nursing conference learning about advances in nursing practice and thinking of how I would use the information to improve care at my hospital. Two days later, I go for a simple eye exam to adjust my contacts, and suddenly, my world starts falling apart.

The sense of sadness was like an ache that would not go away. Night after night, I remember lying awake in bed next to Eric, listening to his breathing. I could hear the faint sounds of Jonathan's gentle snores on the baby monitor beside my bed. Lying there staring at the ceiling, I repeated to myself, "I can't do this. I can't dig my way out of this. There is no way out."

I wanted to cry, but the tears wouldn't come. It was as if I couldn't release the tears. I think crying would have made me feel better, but I was afraid to start, for if I started, I might never stop.

Instead, I found myself lying there, feeling miserable, unable to sleep. The sadness in my soul would penetrate my mind with a few simple words. "Tears rolling down my face." That was the only way I could voice the ache of despair in my chest. "Tears rolling down my face."

Not only was the sadness almost unbearable, the guilt was gut-wrenching. I looked at my husband, the man that I had loved for 16 years, and I felt guilty. He did not deserve this. He did not deserve the responsibility of caring for a wife who could not see. He shouldn't have had to take that on.

I watched Eric come home from a long day at work, grab the grocery list, and trudge off to the store. He did not complain, but his body language said it all. He was tired. He was frustrated. He was worried. He had to do everything. If it required walking out of this house and going somewhere, it was all on Eric.

The guilt was overwhelming for me. I felt like I had failed him. I knew it was not my fault, but that did not make me feel any better.

I worried about our parents. They all took it hard. This was not their dream for me. They were concerned about how we would make it. Living three to four hours away from both sets of parents, they did not live close enough to help with our day-to-day struggles.

They wanted so much to help us, but the distance between us prohibited that.

On top of those concerns, my parents were struggling with an added burden of guilt. This was a genetic disease, and somehow, they felt like they had caused this to happen. They felt responsible. Of course, they were not. Nothing they did caused this to happen, and they could not have done anything to prevent it. I never blamed them for a moment. I knew they would have done anything in the world to have kept this hardship from befalling me. They loved me as much as any parent could ever love a child. They had been the best parents any girl could have dreamed of. No, I did not blame them, but they blamed themselves.

I had asked Dr. Machemer about the possibility of passing the disease onto Jonathan. While he allowed that it was possible, he did not think it likely. Since my form of RP is most likely a recessive trait, the chance of passing it directly to Jonathan is small. For Jonathan to have the disease, that would mean that Eric would also have to carry the gene, an unlikely scenario.

While that was reassuring, there is still a chance the disease could be passed down to my grandchildren or great-grandchildren. The thought of passing the gene onto future generations made me cringe. I couldn't bear the thought of Jonathan having this someday, and I hoped against all hope that Dr. Machemer's prediction of a low probability was correct. Once again though, there was no way to know. Just the thought of the genetics made me want to scream in frustration. It wasn't fair.

I was miserable. I felt sorry for Eric. I felt sorry for our parents. Worst of all, I felt sorry for myself.

During the weeks of the diagnosis, I felt like I was standing on the edge of a cliff looking down at the great abyss below. The threat to my world loomed below me, just waiting to swallow me up, to take away everything. Now that the testing was over and the diagnosis pronounced, I felt myself falling. I was twisting, tumbling, free falling into a desperate pit of self-pity.

CHAPTER 4
The Long Climb Out

A Cross To Bear

It was tough to get up in the morning. I was floundering. Rustling noises on the baby monitor would wake me up from a fitful sleep. I lay there paralyzed with fear, afraid to open my eyes. Would this be the day? Would this be the morning that I would wake up blind?

Blindness consumed my thoughts. It was my first thought in the morning and my last thought at night.

I kept asking, "Why me? Lord, why this? What did I do to cause this? Is this a punishment for some sin I committed? God, where are you? Why are you letting this happen?"

The questions besieged me night and day, playing on a constant rewind in my mind. I was stuck. I could not seem to move on.

One of my friends from church, Marcia, showed up one day with a book. "I saw this and thought of you. I hope it will help you."

The name of the book was "When God Doesn't Make Sense." It was written by Dr. James Dobson.

I thanked her for her kindness. Staring at the book cover, I wondered if the answers to my questions could be found inside this book. A quiet little voice spoke from deep inside me, "Read it."

After getting Jonathan to bed, I opened the book and began to read. The words on the pages seemed to be speaking directly to me, the chapters addressing the questions that I had been stewing about.

The book explained that bad things happen because we live in a fallen and sinful world. Every bad thing that happens is not your fault or your punishment. God allows suffering for reasons we do not entirely understand. What we do know is that God is with us always, walking with us through every moment of our suffering.

God understands our pain and grief. He hurts with us, and He loves us through the hardships. God can take the trials and losses of our lives and work them for our good. He will make good come out of our hard things.

Those words flowed over me, soothing the pain in my wounded heart. I so needed to hear these words of comfort.

These concepts were not foreign to me. I had grown up in church, had read my Bible. The words of Romans 8:28 had been committed to memory years before. "And we know that in all things God works for the good of those who love Him, who have been called according to His purpose" (Romans 8:28 *NIV*). Yet, in that moment, I needed to hear these messages again. I needed to hear these truths presented in a different way.

I remember turning the page and there it was. It was like the words were lifted off the page and spoken directly to my heart. "...My grace is sufficient for you, for my power is made perfect in weakness..." (2 Corinthians 12:9, NIV). Grace, Dr. Dobson was discussing grace. His next words hit me full force as he paraphrased that powerful scripture. "Everyone is asked to endure something that brings discomfort, pain, or sorrow. This is yours. Accept it. Carry it. I will give you the grace to endure it."[1]

I sat there staring at those words, thinking about the cross.

I understood that Jesus who was free of sin had died upon a cross to atone for our sins. He bore His cross to ensure our forgiveness, to set us free from sin, to open the way to eternal life with Him. He loved us that much, that He would die to give us life.

Suddenly, I recognized something I had not considered before.

Jesus had borne His cross for me, but what about me? Was I free from burden in this life? Was I supposed to be immune from adversity or affliction?

Like a light bulb clicking on in a dark closet, the answers to those questions clicked in my mind. No, I was not immune to suffering. I had no guarantee against affliction. Blindness was my cross to bear.

Staring out the window into the pitch-black darkness, I heard these words in my mind, and sighing deeply, I let them fall softly from my lips, "This is your cross. Accept it. Carry it. God will give you the grace to deal with it."

---

[1] Dobson, J.C. (1993). "When God Doesn't Make Sense" (p. 105). Tyndale House Publishers, Inc.

CHAPTER 4
The Long Climb Out

It was time to rise up and stand firm in my faith. God had not left me alone as I had feared. He was right there with me, orchestrating these hard circumstances for my ultimate good. He would make a way for me out of this darkness if I would just trust in Him. God would give me the grace to deal with this. Could I trust Him enough to find my way to peace?

Car Keys

I had always loved to drive. At age 12, I had begged my grandfather to teach me how to drive, which of course, he did, riding around the pasture in his old, beat-up, blue pickup truck. Even before that, as young as 8 years old, Grand would let me sit in his lap and steer the truck as we ambled down the back country roads near his home. I doubt that any teenager in America was more excited than I was on the day I finally got my driver's license. I jumped in my bright blue '62 VW Bug, and off I went. Freedom! I could go wherever I wanted.

Now here I was, 33 years old, chained to my house. I could not leave that driveway without the help of someone else. "How did I get here? I just can't do this!"

Standing at my dining room window, I stared out at my car in the carport, car keys held tightly in my hand. We needed groceries, and I just could not bear the look on Eric's face when I would have to tell him that he needed to go to the store, again. He seemed so tired these days when he got home. "How can I send him to the store again?"

Just a few weeks ago, I was driving all around town. Nothing had really changed with my eyes since then. They were not any worse than they were a month ago. Would it really hurt anything for me to drive one more time? If I could just go and get the groceries, it would save Eric the trip, and I wouldn't have to feel guilty about asking him to go.

I vacillated back and forth in my mind, still fingering the car keys in my hand. Eric and I had talked so many times about it. Neither of us wanted me to give up driving, but we had both heard the doctor's words. "For your safety, Anita, for your child, for the other people on the road." Eric and I had agreed that I should not take the risk of hurting someone else because of something I could not see.

The decision had been made, but that did not make it easy. I was so frustrated. He was so overwhelmed. Not being able to drive impacted everything. Every single errand outside the home was impossible for me to do now.

I understood the rationale, but the reality of it was painful. Letting go of the car keys meant letting go of my independence. That was a hard pill to swallow at age 33. I was an energetic, ambitious, self-directed young woman. I liked doing things my way. I was headstrong and quite capable. Bottom line, I liked my independence.

I have always had a stubborn, independent streak. Even as a little girl, I wanted to do things my way. When I was about 4 years old, my father and I went round and round until he finally broke me of my defiance. I learned that he was the boss, and when he sat me down to explain why I needed to do what he asked, I figured out quickly that I had better listen.

Although I never gave my parents any trouble, that independent streak was still there as a teenager. Even when I met my husband, he learned quickly that I liked doing things my own way. I remember my father shaking his head at Eric and me as we argued over some point of contention. He laughed and said, "Two great hard heads meet." That isn't far from the truth.

Eric and I had dated for five years, even attending college together. We had enjoyed married life for eight years before deciding to start a family. We had been together as a couple for all those years, and still we liked to do our own things. We had very different interests. We enjoyed pursuing those interests and then coming together to do other things as a couple. I liked being independent, and he liked me that way.

CHAPTER 4
The Long Climb Out

When I was upset about something or feeling stressed, I would just take off driving, finding some back country road to explore and take my mind off my problems. Oh, how I loved to drive!

Jonathan was calling me. "Mama! Mama! Where you at?"

I turned my gaze from the window and looked at the keys in my hand. I shook my head and walked into the kitchen, tossing the car keys on the counter. I would not go anywhere today. I would not drive again because I could not risk hurting Jonathan. I had been warned not to drive, and if I had an accident that injured him, I would never forgive myself. Ultimately, Jonathan was my reason to lay down those car keys and never pick them up again.

I knew it was the right choice, but that did not make it any easier to live with.

Spiritual Seesaw

If my emotional state felt like a rollercoaster ride, then my spiritual life resembled a seesaw. One day, I would be on top, full of faith, comforted by my belief in God's amazing grace. The next day, I would plummet to the bottom, my heart sick with fear and weighed down by hard questions.

It was like I took one step up and two steps back. One minute, I had it all together, and the next minute, I was falling apart.

Night after night, I immersed myself in the words of Dr. Dobson's book, "When God Doesn't Make Sense." On certain pages, I would stop and re-read the words again, trying to silence the endless "Why?" questions that I couldn't seem to eject from my brain. I wrote down several quotes, trying to hang on to their reassurance.

I held the tiny blue cross in my hand, remembering how someone I didn't know had made this treasure and sent it to me with a prayer. I stared at the miniature cross and recalled the late-night epiphany that had leapt out at me as I absorbed the words of Dr. Dobson's book. "This is your cross. Accept it. Carry it. God will give you the grace to deal with it." Deep down, I knew that blindness was my cross to bear. I knew that God's grace was with me. I knew that somehow He would see me through, and yet, I felt so weak, so weary. I needed to carry my cross, but it was too heavy. It was more than I could bear.

The little blue cross became a placeholder in my Bible, marking the pages of the eighth chapter of Romans. Again and again, I would look at the underlined verses on those pages.

> "But if we hope for what we do not yet have, we wait for it patiently" (Romans 8:25 *NIV*).

> "And we know that in all things God works for the good of those who love him, who have been called according to his purpose" (Romans 8:28 *NIV*).

> "No, in all these things we are more than conquerors through him who loved us. For I am convinced that neither death nor life, neither angels nor demons, neither the present nor the future, nor any powers, neither height nor depth, nor anything else in all creation, will be able to separate us from the love of God that is in Christ Jesus our Lord" (Romans 8:37-39 *NIV*).

I reminded myself that God can do anything, that He can make good come out of this bad thing, and that I needed to wait patiently and confidently on Him to act. I would tell myself that nothing could separate me from His love.

On good days, I could believe that. On bad days, I would lift my eyes to heaven asking, "Lord, where are you? Why would you let this happen? How in the world can you use this for good? Lord, I'm drowning in the deepest ocean. Why do I feel so far from Your love?"

I felt guilty about my doubts, chastising myself for my lack of faith. "Lord, forgive me. I just don't know what to do. I want to believe, Lord, but why would you let this happen to me?"

CHAPTER 4
The Long Climb Out

I flipped through my Bible to find verses I had underlined over the years.

> "For I know the plans I have for you," declares the Lord, "plans to prosper you and not to harm you, plans to give you hope and a future" (Jeremiah 29:11 *NIV*).

> "Have I not commanded you? Be strong and courageous. Do not be afraid; do not be discouraged, for the Lord your God will be with you wherever you go" (Joshua 1:9 *NIV*).

> "I can do all this through him who gives me strength" (Philippians 4:13 *NIV*).

> "Do not be anxious about anything, but in every situation, by prayer and petition, with thanksgiving, present your requests to God. And the peace of God, which transcends all understanding, will guard your hearts and your minds in Christ Jesus" (Philippians 4:6-7 *NIV*).

Bowing my head, I prayed, "Lord, I know you are there. I know You are with me. I am afraid. I don't want to doubt you. I can't do this on my own. O Lord, why does it have to be this way?"

Some days, I would pray and feel God's peace settle over me. Other days, I just felt desperate and so far from His healing touch. I wanted to trust. I wanted to believe, but the "Why?" questions kept cycling through my head, and it was hard to let them go, to make them stop.

I kept reassuring myself that this was not a punishment for some sin I committed, yet why did I feel so guilty? Somehow, I had messed up our lives, and I didn't know how to fix it.

Despite my hard questions, my doubts and fears, I kept praying. I refused to turn away from God even though I didn't understand. I knew God was real, that He loved me, that He was with me. I couldn't always feel these things, but I chose to believe them anyway. I kept on praying. I kept on hoping for a way out of this pit I found myself in.

I needed to talk to someone. My verbal-processing self needed to say these things out loud. I tried to say them to my pastor, and the conversation helped some, but I wasn't comfortable sharing the depth of my angst with him. I needed someone to talk to that I could be real with, that would hear me out without judging me. Yet so far, I hadn't found the right person or time to discuss my seesaw of faith.

Sister Speak

The phone kept ringing. My friends did not forget. My family kept reaching out. Everyone knew I was struggling. They all knew we were in crisis. I felt their love. It helped. It did not erase the hurt. It did not solve the problems. Still, their love made the burden a bit lighter.

I would soon have to give Lynn an answer about work. I could not keep putting off that decision. Nonetheless, I felt like I had nowhere to turn. For every scenario proposed, there was a myriad of hurdles to overcome.

One morning, I answered the phone to find my cousin Cathy on the line. "I want to come and see you. Can I bring the girls and come up for a few days?"

My heart skipped a beat. A visit from Cathy would be wonderful. Holding back the inevitable tears, I said, "Yes, come!" As I hung up the phone, I felt such relief. I could talk to Cathy. I could really be honest with her. I needed to be honest with someone.

Cathy and I had grown up together. We may have been cousins, but she had always been like a sister to me. As an only child, I had longed for siblings as I grew up. Cathy filled that role. She was eighteen months older, and I had always looked up to her.

As an Army brat, I had grown up living far from our extended family. Still, we traveled back home to South Carolina as often as

CHAPTER 4
The Long Climb Out

we could. Whenever we came home, I spent as much time as I could with Cathy. We were the best of playmates as little girls. As we grew, I tagged along on many of her family's camping vacations.

When I was 15 years old, we moved back to live in SC, about fifteen minutes from Cathy's home. She and I tore up the road between our houses with shopping trips and sleepovers. We were inseparable. We could tell each other anything. She knew me, really knew me.

I could talk to Cathy. I did not have to protect her from my feelings. That's how I felt about everyone around me. Eric and our parents were hurting so badly. "How could I be honest with them? That will just make things worse for them."

But Cathy could take it. I could be honest with her.

It was a sunny afternoon when she and her two precious little girls arrived in my driveway. In typical Cathy style, she headed straight for me with a tight hug and tears in her eyes. "Oh, I'm so glad to see you." The feeling was mutual.

She was like a breath of fresh air, like a soothing balm for my wounded soul. I felt the tension in my shoulders release just a bit, the knot in my stomach give way.

Jonathan welcomed the girls with a call to come play on the swing set. Cathy and I followed them into the yard and stood catching up. I was just so glad to see her.

With three kids in tow, there was little time for deep conversation until after we put the kids to bed. Eric had to go to work in the morning, so he headed to bed at his usual time. Cathy and I stayed up. It was like the sleepovers of old.

I confess that I don't remember the exact substance of all of our conversations, but I remember sitting on our sunporch, she sprawled across the love seat, me stretched out on the couch. The quiet of the night blanketed us. It was like we were the only two people awake on the planet. I opened up to her, letting all my feelings and thoughts flow out. The dam that I had plastered up for so many weeks broke, and all the emotion came pouring out. She listened with the intensity and acceptance that flows from sisterhood.

We talked, and we cried. I don't remember all the words I said, but I remember the relief of sharing what I had been holding inside for all these weeks.

As teenagers, Cathy and I had explored our faith together. We come from a long line of church-going Scotch-Irish ancestors, and faith runs deep in our veins. As we entered adolescence, we struggled with the typical questions of faith. Together, she and I had explored our questions about God, shared scriptures, and attended church together. I knew full well that we shared the bonds of faith.

I do remember opening up to Cathy, putting into words the spiritual dilemmas I had been struggling with. "I know I shouldn't, but I keep asking why. Why is God allowing this to happen? Have I done something wrong? Is this a punishment for some sin I've committed?"

I felt guilty even uttering the questions, but Cathy understood.

She shook her head, "No, you didn't cause this. You didn't do anything to make this happen. Bad things happen. Anita, you know that. You're a nurse. You've seen this with your patients. Bad things just happen sometimes."

How many times had I read those points in Dr. Dobson's book? How many times had I said those words to myself? Yet, when Cathy said it, something clicked. A sense of relief washed over me. A weight had been lifted off my shoulders.

I told Cathy about reading Dr. Dobson's book, sharing some of the highlights. I shared the quote about carrying my cross. I wanted to hear her perspective. She listened intently, reassuring me that the questions troubling me were perfectly understandable.

"You're hurting, Anita. You haven't lost your faith. You're just being human."

We sat in silence for a bit, as we both pondered each other's comments. Finally, Cathy broke the silence. "Anita, you may never know why, but I believe that God will use this hard thing for good. There will be good that comes from it."

CHAPTER 4
The Long Climb Out

"I sure hope so. I can't imagine what, but I hope so."

Cathy didn't have the answers to my questions, but her responses were rooted in faith. Hearing her faith bolstered my own. By voicing her beliefs, she was witnessing to me in a way I so needed at that moment.

It had helped to open up to her. It was safe to vent my doubts and distress. She understood.

We discussed what to do about work. Should I quit and stay home with Jonathan? If I went back to work, how would I get there?

"I just keep thinking that if I can only see for a short time, I want to spend it seeing Jonathan grow up."

I remember her sitting there quiet for a moment. "Anita, you talk like you are going blind in the next year or so. What makes you think that? Is that really what the doctor thinks?"

"I don't know. They don't know. There is no way to know how long I have to see."

"I understand that it's hard to deal with not knowing. I can see you wanting to be home with Jonathan. But I don't think you should live like you are going blind tomorrow. That's not much of a way to live. You are acting like your life is over. You know that's not true. Why wouldn't you do all you can while you can?"

Her words seemed to echo in the quiet canyon of darkness that surrounded the porch. I had no response, for her words had hit home. It was one of those "Aha" moments, when you suddenly get some unexpected insight.

I knew Cathy was right. For nearly eight weeks, I had focused on the loss. I had been consumed by the heartache. For the last couple of weeks, I had wallowed in the pit of self-pity.

My mindset was on the crisis. I was living like my life was over. Every time I thought of the future, I recoiled. It was not the future I wanted. In truth, I had been hiding from that future in the safe cocoon of my home.

Cathy's question had caught me off guard, but her assessment was accurate. I had been living like someone who only had weeks to live.

Because I could not envision this new future, I had boarded up the possibilities. Since the solutions for how to manage without driving were not what I wanted, I had shut them down. I was making my world small, my choices limited, my options bleak.

"Why wouldn't you do all you can while you can?" The words replayed in my mind. I wondered what would it be like to quit fighting the options and start trying out the solutions? Could I really figure out a new way to live, instead of just existing?

I hugged Cathy goodbye the next day, thanking her for her insight and her support. Her perspective had challenged me to think differently about my situation. As she drove away, I stood in my driveway thinking, "Now what?"

Climbing Out

The "why" questions were not answered, but somehow speaking them out loud had turned down their noise level in my mind. Their angst was abating, allowing me to look forward instead of looking back.

Perhaps it was time to let the "why" questions go. I didn't have the answers, and likely never would. Could I accept that and just move on? Could I believe that God would work things together for my good somehow?

I took a good long look at my circumstances. I had fallen into that great abyss, sinking deep down into that awful pit of self-pity. Like the prodigal son, I woke up one morning and found myself wallowing in a pigsty. The only difference was that mine was a pigsty of emotion. I was tired of wallowing in all that misery, but could I really climb out of that pit?

I looked at the precious little boy playing on the coffee table with his Thomas the Tank Engine train. What about him? Doesn't he deserve more than this? He needs a mother to teach and nurture

CHAPTER 4
The Long Climb Out

him, a mother who will give him a good, healthy, happy childhood. How can I be that mother if I am so consumed by regret and resentment?

Could I move past the loss and step out in faith? I wasn't sure, but for the first time in weeks, I wanted to let the heartache go. I wanted to feel better.

It was time to trust God with the plan and believe that He could make it work. I wasn't sure how, but I wanted to move forward. I was sick and tired of where I had been.

Looking back, I would like to say that I let go of those "why" questions and never looked back, but that would not be true. Those haunting questions would occasionally resurface during times of sadness and loss. Still, after my conversation with Cathy, something shifted. Something changed to alter my perspective.

Was it the words I read in Dr. Dobson's book? Was it the prayers and many kindnesses of those who reached out to me in that difficult time? Was it Cathy's witness, her words of affirmation that turned the tide? I don't know, but somewhere along the way, I changed my question. Instead of asking God "Why?" all the time, I began to ask "How?" I chose to reach out in trust and ask God, "How do I move on? How do I live life with this disease? How do I make this work?"

CHAPTER 5
The Road Back To Work

Time's Up

My time was up. I had promised Lynn that I would make a decision before the end of the month. Here it was just a few days before Thanksgiving, and I was no closer to having a firm game plan.

When I had spoken to Lynn several weeks before, she had explained that I could take a family medical leave. This would allow me to take three months off, most of which would be unpaid leave. However, I would still be employed and could return to whatever position might be available whenever I was ready to come back to work.

For the past four weeks, I had used my paid annual leave. That option was coming to an end next week. One way or another, I had to decide. I needed to give Lynn an answer. It was only fair.

In truth, I was sick of thinking about it. Eric and I had debated all the possible scenarios. It was clear that Eric could not drive me back and forth to work. That would mean a commute of over five hours per day. That would be exhausting for him, not to mention the wear and tear on our vehicles. There was no way to time our work hours, let alone drop off and pick up Jonathan from the babysitter at the right time.

There were no public transportation options. While Eric had brought up the idea of carpooling with someone, I quickly discounted the idea. I did not know anyone who worked at the hospital and lived in our area. After all, we lived 30 miles away. Even if I had known someone, I could not imagine imposing myself on someone's commute. That would be asking too much.

Perhaps Eric could find a job in Greensboro, but we both knew that the possibilities were quite slim. He had worked in the Greensboro area for several years, but all the contracts for his particular skill set had recently dried up. He had found a good position in the Research Triangle Park area. Switching jobs did not feel like the right career move for him at the moment.

There was just no easy answer, but my time for debate was up. I picked up the phone and dialed Lynn's number.

I updated Lynn on all the issues and told her I had no idea how to make returning to work feasible. We discussed my taking a leave of absence and how that would work.

"Anita, if you could get a ride to work, would you be willing to come back?"

"I guess so. I think so. But Lynn, how am I going to get a ride?"

Lynn explained that she had shared my story with her supervisors. Everyone was very concerned and offered to help support me in any way they could. Several days later, a colleague of ours contacted Lynn. Fred explained that he had heard about my situation. He had discovered that we lived in the same general area and wondered about offering me a ride to work. He had asked Lynn her thoughts and whether he should call.

"Anita, can I give him your phone number? I know you don't know what you want to do but you could at least talk to him."

My first reaction was gratitude mixed with a humbling sense of surprise. In the weeks since the diagnosis, I was often surprised at the compassion and concern that others had shown me upon finding out the news of my failing vision. People offered help so readily that it almost shocked me. I knew it was a sad story, but I was surprised as to how often people responded with sincere offers of help. Here was yet another surprising offer. Fred and I were colleagues, working on committees and projects together. We shared a mutual respect for each other. Fred was a great guy, but we were not really close friends. Yet here he was going out of his way to offer help.

"That's really nice of him, Lynn, but I don't think I can do that. That's a lot to ask."

"Just talk to him. It won't hurt to talk."

An Offer In Hand

The phone rang. It was Fred. I took a deep breath. After the introductory pleasantries, Fred broached the subject.

"Anita, Lynn shared your situation with me, and I am so sorry to hear about your eyes."

I took another deep breath and thanked him in the reassuring tones I had grown accustomed to using when people expressed their concern for me. While discussing the topic was challenging for me, I knew it was even more difficult for others. They just did not know what to say.

Fred went on, "As it turns out, I don't live far from you, and I'd really like to give you a ride to work."

I sucked in another deep breath. My mind was racing, and I couldn't speak. All I could think was, "How in the world could I ever accept such an offer? It's asking too much."

It was not that I didn't appreciate this kind offer and the acts of kindness from so many others. I was humbled by their generosity. I just didn't want to be in this position. I had always been so self-sufficient. Yet, all that self-sufficiency had flown out the window with four little words, "You are legally blind."

My days of freedom and independence were over. I could not leave my house without the help of someone else. It was killing me, hurting my pride, and making me feel like a burden. Asking for help seemed like asking too much.

I finally mumbled, "Oh wow, Fred." My voice trailed away, and I could not think what to say next.

Fred was prepared to fill the gap and explained that he lived only ten minutes from my house. He would be happy to pick me up and take me back and forth to the hospital each day that I worked. Given my part-time schedule, I was only working three days a week.

"Oh Fred, that is so very kind of you, but I don't see how in the world I could accept such an offer. It's asking too much."

Fred responded, "Anita, I understand how you feel, but before you tell me no, let me tell you a story."

CHAPTER 5
The Road Back To Work

Fred went on to explain that several years earlier, his wife Leah had suffered a serious health condition that required a long recovery period. Her recovery process necessitated that she not drive for six months. While she was ready to return to work, her 45-minute commute was an issue since Fred commuted 30 minutes in an opposite direction. Without family in the area, they were perplexed as to how to manage this scenario.

What happened next totally shocked them. Friends from Leah's work called to offer rides. They worked out a schedule and managed to provide her rides to work for the entire six-month recovery period.

Fred explained, "I could never repay them for their kindness. It helped us so much at a time when we really needed help. I can't repay them, but if you'll let me help you, it will be like paying them back, and that will help me."

His words hung in the air for a few minutes. I sat there trying to digest what all he had just said. That quiet little voice inside me whispered, "Anita, this is your answer."

"Wow, Fred, I don't know what to say to that."

"I know it's hard, but let me help you. I'd really like to."

We talked about the particulars of timing of our work schedules and where we could meet. I told him that I would think about it and talk with my husband. Thanking him profusely, I hung up the phone. Simply stunned by the encounter, I slumped back in my chair, trying to process Fred's offer. "What just happened?"

After some discussion with Eric and a lot of prayer, I called Fred back a few days later and accepted his offer. That was a huge decision. It was the first step in putting the pieces of our lives back together. It meant a return to work, but also required me to accept the help of others. It forced me to acknowledge my loss of independence and to consciously decide to move forward. Accepting that offer certainly was not easy, demanding all the courage I could muster. Life had to go on, and God was offering me a hand.

The First Step

I opened the door from the stairwell and stared down the long corridor in front of me. The nursing unit lay at the end of the hallway. It was my first day back at work.

I had ridden to work with Fred. He had kept me distracted with conversation as we walked through the door of the hospital. Together, we had made our way across the ground floor of the building, headed towards our offices. I had turned off and headed up the stairs alone. I opened the stairwell door and stopped, feeling paralyzed at the sight of my nursing unit in the distance. I had a knot in my stomach. It had been almost five weeks since I had walked through that doorway.

So much had changed in those five weeks. My world had been turned upside down. Just over five weeks ago, I had walked out of that unit wondering what I would learn at my eye appointment at Duke. Now, I knew for certain that my eye disease was real. I had been confronted with the awful news that I was going blind. I had been forced to make the devastating decision that I would never drive again. My whole world had caved in around me. I had spent weeks in a pit of despair.

Now, here I was, five weeks later, in the same place, but feeling like such a different person. I felt like a traveler back from a long journey, weary and oddly disconcerted. It should all feel familiar. I should feel at home. Yet, I felt so out of place, like I had lost my way somehow.

I knew it was time to go back to work. I knew they needed me, and I needed the work. I loved being a nurse. It was an intricate part of me, woven into the very fabric of my identity. I could not imagine giving it up, and at the same time, I was afraid to go back.

I had worked on that nursing unit for over five years. I was a teacher, a leader, a problem solver. The nursing staff depended on me for advice on clinical questions. I would join them at the patient's bedside to assess a situation and determine the best response. "Can I do that now? Will I be able to see things well enough to answer their questions? Will I miss something I shouldn't?"

I thought about taking direct care of patients. It was a very rewarding aspect of my job. I recalled my struggles in performing routine nursing tasks. In the recent months, even the simplest of tasks had become challenging. I had shrugged it off as being out of practice or overly rushed, but now I knew better. My struggles with IV lines or medication delivery were because of my vision loss. The night blindness portion of the disease was causing me to need more light to do normal tasks at night. "I know what is wrong with me now. What if I take care of a patient and miss something? What if I make a mistake because of my eyes? What if I hurt a patient?"

Before, I did not realize what was happening to me. Now, standing there in the hallway, I knew what was wrong. I knew why I had been struggling in my work, and I was afraid. I was scared to walk back into that unit. "How am I going to do this job if I can't take care of patients anymore?"

As if those worries were not enough, I also had a sense of dread about seeing my friends and coworkers. I knew they would all be glad to have me back. "How will they handle this difficult news? How am I going to explain it all to them and not fall apart?"

Even the thought of explaining my eye disease to other people brought a flood of emotions. Watching people's reactions, seeing the sorrow spread across their faces, was enough to undo me.

While I wanted people to understand what was going on, I did not want their pity. My pride couldn't take that. I chastised myself for those prideful thoughts, but there it was. I wanted people to understand what I was going through, but at the same time, I could hardly talk about it. I certainly couldn't talk about it and get my job done.

"So how in the world am I going to walk back in that unit?"

That was all I could think of as I stood there watching the nurses hustle back and forth in front of the open doorway. "Well, I can't stand here forever! Get it together, Anita."

I straightened my shoulders and started walking. I had taken my first steps back into the world of work.

Survived

The day had gone much better than I had expected. I had walked through the doors of the nursing unit and called out "Good Morning!" as was my habit. The unit secretary had looked up, smiled as she recognized me, and called out "Oh, Anita!"

At the mention of my name, heads turned, and I was greeted with warm expressions and kind smiles. Stepping into the nursing station, the hugs began. I had thought that I would fall apart when seeing them all gathered, but instead, it felt like a soothing balm. Sure, there were moist eyes and tight hugs, but no one fell apart. No one asked hard questions. They were just glad to see me.

I guess I had not given people enough credit. After all, these were nurses. They knew exactly how to support, encourage, and love me. I truly felt their love.

After the initial round of hugs, I straightened, assumed my normal work tone, and asked, "So how are things today? What's the census?" Just like that, we shifted to work mode, the angst of my return fading into the background.

There were mini-reunions all day long as I made my way around the hospital. People were caring, but not overly dramatic. They respected my privacy and did not push for details.

It was so good to be with my office mates and of course, we talked more in depth. Seeing Mary was like coming home, and our hug spoke volumes. She was so glad to have me back.

Not only had the work day gone smoothly, but riding with Fred had worked out better than I had expected. Eric had dropped me off at Hardee's near the interstate, and Fred had breezed in and picked me up. He insisted on dropping me at my house on the way home. We had great conversation on both trips, and I found Fred easy to talk to. He was true to his word. His desire to help had been genuine, and that made me feel more comfortable about accepting the rides.

It had all worked out. The day had gone so much better than I had imagined, but I was still a bundle of nerves by the end of the day.

After Fred dropped me off, I stepped through my back door and made my way to my recliner, so glad to be home. It would all be replayed again tomorrow. For now, though, I was content to sit back and snuggle up with my little boy. The work day was over, and I had survived.

A New Path

The next few weeks went smoothly enough. Because of my discomfort with direct patient care, Lynn had removed me from the staffing schedule for now, saying that we could figure things out once I was settled back into work. This was a very generous gesture since someone else would have to cover the shifts I normally worked. Filling schedule holes was no easy task. Although I appreciated the gesture immensely, how long could I reasonably expect this to last? Staffing was part of my job. Could they really pull me off the schedule for good? Was that really fair to my co-workers? I felt uneasy about not pulling my weight, and yet, I was panicked at the thought that I might make a mistake if I went back to carrying a patient load.

On one of our rides home from work, Fred asked how things were going with my job. I explained that the project work was fine, but I was concerned about not being able to staff and the impact on my co-workers. Fred asked if I had given any thought to changing jobs. "Well, yeah, some. But I have no idea what that would be."

"Would you have any interest in working with clinical pathways?"

In the preceding months, the hospital had embarked on a new initiative to improve the quality and cost of patient care. Clinical teams had been charged with developing clinical pathways, which were essentially standardized multidisciplinary plans of care for specific patient populations. I had been involved in the initial work of the cardiology team. I had found the concept exciting, feeling that it had potential to positively impact the quality and flow of patient care.

"We have been considering hiring a coordinator for the clinical pathway program. We need someone to focus on this. We need some energy behind this to get the program moving forward. We thought about you."

I was stunned. I had not even considered such a possibility. While I had heard some discussion about the need for more coordination of the current fledgling program, it had not occurred to me that I might be the right fit for such a role.

Fred expanded further on the proposed duties of the position, and I grew more interested. As he dropped me off at my house, Fred instructed me to give it some thought. I closed the car door with a mixture of surprise and excitement that this might be a good opportunity for me.

Over the next few days, I did give it some thought and prayer. Eric and I debated the pros and cons. There were lots of positives. I would have no staffing requirements which would solve that worry. The hours were flexible. I could do the 20 hours per week in any format I chose. Two ten-hour days were an option, and I could work from home occasionally if I had a transportation issue. The position would report to Fred, and I would work closely with other Clinical Nurse Specialists. I would enjoy those interactions. I had no hesitation about doing the work and found the prospect challenging and exciting.

The downside of the move would be to leave my wonderful co-workers and the nursing staff. I felt very close to all these people, and leaving would be hard. I also loved being involved in patient care, and the thought of stepping away from cardiology nursing tugged at my heart strings.

In the end, the flexibility of the new role tipped the scale. The idea of a new challenge lifted my spirits. There would likely be less pressure and stress with this role, and that would be a healthy change given all my recent life events.

I hardly even interviewed for the job. I think everyone involved had already decided this position would be a good fit for me if I was interested. Within ten days of our initial car ride conversation, I was given the new job title of Clinical Pathway Program Coordinator. Over the next four weeks, I finished up my projects and tied up loose ends. By mid-January, I found myself settling into a new office, my mind challenged with a whole new realm of tasks. I had taken a new path.

Saving The Day

The holidays were bittersweet for me. Emotionally, I had found more equilibrium as I settled into more normal routines. While my vision issues still haunted me, Christmas with a two-year-old was a wonderful distraction. Jonathan was mesmerized by everything Christmas, and the focus on something other than myself was a good thing. For the most part, the events are a blur in my mind, but one story stands out, a memory I still cherish.

After work on a Friday evening, Eric and I loaded up the car and headed for South Carolina. My mother's family always gathered on the weekend before Christmas, and the get-together was scheduled for that Saturday evening. Traffic was bad as we journeyed down the highway, and I knew it would be late by the time we arrived at my parents' house. Jonathan had dozed off in his car seat, and we had ridden in silence for an hour or so. We were about thirty minutes from my folk's house when I peered in the back seat to check on my boy.

Something didn't look quite right. I looked closer at Jonathan's slumped figure. I frowned as I scanned the back seat, then turned further to check the floor. Where was George?

George was Jonathan's faithful companion. He tagged along everywhere, keeping Jonathan company wherever he went. Curious George had arrived at our house when Jonathan was just a few months old. Eric and I had begun reading to Jonathan even as a tiny infant. Although he couldn't yet understand the words, we showed him the pictures and exposed him to the concept of reading.

Soon after we began our reading routine, I had remembered the Curious George books I had loved as a child. Buying several of the book series, I happened upon one of the Curious George stuffed animals and bought it. Although his crib was full of stuffed animals, Jonathan latched onto George.

George slept with Jonathan and ate with him too. He tagged along beside Jonathan as he toddled around the house. When we traveled anywhere, he shared the car seat with his best buddy. Looking again at the back seat, I wondered once more. Where is George?

Then it hit me like a load of bricks. I remembered seeing George lying on the bed next to Jonathan's suitcase, but I didn't recall picking him up. Usually, he was nestled snugly under Jonathan's arm when I tucked him in the car seat, but I didn't recall him being there when I had strapped my little boy in for the ride.

With a sick feeling in my gut, I came face to face with the awful truth. We had left George at home.

Sucking in a hard breath, I turned in panic to my unsuspecting husband and whispered the horrible truth. "We forgot George!"

The terrified look on Eric's face told me he understood the seriousness of the situation. Jonathan would never go to sleep tonight without George, and we were way too far down the road to turn back now. It was going to be a miserable weekend. I thought to myself, "Great! It will be miserable, just like a lot of other days here lately." Clearly, I was feeling sorry for myself again.

CHAPTER 5
The Road Back To Work

Taking a deep breath, I chastised myself for such negative thoughts and forced myself to think of options. Hearing Jonathan stir in the back seat, I formulated a plan and set it in motion.

"Hey buddy, you awake?"

Jonathan nodded as he mumbled, "Uh-huh."

I looked at Eric for moral support and then dived in headfirst.

"Jonathan, did you know that Grandma has a Christmas Bear that lives at her house?" Making eye contact, I nodded emphatically. "Yeah, she does. He's red and blue and he sits in a chair beside her Christmas tree."

Jonathan made affirming noises as he watched me closely, waiting for me to continue.

"But you know what's sad, Jonathan? The Christmas Bear doesn't have a little boy to love him. He is all alone with no little boy to play with or sleep with at night."

I let the words hang in the air before continuing. Jonathan's little face held a sad expression as he considered the state of the Christmas Bear. Seeing my opportunity, I seized the moment. "Jonathan, while we're at Grandma's house this weekend, do you think that you could love on the Christmas Bear? Maybe you could play with him? Maybe he could even sleep with you? Oh, that would be so nice. The Christmas Bear would love that!"

His soft eyes grew wide as he began to nod emphatically. He was deadly serious, a toy soldier signing up for duty. "I can love da Christmas Bear. I love him!"

"Oh, Jonathan, that will be so nice. That will make his Christmas so special! The Christmas Bear will love being your friend this weekend. Oh, that will just be so nice."

I have had many looks from my dear husband over the course of our lives together, but I have never experienced a look of deeper admiration than I did sitting there in that car that night. He was oh so impressed with my clever sales pitch. His sigh of relief spoke volumes.

It worked like a charm. When we arrived at my parent's house, Jonathan tugged on his grandma's hand, "Grandma, where da Christmas Bear?"

A bit confused for a moment, she cast a questioning look at me, to which I mouthed silently, "We forgot George!"

In true Grandma fashion, she quickly read the situation and fell right into step with my well-laid plan. Taking Jonathan by the hand, they headed for the Christmas tree to introduce the bright red Christmas Bear to his new best friend. Jonathan never mentioned George the whole weekend.

In so many ways, I still felt like I was falling apart. Yet, the one thing I felt good at, the one thing that kept me going was being Jonathan's mom. With that episode of motherly magic, I had managed to save the day. Looking back, that may well have been my best "Mommy Moment!"

Finding A New Rhythm

The weeks of winter passed quietly as we adjusted to the new rhythm of our lives. I settled into working two days a week. They were long days, but it was helpful not to have to arrange transportation for a third day each week. I usually ended up with some paperwork to finish at home, but that was easily managed. I did enjoy the challenge of the new position. While it did not offer the exciting fast-paced drama of a clinical nursing unit, it did stimulate my creativity and engage my organizational skills. I found that I was good at motivating teams and keeping projects moving. The role was much less stressful than my old job, and that was a good thing at the moment.

The rides with Fred worked out great. He made me feel at ease, and that helped me get more comfortable with the concept of accepting help. Since he was now my supervisor, our car rides ended up being great opportunities to discuss our work projects. It was a win-win for us both.

CHAPTER 5
The Road Back To Work

Eric did his best to juggle our transportation issues, but it was not easy. He took Jonathan across town to the babysitter each morning that I worked, and then headed to his office. The whole trek took him almost an hour and a half. Then, he did the same trip in reverse each evening. Sometimes, traffic was backed up, and he would be late arriving at the babysitter. Thankfully, Evelyn was so gracious to work with us. She knew what we were dealing with, and she never complained.

We were making the work days work, but it was still a struggle to manage life without my being able to drive. There were errands to run, groceries to buy, doctor's appointments to juggle. There was no way to manage it all without help, but it was so hard to ask for it. Countless friends extended sincere offers of help, but the thought of calling and bothering people made my stomach churn. I fretted over every request I made. Was I being a nuisance asking for a ride? I avoided such outside requests at all costs, but as the weeks progressed, it was clear that was not a workable way to live.

Our families came to the rescue as much as they could. Although Eric's mom Liz was still working full-time, she came down periodically to stay for a day or two and help with errands. My parents began making a monthly visit to help. Of course, it was no great sacrifice to see their grandson so often, and Jonathan loved spending time with each of his grandparents. In preparation for their visits, I would save up as many errands as I possibly could, and Mom, Dad or Liz would run me around town. We were so thankful for their help. It made a dent in the seemingly endless list of things Eric needed to do.

As Eric and I tried to adjust to this new way of life, Jonathan was still our lifeline. He was the bright spot in our days, the positive thing to focus on when everything else seemed bleak. He kept us busy and made us laugh. We needed that laughter to distract us from the harsh realities of the situation.

A Church Family

One of the great blessings of this time was our church family. We had started attending our church shortly after Jonathan was born. There is nothing like a child to make you recall why you need to be in church. You look at that sweet little face and ponder all the things that can go wrong. You want him to have the right values, to make the right choices, to choose the right friends. You want him to be grounded in something solid, not gliding along on the slippery slope that is today's secular society. That's when you think about church.

With working weekends as a nurse, I never really found a church home in my 20's, yet I still clung to my beliefs and prayed often. I found my way to a pew occasionally, but wasn't connected to a specific congregation.

That all changed with motherhood, and soon, Eric and I were attending services regularly at a local Methodist church. About a year before my diagnosis, a new Sunday School class had formed, targeting couples in their 20's and 30's. Eric and I had tried it out and enjoyed the other couples in the class. Our attendance became even more regular as we looked forward to connecting with friends in our age group. Jonathan enjoyed his class, and I was excited that he was learning Bible stories and songs while playing with children his own age.

If I thought the church was a good thing before my diagnosis, I found it essential now. I needed the encouragement. I needed the reminders of God's love and grace. I soaked up the sermons. My soul was hungry for comfort.

The friendships we formed in our Sunday School class were an anchor for me. The class was full of young mothers with kids the same age. Soon, we were making plans for play dates for the kids or a ladies' dinner out.

At this point in the journey, these friendships were a lifesaver. God had sent these women into my life at the perfect moment. I really needed friends to talk to and laugh with. So often, I felt so out

CHAPTER 5
The Road Back To Work

of place, so different from everyone else because of my eye disease. These ladies accepted me without question, making me feel comfortable and part of the group.

God had sent me new friends, and I was so very thankful to have found a church family. Things were far from perfect, but little by little, we were making our way forward.

CHAPTER 6
Learning To Ride

Trapped

The car keys were safely tucked away in the drawer, but that did not stop me from thinking about driving. There were days when I was content to hang out at home, catching up on household chores and playing with Jonathan. My work days got me out of the house and interacting with others. That was healthy for me. Still, there were lots of days where I felt trapped. I had errands to run. I wanted to take Jonathan to play at the park. Yet, there I was, stuck at home, trapped inside those four walls.

My neighbor Tami was my salvation. On Saturday mornings, I would get a call. "I'm going shopping. Do you and Jonathan want to come?"

I had met Tami within days of Jonathan's birth. She lived across the road on a side street, but I had never met her. Working full-time before Jonathan's arrival, I had known only a few of my neighbors. I had no idea there was a young family living that close to us.

Tami's father-in-law also lived across the road with a distant view of our house. One afternoon, he had seen my very pregnant self exiting the car in the driveway, and he had mentioned this observation to Tami. When she saw the baby balloon on the mailbox, she decided to investigate. She and her two-year-old daughter Linsey rang the doorbell with an apple pie in hand. Tami and I hit it off immediately, although Linsey was unimpressed with Jonathan's usefulness as a playmate at that point.

As Jonathan grew and began walking, Tami and I started getting the kids together to play in the sand box or on the swings. Soon, we were taking them to the park or to play in the balls at McDonald's.

By the time of my eye diagnosis, we were the best of friends. Tami was devastated at the news, and in the weeks that followed my diagnosis, she supported us with hot meals, babysitting and a listening ear.

CHAPTER 6
Learning To Ride

It did not take her long to figure out the best way to help us. Tami had wheels, and wheels were what I needed. She soon nicknamed her car, "Tami's Taxi!" Her taxi service would roll into my driveway on Saturday mornings and release me from the bondage of my captivity.

Tami was a Family and Consumer Science teacher at a nearby high school. A very dedicated teacher, she worked long hours each week getting things just right for her students. Saturdays were about shopping. It was her day to get out and about, enjoying Linsey, a good lunch and some retail therapy. Having Jonathan and me tag along just added to the fun.

The kids had such fun together, never failing to find something to play no matter where we went. Linsey was like a big sister to Jonathan, and he hung on her every word.

Those Saturday adventures helped me more than Tami will likely ever know. Because we were such close friends, it was easy for me to ask her for help. I still struggled asking other people for a ride, but not Tami. I knew she was fine with it, and that she really wanted to help. I also knew she would be honest if she could not fit in my request. After one of our excursions, I told her how much I appreciated her help. She smiled and responded that if the roles were reversed, she would want someone to do that for her.

It wasn't just the transportation that Tami offered. It was the "talk time." As we made our way to the shopping mall, I could debrief about what was going on with me. I was comfortable telling her the good, the bad and the ugly. I could be honest with her and not be concerned about glossing over the hard stuff. Likewise, I listened to her life struggles, and we became a support system for each other. Talk time in Tami's Taxi was just what I needed to fight my trapped feelings.

Sinking in Sad

While it had been months since the devastating diagnosis of impending blindness, the pain of that reality would not leave me alone. I thought about it when I woke up in the morning. I recalled it when I looked out the window at sunset or when I stopped to notice a beautiful flower. I would watch Jonathan do something cute and think, "Oh, what if I can't see him do that anymore?"

I tried hard to be brave. I plastered a smile on my face and went on with life, but the ache inside would not go away. The worries for what was to come woke me up at night. The frustration of not driving ate at me. Still, the worst part was the sadness. I felt like I was sinking in sad.

I could get through the days, perform my job duties, even care for Jonathan, but the hole in my heart was always there. I couldn't escape that pang of loss. It followed me everywhere.

I covered it up fairly well, but I knew that obsessing about my eyes was not healthy. My nurse brain told me I should seek some counseling.

One day, my office mate and I were chatting, and she asked, "So Anita, how are you doing with all this?"

I felt my stomach clench like an angry fist. I knew she was expecting an honest answer. "Well, I'm getting through it, but it's just hard. It's so hard not to drive. I hate asking for rides. I just feel so sad."

We talked on for a while, and I opened up to her queries. Her nursing perspective made her reach the same conclusion. "Anita, have you thought about counseling?"

Of course, I had, but the thought of arranging rides for one more place to go made me nauseous.

"Why don't you call EAP?"

EAP was the acronym for the employee assistance program. The program offered employees access to counseling at no cost for several visits. My office mate encouraged me to call. "It's free. What have you got to lose?"

CHAPTER 6
Learning To Ride

Talk Therapy

I made an appointment with EAP and found myself in a tiny conference room facing a counselor. I felt so awkward, almost feeling apologetic for taking up this woman's valuable time. She was used to such discomfort and began with open ended questions. With some gentle prodding, she teased out the details of my story.

I thought it would be hard to tell the story, but it wasn't. I had told the facts of the story many times. The counselor was not satisfied with just the facts though, delving deeper to discover the feelings behind the facts. "So how does that make you feel?"

"I just feel sad all the time. I guess I am depressed."

I remember her quiet smile. "Anita, if you weren't sad or frustrated with news like this, I would think there really is something wrong with you."

She went on to explain that I was likely experiencing a situational depression that was totally understandable given my recent life changes. She suggested we meet again the next week.

We did meet again. At the third visit, the counselor asked me if I felt like these sessions were helpful. I did feel better talking things out. Given that I am a major extrovert, verbal processing is an integral part of my coping strategies. She asked about my support systems and was pleased that I had friends like Mary and Tami to be honest with. "That's good, but I think you might want to consider finding a counselor that could help you process issues as they arise, someone who is trained to help you work through your feelings and concerns. It seems to me that this is a problem that is not going away. You will have tough times that you may need someone to talk to. Why not establish a relationship now that could help you down the road?"

The EAP program typically offered three visits and then made referrals for further care as needed. We talked about my options. Since transportation was such an issue, she suggested that I might contact the hospital chaplain's office. Perhaps one of the chaplains might be willing to see me for counseling.

We ended our sessions together without major revelations or a fix for my feelings, but talking to a neutral party had helped. I promised to give continued counseling some consideration and bid her farewell. The sad was still there, but she had given me some things to ponder.

Getting Adjusted

Several weeks later, I did stop by the chaplain's office to inquire about the option of further counseling. The chaplain that was aligned with my old nursing unit shared that the office did do some counseling on a limited basis. He invited me into his office for a chat, and I shared the facts of my story.

I didn't follow up any further. I'm not quite sure why. I had felt better after talking to the EAP counselor. It helped that she validated my feelings and reassured me that I was responding normally to such a life-altering event. The chaplain I spoke with had been nice enough, but I left his office feeling uncertain. Perhaps I had just not felt a connection with him. Maybe the courage I had mustered to get there failed me thereafter, but regardless, I didn't go back.

I didn't tell Eric about the EAP sessions. I didn't want him to worry any more than he already did. I rationalized that if I felt better, then he would feel better too. For the time being, my angst had abated somewhat, so I put the idea of further counseling aside.

Although my feelings still fluctuated from sadness to frustration, going back to work had certainly helped. Our days had a routine to them, tasks to accomplish, a timeline to follow. I focused on the tasks at hand, what was next on the to-do list. The new routine gave me less time to focus on my troubles.

The rides to work with Fred had worked out better than I could ever have imagined. Fred was so very kind and gracious to me. Our rides were filled with work discussions and planning, making the commute pass quickly. We talked of our hobbies and interests. I thoroughly enjoyed Fred's intellect. It had all worked out so well.

That is not to say that it was easy for me. Eric dropped me off at Hardee's in the morning, and I would watch out the window for Fred. More than once, I sat there wringing my hands. I hated the fact that I needed a ride. I hated that I could not take care of this myself. I was not in control, and I didn't like it one bit. It hurt my pride to have to depend on others. I knew they wanted to help me, and I did so appreciate their kind offers. It was just that I did not want it to be this way. I wanted to do it myself. The frustration of it all tied me up in knots.

I sat there staring out the restaurant window, telling myself to calm down. "Deep breath, Anita. It will be OK. Fred will come, and it will be alright." I would pray, "Lord, you gotta help me. I can't do this alone. I need you." Self-talk and prayers calmed me down and soon I would be at the hospital, immersed in my work, the angst forgotten for the moment.

In the aftermath of my diagnosis as I was dithering over returning to work and figuring out transportation, I had prayed so often, asking God to show me the right path. I had asked Him to work it all out, to show me what to do. Without any effort on my part, Fred showed up offering a ride. After my initial surprise at his ride offer, I began to consider that perhaps God was answering my prayers.

Now, after several months of riding with Fred, I was certain that this ride arrangement had been an answer to all the prayers lifted on my behalf. With his matter-of-fact manner, Fred had been the perfect person to get me started on this journey of rides. I had no qualms about accepting his help. He was truly paying it forward. Fred's kind and generous attitude dispelled my fears of asking too much.

I also enjoyed my new job. I relished the challenges and welcomed the opportunities to learn and grow. I was still working closely with many of my former colleagues and friends, so I felt quite comfortable with these interactions. I enjoyed the autonomy and creativity of the position and found I was good at chasing down the details.

I maintained my close relationship with my former job-sharing partner Mary. We met frequently for lunch, and it was good to have her as a sounding board during this adjustment period. I often visited Lynn and my other friends on my old unit just to stay connected. As winter turned to spring, I was surprised to realize that I was adjusting to my new situation.

Catch It!

The warmer spring days meant Jonathan and I could play outside again. He loved his swing set, and we spent hours swinging and sliding.

On those pretty spring days, I often made two peanut butter and jelly sandwiches and carried them outside for a little picnic. Pulling out some lawn chairs, he and I sat on the driveway and enjoyed an outdoor dining experience.

The carport storage room was full of toys, and Jonathan would drag out a menagerie of riding toys, Tonka trucks and balls. He loved playing catch, but he soon learned that I was a lousy partner for that particular pursuit.

I had never been gifted at sports, always among the last to be picked for any baseball or dodgeball team. I was terrible at catching the ball. I did fine with shooting hoops, and had a brief fantasy about being a basketball star like my mother and her identical twin sister. But you have to catch as well as throw, and one season on the church basketball league convinced me that I had no athletic ability.

Now I wondered. Was I just a klutz or was my inability to catch the ball an early sign of visual field loss? Could I not catch the ball because I couldn't follow it through the air?

It didn't really matter. Though the team selection process of physical education classes created a little childhood trauma, I

CHAPTER 6
Learning To Ride

bounced back just fine. My parents dusted off my bruised ego, and I pursued other interests like Girl Scouts, stamp collecting and reading my Nancy Drew books.

Still, as I tried to play ball with Jonathan, I thought about my difficulties with childhood sports. Like my aversion to nighttime driving, I had never really thought about why I struggled with ball games. It was interesting to ponder.

Jonathan and I did find a solution though. We selected a big, bright red ball to toss back and forth. It was large enough for me to follow it through the air, at least most of the time. Jonathan helped with that too. As he tossed the ball in my direction, he would call out, "Here it comes, Mama! Catch it!"

He wasn't even three years old yet, but he was already starting to take care of me.

Change of Plans

One morning in late March, Fred picked me up at Hardee's as usual. After I was settled in the seat, Fred began the conversation with "Anita, I've got something I want to talk with you about."

A little alarm bell went off in my head. His tone was serious as he proceeded to tell me that he and his wife had made the decision to move to Colorado. They would be moving in mid-April.

My heart went into overdrive. It felt like the wind being knocked out of me. My first thought was a selfish one. "Now what am I gonna do?"

I had just gotten used to riding with Fred, just gotten used to being back at work, and now, Fred was leaving. I swallowed hard and stammered, "Wow, that sounds like a great opportunity. Congratulations." I said the words, but my underlying panic must have been palpable.

Fred was prepared for my reaction. He had delayed sharing his news because he was concerned about my ride situation. He was so

110

concerned, in fact, that he had been searching all over the hospital for other ride options for me.

In response to his queries, a mutual friend offered Fred the information that a colleague of ours, Susan, lived in the Burlington area. Unbeknownst to me, Fred had contacted Susan, shared my situation, and asked about the possibility of a ride for me. Susan was immediately receptive and told Fred to have me contact her to work out a ride arrangement.

While I was stunned at Fred's news of impending departure, I was equally shocked that he would go to such great lengths to locate a ride for me. Fred was working hard to solve my problems, and I was still stuck on processing his loss. I felt very conflicted, pleased for the new opportunity for Fred, but sad that I would lose this good friend. Not only would I lose this wonderful carpool arrangement, but I was also losing my partner in my new work responsibilities. My heart felt heavy as I pondered the loss of Fred's friendship.

Fred's diligence on locating ride options for me simply reinforced what a class act he was. He was truly concerned for my welfare.

While I was so appreciative of Susan's receptivity toward a ride arrangement, the thought of working out new logistics was daunting. Furthermore, while I had interacted with Susan at various hospital meetings, I did not know her well, making her willingness to help me a bit overwhelming.

I knew Susan was a kind and gracious woman, but once again, I felt uncomfortable. "How can I ask such a thing from someone I barely know? It's asking too much."

At Fred's insistence, I agreed to speak with Susan. As I headed off to my office, my thoughts were swirling. "Lord, I just got used to riding with Fred, how am I going to change now? Am I really supposed to be working? Lord, help me. I don't know what to do." Trying hard not to panic, I kept reminding myself to trust God to work this out. After all, He had worked it out with Fred. Still, try as I might, I could not hold back the negative thoughts that had plagued me before. "I hate this. I don't want to ask for help. How can I accept such an offer?"

I could not face making the call to Susan that day, so I put it off. I resolved to pray on it for a bit.

Answer to Prayer

Apparently, God was ready to get this problem solved. The next morning as I walked down the hospital corridor, I heard my name being called. I turned to find Susan calling out to me. With a bright smile, she came closer and said,

"Anita, I'm so glad to see you. Fred told me that you might need a ride to work. I would be happy to help you!"

There was a softness in her kind eyes, her smile warm and caring. She was so genuine. It was clear that she really wanted to help. All my reservations seemed to vanish as I stood there looking into her gentle brown eyes. Instead of voicing all my previous reservations, I found myself saying, "Are you sure?"

In the next moments, we were making arrangements to meet at Biscuitville across town. It turned out that she stopped there every morning to grab a biscuit. Meeting me there would not be an imposition in the slightest. In the afternoons, she could drop me off wherever it was convenient. Her evenings were flexible so that was no problem.

I walked away, shaking my head in amazement, and thanking God for working out yet another ride. It was truly an answer to prayer.

Out One Door, In Another

Fred left a couple weeks later. I wished him well and thanked him profusely for the good deed he had done for me. I knew I would miss his expertise at work, but much more than that, I would miss his friendship. I had grown close to him, and I was sad to see him go. Yet, Colorado was calling, and I wished him farewell.

One day, I stepped out of Fred's car, and the next day, I hopped into Susan's car. Fred had facilitated my transition back to work by helping me feel more comfortable accepting rides from others. His persistence pushed me to believe that I could really do this. I owe Fred a great debt for his support and encouragement at a time when I so needed it.

Girl Talk and God Talk

From the moment I stepped into Susan's car, I knew I had found a new best friend. Our bond was instantaneous. A true GRIT (Girl Raised In The South), Susan's bubbly personality lit up any room she entered. Her sparkling smile and sweet Southern accent put people at ease. You could tell her anything, and people often did. She was one of those people who could bring the sunshine into any situation. She was just what I needed.

Susan's strong Christian faith was like a beacon of light for me in those hard days of adjustment. I looked forward to our rides together. She would always have a good word for me, offering support and encouragement as I dealt with my eye disease and its life-changing consequences.

She listened. She laughed. We talked "Girl talk" and "God talk." Looking back, those times sitting in her car were a sacred space for us to share our stories and struggles as we made our way down the road.

Our conversations were so lively. We were never quite finished with our conversation by the time we got to the shopping mall where she dropped me off. The thirty-minute drive was simply not enough time for all we had to say. Almost daily, Eric would shake his head and laugh at us as we pulled into the parking lot, talking a mile a minute. Susan would then roll down the window, throw up her hand and call out, "Hey Eric! Wait just a minute. We're not quite done. I just need to tell her one more thing!"

CHAPTER 6
Learning To Ride

What a blessing to have found a ride and a best friend all in one beautifully wrapped package!

Other Options

As spring turned to summer, Susan and I began to contemplate travel plans and vacation time. I soon realized that I needed some other ride options for when Susan was on vacation.

Though it still made me nervous, I began mentioning my need for ride options to my friends at work, asking them if they knew of anyone else who lived near Burlington. I asked my family and church friends to pray about this.

After only a few queries, I found out that one of my social work colleagues lived in Burlington. I had known Hope professionally for several years, but did not know her well personally. I gathered up my courage to ask her about a ride. Her broad smile and warm, kind eyes told me that she would indeed be another ride option for me. She was happy to help.

We talked about places to meet and work schedules. I explained that I was riding with Susan primarily, so I would only need her periodically when Susan had a day off. Hope was fine with that plan. Just like that, I had another ride. It was another answer to prayer.

As the summer progressed, I tapped Hope for a ride several times. It worked out great. We had so much in common, and our rides were full of animated conversation. I had made a new friend and found a new ride.

As part of my work duties, I had started meeting with the leaders of other clinical disciplines. In one of those meetings, the conversation turned to where everyone lived. One of my physical therapy colleagues piped up to say that she lived in Burlington. I was so surprised. I had known Susan D. (Yes, another Susan!) for quite some time, but had no idea she lived close to me. It took me a few days to build up my courage, but when I finally asked her, she was thrilled to offer me a ride. It was yet another prayer answered.

I loved riding with Susan D. Her soft-spoken manner calmed my nerves at the end of a busy day. We talked of our families, especially our only children, their interests and issues. Another beautiful friendship was born.

Not only had God solved my ride problems, He had given me several wonderful new friendships. I was amazed by these incredible women. They were each quite different, yet each one offered just the right support and encouragement to help me through my life-altering situation. God had indeed answered our prayers. The interesting thing was that He wasn't finished blessing me yet.

Mentor on Wheels

Several months after Fred's departure, I received a call to schedule a meeting. I was to be part of a team to interview a candidate for Fred's vacant position. When the secretary shared the candidate's name, I was dumbfounded.

About seven years earlier, during my graduate school days in Washington D.C., this nurse had served as a mentor for my Army nurse friend Susan during one of our clinical rotations. Interestingly, she had received both her Master's degree and doctorate from the same university that I had attended. As a past president of my professional organization, she was a highly acclaimed and well-respected leader in our profession. What good fortune that she might be interested in working at our hospital. I could not wait to meet her.

Several weeks later, I did meet Marianne, and she was even more impressive in person. Her keen intellect was apparent, her smile, warm and genuine. Her excellent interpersonal skills put us all at ease, and I walked out of the interview, hoping against all hope that she would take the job.

She did. Within a few more weeks, Marianne moved into her office and set up shop. It was decided that I would report directly to her, although from the outset, our interactions were totally collaborative. We worked as a team, and I knew right away that I had found a new mentor as well as a good friend.

Within days of her arrival, she shared that she would be commuting from Chapel Hill, over an hour's drive each way. Of course, she learned quickly about my eye disease and that I could not drive. She asked about how I was getting to work. When I explained the scenario, she immediately offered a ride. "You know, Anita, I practically drive by your house every day. I'd be happy to stop by and pick you up."

To my amazement, I had another ride, and another wonderful friendship was born. She became my Wednesday ride, stopping in my driveway to pick me up and dropping me off at my house in the afternoons. We stopped for a Diet Coke at the vending machines on our way out the door, and our rides were full of friendly chatter. We talked of our families, friends and travel. She was very fond of Jonathan and loved to chat with him when we got to my house. We planned work projects and debated solutions to problems. I felt like I soaked up knowledge just sitting in the seat beside her. Yes, I had another ride, but even better, I got a mentor on wheels!

Fun On The Farm

As the summer sun climbed high in the Carolina blue sky, so my spirits began to lift. My ride situation was stable, allowing me to relax a bit. I was ready for a road trip! Eric's vacation time was limited, and he couldn't get away. I decided that a trip to South Carolina to see my parents might be just what the doctor ordered. My parents were all too eager to spend time with their only grandson, and volunteered to come up and transport Jonathan and me back to the farm.

As soon as the car came to a halt in the driveway, Jonathan clamored to exit his car seat. He was ready to run! Jonathan raced across the yard, his grandparents trailing closely behind. The cows were gathered along the fence line, munching on their lunch and curiously eyeing the little ball of energy headed straight for them. Jonathan scampered toward the fence, skidding to a stop just shy of the prickly barbed wire. Tiny hand extended in a friendly wave, he bellowed out, "Hey cows! Moooo!"

The cows simply stared, but Grandaddy let out a big guffaw, tickled at his grandson's enthusiastic greeting. Grandma chuckled as she picked up her favorite little fellow to continue the animated conversation with the stoic cows.

My parents had built their retirement home on their portion of the 120-acre family farm that had been my father's childhood home. My grandparents had bought the farmland located in the Upstate of South Carolina in 1937, building a small white clapboard farmhouse to shelter their growing family. No strangers to hard work, my father and his two brothers had grown up as farm boys hauling hay, hoeing cotton, and milking cows. All three sons had pursued non-farming career paths after college, but had held onto the property after my grandparents' deaths. The oldest brother returned to live in the old farmhouse while my parents had built a new home on a portion of the old pasture land.

I chuckled as I watched Jonathan explore the property, his charmed grandparents entertaining him at every turn. He was fascinated with the cows, the tractor and even the lawn mower. I, too, had been fascinated by such things when I was a little girl.

The farm had been the place I called home in my growing up years. Army life had kept us moving to the tune of 29 moves and 25 schools. Two years was the longest we had stayed anywhere. The farm was the constant in my life, the fun retreat that we returned to for weeks or even months each year depending on my dad's assignments. In my youth, I roamed around those rolling hills on foot, on tractor, on lawn mower and motorcycle. In the old blue pickup truck, I had received my first real driving lessons in the pasture that now surrounded my parent's home.

Like Jonathan, I had adored my grandparents, my visits with them packed with fun farm adventures. My grandfather was a hard-working farmer and jack of all trades. He could do anything he set

CHAPTER 6
Learning To Ride

his mind to do. Grand was a master storyteller regaling his sons and later his grandchildren with fascinating stories of his family and his youth. I could sit forever listening to his tales. He loved to spoil me and my cousins, letting us drive any piece of machinery we desired. I loved helping him feed the cows on cold winter days, and devotedly trailed behind him as he did his farm chores. I was his long-awaited girl, and we treasured every minute of our time together.

My grandmother was a serious-minded schoolteacher with a strong work ethic and a deep, abiding faith. Grandmama was an amazing cook, her kitchen always filled with the savory smells of everything from black iron skillet fried chicken to melt-in-your-mouth chocolate chip cookies. Her list of talents was endless covering everything from quilting to embroidery to gardening and beyond. There was nothing she wasn't good at, and she patiently taught me a bit about each of her hobbies. She loved the family history, a fascination she passed along to me.

As I gazed out over the expanse of lush green pasture, I thought about the values of faith, family and hard work my grandparents had instilled in me during all those childhood days on this farm. I recalled the hard times my grandparents had weathered as they raised their family on this land. They had faced the adversities of life with courage and determination. As I pondered my own situation, I knew I needed to face my own struggles with such bravery and resolve. They had survived their struggles, and so could I.

Jonathan was giggling as he ran past his grandaddy, the fields of the farm forming a backdrop for this precious scene. I hoped that Jonathan would learn to love this land as I have, reserving a special spot in his heart for the unmatched treasure of a loving family.

Caterpeg

In early June, I experienced one of my cleaning frenzies as I readied the house for Jonathan's birthday party. I could hardly believe that he would soon be three years old.

The birthday party theme was Sesame Street, right down to the party goods, balloons and a sheet cake covered in the colorful characters. We held the festivities outside in the carport and pulled out all of Jonathan's outside toys to entertain his little friends for the gathering. Our family and friends had a good time visiting while enjoying a slice of pizza followed by cake and ice cream.

Everything went well, except for Jonathan. My easy-going, good-natured child had woken up on the wrong side of the bed that morning and declined to politely share his toys with his guests. He demonstrated an uncharacteristic possessiveness and a distinct lack of manners. His mother was aghast, but everyone laughed it off as, "Welcome to 3!"

When the party was over and the guests departed, Jonathan threw up all over the sunporch carpet. Feeling his forehead, I surmised a fever. Now I knew why he had behaved so badly.

When I shared the story with my cousin Cathy though, she laughed and said, "Oh Anita, I should have told you to skip the three-year-old birthday party. Three-year-old birthday parties are always a mess!"

There was a bright spot in the midst of the birthday party disaster, and it came in the form of a gift from Grandaddy. My father made some grandparent magic when he unveiled an unusual riding toy named "Caterpeg."

From the moment he saw that bright yellow front loader in the driveway, Jonathan was hooked. The Caterpeg became his all-time favorite outside toy. It had a working scoop that he could use to pick up toys and tote them around. He spent hours riding that Caterpeg around and around our circular driveway. Sitting behind the wheel, impish grin on his tiny face, he was absolutely adorable.

CHAPTER 6
Learning To Ride

From that day forward, our outdoor playtime now revolved around the spin of tires on the driveway!

Pool Time

The summer sun had definitely improved my mood. It felt good to play outside with Jonathan, and we had another entertainment option that brought both of us great pleasure. The pool opened.

Eric and I had joined a local pool the summer Jonathan was born. The previous summer, Jonathan and I had made frequent visits to the pool, but that was when I could drive. This summer, our transportation issues presented a new challenge. I called the pool management and made arrangements to purchase a guest pass so I could bring friends with me to the pool. That meant I could ask a friend for a ride and offer her a chance to enjoy a pool day. The pool management was quite supportive of this option, and it was all settled.

My neighbor Tami had the summer off from teaching. She and Linsey transported us to the pool often that summer. The solution offered both a ride and a play date for Jonathan. He and Linsey had a wonderful time playing in the pool, while Tami and I thoroughly enjoyed our poolside chats.

The change in scenery did me good. It was good to be out of the house. I loved the feel of sunshine on my face and playing in the pool with my little boy. Sitting there chatting poolside, I felt like a normal mother, the bondage of my disability forgotten for a time.

Not only was the pool great therapy for me, it was equally important to Jonathan. From the moment we stuck his little feet into the baby pool, Jonathan had taken to the water like a little fish. I hadn't bothered about swim lessons because Jonathan had his own personal instructor, his dad. Eric had taught swim lessons during the summers of our college years. While Eric hadn't started formal lessons with him yet, Jonathan had been jumping off the side of the pool to us, and Eric had practiced some floating exercises with him. He loved being in the deep water and regularly begged me to take him out there to play.

One afternoon, I sat on the end of a lounge chair next to the water's edge while Jonathan played near the shallow steps. As I chatted with the other pool moms, I noticed Jonathan leaning over, sticking his head under water, and paddling his arms with fury. Abruptly, he would stand up, catch his breath, and then repeat the maneuver again. Knowing he was perfectly safe in the shallow water, I didn't intervene, but continued to watch him closely. What was he up to?

After repeating the process five or six times, he moved over to the railing. Holding the railing with both hands, he stretched his body out and began kicking hard, sending sprays of water onto the pool deck near my feet. He stopped, stood up and turned to watch the big kids swimming in the deep water for a few moments. Without a word, he grabbed the railing again and restarted his kicking routine.

I thought to myself, "I think he's trying to swim!" Leaving my perch, I stepped down into the water beside my busy little boy. Reaching for him, I asked, "Hey buddy! Want to go swim in the big water?"

He was all for that idea, and off we went to the other side of the pool. He barely waited for me to jump in the water before flinging himself in my direction. Usually, I would reach out and catch him, but this time, I pulled back when he hit the water, allowing him to sink under the surface for a moment. With lightning speed, Jonathan reached out his arms and began to paddle hard. Adding the kicking action, he propelled himself through the water headed straight for me. I stepped back a couple of steps, and he kept swimming toward me. Amazed, I scooped him up out of the water and exclaimed, "Oh buddy, you're swimming! You're really swimming! Wow!"

His grin was a mile wide as he clasped his little arms around my neck for a tight hug. Pulling his head back to look at me, his eyes gleaming with pride, "I wanna do it again, Mama! I wanna do it again!"

Jonathan's swimming days had begun!

Grandma's Pool

While Eric and I were certainly thrilled about Jonathan learning to swim, there was another person who was even more enthused about this big accomplishment, his Grandma Liz. Since moving to Richmond when Eric was 11 years old, Liz had managed a swim and tennis club in her community. Working from her home office, she managed the business end of the club, but her favorite part of the job was being at the pool. She was involved in everything: hiring and supervising staff, assisting with swim team logistics, managing the clubhouse rentals and facility maintenance, and her favorite duty, running the pool snack bar. Needless to say, Liz lived at the pool in the summers. It was work, but it was also her social scene.

When Liz learned about Jonathan's foray into swimming, she couldn't wait to bring him to her pool. Ever the proud Grandma, she was excited about his newfound skills.

Since August was less busy for her, she volunteered to come down and bring Jonathan and me back up to her house for a few days of fun. Always full of energy, Liz left early to make the three-hour drive to our house. After a little lunch, she loaded us up for the return trip to her place. Wiggling in his car seat, Jonathan was so excited about going to Grandma's pool, and he and his grandma chatted happily about all the things he would do there.

Eventually, Jonathan drifted off to sleep, offering Liz and me a chance to catch up. Liz and I have always been friends. I liked her from the moment I met her, standing there in her kitchen, dishrag on her shoulder, her bright smile a beacon of welcome.

At our first meeting, I had been only 16 years old, having dated Eric just three weeks. He and I had been out for the afternoon when he remembered something he needed from his house. Stopping impromptu, he urged me to come in and meet his mom. Not quite prepared, I had reluctantly followed him into the basement where he immediately stopped at the freezer to grab chocolate chip cookies for both of us before heading upstairs. Liz was no doubt surprised by this unscheduled visit, but her kind face and gracious greeting immediately put me at ease. Between her lively personality and that first bite of her signature cookie, I knew I had come to the right place.

Before long, Liz and Pete's house was my second home. After raising two boys, Liz was delighted to have a girl around the house. Both of us talkative, we had no trouble carrying on a conversation. Compared to Eric's quiet nature, I was a fountain of information, and she loved knowing more about what was happening at school and with our friends.

Not only did Liz welcome me, but Pete and I hit it off as well. Though quiet by nature, Pete always greeted me with a ready smile, and we invariably found a topic to chat about. His dry wit never failed to inject a touch of humor into the conversation. A building supply salesman, he spent much of his life on the road, while Liz managed the household.

Although Liz was raised in New Jersey and Pete, New York State, the two had met in college at Purdue University. After their marriage, Pete did a tour in the Army before returning to upstate New York to enter the building trade. His job necessitated several moves in the New England region while their boys were still young. Their final move was to Richmond, VA when Eric was in middle school.

My relationship with Liz and Pete only grew closer with the passage of time. By the time Eric and I married, they welcomed me into their family as not just a daughter-in-law, but as the daughter they never had. The diagnosis of my eye disease had cut them to the core, and they were ready and willing to do anything they could to help me.

Over the past few months, Liz had made a few quick trips to our house to help us with errands or an appointment, but she was

CHAPTER 6
Learning To Ride

intent on this trip being a fun get-away for Jonathan and me. I was ready for some fun, and it felt good to be in Liz's company.

The minute we arrived, Jonathan was ready to go to the pool, and Liz gladly obliged that request. An avid and extremely talented photographer, Pete grabbed his camera to record Jonathan's swimming debut.

I'm not sure who had more fun. Jonathan was grinning ear to ear as he showed off his swimming skills for his grandparents. Pete grinned with delight as he chronicled the event on film. Liz was in her element, simply delighted to play in the pool with her grandson.

The next few days were lots of fun as Liz and I took turns chasing Jonathan around the pool deck or catching him as he jumped off the side of the pool. He had decided that he was now beyond the baby pool, setting his sights on the big pool instead. Since Grandma managed the snack bar, Jonathan really was a kid in the candy store. All he had to do was point at one of the candy jars, and Grandma would make it happen.

By the time Eric joined us on the weekend to take us back home, Jonathan was a committed fan of Grandma's pool. That suited Liz just fine. We were welcome at her pool anytime, and we would take advantage of that offer frequently in the years to come.

Part 3
Bumps In The Road

SEPTEMBER 1994 – SEPTEMBER 1995

He reached down from on high and took hold of me;
he drew me out of deep waters.

—Psalm 18:16 *NIV*

Part 3
Bumps In The Road

CHAPTER 7
One Wave At A Time

Sad Returns

The summer was over, the pool closed. My teacher friends were back at school. Tami's taxi service was back on a limited schedule. Once more, Jonathan and I were home alone on my days off. Once again, the walls closed in around me. I felt trapped, and those sad sinking feelings returned.

The summer had offered a great distraction, a diversion from the new realities of my altered life. Yet, with the changing of the season, I found I could not escape my sagging spirits.

Eric felt it too. My good humor had vanished, and that sharp-edged tone had worked its way back into my voice. I am upbeat and positive by nature, always preferring to see the glass half full. Now, the glass was half empty, its contents siphoned off by the loss of my car keys. This disease was not only stealing my sight, it was robbing me of my independence.

Fear of the future was ruining the present. I was afraid of going blind, imagining myself as some kind of invalid that others would have to care for. Not only was I losing my retina, I was losing sight of all that was once mine.

I told myself again and again that God would work it all out. I reminded myself to be thankful. Had God not provided multiple transportation options? Had He not provided a good job that offered intellectual stimulation and flexibility? Had He not provided a wonderful babysitter for Jonathan, a beautiful home, a loving family? He had sent countless friends to help us, given us a wonderful church family to shepherd us. Hadn't He blessed me with a fine husband who was trying so hard to take care of us?

"Why can't I just be grateful? Why can't I stop worrying? Why do I just want to scream?"

CHAPTER 7
One Wave At A Time

Without a doubt, the pressures inside me were building. I felt a growing sense of panic in my gut. The years ahead seemed to loom in front of me like a dark cloud. How would we cope?

I tried to smile and look like I had it all together. I made an effort to sound positive, appreciative and pleasant, but my emotions were fast becoming out of control. My frustrations were rumbling beneath the surface, just waiting to erupt.

Though he said nothing, I knew Eric felt their impact. As I grew more frustrated, he grew more grumpy and resentful. The weight of my burdens was dragging us down, draining the joy out of our relationship. It was time for some help.

Caring Connection

As the feelings of sadness and frustration flooded my heart, I knew it was time to reach out. I recalled my previous query about the option of counseling with one of the hospital chaplains. Perhaps it was time to pursue that alternative.

Although I had worked with several of the chaplains in patient care situations, I knew exactly who I wanted to see. I had known Bob for several years, and his kind, compassionate demeanor always put everyone at ease. He had this way of bringing calm to chaos. Bob knew how to listen, projecting a sense of warmth and comfort that made you feel like you could tell him anything. Watching him work with patients and families, I had felt his gentle touch in the midst of crisis. He just had this wonderful way about him. If I was going to talk to anyone, then it would surely be Bob. I called the chaplain's office and made an appointment.

I did not tell anyone I had made the appointment, not even Eric. Uncertain of the outcome as well as the process, I wanted to keep this all to myself for now.

Couch Comfort

On the couch in Bob's office, I waited for him to return from a meeting. Wringing my hands, stomach in knots, I wondered if this was a good idea. When his tall, slender frame filled the doorway, I looked up and smiled. The smile he offered back was one that reached the eyes and warmed the heart. When I saw that smile, I knew I had come to the right place.

Bob crossed the room, clasped my hand in his, and turned to close the door before seating himself in his rolling office chair.

"Anita, what can I do for you?"

I stammered out the story of my eye disease. He listened quietly as I shared the facts of the story. "So how are you doing with all this?"

"Not good."

"Tell me about that."

The floodgates opened, and my pent-up emotions came pouring out. The tears came with the words. That surprised me because I seldom was able to let myself cry. I had long been afraid that if I started crying, really crying, I would never stop.

I don't remember much of what I said or how long we talked. There were no major revelations uncovered. It just felt better to let the feelings out. It felt good to be honest about my emotions instead of covering them up. I spent a lot of time protecting those around me, becoming quite adept at painting a smile on my face so they would feel better. The smile was gone now, and the tears were real.

I left Bob's office, grateful for his caring support, his compassionate counseling. He had reinforced several times that his door was always open for me. Knowing that was a great comfort, for somehow I knew that I would find my way back to that couch sometime soon.

CHAPTER 7
One Wave At A Time

One Wave At A Time

Several weeks passed. Despite my best efforts, I found myself consumed with an overwhelming sense of sadness and loss. I tried to hide the misery, doggedly trudging my way through each day. I could not keep going this way. Something needed to change.

I kept thinking that I needed to go back and see Bob, but I kept putting it off. I'm not quite sure why. Was it just that the work days were busy or was it that I didn't want to face my escalating emotions head on? Regardless of the reason, I procrastinated on making another appointment.

A friend invited me to a weekend women's conference at her church. It was not your average Christian women's retreat. What impressed me was the fact that the women planning this conference prayed for the event for an entire year. They prayed that every decision, every speaker, every aspect of the event would be blessed by God. When you walked into the church, you could feel it. The blessing of the Holy Spirit filled the rooms. It was palpable.

Reviewing the list of concurrent sessions, I selected a class on how to study the Bible. I thought perhaps it would give me a new approach to Scripture reading.

The class was pretty full, and the speaker got things started. Beginning with an apology, she explained that this class had been on her calendar for a year. Along with the event organizers, she had been praying about it every day for the entire year. Despite her best intentions, the past couple of weeks had been some of the most difficult weeks of her life, and consequently, she did not feel as prepared for the class as she wanted to be. Everything had gone wrong. Several of her family members had been ill, and then she herself had required a trip to the emergency room for kidney stones. She was still struggling with this health issue. There had been several problems at her house. From a leaky roof to plumbing issues, things were falling apart in her home. It had all just about gotten the best of her.

The speaker had told the event organizers that she just did not think she could be at the conference. With everything going wrong in such a short span of time, she did not see how she could get this workshop together. The event planners were understanding and reassured her to just take care of herself and her family. Despite their kind reassurances, the speaker could not seem to escape this nagging sense of duty. She prayed about it, asking God to guide her on what she should do. Although she knew she had a reasonable excuse, she could not break free of the idea that she needed to be here to teach her workshop. So she gathered her notes and came anyway. Although she did not feel as prepared as she wanted to be, she would give us her best and hope that it would meet our needs.

There were lots of nods and murmurs of understanding in the room as we moved into the content of the workshop. The speaker offered lots of helpful hints, and there was good discussion.

My Bible was open, but I could not focus on the words. The speaker was teaching, but I could not comprehend the content. While my body occupied the tiny student desk at the back of the classroom, my mind was a million miles away. All I could think about was drowning. I was drowning in a sea of sorrow. Waves of anguish pounded me again and again. I could not figure out how to pull myself out of this sea of swirling emotion. This had to stop. Something had to change. I just had no idea what to do, no idea how to fix this.

Although I kept trying to pay attention to the speaker's words, I found my mind racing in a thousand directions. When the class was over, I dawdled at the back of the room. As the others filed out, I moved toward the speaker with the intention of thanking her for her time and dedication. I wanted to wish her well in hopes that her health problems would improve. As I drew near to the speaker, I murmured something to that effect. I will never forget what happened next.

CHAPTER 7
One Wave At A Time

She looked at me with clear, bright blue eyes and said quietly, "Are you OK?"

Surprised, I stood there looking at her for a long moment. Then, hanging my head in despair, I muttered, "No, not really."

Gently, she touched my arm. "Would you like to talk about it? I just feel like I'm supposed to talk to you."

Eyes glistening with tears, I nodded my agreement. Motioning for me to sit down, she nudged me with a few gentle questions. Before I knew it, my whole story came tumbling out. I did not mean to tell her everything. It was as if the dam holding my emotions at bay collapsed and a waterfall of words came flooding out.

She listened quietly, nodding her head, eyes locked on mine. Those clear, bright eyes just kept encouraging me to continue. I am not sure just how long we talked. Time seemed to stand still. I honestly don't remember what all I told her, nor do I recall much about what she said either. What I remember most was the feeling in that room. A deep, hushed sense of calm enveloped me as we talked. It felt like peace.

I cried, and she cried. I remember talking about my struggles to deal with my eye disease, my inability to drive, and my loss of independence. Explaining how I kept trying to let go of the sadness and frustration, I shared how things would get better, and I would feel stronger for a time, only to find myself crashing once again, starting the downward spiral once more. It was like the same movie scene kept replaying in my head over and over again, and I could never finish the story. I could not get it to stop.

I was sinking. I was sliding down an endless cavern, falling, flailing, with no way to stop.

For the most part, the conversation is a blur in my memory, but there is one moment that I remember vividly. We were nearing the end of our conversation. I looked at her and said, "I just don't know how I'm going to get through this."

She grasped my hand in hers, squeezing it gently, her eyes locked on mine. "You will get through this one day at a time, one wave at a time."

There are moments in your life when everything seems to stop, when you realize something really significant just happened. That is exactly what I felt in that moment. I knew, right then and there, that God was speaking directly to me. He was sending me a message that could not have been more clear. I would not be delivered from this painful affliction, but He would be with me. Every day, every moment, God would be with me.

Before I left the room, we prayed together. As I moved toward the door, she called to me once more. With a bright smile, she said, "Now I know why I had to come today. It was to talk to you."

An Angel Among Us?

I remember leaving that room and stepping into the busy hallway. Leaning against the wall, I closed my eyes to stop the world spinning around me.

"What had just happened? Was that real? Surely, God had been in that room. Was she an angel?" These were the thoughts swirling around in my head.

That's how my friend Mary found me. She had been attending another concurrent session and came looking for me afterwards. From the look upon my face, Mary knew something had happened to me.

I remember telling her some bits and pieces of the experience. I looked up at my tall, gracious friend as she stood there, almost mesmerized, soaking up every word. "Well, now we know why you had to be here today," she said, with that knowing look in her eyes.

Mary's incredible faith had been a rock for me throughout the past year. I knew instinctively that Mary had surmised that the presence of The Lord had been in that room with me.

CHAPTER 7
One Wave At A Time

We found a quiet place to sit and debrief. As I conveyed more of the story to her, Mary listened attentively, taking it all in, her face a canvas of emotion. She was as amazed as I was.

"Anita, this is a sign. God is with you. He will be with you through whatever comes."

A feeling of warmth and light had settled over me. For that moment, the fears and doubts that had plagued me for so long seemed to wash away. I basked in the glow of that light for the rest of that weekend. I knew God had been in that room with me. He had cared enough about my tragedy to show up and soothe my aching heart. It was surely a memory I would carry with me for the rest of my days. Was that kind teacher an angel? I would never know, but I did know I would never forget her words.

"You will get through this one day at a time, one wave at a time."

CHAPTER 8
Riding The Wave

Anniversary Appointment

As October rolled around, I found myself reliving the events of the year before. I replayed the moments, suffered the agony all over again.

I made my way to Bob's office several times, unloading some of my angst upon his steady shoulders. Our talks helped me sort through my feelings, and I always felt better after talking with him.

Eric and I made the trek to Duke to see Dr. Machemer. He was as kind and gentle as he had been the previous year. He was pleased that I had started taking the high dose Vitamin A therapy. He felt that this therapy offered real hope for slowing the disease progression.

The visual field test was repeated, and Dr. Machemer was pleased to report that there was no change in my vision. I breathed a sigh of relief.

"Perhaps now, Anita, you have entered a phase of slow progression. We will hope for that."

Hope for a Cure

At my original visit to Duke, Dr. Machemer had told me to look into the RP Foundation, short for Retinitis Pigmentosa Foundation. A non-profit organization, its focus is on promoting research to develop a cure for this type of blindness, as well as to support people impacted by the disease. (Note: The name was later changed to the Foundation Fighting Blindness.)

I had contacted the organization and added my name to their mailing list. That is how I learned about the upcoming Visions Conference in San Francisco. The conference was held annually to offer updates on the latest breakthroughs in research. Targeting those affected by the disease, there would also be sessions focused on coping with vision loss.

At this point, I was desperate for hope. I wanted to know about the possibilities of a cure for this disease. The opportunity to meet other people with RP sparked my curiosity. Having never met anyone with the disease, I yearned to talk with someone who knew what it was like to live with this threat hanging over your head. I guess I was desperate for encouragement. I hoped such conversations might help me get to a better place.

I proposed the concept of the conference to Eric. Since his aunt and uncle lived in the Sonoma Valley, an hour's drive from San Francisco, we could visit them for two nights, and then head to the conference. When I mentioned the idea to my mother-in-law Liz, she immediately volunteered to keep Jonathan for us.

I hoped the trip would be a good get-away for Eric and me. The past year had put a tremendous strain on our relationship. Between the drama of a new-found life changing disability and the rigors of raising an active three-year-old boy, some marital strain was not surprising. At least, that is what I told myself.

What Can You See?

We flew to San Francisco and rented a car to travel up to see Eric's aunt and uncle. Since my diagnosis, all of our extended families had expressed their concern, continually praying for us and sending notes of encouragement.

Aunt Betty had been one of those supportive people. Steve and Betty welcomed us with their usual hospitality, and we passed a relaxing couple of days in the mountain retreat they called home.

Over the past year, I had often felt other people's discomfort about asking direct questions regarding my vision loss. People were unsure whether to bring the subject up. Would it upset me? Would I want to talk about it? Most people simply avoided the topic, their discomfort so acute.

Interestingly enough, I did not really mind talking about the subject. While discussing my feelings was still quite difficult for me, I was good at explaining the facts of my disease. I did not really mind answering questions about the disease process. It actually felt better to discuss it than to let the subject hang in the air. So often, it felt like the elephant in the room that no one dared to mention.

During the visit, I had answered several questions about my eye disease, but the bulk of our conversation was on lighter topics. Both Steve and Betty had voiced their love and concern for us, but we had skimmed the surface on the topic of my eyes.

As we were packing the car up to leave, Betty had followed us out to chat. I had dressed up for the trip, knowing we would be attending the conference later in the day. Betty complimented me on my outfit and turned to peer closely at my face.

"Anita, how in the world do you do your mascara like that, and you cannot see?"

My first reaction was surprise. What did she mean by "You cannot see..."? Flinching a bit at first, I quickly realized that she was truly perplexed. I had run into this before. Most people had such a hard time understanding what I could and could not see.

The general public often assumes that blindness is "lights out darkness," a total absence of vision. The reality is that there is a whole spectrum of blindness, with varying degrees of vision loss. A person can be deemed legally blind and still have a large amount of useable vision.

I tended to forget these misunderstandings. I also bristled at the word "blindness." In truth, I avoided the term like the plague. The term stirred panic in my gut. It was a label that I did not want to use for fear it would become real. If I did not say it, if I did not refer to myself that way, then it would not happen. I know that makes little sense, but the mind can play lots of games when it does not want to deal with something. Bottom line, I did not want to be blind.

It was hard to describe what I could still see. I used the donut analogy often, explaining that I could see things clearly inside the donut hole. This area comprised my central vision, and though it was only a tiny area, the vision there remained quite good. In fact, my visual acuity could be corrected to 20/20 with glasses.

The ring of the donut covered the area where I could no longer see, while the space outside the donut comprised quite healthy vision. In other words, I had lost my mid-peripheral vision, but retained healthy far peripheral vision. This analogy seemed to help others understand.

I often went on to explain that I could read, write or sew, because these activities used my central vision, one of the areas not yet affected by the disease. However, it was easy for me to bump into things, to trip on a step, or miss a hand extended for a handshake. These activities fell inside the "donut ring" housing the lost portions of my visual field. Since my far peripheral vision remained intact, I could identify images in the far distance or notice someone standing beside me.

Practically, this meant that I could see to put on makeup and find my eyelashes for applying mascara. Seeing colors was not a problem, so I could match up my clothes without difficulty. I could visualize the tiny backs of earrings or thread a needle, but I could miss a child on a bicycle while driving a car. If the child was in the right spot at just the right time, I would totally miss him or her. It was easy for me to run into someone in the hall, just plow right over them as if they were not there. I often missed a step on a staircase and sometimes ran into the corner of a wall. Clear as mud, right?

On that November morning, I remember smiling and trying to explain my visual limitations to Betty, just as I had described them to so many others in the past year. It was difficult to tell if they really understood, but most people nodded and thanked me for my explanations. Likewise, Betty hugged me and sent us off with a wave, and I think, a teary smile.

Visions 1994

Eric and I arrived at the hotel, the lobby housing a large sign indicating "Visions 1994" sponsored by the RP Foundation. There were strips of caution tape on every step to help differentiate one step from another. Extra lighting had been erected in every room to increase the brightness of each room and corridor. There were large signs with bold, dark letters touting directions. Braille maps and signs were scattered throughout the lobby areas. The hotel had done an amazing job preparing for their conference guests with vision loss.

I was less prepared. Everywhere I turned, there were people walking with guide dogs. There were people sporting dark glasses and white canes. Others traveled on the elbow of their companions. I had never encountered so many blind people in my whole life, and I was not quite sure how to handle it.

On the one hand, it frightened me. I could not help but think that one day, that could be me. I might have to walk with a white cane or need a guide dog. I did not like contemplating those ideas.

On the other hand, I was amazed by these people. They were getting around the hotel corridors with ease. They were laughing, talking, visibly enjoying their conversations. They were fully embracing life. Yes, they had a disability. Certainly, they were limited by their disease, but they were not giving up. They were persevering, making the most of where they were and what they could do.

Those observations gave me hope. Yes, hope. Perhaps blindness was not the end of everything as I so often allowed myself to lament. Perhaps it was simply a different way to live, not less, not more, just different.

Such thoughts offered a moment of epiphany for me. It was a new insight, an opening of the mind to something that had been sealed shut, locked away, forbidden to be considered. Gazing around me in that hotel conference room, I was forced to consider that being blind did not mean that my life was over. People all around me were leading full, active lives even though they could not see. Glancing at the guide dog sitting quite calmly at the feet of the lady in the chair beside me, I contemplated that others were making this work, and perhaps I could too.

The conference offered excellent speakers and informative sessions. Researchers shared their findings, explained their avenues of study, their hopes for the future. It was all very encouraging, clearly hopeful, but a long way from a cure. Still, it was something. Things were happening. Scientists were passionate about their research pursuits, and their passion was inspiring.

Perhaps the most helpful event was the coping session with other newly diagnosed patients. We met in a small conference room with a facilitator to spawn the discussion. It did not take much prodding, and soon, we were all telling our stories.

Listening to these stories, I felt such camaraderie, such comfort to hear others talk of their struggles, their angst, their losses. I was not alone. Other people were enduring the same trials, and if they were getting through it, so could I. The group could have talked all night, but the facilitator finally sent us on our way.

Eric had attended the family member session. True to his introverted nature, he said very little about how it went. Although he was glad that my session had been helpful, he remained quiet, as if just taking it all in. After all, he was being forced to consider the same observations that I had encountered, requiring him to contemplate a different reality for me than he would have ever chosen.

There were several moments during the presentations when I felt that nudge, that racing of the heart, that quiet touch on my shoulder. It was as if God was telling me to listen, to be encouraged. "See I am doing a good thing here. See they are getting through this and so can you." His Presence was there with me, and I felt His leading.

I was glad we had chosen to come. It had forced me to deal with the diagnosis head on, to encounter the possibilities of the future.

While I still recoiled from the thought of a cane or guide dog, it was less scary. People were living with this disease, and I could too. There could be life even with vision loss.

Struggling With Stress

The trip had been a good one, but soon, we were back home, mired in the bustle of daily life. We were struggling with potty training a three-year-old who was not so well inclined to the idea. The holidays were almost here, and there was shopping to do and places to be.

I have always been big on Christmas. I love to decorate and enjoy buying gifts. Now I could not go like I wanted to, but must wait for a ride. I made my Christmas list, and then fretted over how I would get it all done without being able to drive.

Eric was struggling with the stress at work. The world of Information Technology (IT) is always stressful. He had been in his current position for about two years, and he loved the challenge. The problem was there was nothing but challenges. Every day held a fresh disaster to solve, a crisis to manage. You can get by on adrenaline for a while, but eventually, it takes its toll.

He was worn out when he came home, but his stress did not stop at the office. His commute was tough on a good day. The traffic could be brutal. Now, that difficult commute was positively grueling with added loops to the babysitter and transporting me across town to meet my rides. On the days I worked, he spent about 90 minutes just getting to work, and then he had to do it all in reverse at the end of a long, stressful day.

As if that was not enough, there were the groceries. They were the bane of our existence. I could save up a lot of the other errands for when Mom and Dad came to visit. I could take care of some things when I was bumming around on Saturdays with Tami, but not the groceries. There was no way to avoid that trip. Before my diagnosis, I had taken care of most of the grocery shopping,

CHAPTER 8
Riding The Wave

although Eric had done it occasionally. Neither one of us liked the task. Now it was like a noose around our necks.

I remember one night in late November. We were out of everything, especially milk and breakfast food for the next day. There was no way to put off the trip any longer. I made a grocery list and cooked supper so it would be ready when Eric walked in the door.

I broke the news to him over the last bites of his meal. He just looked at me. Without a word, he stood up, grabbed the list and trudged out the back door. I felt awful.

Doing the dishes, I watched anxiously for his return. I felt so guilty, but had no idea what I could have done differently. I stood at the window, tears in my eyes, fists clenched in fury. Here came the sentiments I had repeated a million times before. "I hate this. I'm so sick of this. I want to do this myself. He will be so mad at me. Why does it have to be this way? How are we ever going to do this?"

Soon, I saw the headlights in the driveway, and I rushed out to help unload the groceries. Eric never said a word. He didn't have to. The look on his face and the set of his shoulders said it all. He was sick of this. I was too.

Tantrums

The holidays came and went with visits from family and friends. Christmas for a three-year-old was indeed a great adventure. Eric and I thoroughly enjoyed playing Santa. We adored watching the joy on Jonathan's little cherub face as he opened his gifts. As always, he was a source of light for us, a welcome distraction from the stresses of our situation. Jonathan made us laugh. He kept us grounded, pulled together as we shared the joys of his little world. We were so thankful to have him.

That is not to say that raising a three-year-old was without its challenges. In truth, the "Terrible Two's" everyone warned us about were nothing compared to the feistiness of three! Jonathan was

definitely testing his limits. From mealtime to potty training to naps, he was intent on asserting his independence.

While Eric and I set a united front on enforcing proper boundaries with him, Jonathan kept sticking his toe over whatever line we drew in the sand. The problem for me sometimes was that even while he was disobeying me, his little expressions were so cute that I had trouble keeping the smile off my face.

I remember one particular meeting of the minds during church one Sunday morning. Eric was not with us, and I think Jonathan thought he could manipulate his mother. He refused to sit still in the pew, making too much noise for my taste. I corrected him several times, but he returned right back to his wiggly antics. He thought he was safe, for surely I would not discipline him at church. He was wrong. When I reached my limit, I jerked him up, and we trotted down the aisle. His face held a look of horror as I propelled him out the front door onto the front steps where I showed him quite clearly who was boss. I then made it clear that we would repeat this process all over again if he continued to misbehave. Apparently, that little trip down the aisle made an impression because he never acted up at church or anywhere else thereafter.

I couldn't really blame him for his desire to get his own way. There was a strong-willed independent streak running deep in the veins of my son. I recognized that streak. It ran through my veins too. He was testing his limits in an age-appropriate manner, while I was chafing under the limits being imposed on me. Three-year-olds were expected to throw a few tantrums. Adults were supposed to control their emotions and learn to deal with their circumstances in an appropriate manner. I was trying to teach Jonathan self-control, but I was finding it much harder to control my own emotions. Jonathan wasn't the only one who felt like throwing a tantrum.

Stepping Out In Faith

One Sunday in January, I noticed the announcement in the church bulletin stating that it was time to submit playschool enrollment applications for the following Fall. The playschool at our church was highly acclaimed. Eric and I had been talking about sending Jonathan there for four-year-old pre-school. Our babysitter Evelyn had told us upfront that she would love and care for her kids, but she was not a teacher. She had explained that we would need to seek other options if we wanted him to get prepared for school.

Jonathan was such a smart little fellow. He was so inquisitive. Both of us felt he needed more stimulation and preparation for school. I could hardly believe he would be four years old in a few months.

At the same time, we did not want to remove him from Evelyn's house. He had good friends there. He and his little buddy David were such good pals. Perhaps a mix of playschool and Evelyn's would offer the best of both worlds.

If he was going to attend pre-school anywhere, I really wanted Jonathan to go to our church's playschool. I just felt good about it. It felt right.

"But how on earth are we going to get him there? What will we do on the days I work? How can we get him there if I cannot drive?"

The playschool program was three days a week from 9 am to 12 noon. We would need transportation from our house to school on the days I was not working. On Wednesdays when I worked, not only would we need transportation, but we would need a place for Jonathan to stay after school until Eric could pick him up.

The whole prospect was daunting. Still, I really wanted him to go to playschool. So I did the only thing I knew to do. I prayed. "Lord, you know what Jonathan needs. You know the problems we face. If it is Your plan, if You want Jonathan to go to this playschool, then we need You to provide a ride for him. We need Your help. Please Lord. We can't do this alone. We need You. Your will be done. Thank You, Lord."

Prayer lifted, I filled out the application, mailed it and hoped for the best. It was up to The Lord. I did not know anything else to do but wait for God's help.

CHAPTER 8
Riding The Wave

CHAPTER 9
Pivot Point

Time For A Change

We were fighting again. It seemed like Eric and I were always fighting these days. It was not a full-on fight, more of the constant, underneath-the-surface bickering. We seemed to be continually annoyed with each other. The most frustrating part was that neither one of us wanted it to be this way. How did two people who loved each other so much get to this point?

It had not always been this way. We were high school sweethearts who had loved each other since we were 16 years old. Growing up as an Army Brat, my parents and I had moved 29 times with me attending 25 schools. From Panama to Korea to a long list of US Army posts, we had lived a nomadic life. Although our Army life was finished, and we had planned to stay settled near our family in SC, an unexpected job opportunity had fallen into my father's lap. The moving van had showed up at our house one more time.

We had moved to Richmond, Virginia in the summer of 1977. On a hot September day, I had trudged off to my fifth high school, dreading the prospect of being the new kid at school yet again. My angst quickly dissipated when I met the handsome football player in the hallway. I was enchanted from my first glance into those soft, hazel eyes.

Our first date was five days later, and we fell head over heels from that moment on. We dated all through college, and couldn't wait to get married, doing so as soon as we graduated. Starting our married life at age 22, we had enjoyed eight wonderful, foot-loose and fancy-free years together before Jonathan came along.

Of course, like any relationship, it was not always a bed of roses. He and I are very different people. He is an introvert, while I am a way-out-there extrovert. I love people. He would rather be by himself. We have very different interests. We are both very stubborn, independent, and self-reliant.

CHAPTER 9
Pivot Point

Still, we adore each other. He is my other half. He is strong in ways that I am not. He is my rock, my best friend. I am his sunshine, his zest for life. I drag him out of his cave to play and enjoy the treasures of life. It works. In fact, it had always worked well, until now.

With the words, "You are legally blind," our whole world had been turned upside down. The very fabric of our lives had been ripped apart. Unless you were living through it, it would be hard for someone to understand.

In one day, in one moment, with one pronouncement of a diagnosis, everything changed. Interestingly, it was not so much the diagnosis of progressive vision loss that tore at our relationship. While that was devastating, clearly heartbreaking, it was in the future. Certainly, it was hard to get your mind wrapped around it, but you could shun those thoughts away for another day.

The thing that rocked our world, that cut us to the core, was my inability to drive. Giving up driving was killing us.

With my part-time schedule since Jonathan's birth, I took care of the household chores and errands. With Eric's high stress work life, this offered him a chance to regroup on the weekends and enjoy Jonathan. This balance of responsibilities had worked out fine for our little family. After all, I liked taking care of things, being self-sufficient and making our lives run smoothly.

Then suddenly, it was not working anymore. I could not drive. I could not take care of any of the errands by myself. Every doctor's appointment required rearranging the schedule so Eric could take us. Every errand now fell on his shoulders. From the dry cleaning to the bank to the post office, and worst of all, the grocery store, it all suddenly became Eric's duty. He had to do everything. I could come along and take care of the task, but I could not get to that location independently.

He was overwhelmed and frustrated. He was exhausted. He had not signed up for this.

I was so frustrated and miserable. I felt sorry for myself. Guilt consumed me. I despised dumping all this on his shoulders. I so wanted to take care of things, to make it easier for him. I just wanted to do it myself, and I couldn't.

It was killing us. The frustration and resentment were eating away at our souls. Try as we might, we could not seem to deal with it. The frustration and resentment bubbled up, and we lashed out at each other.

We kept trying to work it out, juggling the schedule, re-negotiating the workload, but the compromises never seemed to last. No matter what we did, things didn't seem to get any better, and the resentments kept building.

It was such a vicious cycle. It seemed like we were on a terrible carnival ride that we could never get off. We were both stuck on the ride, screaming inside, and never finding the exit.

We had come to the end of things. We could not keep going on this way. It was time for a change.

It was late one evening when we had the heart-to-heart talk. He was honest. He couldn't keep going on this way. I was so frustrated all the time, and it came out as a shrill fussing to him. He felt like he could never do anything right, that I was never happy with anything he did. I always seemed to want more. Those were his perceptions, and he was at the end of his rope.

I felt like he was grumpy all the time. He was never vicious in his comments, but there was always an edge in his tone with me. I felt the resentment under the surface, and I just couldn't tolerate that anymore. I so wanted to fix it, to make it better, to take away the burden from him, but I had no idea how to do that.

I was so frustrated with my diagnosis and the changes it had wrought on my life. That frustration came out as resentment toward Eric. I didn't mean for it to, it just came out that way.

"Anita, I can't go on this way. I have had all I can take."

"I know, but what are we going to do about it?"

He was ready to walk out the door, but Eric is a man of high integrity and honesty. He had made a commitment to me, and he did not want to walk away. He still loved me, wanted it to work, but he could not continue this way. I still loved him with all my heart. I wanted to find a way out of all this mess, but I had no idea where to turn.

I looked at him squarely in the eye and said, "We need to work this out. We have a three-year-old little boy in there that needs us both. We need to work it out for him. We owe him that."

I suggested counseling, and to my great surprise, he said yes.

Learning to Listen

Two weeks later, we found ourselves in the waiting room of the counselor's office. Sitting there beside Eric, I couldn't help but wonder how in the world did we get to this point? How did two people who loved each other as much as we did end up sitting in a marriage counselor's office, struggling to save our marriage?

Little did I know at that point, but we had just taken a pivotal step, a step that would point us in a new direction. That one choice, the choice to take action, changed the course of the rest of our lives. Though it was not an easy choice, it was the best decision we ever made. It was a choice that made a world of difference in our family and for our future.

We met with the counselor for a total of seven sessions. Not long by many standards, but amazingly, it was long enough to heal our broken relationship. We spent time talking about the circumstances that brought us to this point. We talked about the course of our relationship, about our values, our commitment, and what drew us to each other. Then we got to the crux of the problem, communication. It all boiled down to communication.

The counselor correctly surmised that the change in my level of independence had thrown our relationship off balance. Prior to the identification of my eye disease, I had been so independent and self-reliant. Suddenly, I was forced to deal with a devastating diagnosis, and at the same time, acquiesce to a life of dependency on others. While I had been dealing with the emotional baggage of all that in my previous counseling sessions with Bob, I had not realized how these changes had impaired our marital communication.

We realized fairly quickly that we had developed some unhealthy communication habits. In fact, these bad habits had been in place long before my RP diagnosis. We had always been good at making the big decisions like job changes or moving. For those kinds of discussions, we were on the same page.

It's the little day-to-day stuff that sometimes led to problems. We often played the "Where do you want to go eat?" game poorly. He would suggest a place, and I would suggest another option. He would agree, but act annoyed. Trying to please him, I would throw out more alternatives that only added to his frustration. Without intending it, our poor communication could sabotage a nice evening out.

The same round robin could happen with social engagements. I thrive in a room full of people. He would just as soon be home in his recliner. He would agree to go to some gathering, and then seem bored or irritated. I would get frustrated, and things would go downhill from there.

Such little disagreements were not really a big deal, and we worked through them, but little or not, they added tension to our lives. It's true that opposites attract, but it's also true that personality differences can generate communication issues. Eric and I didn't always navigate those personality differences well.

Before my diagnosis, there were options. If Eric didn't want to go somewhere that I did, it was fine for me to go by myself. I had car keys, and he was good with that. Once Jonathan came along, we had to negotiate child care if one of us wanted to do something solo. It sometimes took some juggling, but we had made it work without any major upheavals.

Enter the inability to drive, and now it seemed like anything could turn into a major upheaval at the drop of a hat. It was bad enough that he had to take care of all the appointments and errands, but not driving changed our social life too. I couldn't go anywhere solo. If he didn't want to go out, then I didn't get to go. That either led to me being frustrated or him feeling guilty. He would agree to things he didn't want to do just for my benefit, but I knew he didn't want to be there, and that upset me too. There was no way for either of us to win in that scenario.

The truth was I didn't like this new reality, and neither did he. We were both angry. We were both frustrated, and we were actively taking it out on each other.

Recognizing these underlying emotions and the impact on our living situation was crucial. We both had to recognize each other's struggles in this new reality. Instead of only thinking about the impact on ourselves, we had to think about their impact on each other. While we were aware of each other's struggles, sitting there in that dark quiet room with the counselor, we both saw the situation from the other's viewpoint. That was pivotal.

Then, the counselor got down to brass tacks. A big part of our communication problems centered around transportation arrangements.

When I needed or wanted to go somewhere, I felt like I had to ask Eric's permission. When I wanted a ride, I would ask the question, "Can you please take me …?" The counselor pointed out that this sounded like I was asking Eric's permission to do something. It put me in the position of a little girl asking her daddy for a ride. It was a very uncomfortable place for me to be.

I had never really thought about it like that before. I knew I felt very uncomfortable asking for his help, but now I could see perhaps why it was so difficult. Better yet, Eric could understand why it was so hard for me.

The counselor coached me on how to ask for assistance in a more "Adult" manner. He suggested rephrasing the question to something like, "Would you be free to take me to…?" That felt more like making an appointment, instead of asking permission.

Then, the counselor tackled a second problem. Eric knew all too well that he was my primary ride option. He knew he needed to provide transportation, but there were times when he was just too tired and overwhelmed to want to do so. When I would ask him to take me somewhere, he would say "Yes," but his body language was screaming "No!" Being a very intuitive person, I knew immediately that he did not want to do what I had asked.

Feeling uncomfortable and guilty for even having asked him to do something, I would begin to back pedal. Although he had just verbally agreed to my request, I would immediately start searching for other options, trying to relieve him of this burden. He would get so frustrated because he had just said yes, and why couldn't I leave it alone?

The counselor pointed out to him that it was very difficult for me to deal with the discrepancy between his verbal and nonverbal communication. He warned us that it would take a long time to change this vicious cycle, but he went on to teach us some strategies.

First, I was to ask my transportation request using the more "adult" language. Eric was to receive my request, think it over carefully, and answer me honestly. "Let your yes be yes and your no be no," the counselor instructed. He followed up with, "Be honest. She already knows when you are not." If Eric answered "yes" verbally to my request, then he needed to make sure that his body language also said "Yes!"

The counselor then turned to me and told me something that I still smile about. "Now Anita, he won't be very good at this to begin with. He may say yes when he really doesn't want to. You will hear yes, and his body language will say no. But until he gets better at this matching game, whatever answer comes out of his mouth is the one you are going with. If his answer is yes, go with it, no matter whether his entire body is screaming no. This is a work in progress, and he will get better at it."

He continued his instructions for me. I was to make the request, listen to his answer, and not offer alternatives unless he replied no.

CHAPTER 9
Pivot Point

"If no is the answer, then you can pursue other options. Perhaps you can pursue other options together, but you must break the habit of jumping ahead and throwing out a long list of alternatives that quite simply overwhelms and frustrates Eric." This behavior of mine wasn't helping the negotiation process, and it was something I needed to change.

It sounds simple, doesn't it? Actually, it amazed us both that all our problems could be boiled down to a series of communication exercises. In order to fix our marriage, we had to improve our communication patterns. It was as simple as that, and yet, it was so difficult to change long-standing habits.

The time with the counselor had clarified our commitment to each other. We were both able to see that our love for each other was still strong. Our marriage was worth working for, and that work began with learning to listen more effectively to each other. The situation we found ourselves in would require lots of negotiation, lots of compromise, but it was not hopeless. There was a lot to be gained by working it out, and the counselor had helped us see just that.

We left the office seven sessions later with the plan. We had been trying the new communication strategies, and they were working for the most part. The counselor warned us that we would revert to old habits from time to time. We would have to help each other recognize when we were falling into bad habits, and then redirect our course.

Our circumstances would not change, but how we chose to respond to them could improve. We were committed to making that change. We were learning to listen, and love had prevailed.

Working Our Way Out

As winter turned to spring, things were better at our house. Eric and I were communicating better. Our newfound communication strategies were helping us navigate our transportation issues.

Although my reality had not changed, I felt better about things. It was easier to ask for what I needed. Eric had a better understanding of how I struggled with asking for help, and in turn, worked hard to be supportive. The counseling had reset our course, and we both felt better about things.

Work continued to be busy for both of us, but we seemed to manage the busyness better. We started doing more fun family things together. Eric and I planned some date nights too, and that was good for our relationship.

Jonathan was working his way out of the three-year-old tantrum stage. This developmental stage had certainly had its challenges, but I was seeing signs that my good-natured child was returning. He was getting his emotions under control. I sometimes wondered if Jonathan's acting out was simply developmental or had he been reacting to the tension in our home. Whatever the reason, it was clear that Jonathan's mood and behavior were improving.

I kept thinking about the plan for playschool in the Fall. I had no idea how to work out all the ride logistics. I wanted it to work out, but was overwhelmed at the prospect. I kept praying, asking God to supply the rides. "Work it out, Lord, please work it out."

As Jonathan and I played on the swing set in the backyard, signs of spring were all around us. From the tiny buds on the dogwood limbs to the bright yellow blooms of the daffodils, the joy of new life was apparent. Joy had found our little family once more. We were having fun together again, and there were things to look forward to like our upcoming family reunion at the beach. For the first time in a long time, I felt a glimmer of hope.

My Girl

After the rigors of the winter, it was time for some fun, and Eric and I were more than ready to get away for a weekend. A trip to Wilmington, North Carolina for Eric's family reunion was just what the doctor ordered.

CHAPTER 9
Pivot Point

This gathering brought together Liz's side of the family who were scattered all over the country. That weekend, they all converged ocean-side to celebrate the birthdays of the matriarch and patriarch of the clan.

Wilmington was a special place for Eric and me. His grandparents' home was our vacation spot for many years. Located only a few miles from Wrightsville Beach, his grandparents, George and Ann, could not have picked a better spot for their retirement home. The proximity to the beach ensured a steady stream of family visits!

George and Ann had raised Liz and her two brothers in Chatham, New Jersey. George was the town doctor in what was then a sleepy small town. After a long and rewarding career, George and Ann retired to Wilmington to enjoy a sunny coastal climate and their passion for golf. Their lovely home soon became the much-loved vacation destination!

My love for George and Ann had begun nearly two decades earlier at a high school homecoming football game held just seven weeks after Eric and I had started dating. From the outset, they had welcomed me with open arms. When my high school graduation rolled around, Ann had invited Eric and me to visit them for a beach weekend. When my father rejected the idea of me heading off to the beach with my boyfriend, Ann had written a precious letter that had assured my dad that we would be fully chaperoned. In her short note penned with proper etiquette, she had made it quite clear that there would be no hanky-panky in her household. After reading the letter, Dad had chuckled, then sighed, and finally acquiesced. Thus began our annual beach vacations at the Pike family home.

Ann was good with a pen. She had sent another one of her letters to three of her oldest married grandchildren in January of 1990 suggesting that it would be a great year for great grandchildren since it would be easy to remember their ages. The letter had been beautifully worded with the perfect mix of humor and mischief. Upon receipt, Eric and I had howled hysterically at Grandma's moxie as did the other cousins. Interestingly enough, each set of cousins brought forth their first child by the end of 1991! Grandma had gotten her way after all!

I had received another one of Ann's letters in the weeks following my diagnosis. Her heartache for me came through in her words. She encouraged me to keep the faith, that God would see our family through this trial, working things together for good even if we couldn't see how now. I treasured her words as I had all of her letters. Ann was a woman of great wisdom and her words never failed to inspire hope.

After all Eric and I had been through in the past eighteen months, the thought of celebrating life with Ann, George and the family I had come to love as my own lifted my spirits to a height they had not achieved in months. This trip was made even more special by the precious cargo we carried in the back seat. Just three months shy of his fourth birthday, Jonathan was entertaining his two-year-old cousin Elizabeth with a book he held up for her to see. He was merrily chatting away, and she was hanging on his every word.

Since Eric's brother Steve and his wife Amy had a conflicting wedding obligation that weekend, I had volunteered to keep Elizabeth and take her to the family reunion. Her great grandparents were chomping at the bit to see her, and I was thrilled to have some time with her. Since we lived several hours apart, it was sometimes challenging to get the two little cousins some play time together.

Jonathan and I had entertained Elizabeth well from the moment she arrived, and she had not whined for her parents once. Since this was her first trip away from her parents, I was a little nervous about bedtime. My fears were unfounded though. She went right to sleep without a peep.

After raising a little boy, I delighted in the opportunity to take care of a little girl. Getting her dressed reminded me of my doll

CHAPTER 9
Pivot Point

playing days. I dressed her up in her precious outfits, my only
struggle, mastering the hair bows.

Liz and Pete met us at the beach, and Liz was so thrilled to help
me shepherd her beloved grandchildren. The kids had a great time
romping around together with Grandma entertaining them at every
turn.

The party was lovely, and a great chance to reconnect with the
family. The most precious moment of the weekend was watching
Jonathan and Elizabeth sit on either side of their great grandmother
as she read them a story. They were mesmerized by Ann's animated
voice, and she was mesmerized by the two of them. It was a perfect
family celebration.

From the moment I had first cradled Elizabeth in my arms, I had
been smitten. It was so much fun to have a little girl in the family, a
chance to play dolls in addition to trains and trucks. I had enjoyed
playing with her at our family gatherings, but that weekend,
Elizabeth and I bonded. When she crawled in my lap and nestled
her tiny head against my chest, my heart melted. From that
moment on, I was her favorite Auntie, and she was my girl.

Less Of A Burden

With summer came the opening of the pool. Jonathan and I had
a place to go and play. Both of us were excited about that.

While I still didn't like it, I now had more confidence about asking
others for rides. Gradually, I had begun to accept it as a fact of life. I
also started to recognize that I could sometimes give back to my
friends. As we rode down the road, I could listen to their worries
while offering support and encouragement. Our car rides were filled
with lively chatter, and I started to realize that maybe my friends
enjoyed helping me. Not only were they getting the satisfaction of
doing a good deed, they were able to enjoy a friendship. These
thoughts made me feel less like a burden.

When Tami was not available to go with us to the pool, I became more comfortable calling a couple of our neighbors for a ride. The pool was only about two miles from our house, so it was not a big-time commitment. I quit fretting so much about asking, reminding myself that they could say no if it didn't suit.

Our kind neighbors were so gracious to help, and I called upon them often that summer. Since Jonathan was a gregarious little boy, everyone enjoyed talking to him. Giving us a ride meant a little car time with a cute little kid, and that was readily welcomed.

Jonathan progressed quickly with his swimming that summer. He did so well in fact, that he was invited to join the swim team. Swimming in the six and under category, he won several races even though he was the youngest child competing. He loved it! His team swim trunks were way too big for his small frame, but his zest for competition was not small at all. He was absolutely adorable, standing on the swim blocks, arms and legs poised to jump at the sound of the whistle. The fierce look of concentration on his face was priceless. Jonathan had found his passion, and our swim team days had begun.

The Open Window

Jonathan and I spent some great pool time together that summer, but as the months passed, my anxiety about what to do about playschool grew. We still had a guaranteed babysitter with Evelyn, so Jonathan had a place to go. This made it less of a crisis, but it was still worrying me.

I had faithfully prayed for a ride to playschool for months. I guess I was hoping that God would just send someone to our door. Perhaps God meant for me to step out in faith. I thought to myself, "How is anyone going to know of my need unless I mention it. Let people know of your need and let God work out the rest."

I summoned up my courage and mentioned my need to another mother whose child would be attending playschool in the Fall. While I was hoping she might volunteer to transport Jonathan, she

CHAPTER 9
Pivot Point

explained that she was not able to help. I was so thankful that she had been honest with me, but could not help leaving the conversation disappointed. "OK Lord, You are just going to have to help me. I don't know what to do."

I could not escape the nudge that I was supposed to act. So I summoned my courage again and mentioned the subject to a friend of mine from church. Marcia was a stay-at-home Mom, and I was hoping she might be interested in keeping Jonathan for us on Wednesdays while I worked. This would solve a problem for us and offer her the opportunity to make a little extra money while still being home with her children. I explained to her that I needed someone to transport Jonathan to and from school as well as care for him before and after playschool. To my great relief, Marcia immediately said, "I could do that." We agreed for her to discuss it with her husband and pray on it. The next day, she called to say she would take the job. I was thrilled! Wednesday down, two more days to go!

Now I needed to find transportation for Jonathan on the days he and I were home together. We needed a ride to church in the mornings and back home at noontime. Perhaps there would be someone traveling to work in that direction that could drop us off. That might mean I would have to go with Jonathan and hang out at the church while he was there, but at this point, I was willing to do whatever it took to make things work.

I decided to ask neighbors if they knew of any options for people traveling toward town during those hours. It seemed a long shot, but what else could I do? Most of my neighbors attended our church and were well aware of our situation. I felt comfortable at least asking them about my dilemma.

On one of our evening walks through the neighborhood, I encountered my neighbor Jerry. I stopped to chat for a bit. Jerry enjoyed talking with Jonathan who followed along behind me in his bright yellow Caterpeg riding toy.

That little voice inside of me said, "Ask him!" I was not sure about this, but had decided to step out in faith and follow such urging. I swallowed hard and asked Jerry if he knew anyone who might be traveling to town during the hours I needed. I went on to explain about the playschool plan and told him of my needs. Jerry was thoughtful for a moment, "Let me think about that and I will talk with Kay too."

Thanking Jerry for any help he could offer, Jonathan and I continued on our way down the street. I was relieved to have taken the step to ask. "That wasn't so bad. OK, Lord, I have made known my need. Please send us a ride, Lord. Please help us."

During one of our evening jaunts, we stepped across the road to visit our neighbors, Robert and Diane. Jonathan loved to climb up in the boat parked in their driveway. They so enjoyed chatting with him. They had no grandchildren of their own yet, so they were delighted to spend time with Jonathan. After visiting for a bit, I summoned my courage and asked if they knew anyone traveling into town in the timeframe I needed. Robert looked up with a smile, "Well yes, I do. Me!" I was so surprised and explained the background further. With barely a moment's thought, Robert volunteered to pick us up and drop us at the church. We would have to leave a little earlier in order for him to drop us off, but he would be glad to do so. "Why don't I take you two on Mondays? Would that help?"

I could hardly catch my breath. He was offering me a ride. I stammered that this would be wonderful as long as it was not an inconvenience to him. He reassured me that it was no problem. "But, Anita, how will you get home?"

"I don't know yet. I haven't got that far."

"Well then, why don't I just pick you up at noon, and I'll come home for lunch?"

I scarcely knew what to say. I was overwhelmed by his generosity. "Are you sure?" I kept repeating the question.

He and Diane both reassured me. "It will be a great excuse to come home for lunch!"

CHAPTER 9
Pivot Point

Monday was solved. I thanked God again and again on my walk back home. Hope was rising in my heart. God was working this out.

Several days later, Jonathan and I were making our loop around the neighborhood. I looked up to see Jerry coming out to meet us. I paused and smiled as I greeted him.

"Anita, I think we have an answer for you. How about if Kay takes you and Jonathan to the church on Fridays? She can run errands and bring you back home after school is out."

You could have knocked me over with a feather. I was stunned. I remember standing there absolutely amazed, "Oh my goodness, are you sure?" He reassured me that it was no problem, and we made plans for me to call Kay with the details.

I walked away with tears in my eyes, so overcome with emotion I could barely walk home. I had stepped out in faith, putting this big problem in God's hands from the outset. I had asked Him to solve it, admitting that the answer was beyond my control. I had asked God for His will to be done in this and then, I had waited. Perhaps not always patiently waiting, but still, I had waited.

God had nudged me to step out in faith and share my need. Despite my discomfort, I had been obedient and done so. What was the result of this act of faith? God had answered my prayer through the kindness and generosity of these faithful Christian friends.

Tears rolled down my cheeks in gratitude, as I knelt down to hug Jonathan. "Hey buddy, guess what? You are going to playschool!"

It was still hard to understand why God had allowed the door to be closed on my driving. I still struggled with that. Yet, in that moment, kneeling there in my driveway, my sweet little boy in my arms, I knew quite clearly that God had opened a window.

One Day At A Time

Right after Labor Day, Jonathan began his new adventures at playschool. Robert picked us up every Monday, and he and Jonathan had wonderful little chats along the way. I rode with them to church where Jonathan and I played in the gym until school opened. Jonathan had a tough time letting me leave, but his teacher helped us through the separation anxiety phase. I entertained myself with walks around the town, chats with church members and reading until Robert returned at lunch time to take us home.

Marcia was a Godsend. Eric dropped Jonathan off in the morning, and Marcia and Jonathan chatted over breakfast. She drove him to school at 9 AM, and he stayed for the lunch bunch program. She picked him up at 2:30 PM, and he came back to play with her children. Marcia figured out quickly that Jonathan liked helping her in the kitchen. Soon, they were baking a cake together every Wednesday to the delight of Marcia's husband who enjoyed sampling their tasty treats.

Fridays worked out beautifully. Kay picked us up in the mornings and dropped Jonathan at church. She often invited me to run errands with her, taking care of some of my tasks as well as hers. Sometimes, we went shopping which we both enjoyed. Kay was so very kind to both of us. Through the help of all these kind people, God had surely opened a window, and I was so incredibly grateful.

Later that September, we took a trip to the beach with Ricky and Laura. Jonathan and their daughter Catherine had fun playing in the sand and sun. My little fish spent hours swimming in the nice community pool. At the pool or lounging at the house, Laura and I had time to hang out and discuss the issues of motherhood.

Ricky found some time to ask the hard questions about how I was really doing. Although clearly improved from earlier in the year, life still felt like a rollercoaster ride. The dips and turns were much less severe, but I still struggled with the ups and downs of my radically altered life. As usual, those little therapy sessions were helpful and thought provoking, and I so valued our faithful friendship.

Late one night, I recall finding some alone time to sit in a deck chair and think about my upcoming birthday. I would soon be 35 years old. I had always thought that by age 35, my life would be settled. By then, surely I would have things figured out, and my life would have a set trajectory for the future. I shook my head, abashed at how wrong I had been. My life was far from settled, and yet, I had so much to be thankful for. As the waves roared in the distance, I felt the sea breeze ruffle my hair. Staring up at the full moon, I sighed heavily, once again reminding myself, "One day at a time, one wave at a time. That's how you will get through this."

I remember bowing my head in prayer. "Lord, thank You for the rides, for all You have done for us. Lord, I'm going to be 35 and I still don't have it all together. I have so much to learn. I don't know what the future holds. I don't know how I will deal with my eyes, but I know I need to trust You. Help me to trust You. Lord, please work it all out."

Part 4
Stops Along The Way

SEPTEMBER 1995 – DECEMBER 1999

See, I am doing a new thing! Now it springs up;
do you not perceive it?
I am making a way in the wilderness and
streams in the wasteland.

—Isaiah 43:19 *NIV*

Part 4
Stops Along The Way

CHAPTER 10
Hazards And Detours

In All Things

"In all things," the speaker said quietly. "Not in some things, not in most things, He said in all things." The speaker was reading from Romans 8:28, "And we know that in all things God works for the good of those who love Him, who have been called according to His purpose" (*NIV*).

I was sitting in the sanctuary at a local women's conference. The speaker had my undivided attention. It was one of those moments when you stop and think to yourself, "This is really important. I am not supposed to miss this."

While two years had passed since my diagnosis, things were far from easy. Yes, I had a good job with flexible hours, a host of lovely women to ride to work with. I had wonderful friends whom I could call on for help. I had a loving family whose caring support had been amazing. Eric and I had worked through our communication issues, and things were better between us. Jonathan was still my delight, my reason to get up in the morning.

The Lord had supplied the rides to playschool, and those arrangements were working out beautifully. So why did I still feel so overwhelmed? Why couldn't I just breathe a sigh of relief, and move on with life?

We had been back to see Dr. Machemer, and the news had been good. My vision had remained stable. I had lifted up prayers of thanksgiving, but there was still no joy or peace in my heart.

While God had surely provided for our transportation needs, I still felt so overwhelmed by the realities of a life without driving. Our daily life took a tremendous amount of coordination. Arranging rides seemed like a never-ending chore. Our friends were all so gracious, so generous with their time, but it was still incredibly difficult for me to seek their help.

CHAPTER 10
Hazards And Detours

It was so hard to swallow my pride and ask for help, so hard to be always dependent on other people. I felt weary. The thought of the years ahead with all those rides to arrange simply made me nauseous. It felt like an endless battle that I could never win.

As if that wasn't enough to make me weary, there was this little issue of eventual blindness. I did not want to go blind. I could not understand why that was necessary. "Why can't I be spared from this very hard thing? What is the point of making me go through this? How can anything good come out of this?"

"One day at a time, one wave at a time." Again and again, I repeated that phrase to myself, recalling the powerful words spoken by the kind conference speaker one year before. After pouring out my heart to her, I had received what I believed was a message from God, a promise of how I would get through this very hard thing. God had shown up with a message for me, a message of hope and faithfulness. Still, as the waves kept tumbling over me, one on top of the other, I felt myself sinking. Those waves were crashing against me, knocking me down, my strength floating away. "Why Lord, why does it have to be this way?"

These were the thoughts that rattled around in my brain, sitting there on that sanctuary pew. There in the midst of all those anxious thoughts was this eloquent speaker talking about Romans 8:28.

I was no stranger to that verse. In fact, I had loved that verse from the first moment I saw it. I was 15 years old and had recently received a copy of *The Living Bible*. Excited, I had determined to read all the way through the New Testament. As I read through the eighth chapter of Romans, I paused to re-read verse 28 several times, then picking up my pen, I underlined the verse in dark black ink.

The year was 1975, and my father had just left the Army due to a reduction in military force. It was a very hard time for our family. Leaving the Army with 15 years of service was not his plan. He had planned to retire once he reached 20 years of active duty. Unfortunately, the economic circumstances following the end of the Vietnam War dictated a large reduction in the number of military personnel. My Dad was among those impacted. It was a devastating blow. We were a military family. That was the life we signed up for, the only life we knew. Suddenly, everything we had counted on was lost. We had to start over again.

I was heartbroken for my Daddy. I was devastated at leaving my friends, torn apart at the thought of moving yet again. Sitting there cross-legged on the bed, my Bible open in my lap, I stared at that underlined verse. Eyes glistening with tears, I thought, "How can anything good come out of this terrible thing?"

Perched on that church pew, reflecting on that moment long past, I knew the answer to my tearful teenage question. That very hard thing for my father had worked out beautifully in the end. After several years of struggle, he had landed a job as a full-time civil servant leading an Army Reserve division. He went on to retire from both civil service and the Army Reserves with full military benefits. My parents had enjoyed fifteen wonderful years living in Richmond, Virginia, before happily retiring back on the family farm in South Carolina. Things had worked out beyond anything we could have ever imagined on that heartbreaking day in 1975.

As I listened to the conference speaker, my mind kept returning to that difficult time so long ago. As the speaker shared her story of pain and hardship at the loss of her husband to suicide, I was deeply moved by her suffering. She described her struggles to cope with this very hard thing. Romans 8:28 had been her lifeline. In studying that scripture, the speaker had focused on the phrase, "In all things." She emphasized that the Apostle Paul did not say that God would work for our good in some things or in most things. Rather, Paul had said that God would work things together for good in all things.

In that moment, I remembered my father, and how crushed he was over leaving the Army. I recalled the pain we all felt in those dark days. Sitting there, twenty years later, I could see how God had taken that very hard thing and worked it for my father's good, for the good of our family.

CHAPTER 10
Hazards And Detours

"So what about your eyes, Anita?" I thought to myself, "Cannot the God of the universe who is sovereign and in control of all things, can He not take this very hard thing and work it out for my good?"

Whether I wanted it to be this way or not, I could not help but think that God would use this eye disease for my ultimate good. There would be a purpose in all of this suffering. I may never know that purpose on this side of heaven, but God knows.

The speaker went on to say that we must decide if we believe that the promises of the Bible are true. If they are true, then they are all true. If they are true, then the words of the Apostle Paul are true. "And we know that in all things God works for the good of those who love Him, who have been called according to His purpose" (Romans 8:28 *NIV*). She paused and looked intently at the congregation and repeated, "Not in some things, not in most things, but in all things."

Those words echoed in my mind, seeping gently down into the very depths of my soul. It was a "God-moment" for me. I knew very clearly that God wanted me to hear those words. He wanted me to trust Him, to hand over this very hard thing, and let Him work it all out for my good.

I have never forgotten that day in that sanctuary. If you talk to my friends, they have heard me quote that scripture time and time again. I always accompany it with the emphasis, "Not in some things or in most things, but in all things." That scripture has become a life verse for me. It has gotten me through thousands of struggles in this journey through blindness. It has helped me through the trials and tribulations of parenting, of marriage, and countless other life difficulties. We achieve wisdom as we age if we are willing to look back and see the patterns for good that God has created in our lives. Seeing those patterns helps us to move forward in a deeper relationship with God. Although life will throw us curveballs at times, we can take courage and strength from the knowledge that in all things God works for our good. Our challenge is to wait patiently and confidently for those good purposes to be fulfilled.

That day in that sanctuary was an important stop along the way. I was still far from the peace I craved, but the message of trust and hope inherent in Romans 8:28 found its way into my aching heart. I was not yet ready to stand on it, but I had heard it, and I would continue to carry it with me as I moved on down the road.

Baby Blues

"That boy is so cute. When are you going to have another one?" The question was an innocent one. The lady had said it so casually, truly meaning no harm. She had no idea that her lighthearted comment could evoke such turmoil in me.

"Should we have another baby?" I had asked myself that question repeatedly over the past couple of years. It was all so complicated.

When Jonathan had turned two years old, I had brought up the subject with Eric. We both adored Jonathan so much. The idea of another baby to love was both enticing and scary. I loved the idea of having a little girl.

Being an only child myself, I favored the idea that Jonathan would grow up with a sibling. I had longed for a brother or sister to play with when I was a young child. Because of those childhood yearnings, I had always said I wanted at least two children. When Eric and I daydreamed about a family in our dating years, we always had two kids in mind.

Once Jonathan came along, we both realized the work involved in parenting. It made us pause and realistically think about having another child. As Jonathan moved into toddlerhood, we still thought it was a good idea, but we were not quite ready to jump in yet.

Then, everything changed. On that fateful day in October 1993, our world was turned upside down. I was going blind. I couldn't drive. Eric had to take over all the errands. Just getting Jonathan to the doctor was a Herculean chore. He had constant ear infections, and it seemed like we were always at the pediatrician's office. Eric and I were both overwhelmed with just managing the routine tasks of life. "How in the world could we handle another child?"

On top of the practical issues, I was concerned that another pregnancy might make my eye disease progress faster. While I had obviously had this genetic disease since birth, the progression of the vision loss had been so slow that I had not even noticed it in my teenage years or my twenties.

During college, I began using reading glasses. At age 25, I progressed to full-time contact lenses due to a slight decline in my visual acuity. My night vision was never great, but it never really limited my activities.

However, all that changed with pregnancy. In the months after Jonathan's birth, both my visual acuity and night vision deteriorated noticeably. Through discussions with my obstetrician and retinal specialist, we learned that while there was no hard evidence, anecdotal reports indicated that other women experienced rapid disease progression after pregnancy.

"What if I get pregnant, and my eyes get worse? How would I take care of another baby? Is it fair to Jonathan to have another child and then lose so much vision that I cannot do the things I want to for him? Would it be fair to the second child? Is it worth the risk?"

I had started high dose Vitamin A therapy almost immediately after the diagnosis. Since the research suggested that this therapy might slow the disease process down, I did not want to risk stopping the Vitamin A, but there was a risk of birth defects if I took it while pregnant.

Finally, what if I passed this disease along to another child? I had not known about the disease prior to Jonathan's birth, but now I knew about the genetic transmission. Should I risk transmitting the gene, or worse still, the disease to another child?

Yes, it was complicated. So many issues must be considered. It was both overwhelming and heartbreaking. I was facing another lost dream, another life plan that was falling apart. I could risk it, but was that fair to Jonathan, to Eric, to myself?"

I remember that dilemma so clearly. I can still feel the heartache of that decision. After several years of debate over whether to have another child, we decided against it. For years afterwards, there was a little pang of loss every time I thought about it. Still, I knew we had made a good decision. I threw myself into being Jonathan's mom and soaked up all the Mommy times with him. It was enough, and I am so incredibly grateful for the blessing of my only child.

Thank Goodness For Grandparents

If friends were our lifeline to manage the tasks of everyday living, then our parents were our salvation. Despite the distance between us, both sets of parents came to visit every chance they could. During our weekly phone calls, they each listened attentively to what was happening at our house. If they picked up on the slightest need, next thing I knew one of them would be planning a trip to help us. I cannot fully express what that support meant to us as we struggled to manage our transportation issues.

My mother-in-law Liz still worked full-time, but she and Pete came as often as they could. Liz showed up at our back door, apple pie in hand, and all would be right with the world. Liz took it upon herself to be my Christmas shopping elf. She would schedule several days in November to come down and take me shopping. I had my list ready, and we raced around getting all my holiday errands done. Not only did the presents get bought, but we had some fun "girl time" in the process. Jonathan loved those visits, especially the apple pies!

My parents continued their frequent visits, usually arriving on our doorstep once every four to six weeks. I had my to-do list ready, and they took me on my rounds.

CHAPTER 10
Hazards And Detours

My parents picked Jonathan up from daycare or playschool and entertained him in the afternoons. More than once, I came home from work to find them all in the driveway, Mom and Dad plopped in lawn chairs, Jonathan racing around in his bright yellow "Caterpeg" riding toy. Picking up a rock or toy with the front loader shovel, he hauled it over and deposited it with Grandma. With a squeal of tires, he would declare, "I'm off, Grandma!"

My mother found projects around the house to clean, and my dad often helped with home repair tasks. With Eric working so hard, their help was a welcome relief. My parents loved spending time with their only grandson and helping me out in the process.

Thank goodness for grandparents!

Trains, Cars And Spaceships

Zoom! The race cars were barreling around the track, spinning, crashing, out of control. Their battered carcasses were flying through the air, the sound effects deafening. Chugging along through the in-field of the oval track, the train was steadily running down the railroad, moving freight cars and passengers to their chosen destinations.

Suddenly, without warning, all sunlight is extinguished, completely obliterated by the massive spaceship hovering like a dark shadowy menace over the earth below. Oh, but wait! Crashing through the atmosphere, just in the nick of time, Luke Skywalker in his X-Wing fighter swarms in, broadcasting a welcome message to the rebel forces that all is not lost. The massive spaceship is the Millennium Falcon come to join the rebels in their battle against the dark side. The galaxy is safe for another day!

All that happened on my coffee table every day, the result of my son's vivid imagination and his quite eclectic assortment of toys! No doubt about it, Jonathan remained our joy. If three-year-old Jonathan was precious, then four-year-old Jonathan was absolutely adorable.

A bundle of energy mixed with a precocious mind and a caring heart, he was the bright spot in our days. Gone were the three-year-old tantrums and what remained was a joy-filled little boy who was the center of our world.

Each morning, he trotted off to playschool in his Mickey Mouse jean jacket, ready to learn his ABC's and play with his little buddies. Well, he did trot off happily after we got past the first six weeks. A serious bout of separation anxiety began on the first day of preschool and continued for weeks. From the outset, he loved school, loved his teacher, loved his playmates, but he hated leaving Mama! In fact, he screamed bloody murder when I tried to drop him off. His screaming fits simply ripped my heart right out of my chest, and I had no idea what to do. Fortunately, his playschool teacher was quite experienced at dealing with such situations, helping both Jonathan and me adjust to this transition. Soon, he was parting from me with a quick hug and a wave, running over to join his classmates.

Preschool was all about exploration, packed full of fun activities and field trips. I relished the opportunity to explore the pumpkin patch with him or check out the fire station. Eric and I delighted in Jonathan's fascination over the colorful characters at Disney On Ice.

Thomas the Tank Engine was a big thing at our house, and had been so for several years. We regularly read a handful of books about Thomas and his friends, and Jonathan loved watching the videos as well. Thomas and his fellow train mates became regular residents on our sun porch coffee table.

Jonathan loved spending time with his dad. My father had introduced Eric to NASCAR races several years earlier, and Eric had started following the sport closely. Jonathan picked right up on this interest, and was soon watching the races with his dad. His attention span was short, but he became fascinated with the colorful miniature race cars. When he started lining up his few cars on the coffee table and racing them around his imaginary race track, his dad got enthused. Soon, Eric's Saturday morning drive to the trash dump became a father-son bonding experience. On the way back home from their errand, the two of them would stop at the racing store not far from our home where Jonathan would rummage through the bargain bin and pick out a little car. That's when the race track took over our coffee table.

Since the original "Star Wars" movie was our first date, Eric and I loved the movie series. We introduced Jonathan to the movies, and before long, the star ships and action figures were flying all over our house. Every now and then, a Star Wars X-Wing Fighter would fly in and destroy the coffee table race track, littering tiny race cars all over our carpet. Yes, it was an interesting assortment of toys, and he was an amazing little fellow!

Lot Of Loss

No doubt about it, Jonathan was my sunshine, but even his bright smile couldn't always keep the dark thoughts away. While I was so grateful for all the help offered by my family and friends, I still found myself struggling. I could not escape the sadness. It was like a shadow that followed me everywhere, overtaking me when my guard was down. I wanted to feel better, to move forward, to leave it all behind, but down deep in the recesses of my soul, that ache just wouldn't go away.

I didn't know what else to do, so I called Bob. That's how I ended up slumped on the couch, shoulders sagging, eyes downcast, my hands wringing the life out of a helpless white tissue.

"Bob, I just don't know what to do. I just feel so sad, and I don't want to be this way. It's like I get to feeling better, and then all of a sudden, I'm back to the beginning. I'm sick of this. Why do I keep doing this all over again?"

I looked up to find Bob watching me, his kind eyes brimming with compassion. He didn't speak for a moment, letting my words have space as he considered his own.

"Anita, you have been through a lot of loss in a short time; the loss of your vision, the loss of driving, the loss of your old job and taking care of patients, the loss of having another child, the loss of your independence. That's a lot of loss, and you have to grieve it. You have to allow yourself the time to grieve."

I nodded my head, knowing that he was right. It was a lot of loss. I understood it, but understanding it didn't make it feel any better.

Fatherly Faith

My Dad and I have always been close. I was a Daddy's girl, and he was my hero. He still is.

My father is a wise man, invariably full of good counsel. He listens well and is deeply thoughtful in his advice. I value hearing his perspective on things before I make a major decision. I love to have deep discussions with him about life. He has taught me so much.

This disease hit my parents hard. It has always pained them to think of the genetic link of this disease, no matter my reassurances that I never give that a second thought. Their self-imposed guilt has been a burden for them both.

One sunny afternoon, Dad and I found ourselves alone in his home office. Dad turned to me with a kind smile and an intent look in his clear, gorgeous blue eyes. "How are you doing, doll?"

"Doll" has been one of his pet names for me since childhood. I knew by his look and the tone of his voice, he wanted a straight answer. No sugar coating was expected.

"I'm OK, Dad. It's just so hard. I hate not driving. Sometimes I just don't know how we will manage it all."

He was silent for a moment. Shrugging his shoulders, he put praying hands to his lips in a gesture that was so classic Daddy. "I know. I know, doll. I know it's hard. But I really think that one of these days, there will be something for this. I really think there will be a cure for this someday. I just feel like it will all work out."

I remember sitting there taking in those words. My spirits rose as I felt their impact, because deep in my spirit, I felt a tiny flicker of hope.

CHAPTER 10
Hazards And Detours

Perhaps somehow, some way, it would work out. I had no idea how, but his words had held hope, and I wanted so much to hang onto that hope.

Would my sight be restored? Would there be some new treatment to stop the disease progression? Perhaps I would just learn to adapt to the vision loss. Whatever the answer, I wanted to believe it would work out.

I had faith in my Daddy's wisdom. Dad has always had great faith in God. I just needed to trust them both.

Stranded

Summertime meant pool time. Jonathan and I loved our pool excursions. When the weather was good, he and I would head to the pool, prepared to stay several hours. Running back and forth to our house for lunch breaks was not an option like it was for the other mothers. Of course, our pool days were dependent on finding a ride. I continued to rely on our friends and neighbors for transport, and they were all so gracious to help us out.

Those pool days were a happy time for us. Jonathan had friends to play with, and I had adults to talk to. He and I had fun playing in the pool together. It was nice to be out in the sunshine, enjoying our friends and each other.

One afternoon, Jonathan and I hitched a ride to the pool with a friend. She and her child could not stay long. I called Eric to ask if he could stop by and pick us up on his way home. He was fine with that plan, and we settled in to hang out until he got off work. It was a beautiful summer day, and we enjoyed our play time.

I was expecting Eric to arrive about 5:30 PM. He would pick us up, and we could head home for supper. Those were the days without cell phones. There was a phone at the pool, and at about 5:30 PM, the lifeguard answered the phone, calling out that the phone was for me. Eric was on the other end of the line, the frustration high in his voice. He had a crisis at work and had not been able to leave yet. "I'm sorry. I don't know how long this will take. Can you get a ride home?"

I could hear the stress in his voice. He was worried about us. He was super stressed over his work. The job was so unpredictable, and there seemed to be a crisis every minute. He wore a pager that went off day and night, leaving him frazzled and weary. He still had to drive the 45-minute commute once he finally resolved the crisis.

I told him I would work on a ride and call him back when I found one. I hung up the phone, feeling my stomach clench up in knots. Here came the mantra that I tried so hard to shut down, but would not go away. "I hate this. I hate not being able to drive. Why does it have to be this way? Now what are we going to do?"

All my friends had already left the pool for the evening. I went back to my chair to think about who I could call. I felt sick at my stomach. It was so hard to not drive. The loss of control ate at me. It should have been easier by now, but situations like this made all the anxiety and frustration flare up. It was like pouring gasoline on a smoldering fire. I just wanted to sit there and sob.

Jonathan got out of the pool and came over to my chair to get his towel. He snuggled up on the chair with me. "When's Daddy coming?"

"I don't know, buddy. Dad had a problem at work, and he is going to be late."

"I hate that job. I want my Daddy."

At the moment, I hated that job too.

The pool phone rang again, and it was for me. Eric was leaving work and would be there to get us as soon as he could. Jonathan and I hunkered down to wait. It was the only thing we could do.

I had felt stranded that afternoon. It wasn't the first time, and it wouldn't be the last. Without car keys, I had no control, and that loss of control was a bitter pill to swallow. I tried to swallow it, tried to accept this new way of life, but situations like this brought my frustration level to a boiling point. Eric couldn't help it. He was trying so hard to take care of everything, but he couldn't control it all any better than I could. I know he felt my frustration simmering under the surface, just as I know he felt it when it boiled over. I regret he had to deal with that. I wish I could have demonstrated more patience, that I could have handled the situation with more grace.

I fretted about rides constantly, dreaded the phone calls I had to make. I hated bothering people, always afraid it was an inconvenience, constantly feeling like a burden. No one made me feel that way. My friends were so gracious, so willing to help. The problem was me. After all this time, I still wished that I didn't have to ask. Yet, if I didn't ask, I would never go anywhere, and that really wasn't an option either. So I picked up the phone, but it still wasn't easy.

So often, I waited for rides with a knot in my stomach. What if they really don't want to do this? What if they are delayed and I miss my appointment? What if they forget?

I had laid down those car keys, but as time went on, it was clear that I really had not let them go.

Mountain Of Frustration

As the summer days melted away, the dark clouds that loomed in the distance creeped closer. Nearly three years had passed since that horrifying moment in the ophthalmologist's office. With God's help, we had overcome so many challenges. My brain could make a list of all the ways God had seen us through, but my heart still ached. I had so much to be thankful for, so why, deep down in my soul, could I not find any peace?

No matter how hard I tried, I could not flee far enough from the mountain of frustration that hovered over me. My anguish over not driving was like acid eating through the core of my being. After this much time, I should have accepted this "new normal," but the reality was far from it. While I dealt with arranging rides on a practical level, the emotional connection to those car keys proved much harder to break. My loss of independence was a constant regret that could spark resentment in a flash. I tried to put out the flame, but it continued to smolder.

There were several triggers for my angst. The start of kindergarten loomed over me like a thick dark cloud filled with all the typical motherly worries of letting go coupled with the dread of more rides to arrange. My yearly eye appointment was just around the corner, and the possibility of further visual decline filled my heart with dread.

While Eric and I were back on the same page, communicating better and even enjoying some occasional adult time together, his work situation was in a downhill spiral, and all three of us were feeling the effects. He was working incredibly long hours, his days made even longer by the grueling commute. On call 24/7, his sleep was constantly interrupted by calls in the middle of the night, and even his weekends were not his own. He was on high alert all the time as one crisis piled on top of another.

His load didn't stop with work either. He felt the pressure to meet our household transportation needs. On top of his normal drop off, pick up duties, there was grocery shopping, soccer or baseball practice, and heaven forbid, the unscheduled doctor's appointment. He was constantly on the road, and he was exhausted.

Between work and home, Eric's days were full of hassles. No small wonder Eric ended up with a bout of bronchitis that led to pneumonia, leaving a new diagnosis of asthma in its wake. He was carrying too much on his shoulders and keeping all that stress bottled up inside. I felt the weight of his burdens and hated dumping all those duties on him. We rolled from one crisis to another, feeling like jugglers trying to keep multiple china plates in the air lest they crash to the floor and shatter into a thousand pieces.

It was all just too much. I was miserable, and yet, I said nothing to anyone. I kept going, but little by little, I was dying inside.

I knew I could, and should, go back to see Bob, but I didn't. I don't really know why. I was stuck, stubbornly holding my ground as if by sheer perseverance I could make things be different. It wasn't working.

When I looked at the future, all I could see was an endless set of obstacles to overcome. All I wanted to do was grab the car keys and take care of it all myself.

No one else could understand how I felt. No one could imagine how the loss of independence ate at me. How could they? I hid it all so well. From the outside, no one would have guessed anything was wrong. I was good at covering it up. But on the inside, I was desperate. Feelings of sadness and anger were dragging me down into that dark and dusty pit of self-pity. I felt so hopeless. I felt so alone.

Crayon Epiphany

On a sunny afternoon, I sat at the kitchen table while five-year-old Jonathan scribbled in a coloring book, the crayons spread out all over the counter. I listened to him amiably chattering away, yet my mind was far away. There was a piece of white paper lying on the table. Mindlessly, I picked up a crayon and began my own scribbles.

Now, let me be clear, I am no artist. Yet, without conscious thought, I began drawing a scene, reaching for different colors. Soon, Jonathan was done with his coloring and climbed down from the stool. It was then that I looked down at my drawing, surprised to see that I had drawn a desert scene, complete with craggy mountains, sandy hills and a large green cactus in the forefront. I sat there staring at the drawing for a long time. "Yes, that's how I feel...Alone in the desert."

As I cleaned up the crayons and papers, I wondered about that drawing. It was so surprising to see what I had drawn, somewhat shocking to have my feelings of sadness and loss portrayed so clearly on a piece of paper. "So if I feel so alone, so hopeless, what am I going to do about it?"

Alone In The Desert

The weeks seemed to come and go, but my internal outlook did not improve. I still thought about that desert drawing, still felt the weight of my misery.

That was how I was feeling when it came time for the women's retreat that I had attended for the past couple of years. At each of the previous conferences, the speakers had shared stories that had spoken directly to my heart. I prayed that this year would be no exception. I desperately needed some words of encouragement.

As I stood there scanning the list of concurrent sessions to choose from, imagine my surprise when I saw that one of the sessions was titled, "Alone in the Desert."

Hmmm...well, of course, I had to go to that one. It turned out that the speaker was a Christian counselor who worked with couples and families who were struggling through all kinds of trials. She herself had encountered multiple tragedies. She said that when we are faced with trials and suffering, our first question is, "Why, Lord, why?" Well, that got my attention. Had I not been asking the same thing?

The speaker discussed our struggle to understand why bad things have to happen. We assume that God is punishing us or that He does not love us. For if He did, then surely, He would take away that hard thing. While God is still good and He does love us, the reality is that He does not always take away that hard thing.

"What if God allows suffering because in the process of dealing with our struggles, we grow in our faith? What if sometimes God allows you to wander alone in the desert, so you can learn what you need to, so you can become the person He created you to be?" The speaker went on to explain that when we are busy, when we are surrounded by people, when we are immersed in the fullness of life, our hearts and our minds are often closed to God's messages. He may try to reach us, but we are too busy or distracted to hear Him. But when suffering strikes, we need God. We cry out to Him. We search for Him, and when He speaks, we tend to listen. When we listen, we open the door for God to work within us, to mold and shape us into the people He created us to be.

She also emphasized that God is not immune to our plight. He understands our agony. He hears our cries, and He weeps with us. He promised that He will never leave us nor forsake us (Hebrews 13:5). But sometimes, God does not save us from our struggles. Sometimes, He allows the trials that result from living in an imperfect, sinful and fallen world. God knows that with His guiding hand, we can navigate the storms of this life and emerge stronger and better equipped for the work He has planned for us. God can take the imperfections, the losses, the hardships of this world and work them together for good (Romans 8:28). "What if God allows us to wander alone in the desert so that He can get our attention?"

I just sat there, stunned. It was like the speaker had read my mind. I felt so alone, although I was surrounded by people. I felt like no one could comprehend my pain. No one understood how hard the day-to-day struggles of not driving were on me. No one could see my fears of going blind, of my whole life changing, of possibly being totally dependent on others. It was terrifying and heartbreaking.

I felt like a well-dressed mannequin in a storefront window. Everyone just passed by unaware of the real me inside that window dressing. No one saw the real me who was a mess, who hated where I was and what I had to deal with. I hated feeling sorry for myself, but I really did feel sorry for myself. I was thirsty in the desert and there was no source of water anywhere to quench my thirst.

I could not blame anyone for not seeing my pain. I did not share it. I protected everyone around me, especially my loved ones. They were tired and hurting too. Why should I add to their suffering by telling them how lousy I felt? So I kept my anguish inside, locked away from everyone. No small wonder that I felt alone in the desert.

Listening to the speaker's words, I had an epiphany. I suddenly realized that I was not alone. God was with me. He knew my every thought, my every need. He walked this desert road with me. He would provide the water for my thirst if I would just reach out to Him.

Silently, I prayed, "God, help me through this. Show me what I am supposed to do. Lord, work it all out, because I cannot do this alone."

The speaker posed another question. "What if God uses our desert places to plant new seeds of growth?"

Sitting there in that classroom, I wondered what God might do with this desert place I found myself in. It was then that the speaker explained about the rocks.

The speaker held up a basket of tiny rocks, each hand painted with a scripture. She had spent the last year selecting the verses, painting the verses on the rocks and praying that God would allow each person in her class to select the rock with the scripture that was meant for them. Then, she prayed with our whole group that these stones would be a source of comfort and hope, reminding us that God knows exactly where we are in our spiritual desert. He stands ready to guide us along the path He has ordained for us.

I filed past the speaker and plucked my rock from the basket. I held the flat, dark brown stone in the palm of my hand. In tiny white letters, "Hosea 10:12" was painted delicately on one side of the stone. I could not wait to grab my Bible and find this verse.

"Sow righteousness for yourselves, reap the fruit of unfailing love, and break up your unplowed ground; for it is time to seek the Lord, until he comes and showers his righteousness on you" (Hosea 10:12 *NIV*).

As I pondered the verse, I could not escape the idea of planting, sowing seeds, reaping fruit. The directive was clear. Plow up your unplowed ground. Get ready for what God is planting in your life. How? It is time to seek the Lord until He comes and showers His righteousness upon you.

CHAPTER 10
Hazards And Detours

I could not help but think that God was planting something new in my heart. He was calling me to seek Him, and He would get me through. He was telling me that He was changing my life, that He was orchestrating my circumstances for something more, something good, for His good purposes.

In that moment, something clicked inside me. I knew God was working. I knew God was with me. All I needed to do was to trust Him. I needed to let go of my regrets, resentments, fears and worries. I needed to place my trust in God alone and He would lead me out of this desert place.

On that day long ago, I had felt so alone, so lost in that desert place inside my heart. Yet, God was using that desert place to get my attention. That time in my life was a waiting period. God was working, but I could not see it just then. He allowed me time to dwell on my anguish. Perhaps he allowed me to get tired of wallowing in that pit of self-pity that so frequently consumed my thoughts. Perhaps He used that time for me to finally get honest with Him and with myself.

My heart began to change, to grow tired of misery, to desire something more. I found I wanted what God had planned for my life more than I wanted to stay stuck in my misery. God walked with me down that desert road, using that waiting period to plant new seeds of growth. With His perfect timing, those tiny seeds would eventually be used to yield a harvest of good fruit.

CHAPTER 11
Everybody Has Something

Starting School

Backpack slung over his shoulder, five-year-old Jonathan was standing at the back door, his face bright with excitement. "Are you ready, Mama? Let's go!"

I looked into his big brown eyes, and knew for sure that I wasn't ready. It was the first day of kindergarten, and I just wasn't ready.

Through all the struggles over vision loss, Jonathan was my sunshine, the light that kept me going through so many dark days. When I was frustrated with not being able to drive us somewhere, he would blurt out something cute and I would be reduced to giggles. He kept me busy from dawn to dusk, a welcome distraction from my woes over vision loss. To say that we were close is a tremendous understatement.

Jonathan's preschool experience had been good for both of us. Since the preschool was located at our church, I knew he was safe, well cared for and learning good things. The year had flown by and soon, he was dressed in his little white robe and walking down the aisle for playschool graduation.

Our summer play time passed quickly, and before I knew it, I was buying him a new Jeff Gordon racing backpack for the start of kindergarten. Being two years older, Jonathan's best friend Linsey had been telling him all about school, and their favorite playtime game that summer was "school" with Linsey as the teacher. Jonathan was excited about this new adventure. Jonathan's mom was less excited.

Worried about a resurgence of the separation anxiety he had demonstrated at the start of preschool, I was apprehensive about the first day of school. "What kind of teacher will he have? Will she be able to help Jonathan make the transition to this new school? Will he make friends? Will he fit in with the other kids?"

CHAPTER 11
Everybody Has Something

In truth, I was having trouble with the idea of letting him go. I adored him and didn't want him to grow up so fast. We had so much fun together. I knew I would really miss him at home.

On the first day of school, Eric took the morning off so that we could take Jonathan to school together. Jonathan bounced out of bed with a bright smile, ready for his new adventure. Grabbing his new backpack, he marched into school ten feet ahead of us, determined to prove that he was a big boy now. When we reached his classroom, he went straight in, greeting the teacher with a smile. He never even glanced back at us. As we made ready to depart, I had to call his name just to get his attention. He ran over, gave us a quick hug and raced off to play at one of the learning centers.

No tears, no drama, except for Mama. I remember following another mother out of the school. As we stepped onto the sidewalk, I let out a loud sigh. She turned back to look at me with tears in her eyes. "They're just too little to leave them like that."

"Yeah. Yeah, they are."

We both sniffled as we made our way to our cars. School had started.

Helping Hands

While the adjustment to kindergarten created some emotional drama for me, it had posed some practical dilemmas as well. Once again, the issue of transportation had reared its ugly head.

Earlier that summer, my worries about school had escalated. I had talked over my turmoil with my best friend Tami. As we sat poolside on a late June afternoon, I let my fretting have a voice. "How on earth are we going to get Jonathan back and forth to school?"

The week before, Jonathan and I had attended the kindergarten assessment day at his soon to be elementary school. While Jonathan participated in the learning assessment activities, I spoke with the assistant principal about bus transportation. I was a little nervous about my kindergartener riding the bus. I remembered all too well the bullying I had endured on some of those school bus rides. Would Jonathan get picked on by the older kids? Not only that, what was the bus schedule like?

While the assistant principal reassured me about the supervision and disciplinary process on the bus, the bus schedule proved to be a more challenging dilemma. The timing of the bus route would not match up with my ride schedule. Eric had to transport me across town to meet my rides at about the same time as the bus came through our area. There were no other kids in our neighborhood riding the bus. Jonathan could not wait for the bus alone.

Once again, Tami came to the rescue. After updating her on the schedule conflicts with the school bus, Tami offered her help without a moment's hesitation. "I'll take him to school for you. I'm going anyway to take Linsey. It's no problem."

We quickly hatched a plan. On the days I worked, we would drop Jonathan off at her house before heading across town to meet my rides. On my off days, Tami would swing through my driveway and pick Jonathan up for us. She would drop the kids off at the elementary school before heading to her work at the high school. It was a perfect solution.

Now to the next problem. How do we get him home? Enter another set of helping hands. Tami's mother-in-law Mildred was also our neighbor, her home located behind Tami's house. Jonathan and Linsey frequently visited Mildred and her husband Isaac. Linsey had quite a collection of toys there as Mildred had provided her daycare since birth. It didn't take long for Jonathan to occupy the status of adopted grandson. Since Mildred picked Linsey up from school daily and cared for her until Tami finished her work day, she readily volunteered to chauffeur Jonathan home on the days I did not work. Dilemma #2 solved.

The final child care crisis was solved by yet another set of helping hands. Several years earlier, I had met Kim S in my Sunday School class, and we had formed a close bond during a mom's Bible study group. Blessed with the gift of hospitality, Kim went out of her way to make me feel included, readily offering a ride to an event before I even had to ask. Her bright smile and fun-loving nature put me at ease about accepting her help, while making it a pleasure to be in her company.

Kim lived about five minutes away, and her oldest son attended Jonathan's school. A stay-at-home mom, she provided child care for a couple of children in her home. We worked out an after-school care arrangement for the days I worked. What a blessing! Jonathan was safe and well cared for, and he adored playing with her two boys for a few hours after school.

Once again, our friends came to the rescue. As I have said so many times, I don't know how we would have survived without the help of our friends and neighbors. God worked it all out. His grace was sufficient, supplying our needs, one ride at a time.

Wise Choice

The whirring sound of bicycle wheels reached my ears. I couldn't stop the grin spreading across my face as Jonathan blew past me, his blue and white bicycle helmet bobbing up and down as he pumped the pedals. The boy certainly had a need for speed. As he dashed past, he flashed that mischievous little grin that never failed to tickle my funny bone.

We were taking our afternoon walk, burning off energy after his long day at kindergarten. It was a beautiful fall day, the waning afternoon light flickering amid the reds and golds of the turning leaves. As the gentle breeze ruffled my blonde hair, I caught the telltale scent of autumn in the Carolinas, that earthy mix of fallen leaves and fading summer flowers.

I should have been enjoying the array of autumn color along our street, but my mind was miles away, plotting and fretting, actively searching for an easy solution that thus far had eluded me. It was time to sign up for soccer, and I was dreading it.

During his preschool year, Jonathan had played soccer for the first time, running up and down the field in a pack with his teammates. He seemed to enjoy the game, but should I sign him up for it again?

Most of Jonathan's little buddies were playing soccer or baseball. Eric and I wanted him to participate in all the normal boyhood sports, but our family situation was anything but normal. We were making the ride situation work, but both of us felt like overworked jugglers as we struggled to meet the daily demands for transportation. Adding one more place to go created yet another hurdle, and after-school sports felt like a giant leap.

It wasn't just about soccer. There was baseball and swimming to consider too. Jonathan had participated in all three sports the previous year. He enjoyed it all, grinning with gusto as he kicked the ball or swung the bat. Eric and I enjoyed it too, once we finally made it to the field and could settle on the bleachers to watch the game. Jonathan had surprised us with his zest for swimming, demonstrating an unexpected talent for backstroke. He fell in love with swim team, and his stance of fierce competitiveness on the starting blocks was a priceless sight to behold!

Three sports might have been doable, if the seasons had not overlapped. Soccer games were not finished before baseball practices began. Swim practices kicked off smack in the middle of baseball season. While coordinating rides to practices and games presents a challenge for all working parents, it was a nightmare for us.

I worked hard to find rides to practices, and Eric did his best to get there to pick us up or to watch a game. With his long commute, it was difficult for him to get home in time, adding one more stressor to an already long list.

Just the thought of soccer made me cringe. It was one more place to go, one more ride to arrange in a list that never seemed to end. I just wasn't sure we could handle it, but I didn't want to shortchange my son.

CHAPTER 11
Everybody Has Something

As we made a lap around our semi-circle street, I mulled over the situation without progress. It was time to talk it out with Jonathan. At five years old, he was well aware of our transportation hurdles. Perhaps I could find out what he was really interested in doing, and that might simplify the situation.

As Jonathan cycled along beside me, keeping pace with my steps, I decided to pose the question. "Hey buddy. I've been thinking. You know how last year we did soccer, baseball and swimming?"

"Uh-huh," he murmured as he nodded his helmet-covered head.

"Well, you know that was really hard for Daddy to get you to all those practices and games. It was hard for him to get home from work in time. Do you remember how sometimes we had both soccer and baseball going on at the same time?" I paused to see if he was following my thoughts.

"Yeah," he nodded again, closely tracking the conversation.

"I was just wondering which sport you really like. I'm kind of thinking maybe you might have to choose just one sport. You've tried all three now, so you know what they're like. I think to help Daddy, it might be best if you just picked one thing."

I was watching Jonathan closely as I made my little speech. I wanted to be sure he was following my points, and that my proposal wasn't upsetting him. I could tell by his serious expression that he was giving the matter his full attention. His sweet little face showed no sign of distress.

"So, buddy, if you had to choose between soccer, baseball or swimming, which one would you choose?"

He was quiet for a moment, brow furrowed, tiny jaw clenched in concentration. With a heavy sigh, he began, "Well, soccer is too cold. Baseball is too hot. But swimming is just right. I think I'll swim!"

The smile he flashed in my direction told me that he had made up his mind, and he was good with his choice. I had to steel myself not to laugh out loud at the precious way he had come to his decision.

"Well OK, buddy! We'll swim!"

The smile I flashed back at him was genuine, filled to the brim with gratitude. As we cruised on down the road, I breathed a sigh of relief, allowing the knot in my tense shoulders to relax a bit. I felt like I had just dodged a bullet.

I had proposed a hard choice for a little guy to make, but Jonathan had settled on a decision with a maturity far beyond his age. There was no whining, no crying, and he never brought the subject up again. He was going to be a swimmer, and he was good with that decision. He made the compromise out of love for his daddy, and perhaps his mama too. Even at his young age, he understood the heavy toll that a life without car keys took from me. He was doing his part to help us, and he had made a wise choice.

Looking back, this was a pivotal decision. Choosing to simplify our schedule by selecting one sport brought down the stress level of our entire family. Not only did it save driving time for Eric, it gave Jonathan more free time to play at home. Even at that young age, he didn't like to rush. I could enjoy being home with him in the afternoons, then we could have dinner and a relaxing evening to follow. The swim practices in the summer were easily managed as were the weekly swim meets. While our swimming commitments would grow with time, we stuck to our one sport decision, and that proved to be a wise choice.

Granny's Gone

My mother's voice was on the other end of the line, soft and sad. "Anita, Granny's passed." I knew the time was coming, but my heart sank in despair. My beloved granny was gone.

Mama had been at her bedside, holding her hand until the very end. She had gone peacefully, leaving the bondage of her hospital bed to pass safely into her Heavenly Father's arms. I was sad, but I was certain. She was where she was supposed to be.

Granny had always been there for me, ready and waiting with her expressive eyes, bright smile and open arms. She was the kind of grandmother that made you feel safe, cozy, comfortable. I had stayed with her so often that her little five room house in the small Southern mill town of Pelzer, South Carolina felt like home.

She and my papa had raised four children, two boys and two girls, in that little white clapboard mill house that backed up to the railroad tracks. They worked hard to make ends meet as they staggered their shifts at the textile mill just down the street. There was never much money, but they made the best of it, filling the house with love instead of coins or cash.

Their family was a bit of a novelty, having the only set of identical twins in town, my mother and her sister Tina. Since Granny dressed the girls alike, most people couldn't tell them apart; this challenge made even more difficult because the sisters were inseparable. In their teenage years, the girls became high school basketball stars, their ample skills further aided by the fact that opponents could not figure out which one was which and who they were supposed to guard.

Papa was the love of her life, and their years together had been happy ones. They shared a tight bond that did not diminish with the passage of time or the struggles of life. Granny was a woman who was more than comfortable speaking her mind. Papa was the only person capable of silencing her opinions by simply speaking her name. She admired him all her life, long past the days his handsome 6'4" 250-pound frame could fill up a doorway.

Granny was a bad diabetic, learning of her diagnosis by ending up in a diabetic coma. A young doctor fresh out of school recognized her life-threatening condition and responded quickly and correctly. Interestingly, he was just covering for the town doctor's vacation when he was called to treat her, no doubt saving her life. This occurred in her mid-50's and she never really bounced back completely.

Leaving the textile mill work after that life-threatening episode, Papa took care of her, and she adopted "the sick role" for the rest of her surprisingly long life. We lost Papa to heart disease in his early 60's, and Granny lived the rest of her years as somewhat of a shut-in.

She was an avid watcher of soap operas. A random stop by her home in mid-afternoon would find her in her beloved recliner glued to her "stories." She also enjoyed a good nap, though she would never admit to it. If we happened to catch her in the bed in the middle of the day, she would always claim, "Oh, I was just putting the drops in my eyes!"

Granny's other grandchildren lived close by, seeing her often, but my visits were fewer and farther in between. Growing up as an Army brat, we often lived far away, but that did not deter the bond between Granny and me. Whenever we returned from some faraway Army post, I camped out at her house. She and I slept together in the big bed in her front bedroom, me falling asleep to stories of her childhood. She regularly regaled me with tales of life on the family farm and her years living with her siblings after being orphaned as a little girl. Tough times had forced her into the mill at a young age, working in the spinning room most of her life.

She had a merry laugh, and a savvy sense of humor that would pop out when least expected. On the day of Papa's funeral, my father snapped a picture of her six grandchildren all standing together in a line. When Dad showed Granny the picture, he remarked, "Granny, now there's a good-looking bunch of kids."

Granny looked up, a little smile playing on her lips. "Well, there ain't never been no ugly Revis babies!"

She knew how to chat with children, never failing to entertain me. Seated comfortably in her recliner, Granny played Barbies with me. With my dolls spread on the carpet below her feet, she would ask, "What's Barbie going to do today? Why don't you put that dress on her?" Somehow, she always managed to play Barbies beautifully without ever leaving her recliner.

When my father was in Vietnam, Granny traveled to our house every night to stay with Mama and me. My mother was nervous staying out in the country alone, so Granny became my roommate. We became roommates again during my junior year of high school.

CHAPTER 11
Everybody Has Something

When my father's work necessitated a move to Richmond, I stayed with Granny for three months to finish out the school year. How many nights did she send me up to the local fast-food joint to pick up a plate of fried chicken and biscuits? We would then chat animatedly at the kitchen table as we munched on her favorite meal. She liked having me around, and our tight bond grew even more snug in that season of life.

Outliving all my other grandparents, Granny was the only one to see me become a mother. I remember her bright smile when I laid Jonathan in her arms for the first time. Mom and I had my father take a picture of the four generations gathered in and around her old faux-leather recliner. Her eyes were full of sunshine mixed with tears as she gazed into her great grandson's precious face.

It broke Granny's heart when she learned about my eye disease. She handled it all in the stoic way she dealt with most of life's troubles, but she grieved it nonetheless.

I learned so many things from my granny, life lessons I still carry with me, but I also learned what I didn't want to do. Between her health issues associated with diabetes and her having never learned to drive, Granny was housebound, trapped in that little house until someone showed up to visit or take her to the doctor. Her world became so small, her dependence on others so great. While there were reasons for her limitations, she never made an effort to promote her independence. In fact, she assumed the sick role and never seemed to regret it.

That was not how I wanted to live. Our situations had similarities; not driving, health issues, dependence on others for assistance. Yet, Granny never fought to change that, to do more, to live beyond the boundaries of her home. My eye disease altered my lifestyle, stolen my driver's license, and forced me to accept help from others, but I will not let it win! I fully intend to do all I can, while I can, for as long as I can. I do have a lot of Granny in me, but on this mindset, we were miles apart.

Granny's funeral was Jonathan's first experience with death. At five years old, I wasn't sure how he would handle it. Of course, he knew Granny, but he wasn't particularly close to her, and therefore, perhaps this would be an easier first experience with death.

It was a bitter cold morning in January of 1997 when we gathered in the cemetery chapel for what would have been a graveside service had the weather been better. I can still see young Jonathan dressed in his little sport coat and tie standing at the back of the room chatting with various family members. I wondered if he even understood why we were there.

Granny's last few years had been spent in a nursing home after not fully recovering from a fractured hip. The Baptist preacher who had visited her in the facility delivered a beautiful eulogy with an uplifting message. His remarks hit home when he said, "She is home. She is free. No more insulin shots. No more needles. No more diabetes. No more pain. No more tears. She is home now. She is free."

Apparently, Jonathan understood more than I thought. As I tucked him in bed later that evening, I talked about how Granny was happy in heaven, and he nodded and said, "No more needles!"

Granny was free, and in her eternal home, but a part of her is still with me, there in my memory. I remember all our times together, her stories and our giggles, our slumber parties and the fried chicken meals we shared. I glimpse my smile in the mirror, and realize it looks a lot like hers. I am like her in so many ways, yet different in others. She may be gone from this earth, but she will never depart from my heart.

Everybody Has Something

"Anita, you're not going to believe this!" Mom's voice exclaimed from the other end of the phone line. My parents had called with exciting news. They had won a trip, courtesy of their investment firm. The trip offered an all-expense paid weekend at a five-star hotel in Richmond, Virginia, the home office of the company. As

CHAPTER 11
Everybody Has Something

part of a recent promotional challenge for the company, my parents' names were selected to be honored guests at the firm's annual awards luncheon.

Richmond was a special place for my parents, having lived there for fifteen years prior to their retirement. They eagerly accepted the invitation, not realizing what was in store for them that weekend.

In their meetings with their investment broker, Mom and Dad had shared their financial goals, one of which included ensuring financial security for their daughter. Explaining about my eye disease, they expressed their concerns about how long I could continue working, given the progressive nature of the vision loss. My parents wanted to ensure that I would be provided for, should I need that support.

As my parents worked closely with the broker, he became well aware of my story. Little did my parents know, but he had a surprise up his sleeve.

At the awards luncheon, their broker unveiled his surprise. Standing at the podium, he introduced my parents and shared some of their story. To their amazement, he presented them with a book written by the firm's founder, Jim Wheat. It turned out that Mr. Wheat also had Retinitis Pigmentosa. He had lost the majority of his vision by his college years. Despite his blindness, Mr. Wheat founded this very successful investment firm. The employees shared amazing stories about Mr. Wheat, explaining that the book was his biography. It was their hope that his story would be an encouragement to my parents and to me. My parents were deeply touched by this gracious gift as well as the stories that the staff shared about their former leader.

I can still recall the excitement in my parents' voices when they called me upon returning home. I remember the little shiver that ran up my spine as they told the story. I could not wait to get my hands on that book. Since this eye disease is so unusual, it is rare to meet someone who has suffered through the same experiences. I was anxious to learn about Mr. Wheat's challenges and how he overcame his obstacles.

Several weeks later, I traveled to my parents' home and picked up the book, appropriately titled "A Hand Well Played: The Life of Jim Wheat, Jr."[2] Late one night after getting Jonathan tucked in bed, I nestled under the covers to dig further into Mr. Wheat's fascinating life. That's when I came across a story that I will never forget.

The story told of a party where Jim Wheat encountered an old friend he had not seen for a long time. His friend shared that he had recently been diagnosed with Multiple Sclerosis. Jim was devastated, and the wounded look upon his face must have reflected his heartache over this news. Noticing Jim's crestfallen expression, his old friend placed his arm around Jim's shoulders, saying, "It's okay, Jim, everybody has something."[2]

Those words stopped me in my tracks. I looked up from the page, staring across the lamp lit room. The words had touched something deep within my heart. It was a moment of absolute clarity, as if something inside me clicked. Those words were so true. "Everybody has something."

With those three simple words, I felt my whole perspective shift. I had spent so much time feeling sorry for myself about my eyes. I covered it up well, but nonetheless, I did feel sorry for myself. In that moment, I realized that everybody does have something difficult that they must face. We all have hard things in our lives. Mine was a health issue, while others might be burdened with a difficult relationship, financial struggles, a sick family member or a challenging childhood. Whatever the source, everybody has something.

Looking back, this was a pivotal moment. The road ahead would not be easy. Thereafter, there were plenty of times filled with sadness and frustration, but somehow, telling myself that "Everybody has something" made it all just a little bit easier.

---

[2] Wheat, Jr., J. (1994). *A Hand Well Played: The Life Of Jim Wheat, Jr.* Cadmus Publishing in association with Wheat First Butcher Singer, Inc.

CHAPTER 11
Everybody Has Something

This insight gave me more compassion for others. I began to think more carefully before judging another person's behavior. What kind of baggage might that person be carrying that would cause such behavior? My "something" is obvious. That person's "something" may not be so obvious, but it still causes heartache. This humbling realization has helped me extend grace when I might not have been so inclined.

It is amazing how one moment can change your perspective so significantly. It was without a doubt, a God-moment. The course of events that brought that book into my hands, and the power of that one story to so dramatically impact my life could not be the result of anything but God at work. I know full well that God intended me to find that story nestled in the pages of that inspirational biography about a man who overcame hardship and loss to pursue an abundant life. God wanted me to gain some much-needed perspective, a life lesson I have never forgotten. After all, "Everybody has something."

Biscuits and Sweet Tea

The morning sun blinded me as it poured through the windshield, and I hastily reached for the sun visor. Juggling my extra-large cup from one hand to the other, I maneuvered into the seat and grabbed the seat belt. Beside me, Susan mirrored my actions, depositing her Biscuitville bag on the console as she placed her bright yellow cup of hot coffee in the cup holder. The conversation was already flowing as we finished settling into our seats, ready to begin our ride to work.

Susan, always impeccably dressed, was covering her lap with the stack of napkins she had snagged from the store counter. Once her lap was sufficiently covered, she grabbed her brown bag, pulled out her plain butter biscuit and nestled the bag, then the biscuit wrapper on her napkin-laden lap. She was telling me a story as she ran through this well-rehearsed morning routine. Pausing to take a bite of her biscuit, she released her usual moan of delight before returning to her story. Putting the car in gear, she backed carefully out of the tiny, bustling Biscuitville parking lot and maneuvered the vehicle onto the road. Now settled on the main road, she reached for her coffee cup. Flashing her glowing smile at me, she blurted out, "Oh Anita, I wish you loved coffee. Then we could share this lovely ritual together!" I chuckled heartily and held up my bright yellow cup, "That's OK. I've got my sweet tea, and all is right with the world!"

That's how my morning rides with Susan started. Every day held the same rituals. Every day offered the same hearty conversation.

While my friend and mentor Marianne provided my Wednesday ride, Tuesdays were about Susan. From the very beginning, Susan had opened her heart as well as her car door for me. Her strong faith mingled with her genteel Southern manners were a great comfort to me as I rebounded from the assault of my eye disease. Her words of encouragement and listening ear played a major role in my healing from the wounds of my losses.

As she munched on a bite of her biscuit and sipped her beloved cup of coffee, Susan shared a good word and often a good laugh. I hung on her every word, starving for the solace her kind spirit offered. With every mile I spent in her company, my heavy heart became a little lighter.

As the months, then years, rolled by, I often wondered how I could repay her for her many kindnesses. As time marched on, the struggles of life afforded me several opportunities to reciprocate.

Susan and her husband had wanted children desperately, but thus far, their attempts to start a family had been unsuccessful. Soon after our ride journeys began, she had shared the story of a failed adoption. My heart broke for her as she lamented over this loss.

They had decided to pursue another private adoption, and Susan shared her hopes and her concerns about the process. I prayed along with her that this adoption would yield the baby of their dreams, but once again, the birth mother changed her mind. Susan

CHAPTER 11
Everybody Has Something

was crushed, and our ride time offered me a chance to comfort her as she had done so faithfully for me. We mourned that loss together just as we had mourned my vision loss.

Susan adored Jonathan, and when we met my boys at the mall after work, Susan would carry on an avid conversation with him. "Hey Jonathan! How are you doing today?" His brown eyes would light up at the sound of her voice, spurring the little fellow to launch into some tale that invariably brought a chuckle out of Susan. I watched these interactions with a tug upon my heartstrings, knowing full well how much she wanted a boy or girl of her own.

True to her indomitable spirit, Susan soon bounced back, and she and her husband pursued another adoption through an agency. As we rode down the road, I listened to the overwhelming hurdles they had to overcome to qualify for the selection process. When I looked at my little boy, I was struck by how easy it had been for me to conceive a child compared to the hoops and heartache my friends were enduring. Here was another glaring example of "Everybody has something."

I recall the day I slid into the car to find my friend's face full of joy. My heart soared with the news that they had been approved for a future adoption. Now we just had to wait for God to send them their baby.

The future seemed bright as we anticipated a baby to arrive. Then came that September day when the very ground beneath our feet was yanked away, sending our hearts plummeting to the depths. Susan was horrified. At the age of 37, she had found a lump in her breast. Within a few days, she was whisked away for a lumpectomy, closely followed by a series of radiation treatments, then oral chemotherapy.

Visiting her following the surgery, then listening to her descriptions of the radiation process, the whole thing felt surreal. How could this be happening to my young friend? She was only a year older than I.

My spirit struggled over this untimely onslaught, but Susan soldiered on. She handled it all with a grace and determination that testified to her tremendous faith.

While Susan toughed it out and kept a positive attitude, she did share her struggles with fear and anxiety. Though my eye disease was not life threatening, I could so relate to Susan's struggles with fear and loss. The table was now turned, and I could offer her the support that she had so generously offered me.

On a cold December evening, I recall the little victory party we held in her car as we celebrated the completion of her radiation treatments. We rejoiced and prayed together as we considered the preceding months of adversity. Susan was determined to put this harrowing episode behind her and move on with her life. I remember exiting the car, a prayer on my heart, "Now Lord, it's time for a baby."

Apparently, God agreed. Just weeks later, they got the call. Their baby boy would be born in January and delivered to them in March. Words cannot express the joy we shared at this blessed answer to long-lifted prayers.

Her work friends and I celebrated this glorious news with a joy-filled baby shower. I recall standing in the well-decorated conference room sipping punch and smiling as Susan opened a huge stack of gifts. I wasn't the only one smiling. The room was full of colleagues and friends filled with excitement over the upcoming arrival of the long-awaited infant.

Susan picked up the little gift I had brought and smiled. I grinned back, knowing that the real gift was still in my pocket. Once the "Oohs and Ahhs" had subsided, I stepped forward with the card. A quizzical look on her gorgeous face, she took the card from my hand and began to open it.

I had thought long and hard about my choice of gifts. I wanted to give her something precious, for she had been such a precious friend to me.

Susan began reading the card silently, tears forming in her tender brown eyes. The card explained that I had transferred a week of my paid annual leave to her account, allowing her an additional week to stay home with her newborn son. "Oh Anita! Oh Anita!" Susan exclaimed as she crossed the room to hug me. "Oh Anita! This is wonderful! Thank you!" Looking into her wet brown eyes, I knew that I had found the perfect gift.

On a sunny March afternoon, Jonathan and I sat at the kitchen counter sharing an after-school snack. I was watching the clock, just waiting for the stroke of three. When the hour finally arrived, I grinned at my small son seated beside me, exclaiming with joy, "Jonathan, Miss Susan's baby is here! Her baby boy is home!" He joined me in sending up a cheer, clapping our hands together with delight. I'm not quite sure if he understood it all, but he knew enough to know it was good news.

It was good news, indeed, most excellent news! For at that very moment, the social worker had marched up the sidewalk and delivered a beautiful baby boy into his mother's loving arms. Swaddled tightly in a warm blanket, God had answered a whole host of prayers.

Professional Passion

Young people are encouraged to find their calling. They are told, "Pursue your passion!" Many never find a job that they are passionate about, but settle for making a living at something.

I am one of those rare individuals that found their calling. I was born to be a nurse. From the moment I donned my candy striper uniform as a hospital teen volunteer, I was drawn to helping people. Walking those hospital corridors felt right, like I belonged there somehow. Once I put on that student nurse pinafore, I never considered doing anything else. Nursing was my passion.

While my eye disease had impacted my ability to provide direct bedside care to patients, it had not robbed me of my profession as I had initially feared. Once my job was changed to a more consultative, project management focus, I was able to perform my role without limitations. Because my central visual field was still quite functional albeit small, I was able to read and write with ease. With a few modifications to the computer, I could function normally. I compensated so well for my visual field loss that most people at work had no idea that anything was wrong with me. My only obvious restriction was my inability to drive, and that limitation was invisible to most of my colleagues. No one knew what I went through to get to the hospital, but once there, I was just like every other employee.

In those difficult days of adjusting to my vision loss, nursing was a wonderful distraction. Being an "all or nothing" sort of person, I threw my energy into my job. It gave me something to occupy my mind and kept my thoughts off of my worries.

To some degree, it was a control issue. I could not control what was happening with my eyes, but I could control my work. I could work hard and make a difference. I could fix things for other people, even if I couldn't fix my own situation.

When I took the job as Clinical Pathway Program Coordinator, I was interested in the project, but must admit that I was not really excited. I loved my old job. Leaving the clinical nursing setting had been painful. I missed the teaching, missed being at the bedside with patients.

Still, I had signed up for this new role, and true to my personality, I was determined to make this new program successful. As I threw myself into the new duties, I soon found that I enjoyed the work. I took great satisfaction in giving it my best.

In my new role, I was privileged to work closely with my close friend and "mentor on wheels," Marianne. Not only did Marianne offer me a ride to work each week, she offered me countless opportunities for professional growth. Marianne paved the way for me to speak about our clinical pathway program at various local and regional conferences. She encouraged me to submit a poster presentation to the national conference of our professional organization. When my poster was accepted, I was thrilled.

CHAPTER 11
Everybody Has Something

At the conference, Marianne introduced me to a variety of well-respected leaders in critical care nursing. My poster was greeted with great interest. The concept of clinical pathways was new, and many organizations were struggling to get their programs started. As I interacted with other colleagues, many were impressed by my work and interested in my ideas for enhancing their programs. By the time I left the conference, I had an offer to publish a book describing our clinical pathway program. I was absolutely amazed!

I signed the book contract within a few weeks of Jonathan starting kindergarten. The book was a blessing, because it distracted me from the blues of letting my little boy head off to school. I continued to work two days a week while writing the other three. I finished the writing phase in five months, and the final book was published in May of 1997.

While I was writing the book, Marianne encouraged me to submit an abstract for a pre-conference presentation at our national conference. It would be a great opportunity to showcase the contents of my book and share successful strategies with other nurses trying to develop their own clinical pathway programs. The abstract was accepted, and in late May of 1997, Marianne and I presented a full day presentation to a roomful of colleagues. My book was on display in the conference bookstore, and I even had a book signing session.

Never in my wildest dreams would I have expected such exciting professional opportunities. So many doors were opened for me, and I was honored to be able to share my work with other colleagues. I had thought my career was over on that day in 1993. To my great surprise, the opportunities were just beginning.

Home Office

Jonathan's kindergarten year held another unexpected blessing. After three years of an exhausting commute, Eric was offered the option to telecommute from home. He jumped at the chance.

We converted a room in his workshop into a home office. His commute went from three hours per day to a mere stroll across our backyard. He still had to drive me across town to meet my rides in the mornings and return to pick me up in the afternoons, but that was nothing by comparison to the trek he had been making previously. Eric was able to drop Jonathan at school when necessary and pick him up easily from his after-school care.

The new arrangement was an incredible blessing for all of us. We had less hassles on my work days. Eric was close by in case Jonathan needed anything during the school day. On the days I didn't work, Eric and I ate lunch together and could run short errands. When he finished his work day, Eric was home in less than three minutes, and we had more family time together.

The past three years had been such a struggle for both Eric and me. The threat of eventual blindness was always a worry, but it lived in the background. The transportation challenges wore us both out. Eric spent an incredible amount of time in the car, running us here and there, constantly trying to balance the needs of his family with his incredibly demanding job. The commute was a killer and a constant source of stress. I spent hours working out rides or fretting about how to work them out. It was exhausting.

We had struggled over the hurdles, endured the exhaustion, and suffered through the heartache. Now with the opening of this home office, our circumstances changed dramatically, all for the better.

Again and again, I had prayed for God to see us through our challenging circumstances. The divine intervention I had sought so often had arrived. Eric's telecommuting opportunity was an absolute Godsend.

Sigh Of Relief

At the hospital one morning, I turned a corner and ran straight into Bob. While I had continued to visit Bob's office from time to time, our counseling chats had become much less frequent. It had been months since we had last chatted, and now here I was gazing up into his kind eyes and warm smile.

"Anita, how are you doing?"

People ask that question countless times each day, often without any emotion or even genuine concern. It's a greeting, nothing more. But not Bob. When he asks how you are, he really wants to know.

So here he was asking the question, his voice gentle, his tone sincere. We may have been in a bustling hallway, but he had this unique gift of making me feel like the only person in the world that mattered at the moment.

So many times before, I had teared up and poured out my angst at his gentle question. Yet, this time, thankfully, I could answer him with a smile. "I'm good. I'm really doing good!"

I went on to explain about Eric's telecommuting situation, and how positively it had impacted our daily life. The logistics of meeting my work rides were so much easier. Running errands was no longer such a hurdle. Even the grocery store trips were more manageable. Eric could take care of things on his lunch hour or immediately after work. Without the long commute, his stress level was greatly lessened, and he was so much happier.

The change in his attitude helped improve my own. It was like someone had taken the top off the pressure cooker we had been living in, and the steam now released, we could taste life differently.

Clearly, I was coping more effectively with the realities of my eye disease. I still hated its presence, but I wasn't dwelling on it so much. Life was so full in so many ways, and I chose to keep on going, focusing on the good stuff instead of my limitations.

Our family's frustration level had plummeted in a positive way, and both Eric and I were breathing a sigh of relief. The bright smile on Bob's face told me that he could sense the relief in my countenance. As I thanked him again for all his help, he patted my shoulder. "My door is always open for you. Come see me if you need me."

I nodded my head, knowing full well that he meant it, and that support, in and of itself, brought another sigh of relief.

Meeting Mickey

Jonathan stood stock still, soft brown eyes staring up in wonder. Towering above him loomed an enormous set of ears joined by a pair of dancing eyes. Sporting a mile wide grin of greeting, Mickey Mouse was peering down at my little boy, white gloved hand outstretched in welcome.

It took several moments for Jonathan to take in this much anticipated meeting, but soon, he had his bearings and latched onto Mickey's outstretched hand for an enthusiastic shake. Eyes like saucers, he turned his head toward me, "Mama, it's Mickey!"

May of 1997 was a special month for our little family. Professionally, I was thrilled to deliver my presentation at the national critical care nursing conference. In the conference bookstore, I lifted my newly published nursing book off the shelf and held it in my hands. The sense of professional accomplishment evoked a giddy mixture of pride and amazement. But the thing that put me over the moon was the chance to meet Mickey.

The nursing conference was held in Orlando that May, and I traveled to Florida with another colleague, staying in the conference hotel. When the conference concluded, the plan was for Eric and Jonathan to fly down and meet me at Disney World. Eric and I had honeymooned at Disney, but this was Jonathan's first trip. I am not sure who was more excited, Jonathan or his parents.

After completing my conference events, I took a taxi to the Disney property. When the cab pulled up to the entrance of the magnificent Wilderness Lodge, I was quite sure I had stepped into a fairy tale.

Their flight delayed, I waited nervously in the grand lobby for my boys to arrive. When Eric's large frame filled the auspicious timber-lined doorway, closely trailed by my little boy's mesmerized face, I knew our amazing adventure had begun.

Everybody Has Something

Having spent weeks plotting and planning our Disney experience, I had mapped out our agenda carefully to avoid long lines and cover the maximum amount of ground. Jonathan's eyes were quarter-sized when we stepped through the gates of the Magic Kingdom. That's when Jonathan met Mickey Mouse for the first time, and the three of us were all smiles as we huddled together with Mickey for our inaugural photo op!

As part of my careful trip planning, I had fortuitously purchased a meal plan. While redeeming our meal plan coupon at a fast-food venue, I learned that we could use our meal pass at any restaurant on the property. To my great surprise, even character meals were covered. No further nudge required, I got busy making reservations for character meals all over the parks. We ate breakfast with Steamboat Mickey and lunch with Winnie the Pooh. On and on, our meal adventures went, having a few private moments with the whole cast of characters. Even Eric embraced the excitement, particularly enjoying his dining experience with the dazzling Pocahontas.

At one of our first stops, I spied an autograph book on a gift shop shelf. Armed with pen and book, Jonathan trotted off on a mission to gather every signature he could. Of course, every autograph came with a darling photo opportunity, and we snapped pictures of him all through the park.

One of my favorite moments was when we visited Mickey's house. To five-year-old Jonathan, Mickey Mouse and all his friends were real, lifted off the TV screen and standing right beside him. When he stepped foot in Mickey's house, he was absolutely spellbound. This was really Mickey's house, and he could touch all his things. The look on his face was priceless!

Eric and I have always been big rollercoaster fans. On one of our early dating trips to a local amusement park, Eric figured out that he had a thrill seeker seated beside him, and that suited him just fine. He and I made a habit of riding rollercoasters whenever we had the chance.

Rough Places Smooth

On this trip, it was time to introduce our son to the thrill of rollercoasters, and we both wondered silently how he would react. We need not have worried.

Making our way to Future World, we found the line for Space Mountain. Measuring his own height, Jonathan proudly declared that he was tall enough to ride. Seated beside Eric, he grinned at me through the crack between the seats. He was ready to roll!

The ride began, and our car twisted, turned and tumbled along the winding track, bright lights flashing as we flew through the darkness. I held my breath, not out of fear, but more anxiety as to how young Jonathan would weather this new experience. As he pounced onto the exit platform, I had my answer. He was dancing with excitement, his cherub face adorned with a brilliant smile, "Daddy, can we go again?"

I should have known then that my son would be an adventure seeker. We must have passed on the thrill-seeking gene in his DNA.

During one of our shopping sprees to take a break from the heat, Jonathan and I found the perfect gift for his dad. After sneaking to the register to purchase it, the two of us presented Eric with his very appropriate "Grumpy" hat. The three of us erupted into a fit of giggles, and Jonathan's dad wore that hat with pride. It turned out to be his ticket into the afternoon parade. When one of the performers saw his hat, she grinned and remarked, "Grumpy? Well, we can't have that!" Tugging his hand, she pulled Eric into the parade much to the delighted cheers of his wife and five-year-old son.

But Eric's most inspired "Daddy moment" actually came later. Each day as we cruised around the park, Jonathan would repeat the same phrase two or three times, "I want to go to the Magic Kingdom!" Invariably, one of us would patiently reply, "Buddy, we are in the Magic Kingdom!" Still, the comment didn't cease.

On our last day in the park, we paused to rest on a bench overlooking Cinderella's castle. Here came Jonathan's daily mantra, "I want to go to the Magic Kingdom!"

CHAPTER 11
Everybody Has Something

Slightly perturbed, Eric bent down to peer into his little boy's bright eyes. "Jonathan, where is the Magic Kingdom?" Leaping to his feet, our young son pointed emphatically straight toward the towering castle, exclaiming, "There, the Magic Kingdom!"

Both our mouths dropped open in surprise as we finally understood our son's persistent request. "Ahhh...Yeah, we can go there!"

Grabbing each of his tiny hands in ours, the three of us trotted off to visit Cinderella's sparkling home. Our trip to meet Mickey was finally complete, and the three of us headed home, having lived happily ever after for a few precious days.

Compromises

I was washing windows. In typical six-year-old style, Jonathan was happily playing in the carport with his tiny race cars, racing and wrecking them with zeal. I needed to get to the window inside our carport, but our truck was parked directly in front of the window. Deciding to just move the truck out of the way, I went into the house and grabbed the truck keys.

Walking past Jonathan, I headed for the driver side of the truck, calling out, "Hey buddy, you stay right there while I back the truck out."

Opening the door, I climbed inside and cranked the truck. Glancing up, I saw Jonathan running up beside the truck, waving his hands frantically. I paused and rolled down the window, questioning, "What?"

"No, Mama, you can't drive!" Jonathan's face was flushed, his eyes wide with fear.

I smiled back in amusement. "It's OK, buddy, I can do it," I said reassuringly.

I backed the truck out of the carport and turned off the engine. Jonathan was still standing there in the carport, hands on his hips, a very worried expression on his face. "What's wrong, buddy?"

"Mama, you can't drive," he said, shaking his head emphatically.

I laughed out loud. I just couldn't help it. Squatting down, I put my arm around his shoulders. "Jonathan, I know how to drive, I just don't drive anymore because of my eyes, but I used to drive."

Jonathan stood there staring at me, still puzzled, trying to work it all out in his little head. "You stopped driving because your eyes got sick?"

"Yeah, I used to drive. Do you not remember me driving?"

He shook his little head. He had no memory of that. Shrugging his shoulders, he said, "OK!" And that was that. No further questions. He ran off to play with his cars.

A little smile playing on my lips, I moved the ladder over to the window and resumed my cleaning task. "Imagine that? He doesn't even remember me driving," I thought to myself as I sprayed the glass cleaner on the window. "He was so little when I quit. He doesn't even remember."

Memories flooded my mind. I remembered the time that I walked across the kitchen floor and tripped on his little green and yellow wooden tractor. The tractor had gone flying across the room, and the axle for the large wheels had snapped in half. There were tears in Jonathan's eyes as he examined the broken tractor. Squatting down to hug him, tears streamed down my face. "I'm sorry, buddy. Mama didn't see that. I didn't mean to break your tractor."

I recalled the time when I crossed the kitchen floor to pass beside the spot where four-year-old Jonathan was playing with his little race cars on the kitchen rug. Suddenly, he jumped up and threw his hands up in the air. "Stop Mama, don't fall," he exclaimed as he stood in front of his cars, barring my way past. He was so adamant. I couldn't stop a little smile curling on my lips. He was determined not to let me fall and hurt myself, but no doubt, he didn't want me breaking any more of his toys either.

In truth, I was surprised at how quickly he learned that I could not see things on the floor. We solved the toy problem by keeping the bulk of his toys out on our sunporch. When entering that room,

CHAPTER 11
Everybody Has Something

I was careful to avoid any items on the floor. When he did play in the kitchen, I was always surprised at how quickly he would grab his toys if I started to cross the room.

Compromises... we had made so many compromises, so many adjustments to deal with the ramifications of my vision loss. Even my little four-year-old boy had made adjustments to keep his mama safe and his toys unbroken.

Watching my now six-year-old Jonathan playing in the driveway. I thought about the urgency of his protest for me not to back the truck out of the carport. He wanted me to be safe. He wanted the truck to be safe too. He was no doubt looking after that for his daddy's sake!

I was struck by the fact that he accepted my eye disease without question. For him, there was no questioning of "Why?" It's just the way it is. He had grown up with this. He had no memory of things being any different. He accepted my not driving as a fact of life.

What a contrast to me. I understood the diagnosis, the physical limitations, the rationale for the decision to not drive. I dealt with this reality, but I still struggled with it. I wondered if I would ever get to the point of accepting it in the simple way Jonathan had. "Only time will tell," I thought with a sigh. For now, there was nothing to do about it except to keep on going. I shrugged my shoulders and went back to washing windows.

Lovey-Dovey

Stepping through the double doors of the restaurant, I came to a sudden halt. Sensing my pause, Eric threw a quick glance my way. Instantly, he knew what the problem was. The sudden change from bright light to dark had temporarily blinded me.

This was not a new occurrence. It happened frequently, and he knew just what to do. Reaching for my hand, he tugged me toward him, and feeling our shoulders touch, I moved my hand to just above his elbow. Propping out his arm, I latched on, and without a word, we stepped forward into the dimly lit dining room.

By this point, such maneuvers had become a well-choreographed dance for us. As my night vision worsened, navigating dark environments became more challenging. Eric offered the solution. Propping out his elbow in a courtly gesture, I would tuck my arm in his and snuggle into his side. Nestled tightly, arm in arm, we made our way through dark restaurants and movie theaters.

When space was tight between tables or on a crowded street, Eric would grab my hand, tuck it behind his back, and I would trail along behind him like a tight shadow. Without need of formal training, Eric became my sighted guide.

We became adept at these little maneuvers, and soon walking in tandem was just a normal way of life. It wasn't really a sacrifice. Snuggling up to his side was a pleasure, even if it soon became a necessity.

Though I could not see other patrons clearly, I could sense their stares as we paraded into a room, me nestled tightly at Eric's side. Amused by their unguarded interest, I would offer a mischievous grin as I whispered in Eric's ear, "They think we're all lovey-dovey! Little do they know!"

The comment always provoked a little chuckle as he weaved me across the bustling venue. We may have appeared as lovebirds, and of course, we were, but the invisible reality was that we couldn't travel any other way.

We learned to move rapidly together, reading each other's body language as we shifted back and forth around obstacles. Eric was comfortable with me at his side. He could keep me safe and protected. A big John Wayne fan, he takes his duty to protect and serve seriously. I never minded his protective gestures, appreciating his willingness to get me safely wherever I wanted to go. Besides, I liked walking arm in arm, and he did too. Who knows? Maybe I improved his status!

CHAPTER 11
Everybody Has Something

Kite Strings

The bright blue and red kite bobbed up and down, gliding on the ocean breeze. Eric was gripping the kite strings tightly, his large hands resting on top of Jonathan's tiny ones. Eric was trying to teach Jonathan how to fly a kite, but the whipping winds were proving to be a challenge.

I stood in the sand looking up at the colorful kite framed against a gray cloud-filled sky. Watching my boys strain to keep the kite aloft in the strong wind made me smile.

We had rented a beach house at Wrightsville Beach for a week, my parents joining us for a few days of fun in the sun. Our close proximity to Wilmington made visits with Eric's grandparents an added blessing. George and Ann had greeted us enthusiastically, enjoying the chance to spend time with their great grandson. Ann loved children, and she and Jonathan enjoyed chatting together.

My parents adored being with Jonathan, although they aren't particularly beach people. Grandaddy rode the waves with his boy for a bit and taught him a few card games around the kitchen table. Grandma found her perch on the balcony that overlooked the public beach access and was happily entertained for hours watching what people hauled to the beach. She claimed it was fascinating!

Jonathan had grown so much that year, both physically and developmentally. He was headed to first grade in a few weeks, and I was mourning the end of our summer break.

It had been a busy summer. Swim team had consumed our summer schedule. Not quite realizing what I was signing up for, I had agreed to help another mother coordinate the swim and dive team. I was way underprepared for the amount of work required to organize the meets and practices. It turned out to be way more than I had bargained for, but the smiles of triumph on the children's faces when they won a race or improved their times made the effort more than worthwhile. At the recent swim team banquet, I had committed to the role for another year. Perhaps I was crazy, but swimming was clearly Jonathan's talent and passion, so I might as well dive into the water with him.

He had done so well that summer, winning his events and improving his times. He was a natural at backstroke, regularly sailing past his opponents. With swimming clearly his passion, we had decided to sign him up for more instruction at a twice weekly stroke school at the year-round community pool. We had worked out a carpool plan with a few of the other pool moms. I hoped it would be good for Jonathan, and not too much for us to manage.

As the kite bounced up and down above the sandy shore, I thought about how our lives had bobbed up and down the past few years. So many times, I had felt myself falling, spiraling out of control, bracing for impact. Could we survive the head winds that kept stalling our progress forward? Could I live with the loss of independence, the anguish of impending blindness, the frustration of my limitations? Could our marriage survive these gale force winds?

Eric and I had struggled to stop the spiral, to lift ourselves up and catch the breeze once more. Standing there, toes in the sand, watching my large and small boys work to keep control of the kite, I realized that we were making it. We were dealing with the challenges and making things work. Eric's job change to telecommuting had helped immensely. Time and prayer had given me perspective. My faith had grown, and my fears no longer dragged me down.

God was working things together for our good. We were managing to stay aloft, and sometimes, perhaps every now and then, just like the blue and red kite above my head, we were soaring.

CHAPTER 11
Everybody Has Something

CHAPTER 12
The Box On The Shelf

School Mom

"Mama, you coming to school today?" Jonathan asked as he bounded down the back steps to Tami's waiting car.

I smiled at this question, because my presence at school was becoming more and more frequent. One of the best things about my part-time schedule was being able to help out at school. With Eric working from home, he had the flexibility to take a short break and drop me off at the school for my volunteer work.

What had started out as helping with classroom holiday parties had quickly turned into more. Before I could bat an eye, I was chaperoning field trips, tutoring students, and shelving library books. My library time rapidly morphed into coordinating the book fair.

When the kindergarten teachers learned that I was a cardiology nurse, they asked if I could do a show-and-tell time about being a nurse. I donned my uniform and brought my stethoscope for the children to listen to their heartbeat. I got creative and designed a "Heart Smart" game to teach the students about how the heart works. The presentation was a huge success, requiring repeat performances with every new school year.

Jonathan loved it, and so did I. He was thrilled to have me around during the school day, beaming with pride that his mother could do all these things. He loved when I ate lunch in the cafeteria with him. More than once, I overheard him bragging about his mother being a heart nurse. His admiration tickled me and spoke to the tight bond we shared.

While all my volunteer roles were a great help to the overwhelmed teachers and librarian, they offered wonderful opportunities to positively impact the school environment. I knew my hospital work was important, but when I worked with those kids, helping them succeed with school work or just have a fun day, I was quite certain that was some of the best work I would ever do.

Against Medical Advice

It was time for my yearly eye appointment at Duke. Each October since my diagnosis, I had returned to see Dr. Machemer for an evaluation. At each visit, he had examined me with his kind, gentle manner, answering our questions in his reassuring way. Much to his relief and ours, my eyes had remained stable with each exam. Thankfully, his prediction that I had entered a phase of slow disease progression had been correct.

At my last visit, Dr. Machemer had shared that he would be retiring several months later. He explained that there would be a new retinal disease specialist coming, and I would be scheduled to see the new physician. Eric and I thanked Dr. Machemer profusely as we left his office that day. The words were inadequate to address how much he had helped us. I was truly sad to see him depart.

A month before my appointment the next year, a letter arrived introducing my new physician and indicating my appointment date. I wondered how this new doctor would compare to Dr. Machemer. She would have some big shoes to fill.

On the day of my appointment, I was nervous as I sat in the crowded waiting room. When my name was called, I was ushered into the exam room and introduced to a petite, dark headed, young woman in a white lab coat. Briskly shaking my hand, she motioned for me to sit in the exam chair. With little fanfare, she launched into questions about my medical history, her eyes only occasionally meeting mine as she glanced up from my chart. Once her questions were answered to her satisfaction, she stood and began her optical exam of my eyes. Her manner was quiet, focused and devoid of any TLC. She was all business.

Finishing her eye exam, she questioned me about my decision to take high dose Vitamin A therapy. She explained that this therapy had been linked to birth defects. "Are you aware of this risk?"

"Yes, I have read about that."

"Are you planning on having more children?"

"Well, no. We are not planning that at this point."

Looking up with a furrowed brow, she shook her head and went on to say that she could not support my taking Vitamin A therapy unless I took permanent steps to prevent any future pregnancies. With a direct stare, she informed me that I should stop the supplement immediately.

"But there is nothing else I can do to prevent my vision from getting worse. I don't want to stop taking it. It's the only thing I can do for this."

"Well, then you will be taking it against medical advice."

Her words hung in the air as we stared at each other. I was so taken aback, so disturbed by her abrupt manner and her adamance about this issue. I didn't know what to say, but I could feel the hair on the back of my neck standing up, straight and tall.

"Well, I will think about what you've said, but I don't see stopping the Vitamin A."

"Then you should consider sterilization measures. I am documenting that I have advised you against taking Vitamin A."

With that, she snapped my chart closed and instructed me to return in one year for follow-up. With an abrupt "Thank you," she opened her office door indicating it was time for me to leave.

She was certainly not Dr. Machemer. In a bit of a daze, I stepped out into the hallway. "What in the world was that all about?"

Another Option

"What? That's unbelievable!" Marianne's face was a mask of outrage. She simply could not believe the story of my eye appointment.

CHAPTER 12
The Box On The Shelf

I had stewed over the doctor's inflammatory comments all night, and by the time I slid into the passenger seat the next morning, my anger had reached a fever pitch. My chauffeur and mentor drove us to work in stunned silence as I relayed my infuriating tale. The more I talked, the angrier I became. I had already experienced an uncaring ophthalmologist once before. It seemed that I was destined to experience another one.

I could not believe her brusque attitude, nor her insistence on pressuring me to come off Vitamin A. I was incensed at the way she challenged me on my childbearing options and simply rejected my concerns about stopping the supplement.

That doctor had no idea what it was like to have an incurable disease. There was no definitive treatment, no surefire approach to stop the descent into blindness. The only option I had available to me was Vitamin A. While it would not cure the disease, it could slow it down. How could I not take this vitamin? It beat the alternative which was to do nothing.

Marianne listened attentively to my angry rant joining in with occasional murmurs of frustration at this physician's attitude. Then, she made a suggestion. "Have you ever considered pursuing a clinical trial at NIH?"

Marianne had worked at the National Institute of Health in Bethesda, Maryland for several years and explained about their clinical trial process. She offered to reach out to some old colleagues and get the contact number for the National Eye Institute.

I had never considered going to someplace like NIH. With Duke Eye Center right down the road, it was an easy option for us. This experience had made me reconsider that decision. After some further contemplation, I accepted Marianne's suggestion to explore another option.

A New Plan

Marianne obtained the contact information for the National Eye Institute and passed it along to me. I made a phone call to inquire about the process for being evaluated by one of the clinic physicians. There were several steps to the process, and I made an appointment for the following September.

All of our parents were pleased that I was pursuing another opinion, particularly in such a major research center. True to her heavily entrenched planning gene, Eric's mom immediately began hatching a plan even though the appointment was months away.

Given that Jonathan would be in school at the time of the appointment, Liz volunteered to accompany me on the trip. Since NIH was only a two-hour journey from her home in Richmond, Eric and I could come up for a weekend visit, and then Liz and I would head to Washington, DC on Sunday afternoon. After the appointment, Liz could bring me the rest of the way home on Tuesday. It was a complicated plan, but we thought it would work.

September rolled around, and we traveled to Richmond that weekend as planned. Liz and I departed Sunday afternoon and made our way up I-95. We were happily chatting away when smoke began pouring from the engine. Steering the car became difficult. Something was terribly wrong.

We made it off the interstate to a small convenience store.

My mind was racing, trying to devise a plan. I found a pay phone and dialed an old friend who lived not too far away. Since Eric and I had lived in the D.C. Metro area when we were in our 20s, we still kept in touch with old friends in the region. In about thirty minutes, Sandy drove up like a knight in shining armor and took charge. We had the car towed to a service station for repairs. Sandy insisted on taking us to dinner, and we met up with his lovely wife Ann. After a nice meal, he herded us into his car and drove us the rest of the way to our hotel in Bethesda, Maryland. Sandy had certainly saved the day!

CHAPTER 12
The Box On The Shelf

Arriving about 9 PM, we found that the hotel had a problem with their water pipes, and there would be no running water for the night. I was starting to think that coming to NIH had been a bad idea.

Inaugural Visit

That assessment changed the next day when I arrived at the National Eye Institute. The staff greeted me with friendly professionalism. After a thorough history and physical, the battery of tests began. I barely had time to eat lunch as the testing was long and intensive. At the end of a very full day, the kind doctor explained their findings. The results were in line with the previous year, and the disease thankfully remained stable.

The doctor was careful to explain all the results, taking time to ensure my questions were answered. I asked about Vitamin A and received a strong recommendation to continue. While she concurred that the risk of birth defects was a concern for all women of childbearing age and caution was warranted, she refrained from any imperative statements, suggesting only that I give some thought to family planning issues.

In contrast to my frustrating doctor visit the year before, this eye appointment provided clarity for my questions and offered encouragement about the research avenues. I could not have had a better experience. I left the clinic at 5PM exhausted, but very glad that I had come.

Since the car was still in the shop, my father-in-law Pete came to retrieve us. I finally made it home on Tuesday, relieved that I had pursued another option.

Looking back on that inaugural trip to NIH, I remember the anxiety associated with that visit. The tests were grueling, and waiting for the results was agonizing. It was so hard to calm myself down, to not panic over what the doctor might have to say.

Rough Places Smooth

I wish I could say that the yearly eye appointments got easier with time, but they have not. For sixteen consecutive years, I traveled to NIH, and it never got easier. Every year, I would spend several months beforehand dreading the visit, fearing news of disease progression. While the clinic staff have always treated me with the utmost care and compassion, that did not lessen the anxiety of the process. Afterwards, I was jubilant if the news was good and depressed if the news indicated further vision loss.

Though my visits to NIH became less frequent over time as clinical protocols changed, the battery of tests remains intense, and the day wears me out. Liz has been my faithful companion on almost all of my trips to NIH. Her presence made the difficult day a little brighter. She would have breakfast waiting for me after my lab work was complete. When I finished some grueling test and returned to the waiting room, Liz would be ready with a cold drink and a cookie. Her loving care was such a comfort.

I could not have asked for better in-laws. Liz and Pete have always been so supportive. They wanted so badly to help us, and the NIH trips became a wonderful way to do so. Liz looked at the trips as our girl time, and despite the stress of the eye appointment, we managed to have fun being together. After our car disaster, we switched to train travel, enjoying the opportunity to sit and chat without the stress of driving. Liz has been such a blessing to my life, and I am forever grateful for her loving support through all the ups and downs of the journey.

CHAPTER 12
The Box On The Shelf

Girlfriends

Setting down her cafeteria tray, my tall, gracious friend Mary bent down for a quick hug of greeting before joining me at the lunch table. Sliding into her seat, she asked, "So what's up?" I opened my mouth with the answer, and the conversation flourished from there.

That's how it's always been with Mary. Our tight bond only strengthened with time, forging a sisterhood that has far surpassed mere friendship.

Lunchtime at work offered the opportunity for connection, and we took that opportunity regularly. Mary continued to be my bright light at work. We shared everything we encountered, from the mundane to the miraculous, the social and the spiritual. She was my faithful sounding board, always ready to listen, frequently finding a way to interject some humor into the situation. Her counsel was thoughtful and profound, steeped in a faith that both taught and comforted me. While I could seek out Bob for counseling anytime I needed it, I found myself turning to Mary more and more often when my woes over vision loss weighed me down. With her, I could vent my angst, and more often than not, that was enough. Beyond that, we just had fun being together, sharing mutual interests and seeking new adventures. Whatever we found to do together, there was always laughter involved. That has been good medicine for me.

Leaving the lunchroom, I headed down the hallway, greeting co-workers as I went. I was struck by the wealth of strong friendships I enjoyed both inside and outside of the hospital walls. Working in a hospital full of caring nurses lends itself to easy, supportive friendships. Along the way, I met so many wonderful women that I could call on for a listening ear or a hearty laugh.

My ride partners were all lovely women who became fabulous friends. Our travel time was filled with lively conversation. We shared our joys and sorrows as we rolled down the road.

Rough Places Smooth

After several years of our road trips together, Susan switched to a weekend option position in the emergency room. This schedule change afforded her more time with her young son, but we both mourned the loss of our roadway chats. Though we saw each other less frequently, our friendship remained as strong as ever.

As Susan transitioned to her new schedule, I continued my rides with Marianne, adding in time with Hope and Susan D when Marianne's schedule differed from my own. I gradually met a few other colleagues that I could also ride with in a pinch. Not only did all these women get me to work, but they got me through the ups and downs of daily life. The blessing of these beautiful friendships was a constant reminder of God's grace in action.

Tami continued to be my chief confidante and shopping buddy. Living so close to one another, our lives became closely intertwined. We had walk talks through the neighborhood and play time with the kids. Snow days offered opportunities to sample one of Tami's signature cakes and some hot soup at her kitchen counter. There were Friday night pizza parties at one house or the other, and late-night chats on her patio. Her extended family adopted us, and we were on the standing guest list for Sunday family dinners. Her parents, Hilda and Danny, made certain that we were invited to all the holiday celebrations, even including our parents when they were in town for a visit. Jonathan became the adopted grandson, and Hilda lovingly referred to me as her other daughter. As the years progressed, Tami and I became so close that Eric began referring to us as sisters, an absolutely perfect description.

Early on, I had forged friendships with the women in my Sunday School class. Bonded by motherhood, we planned play dates and birthday parties. We saw each other at circle meetings and Bible studies. Our Mom's Night Out meals became a monthly highlight, and soon, there were fifteen or more ladies getting together to chat over dinner.

As our children grew, so did the bonds of our friendship. We planned beach trips together and shopping days around town. Once the kids entered school, we planned Friday lunch dates and parties with our spouses. We worked on mission projects and socialized at church covered dish meals.

These women accepted me without question. My vision issues and driving restrictions were never a burden for them. Rather, they were quick to volunteer to pick me up or take me home. They grabbed my arm in dark restaurants and warned me about upcoming curbs, all without ever ceasing the constant stream of lively conversation. Their cars knew the way to my driveway. There's no telling how many gallons of gas they wasted parked in my driveway, motor running, while we finished that last bit of conversation. One of those late-night driveway chats outlasted my friend Pam's car battery, leaving her stranded. I can still see the smirk on Eric's face when I summoned him from his recliner to come to our rescue. He has never let Pam or me live it down!

Looking back, what a Godsend all these women have been to my life. Those friendships have grown deep roots over these 28+ years. They have brought me such joy and comfort. These women have pitched in when there has been a crisis. They have made me laugh when I so needed a good, hearty chuckle. We have shopped and traveled, sung and danced, mourned and wept together. I truly don't know what I would have done without my girlfriends.

Riverside Query

"So how are you doing?" Ricky was looking me straight in the eye as he asked the question he had often asked before. Like my friend and counselor Bob, Ricky's question was not a mere greeting. He wanted an honest answer.

The four of us were lounging under the canopy of his boat, watching our three kids splash around on the river shore. It was a gorgeous summer day on the water. Ricky had anchored the boat near the edge of a small island, allowing Laura, Eric and me to kick back in our seats and relax. Their two children were having fun playing games with Jonathan in the shallow water.

Ricky was waiting for his answer, just as he had waited on that October afternoon so many years before. In those agonizing days following my devastating diagnosis, he had urged me to open up and express how I really felt. He had told me then that "This is a big deal, a really big deal. It's OK not to be OK."

Now he was at it again, and he wanted my honest answer. He had asked the question from time to time, although not with every visit. We saw Ricky and Laura quite often when we traveled to Richmond to see Eric's parents. The past few years had been busy for them as they guided their children through the preschool years, but they had managed to visit us occasionally as well. Our times together were always full of laughter and catch-up conversation. Today, Ricky was intent on a more serious discussion.

I met his gaze and smiled. "I'm good. Actually, I'm doing really good." And I was. Life had settled into a good rhythm for me. I enjoyed my work, particularly the flexible part-time schedule. Having Eric work from home had truly been a Godsend, reducing our stress levels by astronomical proportions. This new schedule allowed us some adult time together, affording even an occasional lunch out. The transportation scenarios were so much easier. Jonathan was at a fun age, and the three of us enjoyed doing things together.

I was still coordinating the summer league swim team, a very time-consuming job that I thoroughly enjoyed. I continued to teach an adult Sunday School class, an occasional Bible study group, children's church and Vacation Bible School. I had learned that teaching was one of my spiritual gifts, and there seemed to be endless opportunities to use that gift in the church, school and community.

The desire to help people must be written into my genetic code, and being involved in the volunteer opportunities gave me a sense of purpose. It fed my soul. They also opened up an avenue to reciprocate for the many kindnesses sent our way, a channel to pay it forward.

The Box On The Shelf

It all kept me busy, but I had learned that was not such a bad thing. Distraction was a good coping mechanism for me.

I shared these thoughts as we sat riverside with our best friends. Then Ricky asked, "How are your eyes?"

"The doctors say they are stable for now. I struggle with some things, but have figured out how to accommodate for them." I went on to explain about the computer accommodations the hospital had set up for me, and how these adjustments had helped me in my work. My central visual field was small, but still quite healthy, so reading and fine motor skills had not been impacted. Trip hazards were one of my biggest challenges at that point, that and of course, not driving.

Eric piped up and said, "She does alright as long as she doesn't get in a hurry. That's when she misses stuff or knocks things over."

I looked squarely into Ricky's eyes as I said, "I have come a long way. It's still hard sometimes, and I do get down about it, but overall, things are so much better. I just keep on going."

As Ricky loaded us all up for the trip back to the dock, he had the answer he had searched for. Traveling down the river, I offered a silent prayer of thanks. It felt like God was sending a smiling response as He weaved a blanket of pink, orange and gold around the setting sun as it kissed the riverbank. Things really were better for me, and I was thankful.

The Box On The Shelf

I had been teaching our adult Sunday School class for several years. What had started out as a little offer to help out on occasion became a regular teaching gig. While it did take time to prepare the lesson, I found that I enjoyed learning the content. The job made me dig deeper into scripture, and that was a very good thing.

One Sunday morning, I found myself teaching a full house. Most of the class participants were now close friends, so I felt comfortable leading the group. I confess that I do not recall the exact topic of that lesson, but I remember a moment during that class so clearly. It was an "Aha" moment.

We were discussing coping with hard things in our lives. I brought up the issue of my eye disease as an example. My friend Kim F spoke up and asked, "So how do you deal with that? How do you not let it overwhelm you?"

The question caught me a bit off guard. I paused and thought for a moment. The words that came out of my mouth surprised even me. "I don't know. It's hard to explain. I can't live thinking about the disease all the time. I just have to go on with life. Sure, I feel sad and worried a lot, but I can't live there. It's like there is this shelf in the back of my mind, and there's a box there, just sitting there on that empty shelf. When I get sick of being sad, when I get tired of being frustrated and worrying all the time, it's like I take those feelings and pack them up in that box and put them on the shelf. They don't go completely away. The feelings are still there. I still can see them there inside that box. I just don't have to dwell on them every day. I put them in the box, and I go on with life."

Looking back, I had no idea how that one analogy would so profoundly impact my coping abilities. Until that moment in that classroom, I had never put those thoughts into words. Yet, deep down, I was aware of packing those emotions up and setting them aside to deal with later. If I hadn't done so, I would have drowned in the pool of those swirling emotions.

Somewhere along the way, "The Box" became my coping strategy. Perhaps you might call it denial, but that was not quite right. I was well aware of the disease. I knew it every time I opened my eyes.

It's just that I couldn't deal with the ramifications of the diagnosis every minute of every day. I couldn't live there. I had a little boy who needed me, a marriage to nurture, a demanding career that necessitated my focused attention. I had things to do, and I could not afford to wallow in a pit of self-pity or spend my time wailing about my worries. I had a life beyond this disease. So I packed up those emotions and put them away. It worked, most of the time.

Life Goes On

It had been four years since I had attended the Visions Conference in San Francisco. I read the research updates regularly, always hoping for concrete progress toward a cure. Part of my coping strategy hinged on finding a definitive treatment for the disease. I kept telling myself that perhaps they would discover a treatment, and I would be spared the suffering of further vision loss.

My parents also closely followed the research updates. When the flyer for "Visions '98" came in the mail, my mother called to ask if I was interested. To my surprise, she wanted to accompany me. She proposed that we attend the conference in Chicago and visit my first cousin who lived there.

While I readily accepted the invitation, I could not escape my surprise at my mother's interest in the conference. My mother had taken the news of my diagnosis so hard. The guilt over passing along a diseased gene to me weighed her down. No amount of protestations on my part could assuage the weight of that guilt. She worried so much about my situation and my future. That she would want to go and mingle with others with the same disease shocked me, for she regularly avoided discussing her feelings on the subject.

Being a mother myself, I could understand her pain. She wanted so much to protect me, to fix things, to make the problems go away. Mothers have that maternal instinct to save their young from all manner of threats. Mom felt powerless to solve my situation, and that burden was a heavy load for her. If coping with the disease was hard for me, the impact on my mother's life was magnified ten-fold.

As we caught our flight to Chicago, I could tell my mom was determined to make this a fun girls' trip. Our hotel room was elegant and located close to the downtown Chicago shopping district. Having my cousin close at hand was indeed a wonderful bonus, and we spent lovely evenings dining outdoors in the pleasant summer air. Such distractions offered a good balance to the weight of the conference content.

While listening to the research updates was certainly encouraging, it was also a bit daunting to be immersed in the reality of the disease. Everywhere I turned, people were using guide dogs or white canes for mobility assistance. I had not been in the presence of so many blind people since the Visions conference I had attended four years earlier.

I may have been intellectually prepared for the content and surroundings of the conference, but the emotional angst was a different matter. As I watched a young woman with a guide dog, I could not help but think, "Will that be me someday?" As I followed a man with a white cane down the hall, I wondered if I would have to use one of those canes one day.

My mother seemed to handle the sights and sounds of the conference with relative ease. She attended some sessions for family members and seemed encouraged by the interactions. I kept any emotional angst well camouflaged. I did find many of the sessions helpful, and this seemed to comfort Mom.

It was at the awards dinner that I encountered a moment of epiphany. Mom and I were seated at a table with some pleasant dinner companions with whom we shared good conversation. The room was filled with people with varying degrees of vision loss. There were white canes lying folded beside chairs, and guide dogs sitting quietly at the feet of their owners. These individuals were enjoying their meals, engaged in lively conversation, laughing and talking as if it was the most normal of days. As I sat there taking in my surroundings, I marveled at the resiliency of these people who were living full lives despite their disease. They were not shut up in the four walls of their homes wailing, "Woe is me." They were engaging, interacting and overcoming. I thought to myself, "Life goes on."

CHAPTER 12
The Box On The Shelf

Four years earlier, I had sat in a similar room, sharing a meal with a handful of visually impaired people. Guide dogs and white canes had littered the floor beneath my feet. I had sat there, feeling uncomfortable and yet, encouraged, both emotions wafting through my soul as I pondered my new reality. So much had changed for the better in four years, yet the struggles remained.

Gazing at my table companions, I considered the significant life challenges they faced. Yes, the disease had no doubt altered the course of their lives. Still, they were not giving up. They were moving on, and if they could do it, then so could I. My vision loss had certainly changed my life, but there were options and opportunities to pursue in the days to come.

Deep in my heart, I felt God nudging me, reminding me that He has a purpose for my life, and I needed to trust His plan. Glancing around that large dining hall, I thought, "Life goes on, and whatever lies ahead, I need to keep on keeping on."

Cousin Connection

The traditions of our Scots-Irish ancestry run deep in my father's family. The Pedens have always been fascinated with genealogy. Family ties are kept with reverence. Whenever two or three of my family are gathered together, the subject of family connections invariably comes up. As it turns out, this need to keep in touch yielded an important discovery.

My cousin Martha called my mom one afternoon with some surprising news. Martha and my grandmother were first cousins, and we had always maintained a close family bond with her. Keen on maintaining family connections, Martha often touched base with distant cousins.

It was in one such phone call with her second cousin Terry that Martha found the first RP connection in our family tree. As the cousins delivered the family updates, Terry shared the upsetting news that her nephew Bob had recently been diagnosed with a devastating eye disease. Recalling my diagnosis five years earlier, Martha asked for more details. She caught her breath in surprise when she learned that he also had Retinitis Pigmentosa. Like me, Bob, three years my junior, received his diagnosis at the age of 33.

While Terry knew my father, they had not spoken in years, and she had never met me. I knew nothing of this portion of the family and had never heard of Terry or Bob. Though distant cousins, we were strangers to one another. After a lengthy discussion, Martha and Terry decided that they needed to forge some connections between Bob and me.

Martha immediately called my mother to share the connection and pave the way for Terry's call. My mother and Terry had a long conversation about my diagnosis and the similarities to Bob's experiences.

Scrutiny of the family tree revealed that our great grandmothers were sisters. Bob had also noted a series of unusual symptoms, and a routine eye exam had prompted a further work up. Like me, Bob had poor night vision, problems with running into obstacles and missing objects in his surroundings. The findings were consistent with visual field loss. Bob and his wife had just started their family with their first son born about 18 months earlier. The similarities between our stories were almost uncanny.

My mother called me immediately to let me know of the connection. I was so shocked, and yet, there was a bit of comfort in the discovery. Up to that point, I knew of no one in either side of our families with this disease. While the doctors had postulated that the genetic origin of my disease was likely a recessive trait, they could not rule out a gene mutation. If the disease was passed to me through a recessive trait, the likelihood that Jonathan would be saddled with the disease was very low. However, if I had the disease due to a gene mutation, the likelihood I could have passed the disease to my precious son was much higher.

Knowing that I had a third cousin with the disease meant that the disease was most likely carried by a recessive trait. While future generations could be affected, the immediate threat to Jonathan was significantly lessened. That was a source of comfort for me.

The idea that there was another family member out there that could understand my struggles from a personal perspective was also comforting. At this point, I knew no one with the disease personally. There was no one to commiserate with, no one who could understand the challenges. Given that I was farther along on this journey, I hoped that I could offer some support and encouragement. I would have welcomed such support in those early years of my diagnosis. I longed for the opportunity to meet Bob and his wife.

Several months later, Eric and I traveled to Richmond, Virginia to meet Bob and Myra. They invited us to dinner at their home, and we took Jonathan with us. While Jonathan played with their young son, Bob and I shared our stories. We were amazed by the similarities in our journey. Though much of the talk was serious, we found occasion to laugh as well. I found Bob to have a good sense of humor that matched my own. In just one evening, I felt I had found a new friend, for we had an unusual bond that would connect us together for the rest of our lives.

Looking back, that dinner meeting forged a lifelong friendship. While distance does not afford us frequent opportunities to visit, we always touch base at Christmas, sharing the update on our families as well as our disease progression. Over the years, we have conversed by phone or email, offering each other a unique type of support. We understand each other in a way others cannot comprehend, and that has been a comfort for both of us.

I encouraged Bob to pursue an evaluation at NIH, and we both have been followed there for many years. We are both enrolled in a genetic study, and it will be interesting to see what findings may come from that someday. While I would never wish this disease on anyone, I am grateful to have made this connection with the cousin I never knew. It has been a good connection for us both.

Photo Op

I lurched forward, my body responding to the sudden stop. Within seconds, the car was in park, and the door thrown open by our driver. Beside me, Jonathan was unbuckling his seat belt, scrambling for the door, without waiting for permission.

This was not the first time. In fact, the scenario had been repeated countless times as we motored around the Oregon countryside with our old Army friends, Susan and Bill.

It was our summer vacation, and Jonathan was eight years old. As part of a two-week jaunt to see Oregon and Washington state, we were enjoying some quality time with some of our oldest friends.

Jonathan had bonded with Bill on one of our previous visits, taking easily to Bill's enthusiastic personality. Bill is one of those guys who can make any situation fun, and Jonathan followed him around like a puppy dog. An avid photographer, Bill was always on the lookout for a good photo opportunity, and Jonathan provided perfect subject matter for his camera lens.

Camera in hand, Bill was calling, "Come on, Jonathan, time for a photo op!" Jonathan raced after his idol, the two of them grinning from ear to ear, as they scurried to a picturesque spot that had caught Bill's eye.

Susan just rolled her eyes and chuckled as she watched Bill set the scene, with Jonathan turning this way, then that, following Bill's commands, all in search of the perfect picture. Eric and I sat in the car, laughing at the two of them, not sure which was the kid, the one posing or the one taking the picture. They were the dynamic duo, trotting off bravely to capture some new image. There is no telling how many pictures Jonathan posed for on that trip!

Our little nuclear family took a few days to explore the mountains of Washington state, meeting up with our West Coast cousins for a brief reunion in the quaint German village of Leavenworth. We loved strolling the streets of the village, checking out the shops and restaurants. Jonathan and his cousins found the

CHAPTER 12
The Box On The Shelf

big hill in the village park, and they spent hours chasing one another up and down it while the grown-ups chatted on a park bench.

On one of our strolls, I had spied a store filled with authentic German nutcrackers, and later, we returned to browse through the store. My fascination with these whimsical works of wood had started years before, and Eric had bought me several as gifts along the way. I had never seen so many nutcrackers in one place, and the three of us roamed the aisles in a state of wonder, pointing from one character to the next. They were adorable.

Several years earlier, I had begun collecting snowmen, filling the house with their happy little faces at Christmas time. As friends and family learned of my snowmen fetish, that became their go-to gift for me. Jonathan loved picking out a new one for me each Christmas. Every season, I added new figures to my snowman collection, and my winter displays expanded to touch every room in the house.

So it came as no surprise that when I rounded the corner and saw the set of snowman nutcrackers, I squealed with delight. Mr. and Mrs. Snowman smiled at me from the shelf, and I fell in love. Beside me, Eric was smiling at my joy over this unique find, but one look at the price tag made me shake my head in defeat. Eric lifted the tag and looked, then putting his arm around my shoulders, he whispered, "Let's get them. You'll never find anything like this again."

My eyes were wide as I turned to look up at him. He was serious, and yes, he was spoiling me. My heart leapt with joy, not just for the gift, but for the love that spurred its purchase. We had come a long way in the past few years, and I lifted a small prayer of thanks even as I gave him a kiss of appreciation.

It was a happy trip for our little trio, laughing and exploring new sights together. We returned to Susan and Bill's house for a few days before flying home. It was then that I got the call.

Since our family traveled on a "no news is good news" policy, I was immediately concerned when I heard my father's voice on the other end of the line. Dad explained that my mother had experienced a strange episode of confusion with motor and speech changes. He had rushed her to the emergency room where a diagnosis of TIA or mini-stroke was delivered. Thankfully, all her symptoms had quickly resolved, and she was scheduled for a visit with a neurologist in a week.

I was shaken as I hung up the phone, my mind racing with worrisome possibilities. My nurse brain was in overdrive. My mom was only 61 years old, quite healthy and physically active. How could this be happening?

I was glad to have Susan, a fellow cardiology nurse, to discuss my concerns with, and her reassurances helped me settle down. We headed home two days later, my mind still fretting over my mother's health.

Sad Eyes

One week later, I had another phone call from my father. This one put me in a tailspin.

I was in a meeting at work when one of the secretaries called me to the phone. Dad was on the line, calling from the hospital. I knew Mom had her neurology appointment that morning and had been anxiously awaiting a report. I was unprepared for the report that followed.

Apparently, Mom had been sitting in the neurologist's office answering questions when my father noticed some unusual behavior. Always the proper lady, my mother was answering the doctor's questions with only a "Yeah." My father had looked at her quizzically. Mom would never respond to a doctor with such a casual choice of words. Her normal answer would be a polite yes or no, but never "Yeah." Dad quickly ascertained that something was wrong. The neurologist sprang into action, determining that my mother was having a seizure. Within minutes, Mom was whisked away to the emergency room where anticoagulant therapy was immediately initiated.

CHAPTER 12
The Box On The Shelf

Further evaluation revealed that Mom had suffered a stroke affecting her speech center. Thankfully, she was moving all extremities and following commands, but she was unable to speak.

My heart plummeted to the floor, ripped out of my chest in stunned disbelief. How could this be happening? She was only 61.

With a shaky hand and a promise to come down there as soon as possible, I hung up the phone. I began making some fast arrangements and soon, the three of us were headed for South Carolina.

I found my mother lying in a hospital bed, looking up at me with a glimmer of a forced smile. Her big brown eyes held a deep well of sadness, the heartache so evident that I felt myself in danger of falling into that great abyss.

When I took her chilly hand in mine, she responded with a reassuring squeeze so typical of the mother I adored. She was worried about me, comforting me with a hand clasp even if she couldn't offer me consoling words. I knew by the size of her moist brown eyes that she was afraid. So was I.

It was clear from the outset that she understood what we were saying, but she couldn't speak a response. Her nonverbal recognition of our queries and comments was an encouraging sign, but the doctor advised us that only time would tell what her recovery would be like.

I sat heartsick in the uncomfortable chair beside her bed. As she napped, I listened to the hum of the IV pump as it slowly delivered the blood thinning medication. All I could think about were the stroke patients I had cared for over the years. I had witnessed the devastating damage a stroke can wreak upon a life, and my stomach clenched at the thought that I might never hear Mom's sweet voice again.

"Please, Lord, please. Let the meds work. Let her speech come back. Please let her be alright. Lord, we need her. I need her. Please."

240

The prayer played on a constant loop as I sat by my mother's bedside. I had sent Dad home with Eric and Jonathan, knowing that I could not stay forever, and that he would have to shoulder the burden of care in the days to come.

Thankfully, that burden was not as great as we initially feared. By the grace of God, my mother began to slowly respond to the treatment. After about 48 hours, she was able to form one- or two-word responses to our queries. Within the next few days, she was speaking in short sentences. Our wounded hearts lifted with hope that she might recover her lost speech.

She did, but it took a long time, and lots of hard work and speech therapy. After several months, her speech had improved dramatically, but she still struggled with finding the right word or pronouncing a word correctly. She also had some struggles with decision making, finding it easy to get overwhelmed with too many choices. Simple things like grocery shopping became challenging.

In the months that followed, the losses and limitations took their toll. Although she made steady progress, her spirits began to sag. Because of the seizure, Mom was unable to drive for six months. Restless after a few months at home, she called me one day lamenting about the driving restrictions, saying, "I knew it was hard for you, but now I really know."

She was blessed with lots of support during her long recovery. My father was her faithful caregiver, transporting her to appointments and helping her with her therapy. Between work and school, our visits were more limited than I would have liked. Not being able to drive myself to see her added to my worries and frustrations, but Dad handled it all in true soldier fashion. Their church family was a wonderful help to them with loads of cards, calls and tasty meals.

My mother's twin sister lived close by, and she was a strong source of support in her recovery. Mom and Tina shared a magical connection, reading each other's minds and finishing each other's sentences. Now Tina was both consoling Mom's wounded spirit and speaking the thoughts her sister struggled to share.

The Box On The Shelf

Tina and their cousin Trudy rallied around my mom, and their support meant so much to my father and me. It was a slow process, but God worked a major miracle in her, eventually restoring her to near normal function. While she still struggles with word choices and pronunciation from time to time, these difficulties go often unnoticed by most people. Her recovery has truly been a miracle for which I am forever grateful. Standing at her bedside in that hospital room, I thought I had lost my mother's precious voice, but God answered our heartfelt prayers and gave her back to us whole once more.

Fireplace Reflections

The golden flame flickered, dancing merrily upon its floor of red-hot coals. I smiled, enjoying the warmth of the fireplace as I gazed out the picture window at the winter wonderland just beyond the glass. It was good to have some downtime, a chance to rest and reflect.

So much had happened over the course of the last six years. My life had changed in countless ways. There had been so many trials, so many challenges, but there had also been so many blessings.

We had come to Pipestem State Park in West Virginia to celebrate the holidays with the Sherer clan. This trip had been our Christmas present from Liz and Pete. Dispensing with the usual toys and gifts, Liz had planned a three-night getaway for us as well as Eric's brother's family. She had rented three cabins, one for each family. This allowed the children space to play and nap, but offered plenty of opportunity for the whole family to gather by the fire and enjoy one another.

It was a treat for Jonathan, age 8, to hang out with his cousins. Since Elizabeth was two years his junior, they had been pals from the moment of her birth, acting more like siblings than cousins. Now Jonathan had a new playmate, Ben. At 21 months old, Ben idolized Jonathan, trotting around after him everywhere. The boys played cars together by the fire, and Ben loved the attention. He was a precious little fellow, capturing my heart with those big brown eyes.

Liz was enthralled with her grandchildren, shepherding them through the snow to the lodge to play in the game room or run their little cars down the long open hallways. The whole family turned out for hours of sledding, then returned to Liz and Pete's cottage for fireside visits made even more special by the presence of Grandma's fabulous cookies.

It was perfect. The kids had a blast, and the adults had time to read, rest and reflect. It was a wonderful chance to reconnect.

Steve and I had always been friends. He was only 14 when Eric and I started dating. He and I bonded immediately, even though he and his brother were still engaged in the typical teenage sibling rivalry. Steve became my little brother, maintaining our connection through his high school days. When he joined us at JMU, he and I kept up with each other. However, with our entry into the workforce and the distance between our homes, we had spent less time together in recent years. Our wintry walks and fireplace chats were a welcome way to rekindle our relationship.

Then there was Elizabeth. I may not have birthed her, but she stole my heart from the first moment I laid eyes on her. I had always wanted a daughter, but that wasn't in the plan. So Elizabeth became my little girl.

While I was enamored with her from the moment of her birth, she really latched onto me firmly the weekend she spent with us when she was two years old. From that visit on, she was drawn to me, crawling in my lap for a story or wrapping her tiny arms around my neck in a precious hug. We didn't have the luxury of seeing each other often, but when we did, it was special.

Always adoring dolls, my father had sent me quite a collection from all over the world. Now, I had a little girl to play dolls with. For every birthday and Christmas, I spoiled Elizabeth with dolls and clothes, delighting in every opportunity to play with her. Children know when they are loved. Elizabeth felt my love, and she loved me back. I held the honored status of favorite Auntie!

Enjoying the quiet moments by a late-night fire, I gave thanks for this time with our extended family. What a treat it was to be together. I thought about all the struggles over the preceding years, but decided that they paled in light of the good things. God had been with us through it all, working all things together for good. Glancing at Eric, reading in the chair beside me, our precious Jonathan slumbering in his warm bed in the adjacent room, I could not be anything other than grateful.

Looking back, that first trip to Pipestem was a blessed moment for our family. We all loved our time together so much that Liz and Pete made it an annual tradition. For the next fourteen years, we returned to those cabins extending our visits from three to five nights. Those trips were the highlight of the holidays for the kids as well as the adults. We bonded together as a family, forging connections that strengthened us all for the various challenges that came thereafter. Nowadays, no family gathering is without some mention of our years at Pipestem. It was the best Christmas present any of us ever received.

Part 5
Turning Points

JANUARY 2000 – DECEMBER 2009

I will be glad and rejoice in your love, for you saw my
affliction and knew the anguish of my soul.

—Psalm 31:7 *NIV*

Part 5
Turning Points

CHAPTER 13
The Box Comes Down

Time's Running Out

The trouble with chronic diseases is that they are chronic. They don't go away. The disease never leaves.

It's the unknown that gets you. There is no way of knowing when the disease might flare up again, when the symptoms might worsen, when the treatment might fail. The unknown makes coping with the disease so much harder.

Retinitis Pigmentosa is a chronic disease for which the unknowns are endless. There is no way to know the pace or the pattern of visual field loss. Will central vision be lost before losing peripheral vision? Will all vision be lost, or will some vision be retained? Will there ever be a treatment for this disease? How will I cope when the disease progresses? For those living with RP, there is one question that haunts your soul, "How long do I have to see?"

In the first few years following my diagnosis, the questions played in my head like a broken record. Living with the endless list of unknowns was maddening at times. There is always this sense that time is running out.

As the years moved forward, the constant replay of questions abated somewhat. There were stretches when I could turn off the record player, silence the persistent noise. However, with every eye appointment, the questions would come blaring out again, their clamor deafening. When the exam revealed that my vision remained stable, my angst would dissipate, and the questions would retreat into the periphery of my mind.

In those first nine years, there was minimal disease progression. Still, that sense of time running out never left me. It felt like being trapped inside an hourglass, the sand slowly slipping through my fingertips. With every grain of shifting sand, that question returned, haunting me, "How much longer do I have to see?"

CHAPTER 13
The Box Comes Down

Travel Bug

The question of "What's on your bucket list?" is a common one, shifting our thoughts to our fantasies for the future. It makes for interesting table talk. However, for me, the question was poignant, hitting a deep chord within my soul. This was not a topic reserved merely for mindless banter. This hit home, evoking serious thoughts about the future.

Though I tried, I could not flee from the thought that there were all these things I wanted to do, and my time to do them was growing shorter with each passing day. There were so many places I wanted to see while I still could.

The travel bug bit me early. Growing up as an Army Brat, our 29 moves afforded wonderful opportunities to travel all over the United States, as well as South America and Asia. I had tasted of that great big world out there, and I wanted more.

Travel was a joy Eric and I had always shared together. The anticipation of an upcoming trip kept us entertained for months beforehand. We adored the sights and sounds of new places, thrived on the opportunity to explore.

When Jonathan came along, we thought we would just take him along on our travels. We quickly learned the flaws in that assumption. Little boys don't love car seats. Little boys require tons of gear and don't function well with lack of sleep. Learning from our mistakes, we determined that visits to the grandparents would be the extent of our travels for a while.

During Jonathan's preschool years, we ventured further, planning family visits to the beach. When he turned five, we made our inaugural visit to Disney World, where all three of us had an amazing time. The trip was such a success that we began to contemplate that perhaps Jonathan was getting old enough to pursue other travel adventures.

It was after a trip to NIH for my yearly eye exam that the travel bug really bit me once more. The news had not been good, with my vision showing some slight deterioration. While I had steeled myself for the possibility of such news, my heart sank. All those fears of time running out hit me full force. That bucket list began to invade my thoughts. Perhaps it was time to get started seeing those places I really wanted to see.

It was on one of our drives to visit the grandparents that Eric and I had the travel conversation in earnest. While Jonathan napped in the back seat, I brought up the subject. "I've been thinking that maybe we should go see some of the things we've always wanted to see. Maybe we shouldn't put that off. Maybe we better go see them while I can still do it, while I can still see them."

I wasn't sure how Eric would react to such honest disclosure. We seemed to avoid such talk of the future, neither of us wanting to say out loud that the day might come when I would lose my vision. The "blind" word was never used. Neither one of us could stand to go there.

Apparently, Eric was thinking along the same lines. Instead of spending the money on a beach house, he proposed that we explore other places. His sentiments were music to my ears, and we began to daydream about where we wanted to go.

While the impetus of the conversation had been uncomfortable, it was good to know we were on the same page. As the miles passed by, my heart lifted, my focus shifting from sad realities to exciting possibilities.

That conversation occurred around the time that Eric was knee deep in preparing for the Y2K computer conversion. Working for a telecommunications company, it was all hands on deck, upgrading the software to handle the calendar shift to the new millennium. Given the long hours of preparation, his company promised bonus incentives to both thank their employees and encourage retention after the crisis passed. As a stress reducer, Eric began to fantasize about where we could go once he survived the aftermath of Y2K.

CHAPTER 13
The Box Comes Down

In late January of 2000, he announced that we were going on a Disney cruise. He didn't need much of a sales pitch to win Jonathan and me over to that idea.

Traveling with Mickey Mouse was just what the doctor ordered. Sitting on the ship deck, relaxing under a star-studded sky, Eric and I started dreaming about travel. Eric put forth his proposal. "Let's go while we can. Let's see all that we can while you can still see it all."

There was no argument from my tent. I was ready to travel. The next year, we hit the first stop on my bucket list, London, England. I grew up reading books about England and Scotland, always dreaming of the day when I might walk those city streets and step foot in those ancient castles.

It was early on a cloudy winter morning, when the three of us emerged from the subway, rising up out of London's Tube. After just a few brisk steps along the crowded side street, I found myself standing in the heart of Trafalgar Square. Traffic was buzzing all around us, double decker buses and black cabs bustling past. I spied the red phone booths and caught my breath in delight. The spires of Parliament stood in the distance as Big Ben chimed the hour. I twirled around, arms open wide, a broad grin lighting up my face. I had made it. London was all around me.

Life is a series of moments. Most pass by without notice while a few are etched on our memories forever. This was such a moment. I was in the heart of a city I had always wanted to visit, and I could see it. I could look all around me and treasure each image. Standing there, bright smile on my face, heart beating fast, I thanked God for this most precious moment.

Our travels had begun!

Looking back, our focus on travel was one of the best decisions we ever made. As the years progressed and my vision gradually declined, I am so thankful for the privilege of seeing so much of the world. We made travel a family priority. Eric and I decided that saving such trips until our retirement years was simply too great a risk. Foregoing some of the typical entertainment expenditures, we budgeted our money to allow us to travel.

Not only did we enjoy the adventures, our trips created a strong family bond between the three of us. To this day, we never gather together without some mention of a family adventure experienced in some faraway destination. The travel shaped Jonathan's perspective on life, offering a taste of other places and cultures.

Traveling together, we made memories. Those memories are etched upon the walls of my mind. No matter the condition of my retina, I will always have that vision of Big Ben towering above me. Retinitis Pigmentosa can never steal that away.

Heart Talks

After six years in my clinical pathway program coordinator role, I found myself bored and restless. While the position had offered me countless professional opportunities, and the program had been extremely successful, it was time for a change.

The truth was that I missed patients. I missed taking care of people. That was my calling. I loved the clinical side of nursing, and I longed for something with more patient interaction. I knew my eye disease prevented me from most hands-on nursing roles, but I wondered if there was something else available that might fill the void in my heart. I began to pray for the right opportunity, for God to open a new door.

While I lifted up prayers, I began to check the job postings, mentioning my restlessness to a few of my colleagues. During one such conversation, I was thrilled to learn that the hospital had recently been awarded a federal grant to promote heart disease awareness and prevention. This new program focused on raising community awareness and promoting heart healthy lifestyle changes. My ears perked up at just the thought. I could get passionate about this!

Even better, the program coordinator was searching for a health educator to teach community classes and conduct health screenings. With my experience in cardiology nursing and my teaching skills, I figured the role was right up my alley!

For months, I had been praying about a new job opportunity. From the moment I saw the posting on the job board, I had a feeling that this was the next step for me. However, my enthusiasm was dampened when I recognized there were several huge obstacles to overcome.

First of all, assuming a full-time position would create too many challenges for our family. Arranging rides for even my limited part-time schedule was daunting. Furthermore, Eric and I still valued my time at home with Jonathan.

A full-time position was not an option, but something in me was not willing to throw in the towel just yet. I stepped up my praying about this. "Lord if this is the right thing for me, then let me find the right way to work this out. Open the door for me, Lord, if this is Your will."

After speaking on several occasions with the outreach program coordinator, I managed to sell the idea of dividing the full-time position into two half-time positions. Having job shared my previous role with Mary, I could identify major advantages to employing the same strategy for this new program. Two part-time health educators would allow for more flexibility with health screenings and class offerings. There would be two people available to cover classes in different locations or at varying times. For health screenings, two nurses could see twice the number of participants. Clearly, based on the needs of the program, two would be better than one, and the overall cost would be the same.

My sales pitch worked, and I was tasked to find a partner. While thrilled with receiving this affirmation, I had no idea where to look. Apparently, God was already at work. Within a matter of days and a few well-placed conversations, I identified another cardiology nurse who was interested in both the program and a part-time schedule. We proposed the option to the powers that be and received the nod of approval.

While I was elated, I knew I was still not out of the woods. The second obstacle was a bit daunting. The health screenings and community education classes would be offered all over the county. Transportation would be an issue for me. While my partner Joan could easily drive to a class location, I did not have that option. "How am I going to get there?"

It turned out that an accommodation from my previous position paved the way for the solution. During my years of leading the clinical pathway program, my work required increasing travel to other hospitals within the health system. Since I was fully capable of performing all aspects of the job with the exception of my own transportation, it was deemed by my supervisor that the hospital would provide cab fare reimbursement to cover my travel. This was considered a necessary accommodation under the requirements of the Americans With Disabilities Act (ADA). While my taxi travel had not been excessive with my previous situation, this new position would require significant cab fare reimbursement. I made a request for this accommodation to be considered. After some review and discussion, it was decided that the precedent had already been set, and that continued reimbursement for my unique travel expenses was appropriate. Furthermore, given that my partner would receive mileage reimbursement, cab fare reimbursement would be an acceptable modification.

Just like that, God had overcome the obstacles, and within only a few weeks of expressing my initial interest, I had a new job! I was simply amazed. An exciting new opportunity awaited me. Once again, God had worked it all out.

Taxi Tours

With the new year came the new job. After a few weeks of planning, my partner Joan and I started offering classes in the community. It was time to take a taxi.

I had met several of the cab drivers previously, but my frequent trips introduced me to several more. I soon bonded with two

CHAPTER 13
The Box Comes Down

gentlemen who became my go-to drivers. Mr. Brown was a genteel African American in his late 70's who had been driving a cab for 50+ years. He greeted me with pristine manners and was totally dependable. He truly was a gentleman, and I admired him greatly. I learned all about his life and family as we made our way across town. I looked forward to our little chats.

Tom was a 70+ white bachelor with a crusty exterior and a heart of gold. A bit of a character, he would regale me with stories of the old days and a few salty comments from time to time. Though he never said it, I know he liked me and enjoyed the fact that I called and requested him by name. He took care to return to my class location early so as to be waiting when I walked out. He was insistent about where to drop me off, always considering my safety first. He, too, became a good friend.

While there were many others who chauffeured me around, I always requested these two drivers first. Regardless of who picked me up, over the course of that four-year grant, I never missed an appointment or was left stranded. I remain convinced that God rode in that back seat with me, and my taxi tours always arrived safely at their appointed destinations.

Looking back, that healthcare educator role was one of the most gratifying positions I ever held. During my previous administrative position, I had longed for interaction with patients and families. I had really missed that part of nursing. As I educated community residents on heart disease prevention, it felt like I had returned to direct patient care. Though I was not starting IVs or interpreting heart rhythms, I was counseling and teaching patients and their families how to keep their hearts healthier. I simply loved the teaching opportunities.

An added bonus was the opportunity to work with my partner Joan, and Kristen, the program coordinator. The three of us made a wonderful team, and even better, we became close friends.

When RP had entered my life, I thought that the door to clinical nursing was closed forever. It was a huge loss, one that quietly ached inside me for a long time. With this wonderful work opportunity, God had not only opened a door that was previously shut, but He led me down a whole hallway of possibilities. While the threat of losing my vision never completely abated, I launched my energy and intellect into that program, and in turn, that work brought me pure joy. While I was helping other people keep their hearts healthier, I found that my heart was also healing from its devastating wounds.

Nowhere To Go

It was a splendid September morning, the sky painted a bright, cornflower blue that held the promise of a delightful day ahead. White puffy clouds floated across the autumn sky as if to showcase their splendor. Though the air was warm, the humidity was down, offering a welcome relief from the typical summer swelter of Washington, D.C.

My spirits were high. I was headed home, so thankful to have completed my yearly eye exam the day before at NIH. This yearly trip was always so stressful as I waited to learn whether my vision had declined further. The news yesterday had been good, no further changes in my vision.

On this particular morning, I woke from a good night's sleep filled with the joy of a new day. I checked my train tickets, confirming our departure time. The train was scheduled to leave Union Station at 10:20 AM. The date was September 11, 2001.

My traveling companion was my mother-in-law Liz who had served as my faithful supporter on these trips for the past five years. While the purpose of the trip was stressful, the chance to enjoy some girl time with Liz was a welcome treat. Once the testing was complete the day before, we had ventured out for a nice dinner, then retired to our hotel room to chat before bedtime.

On this fine morning, we were up early, preparing for our journey home. Liz and I gathered our things and made our way to the hotel lobby to catch the 7:30 AM shuttle to the Metro. Having

CHAPTER 13
The Box Comes Down

done this before, we wanted to allow plenty of time to navigate the rush hour sojourn to Union Station.

Our Metro ride was uneventful. Exiting the subway, we headed to the food court to grab some breakfast. Snagging muffins and drinks, we sat down to munch and chat. As was our custom on these yearly trips, we planned to stroll through the Union Station shops prior to catching our train. Thankfully, the ease of our morning commute had left us plenty of time to shop. It was only about 8:20 AM and our train wouldn't leave for two more hours.

Dragging our suitcases, we stepped into several of our favorite shops, just browsing and passing the time. Liz mentioned that she needed a brightly colored luggage strap for her upcoming overseas travel. She recalled seeing a luggage store on the lower level, and we went in search of it.

Locating the luggage shop, I trailed Liz into the store, taking over care of the suitcases while she looked for her strap. Noticing the absence of any sales clerks up front, I peered curiously around a suitcase display to follow the sound of hushed voices near the back of the store. Spotting the two sales clerks, I noted that they stood gathered around a small television, their backs to me. Suddenly, one of the clerks let out a stifled cry, while the other exclaimed, "Oh, no!"

My curiosity got the better of me, and I wheeled the trailing suitcases toward the television screen. Liz had found her bright pink straps and joined me at the sales counter. Raising my voice to grab their attention, I asked the store clerks, "What's going on?"

The two clerks turned in unison, their faces awash in bewilderment. "A plane just crashed into one of the Twin Towers."

As they stepped back from their previous viewing post, Liz and I could see the TV as the news program replayed the moment of impact. Images of the plane burrowed into the side of the massive tower covered the screen as we stared in disbelief.

Liz and I stood there, glued to the TV, as we watched the news cycle evolve. Several minutes passed before we jerked ourselves out of our shocked stupor. With effort, the clerks turned from the screen to ring up Liz's purchase. No longer in a shopping mood, we slowly departed for our train gate, sharing our shock and sadness at what had just happened.

Reaching our gate about 9 o'clock, we found seats and settled our luggage. We took turns visiting the restroom, and then I wandered up the way to grab a Diet Coke to nurse on our train ride. Passing by the shoeshine stand, I heard the crackle of a small radio. With no televisions inside the gate area, people were huddled near the radio for news updates. Seeing the gathering crowd, I stopped to ask for an update.

"Another plane has hit the tower. It hit the other tower."

"They've both been hit. Both towers have been hit!"

A chill ran down my spine as the impact of those statements rebounded in my mind. With a sick feeling in my gut, I knew instantly that this was no accident. "It must be a terrorist attack. Something awful is happening!"

I stood listening for a few more minutes, shaking my head in horror, wondering how in the world such a terrible thing could happen. Realizing Liz would be worried, I headed back to my gate. As I delivered the news, Liz stared at me in shock. "What on earth is going on?"

The news was spreading quickly amongst the waiting passengers. The buzz of conversation around us climbed to a rumble as anxiety levels soared. Faces were drawn and worried as we sat there waiting for our trains to arrive.

After a few minutes of fretting, Liz decided we needed a cookie and wandered up the way to the bake shop. Cookies in hand, Liz was headed back to the gate when several men came bursting through the main entrance to the station, screaming, "They've hit the Pentagon. A plane has hit the Pentagon."

Liz stared in horror for a moment and then rushed to find me, revealing the awful news, fear palpable in her voice. She was barely settled in her seat when we heard the announcement over the loudspeaker that struck fear in our hearts. "All northbound train

CHAPTER 13
The Box Comes Down

service has been cancelled. All trains departing for the northeast sector have been cancelled until further notice. Southbound trains will continue as scheduled."

I knew full well this was not a good sign. Since we were headed south to Richmond, Liz and I were relieved to hear that our train was still scheduled for an on-time departure. It wouldn't be long now before they would announce the boarding call.

Liz asked me to call my father-in-law Pete and tell him to turn on the TV. "He won't even know anything is happening." Pulling out my cell phone, I realized with a cringe that I had forgotten to charge the phone the night before. When Pete did not answer the phone, I left a quick message, hoping to save as much of my limited battery as possible.

The train we were ticketed for was the Carolinian offering southbound service to Charlotte. Liz would ride as far as Richmond where Pete would meet her. I would continue on several more hours until arriving in Burlington, NC where Eric and Jonathan would meet me. The knot in my stomach coiled even tighter as I wondered whether the current circumstances might delay our train, but so far, the board showed an on-time departure.

Soon, the boarding agent called our train, and we gathered our things and joined the forming line. Tickets checked, we moved through the double doors, making our way to the escalator that led down to the train platform below. Our train was there, waiting, and I felt a note of relief at spotting it. I was ready to get out of there.

With assistance from the conductor, Liz and I boarded the train, found two vacant seats and stored our small suitcases in the overhead compartment. Slumping into our seats with a sigh, we both agreed we were ready to get home.

It had been no more than ten minutes since we had stepped on the train when we heard the conductor's voice making an overhead announcement. "Attention all passengers, this train is now out of service. You must gather your personal items and exit the train immediately. Amtrak staff are waiting on the platform to assist you with directions. Please proceed to the nearest exit immediately."

Liz and I looked at each other in shock and confusion. Not for the first time that day, we muttered, "What in the world is going on?" Obediently, we collected our luggage and headed for the exit.

Stepping off the train, we heard the calls of Amtrak personnel directing us to move quickly to the waiting escalator. By this time, my nerves were on edge, and you didn't have to tell me twice. I scurried toward the escalators with Liz right behind me.

Reaching the upper platform that we had crossed only moments before, we encountered several staff members pointing directions and ordering us to move quickly down the corridor. I paused for a moment, allowing Liz to catch up.

Glancing through the glass window of the station gate door, I was shocked to find the train terminal completely empty. Not fifteen minutes before, the station had been teeming with people waiting for trains. Now, there was not a single soul in sight. An eerie feeling washed over me as I stood there transfixed on the deserted scene.

My stomach fell to the floor with the next sight. Uniformed police officers armed with automatic rifles were patrolling the station corridors. Paired with police dogs, the policemen were moving quickly up and down the aisles of the station gates. I caught my breath in shock. Growing up as an Army brat, I knew about that kind of firepower. This was not a drill. Something was terribly wrong.

The Amtrak staff was shouting for us to move along quickly. I tore my eyes away from the scene inside the station and began to move rapidly down the corridor, my mother-in-law trailing closely behind. The knot in my stomach grew as a station official directed us to take the escalator down to the underground Metro station. I had already started processing what was happening. If those were bomb-sniffing dogs, we needed to get out of there fast. As I ascertained that we were being directed down into the Metro, my chest tightened in panic. If there was a bomb in this station, the last

CHAPTER 13
The Box Comes Down

place I wanted to go was further underground. Yet, there was nowhere else to go, no time for argument. We did as we were told.

Once arriving in the subway station, I realized that the staff was pushing us toward the Metro exit leading to the street outside. I stepped up the pace, ready to get out of that building. I was totally unprepared for the scene that awaited us.

On the streets outside, there were hundreds of people clogging the sidewalks all around the station. People were wedged on every available surface in order to stay out of the streets. Bumper to bumper traffic was at a standstill on every road within view. Horns were blaring. Several city buses were stuck in the traffic circle near the station, the roar of their idling engines nearly deafening. Exhaust fumes from the throng of cars clogging every inch of roadway wafted up from the street, making my eyes water and my nose turn up in disgust.

I stood there staring, not knowing where to go, what to do, as if I had somehow stepped into a movie scene without the benefit of reading the screenplay beforehand. It was surreal. Nothing made sense. My mind struggled to take it all in.

The sound of the policeman's whistle brought me back to reality as the officers shouted for us to move along away from the building. Liz and I looked at each other in bewilderment. Where were we to go? Every inch of concrete was covered in wall-to-wall people.

The police officer was insistent with his orders, forcing us to inch our way forward, wheeling our luggage in between the jammed traffic. Reaching the concrete slab in the middle of the traffic circle across from the station, we weaved our way through the crowd to find a small patch of real estate upon which to perch. A buzz of mumbled conversation emanated from the people standing nearly shoulder to shoulder all around us, suitcases at their feet. Knowing they must have been evacuated from Union Station, Liz asked several people, "What's going on? Why did we have to leave the station?"

"I'm not sure. The police just told us to leave immediately."

"Bomb threat is what I heard."

"Yeah, I heard someone say a bomb threat in the station."

The crowd ebbed and flowed as people moved off to other locations trying to find a better spot to wait. Voices all around us crackled with little sound bites of news.

"I heard the Twin Towers collapsed."

"They say there's other planes out there, maybe more hijackers."

A woman with a handheld radio stood several feet away from me. I inched closer to her and asked, "What are they saying? What's going on?"

"A plane has hit the Pentagon. They're shutting down all the government buildings, evacuating everyone. There still might be other planes out there."

I stared at her in disbelief. I couldn't seem to take it all in. Just the same, my eyes flew to the sky, searching for clues. Tall federal buildings loomed in front of us, but I knew the direction of the Pentagon from where I was standing. I had lived in D.C. in my twenties and was quite familiar with my surroundings.

My stomach clenched in panic as I saw it. There in the distance, amidst that cornflower blue sky, was a trail of dark black smoke. I felt sick. This was really happening. The unimaginable was taking place. I thought, "What if there is another plane?"

I turned my head in what I knew to be the direction of the Capitol building. It took a nanosecond to begin to process the scenarios. The most likely target would be the U.S. Capitol. I had flown enough times into National Airport to know that the Capitol building and the Washington Monument stood out like beacons from the air. You could not miss them. If you were a terrorist bent on weaving destruction, those would be easy targets. Come to think of it, the White House was another prime target. The fear bubbled up as I internalized that all those places were just blocks from where I was standing. I couldn't stop the chilling thought that came next. "If a plane hits one of these places and we are standing out

CHAPTER 13
The Box Comes Down

here with no cover to shield us, we are in trouble. Flying debris
from the Capitol could kill us. We're just sitting ducks."

With an ever deepening sense of dread, I realized that there was
nothing we could do. There was nowhere to go, no shelter to seek.
We were stuck out here on the street, at the mercy of whatever
comes next.

I wanted to call Eric, but was worried about how much battery
charge I had left in my phone. I dialed anyway, only to find the busy
signal indicating there was no service. Asking others around me
about their cell service yielded the same findings. There was no way
to call anyone.

So we waited. Standing in the hot September sun, listening to
the roar of the standstill traffic, we just stood like statues and
waited. There was nothing else to do, but try to stay calm and pray,
and pray I did. I prayed hard. Over and over again, the words played
on a constant rewind in my head, "Lord, help us!"

Hours passed. We had no water, no restrooms, no official
updates on what was happening. Though moving at a crawl, the
traffic did inch forward and, over time, the streets began to clear.
The crowds thinned out some, though I had no idea where all those
people went. Eventually, Liz and I made our way over to the steps
of a federal building and found a seat with a tad bit of shade.
Devoid of sunscreen, our cheeks and noses were beginning to burn
from the sun's unrelenting rays. Without food or drink since
breakfast, we were hot, thirsty and hungry. I remembered I still had
part of my Diet Coke in my bag and pulled it out for us to share. Liz
located the chocolate chip cookies she had bought that morning.
She pulled out the well warmed cookies and we munched on them,
licking our fingers to cleanse the oozing chocolate from our hands.

Positioned across the street from Union Station, we could watch
for any signs that the building might be reopened. We waited. We
worried. We prayed.

We did debate our options from time to time. "If the station
remains closed, should we try to go back to our hotel and see if

they have a room? But how could we get there? Maybe we could find a pay phone and call our old friends to meet us somewhere? Maybe they would let us stay with them until we could get out tomorrow. Will the train even run tomorrow? What happens if it gets dark, and we are still out here on the streets of D.C.?"

We wondered for the hundredth time that afternoon when we might hear some news from the station officials. We were not the only ones waiting. Hundreds of other passengers, suitcases stashed beside them, were positioned all around us on the steps of adjacent buildings. Surely, they would let us know something soon.

"What must Eric be thinking? And Pete? They must be worried sick." Still, there was nothing to do about it. There was nothing to do but wait and worry.

As the sun shifted, throwing long shadows over the concrete, the sound of traffic slowly diminished. There were no cars on the streets around us, no roar of buses within earshot. It began to feel like we were the only people still left sitting in downtown D.C. For almost six hours, we had sat there without food, water or a restroom. By this point, we were miserable and working on just plain numb.

Finally, close to 5 PM, we began to see movement near the station doors. Police officers were moving back and forth, near the entrance. We watched as other passengers approached the officers, and one by one, they began to form a line near the door. The officers started waving a security wand over each person and their cargo. Liz and I collected our luggage and trudged toward the station. Making it inside, we made a beeline to the bathroom.

That need relieved, we went in search of water. The stores were all closed, though it looked like a few might reopen. The water fountain did the trick for the moment. I tried my phone again, the battery nearly drained. I hoped there might be cell service soon so I could call home. Hopefully, I would have enough battery charge to make the call.

Amtrak officials were busy updating passengers and posting information. All northbound trains remained cancelled, but they

CHAPTER 13
The Box Comes Down

would be running a few southbound trains that evening if all went as planned. We settled in to wait some more, though at least we had more comfortable seats.

Within an hour or so, we received word that there would be a train to Richmond leaving at 7 PM. Directing us to the same gate we had passed through earlier that day, we were told to wait there for further updates. We had already decided that if we could get to Richmond that night, I would get off and go home with Liz. She and Pete could drive me home the next day. If we could just get out of there, I wanted no further part of public transportation for a while.

I tried my phone again and there was cell service. I made a quick call to Eric. His voice was shaky as I quickly explained the train update and reassured him we were OK. He would call Pete with the news.

There were no televisions or radios for us to learn about what was happening. The best news source available was the gossip line from our fellow passengers who were randomly reporting that they had heard this or that. We should have been hungry, but the stress of the day stole any appetite we might have had.

Close to 7 PM, we were called by the ticket agent that the train was now boarding. I had a weird moment of déjà vu as I stepped through those same double doors I had walked through eight hours earlier. Quickly, Liz and I crossed the upper platform toward the escalators. As we descended slowly to the lower platform, I felt an eerie tingle. The platforms below had this uncanny sense of quiet. The usual complement of trains was absent, and you could feel it in the air. I must admit a sense of trepidation as I stepped onto the train. Stabs of fear kept needling me. "Is this train safe? Should we be doing this? Are we going to get there OK?" But there was nothing else to do. Our only option was to spend the night in the station, and I wanted no part of that. I wanted to go home. I wanted out of there.

All passengers boarded safely, the train began its slow progress out of the station, exiting underground through a tunnel. Within a few minutes, we popped out of the tunnel preparing to merge onto the 14th Street Bridge. Looking out the window, I could see the streets of D.C. interspersed between the facades of the various office buildings that skirt the Capitol Mall. There was no one on the streets, no cars, no pedestrians. It was empty, completely devoid of any signs of human life.

I caught my breath in shock for I knew the streets and sidewalks should be teeming with people at this point on a normal day. As we approached the bridge, I spied I-395 to my left, not a car in sight. "Had we lived through the Apocalypse and we were all that was left?" It felt like being stuck in the middle of one of those terrifying end-of-the-world movies.

Passing over the Potomac on the 14th Street Bridge, the train made its turn southbound. It was then that I saw it. I let out a gasp of horror as I caught sight of the Pentagon, black smoke rising from its walls, emergency vehicles scattered amongst the debris that covered its giant parking lots. The glimpse was brief, barely time to take in the sight, but the shock would last for days. This horror had really happened, and it had taken place just a few miles from where I had stood in the hot sun for most of the day. I shook my head in disbelief, and for the millionth time, offered up my prayer, "Lord, help us. Help us, please."

The train ambled slowly southbound, just barely creeping forward. Asking a conductor about the speed, he replied that we were following a search party, whose duty was to scan the tracks to ensure there were no bombs or hazards on the railway ahead. We could not exceed 35 mph between D.C. and Richmond. I nodded and gulped down the acid that had leapt from my stomach at the import of his words. Fear reared its ugly head yet again, as I thought, "Good grief! The danger is not over yet."

As the conductor moved away down the aisle, Liz just looked at me with wide eyes of disbelief. We were both out of words at the moment. We rode in relative silence the rest of the journey, praying silently and trying to sort through the events of the day.

CHAPTER 13
The Box Comes Down

Finally, the conductor called out that Richmond would be our next stop. We collected our belongings and made ready for departure, hoping all the while that Pete had found out about our pending arrival and would be waiting for us at the station.

As my feet touched the concrete platform, I said a prayer of thanks to be out of Washington. When we found Pete waiting outside the station, Liz and I both let out a "Thank God!"

The car ride to their house was a bit surreal as Pete shared the news of the day with us. Though we had lived through it in the heart of the Capitol city, we knew little of the events in New York City and nothing of the foiled hijacking attempt and subsequent crash in Pennsylvania. My mind reeled as I realized that the brave men and women of Flight 93 had saved our lives. Had that plane made it to Washington and hit the Capitol, we would be dead. Standing on that street corner with nowhere to go, the falling debris would have killed us.

Still, the real shock came once we had arrived at their house and turned on the television. A sick sense of horror washed over me as the images replayed on the screen. My mind was spinning just trying to comprehend the enormity of the tragedy.

Of course, I had called Eric the moment I stepped foot in the house. So relieved to hear his voice, tears flooded my eyes. He was OK, and so was Jonathan. They had been worried sick about us. I could tell from the sound of Eric's voice that the hours of watching the news unfold and not knowing our whereabouts had been devastating for him. He had been watching the news when the first plane hit the Twin Towers. His shock had morphed into panic when the news of the Pentagon attack hit the air waves. Like me, Eric was familiar with the landscape of downtown D.C. He knew how close Union Station was to the Capitol. When the Pentagon had been hit and there was talk of another plane on its way to the Capitol, Eric was practically apoplectic. All he could think was that the plane was headed right toward me and he was powerless to do anything. Like me, he had to watch, wait and pray. Yes, my day had been horrific, but so had his.

I thought I would not sleep that night, but the rigors of the day had left me exhausted. After a small snack, I made my way to bed. While I did sleep, my dreams were filled with buildings on fire and blown-up trains. It was a fitful sleep, and I was glad to leave it when the morning light streamed in the bedroom window.

It was decided that Pete would drive me home, while Liz attended to her work. The sunburn and dehydration of the day before had left her feeling poorly. With a tight hug, I left Liz in the driveway, both of us still reeling from the surreal disaster that was yesterday.

The ride was quiet as Pete and I listened to NPR and tried to process the events that had unfolded. Home had never looked so good as when we pulled up in our driveway that morning. Jonathan was at school, but Eric was waiting for us, his face awash with relief at the sight of me.

Pete refused to stay for lunch despite our invitation. After a brief break, he snagged a Pepsi to keep himself awake and headed back to Richmond. He was ready to get home. I couldn't blame him. After all that had happened in the last twenty-four hours, the only place anyone wanted to be was home.

Waving goodbye to my father-in-law, Eric and I turned to head back in the house. Falling into my favorite chair with a heavy sigh of relief, I thanked God that I was safe and sound, home at last.

Grateful

The gust of wind caught the flag just right. As if suddenly called to attention, the flag unfurled, stretching out to its full length, proudly showcasing its Stars and Stripes.

The November sun was surprisingly warm on my face as I stared upward at the massive flag framed against the Carolina blue sky. The laughter of children floated through the air as I sat on the park bench looking up at the flag. Chaperoning Jonathan's fifth grade field trip, we had traveled to Asheville, NC to tour the Biltmore House. We should have been in Washington, D.C., but the events of 9/11 had changed all that.

As the flag floated on the gentle breeze, my mind was flooded with images of that September day; the eerily quiet train platform, the silent streets, the smoke rising from the Pentagon. I thought of all those who were lost and all those who had saved so many on that tragic day. As I had done so often in the preceding weeks, I considered the heroes of Flight 93, convinced that their brave actions had saved my life as I stood stranded on the D.C. streets. My life had been spared while so many had been lost. God still had a purpose for my life, and I resolved once more to do all I can, for whoever I can, while I still can.

Two days later, I stood hand-in-hand in a circle of Tami's extended family gathered together to celebrate Thanksgiving. Eric, Jonathan and I had long since been adopted into this wonderful family, and the privilege of belonging was not lost on me in that moment. As each one of those gathered around the circle shared a word of thanks, I searched for words, finding it hard to convey the depth of my emotions.

I was standing there, surrounded by my loving family, alive and well, while so many were not. All I could think was, "Grateful. I am just so grateful."

Miracle At Sea

The events of 9/11 were a poignant reminder of the preciousness of life, bringing to mind once more the importance of my travel bucket list. That's how our little family of three found ourselves standing on the deck of a touring boat in the frigid waters of Alaska's Inside Passage.

The boat swayed to and fro, as the churning waves slapped against the hull. Standing at the rail, I waited and hoped. The captain had spotted a pod of whales in the distance. By law, we could sail no closer to the creatures, but as the captain jokingly remarked, that didn't prevent the whales from finding us.

The passengers on the touring vessel maintained a hushed silence, just waiting for the whales to resurface. Suddenly, the boat heaved violently, water crashing hard against the hull. Just yards from my viewing station, the magnificent creature soared out of the water, showcasing its gigantic torso before descending headfirst into the depths below.

I caught my breath in amazement, but the show was not finished. In a fluid motion befitting a ballroom dancer, the whale flipped its tail up out of the water, pausing for an instant, as if to offer a graceful bow before exiting the stage. In a flash, the tail was consumed by the sea, and the whale disappeared from view.

I was awestruck. I had come to Alaska to see the sights, and I had just witnessed a miracle at sea.

The whole trip had been an amazing adventure, from the train ride to Denali Wildlife Refuge to the cruise down the Inside Passage. We had seen the Hubbard Glacier shed part of its icy frame and watched Orcas surf on the ship's bow wave.

Every evening, the three of us discussed what was our favorite thing. I had trouble deciding, for I had loved every minute. Just when I thought it couldn't get any better, there would be a new treat in store, and now, I had met a whale, up close and personal.

The Box Comes Down

With the end of summer came my annual eye appointment. On a warm September day in 2002, it felt like a knife had been thrust into my gut as I listened to the ophthalmologist's words. I heard the doctor say it, but I didn't want to hear it. There had been a significant change in my eyes. Over the nine years since my diagnosis, there had only been slight changes in my visual field. On that warm autumn afternoon, I was not prepared for this bad news.

I knew it could happen. In a way, I knew I was living on borrowed time. Still, you always hope for another year or even another five.

CHAPTER 13
The Box Comes Down

You cannot help but hope for that. After nine years of only slight changes, I suppose I was lulled into a false sense of security. It's easy to tell yourself that things will never change, but that, alas, was a forlorn hope.

On this particular trip to NIH, Jonathan and Eric had traveled to Washington, D.C. with me. Given the traumatic events of the 9/11 tragedy the year before, I decided to handle the trip a bit differently. I suppose I was hesitant to repeat the usual train trip, given the replay of memories that still haunted me from time to time.

There was another reason. Jonathan's 5th grade school trip to the Capitol had been cancelled in 2001 due to the September 11th events. Since he had missed that important educational opportunity, Eric and I wanted to give Jonathan the chance to see the museums and monuments, to understand more of our nation's history. The events of the year before made that desire even more poignant for us. So we decided that we would give Jonathan a private tour of the city's highlights.

After enjoying a great weekend together sightseeing, I had decided to go to NIH alone on that Monday. That way, Eric and Jonathan could take in some more historic sites while I saw the doctor.

I was fine with that plan. That is, I was fine with that plan until the doctor told me the bad news. Then I was overwhelmed and devastated. Suddenly unable to control my emotions, I fell apart right there in the exam chair. I had never done that in a doctor's office, always managing to keep my emotions in check, but somehow on that day, I could not stop the flood of tears that came with her words.

For the first time in all these years, I had come alone to the clinic. Of course, this would be the time when things would go awry. This would be the very time when I would fall apart. The staff tried to comfort me as I forced myself to get it together and exit the eye clinic, but once in the taxi, a stream of silent tears flowed down my face.

Reaching our hotel, it was all I could do to get upstairs to our room and fall on the bed in a sobbing fit. My boys would be back soon. I had to get myself under control. I did not want Jonathan to see me this way.

By the time the guys returned to our hotel room, I had managed to pull myself together, even telling Eric the news without falling apart. We had dinner plans with an old friend that night. I donned the mask I was so good at wearing and passed the evening with surprising composure.

My exterior may have been calm, but my interior was a mess. All those emotions I had packed away so neatly in that box on the shelf were not so safely tucked away anymore. The box had come down. It lay alone on the floor, flaps wide open, its contents spilling out unabated.

The sadness was overwhelming, the fear, crippling. My mind kept replaying the doctor's words. I wanted to scream in frustration, to yell, "It's not fair!"

The ride home was quiet the next day. My thoughts were swirling, and all I could do was just stare out the window. The lump in my throat felt like a boulder wedged in the midst of a raging river of emotions, the rush of water pushing to be released, seeping out its contents in the tears that I tried so hard to blink away.

I suffered my anguish alone. The need to protect my family from the depths of my emotions was fierce. I so didn't want to lose it in front of Eric, and especially not with Jonathan riding happily in the back seat. He should be basking in the glow of boyhood, not seeing his mama cry. Undoubtably, Eric felt my angst, but I could not voice my pain, even to him.

There was nothing anyone could do about it anyway. No one could make this disease go away. It would remain, lurking in the shadows, waiting for its next chance to steal more of my sight.

CHAPTER 13
The Box Comes Down

At home the next day, we sent Jonathan off to school. Both Eric and I had taken an extra day off from work to recover from the trip. I was exhausted. I was miserable. He could see it on my face.

We did not say much that morning, but I finally went and crawled back in bed. Eric came and laid down beside me, wrapping me in his strong arms. At the touch of his embrace, the floodgates opened. I could stop neither the tears nor the words. Years of pent-up anguish came bursting out. "I don't want this to happen! I can't do this!"

Over and over, I repeated the words, my tears pouring out in torrents of pain. He just held me close, stroking my hair, letting me shed all those long-forbidden tears. He was silent, no doubt uncertain of what to say, but there was no need for words. I just needed to empty out that long sequestered box.

Looking back, that was a rare moment of honesty. Why had I spent so much time hiding my pain? I wanted to protect my loved ones, but not being honest about my feelings did not really help anyone.

The box on the shelf had served its purpose, allowing me to set my emotions aside and get on with life. However, I could not ignore my feelings forever. I guess it was just time to open the box.

That day, I learned that sharing my feelings was far better than bottling them up. My loved ones knew when I was hurting anyway. Being honest was far better than all of us trying to dance around the elephant in the room.

I cannot say that it was an immediate transformation, but gradually I began to talk more openly about my feelings. My counseling sessions with Bob helped me understand that honesty was much better than subterfuge.

Burying your feelings is not the answer. It does not release the pain, nor does it protect those you love. It does not make the problem go away. It just adds to your misery.

Finding a safe place to talk about the painful circumstances in your life is a much better strategy than struggling through them

alone. It's a step toward healing. The circumstances don't necessarily change just because you open up, but the pain is somehow more bearable when it is out in the open.

As time went on, not only did I share my feelings with Eric, but I became more open with Jonathan. I began to share my anxiety over an upcoming eye appointment or my worries over future vision loss. I didn't belabor it, but I didn't sugar coat it either. He listened attentively with a maturity far beyond his age. At some point, he coined a response that both surprised and comforted me, a reassurance he still offers when the subject comes up, "It'll be OK, Mom. It'll work itself out."

Just Hanging Out

While not driving presented daily obstacles for our family, there were some surprising benefits. Because I could not hop in the car and run all over town, I was forced to spend more time at home. As the years went by, that time at home felt less like a punishment and more like a blessing.

No longer able to dash to and fro running errands on my off days, I used the quiet time at home to wind down. Prone to overcommitment, I had a tendency to take on too much volunteer work. The forced time at home not only helped me get the projects done, but also allowed me to slow down the pace and regroup. That was healthy for me.

Still, the most surprising blessing of those days at home was the time with Jonathan. He and I spent lots of time just hanging out. When he was younger, we played board games or worked puzzles. We played on the swings or enjoyed a hike around the neighborhood. After school, we shared a snack and talked about his day. As he got older, we found movies to watch together.

No matter what we found to do together, we talked. Both extroverts, there was no shortage of conversation between the two of us. I told him stories of my childhood, and he listened with rapt attention. We passed the time in conversation as we waited for

CHAPTER 13
The Box Comes Down

rides to swim practice or other activities. Even on pool days, Jonathan would hang out with me, chatting on a deck chair or in the water if none of his swim buddies were around. No doubt about it, we were tight.

Well into his middle school years, he still enjoyed us reading together. We read all sorts of books, sometimes taking turns reading aloud to give him some extra practice. We loved the "Narnia" series and "The Little House On The Prairie" books. He was in the sixth grade when we tackled the first Harry Potter book. He had started it on his own, but quickly found the accented dialogue hard to comprehend. Inviting me to read it with him, we made it through the first sixty pages before deciding that his dad would love this book. After enlisting Eric to join us, the three of us sat together each evening reading the book out loud. The first book complete, we dove straight into the second one. Soon, Jonathan was racing to the locker room after swim practice in order to get home early enough to read Harry Potter. We continued on through all seven books, finishing the last book his junior year of high school. It was a precious family time that I will always treasure.

All that time together opened up bridges of communication that remained open even throughout middle and high school. As is typical of the early teenage years, he grew quieter, giving more one syllable answers than the longer narratives of his younger years, but he never clammed up completely like some kids do. I could still get him to talk to me. Sitting on the porch or in the recliners, I could ask an open-ended question, and he would open up.

Sure, it would have been nice sometimes to pick him up from school and grab a milkshake just for fun. I would have loved for him and me to celebrate the end of the school year with a little outing. Yet, I wonder if I still had those car keys would I have been tempted to spend more time running around, and less time just talking with my son? In retrospect, that time at home had its distinct benefits. For all the difficulties of not driving, I never regretted the amount of time Jonathan and I spent together, just hanging out.

Celebrating A Century

On a beautiful spring afternoon in 2003, sunlight streamed through the bank of windows that brightened up the recreation room in the nursing home. I couldn't stop the grin from spreading across my face as I observed my precious family all gathered around the large table. Just shy of his twelfth birthday, Jonathan and his cousin Elizabeth, now age 10, were giggling at some pre-teen humor as they stood beside their great grandmother's wheelchair. Pete's mother Dorothy was watching five-year-old Ben with fascination, and Ben was gazing with equal fascination at the cake container his Grandma Liz had just placed on the table. Ben had a sweet tooth a mile long, and the mere thought of the cake inside the box made him squirm with glee. As Liz pulled the beautifully decorated birthday cake from the container, Ben's gorgeous brown eyes snapped to the size of silver dollars!

Eric and his brother Steve were having a guy chat on the other side of the table while Pete took his usual stance, camera in hand, ready to chronicle the big event through his lens. As I readied the party goods, Liz retrieved the three candles she had purchased for the occasion. Holding them up to Ben, she asked him to call out the numbers.

"One! Zero! Zero!" Ben called out with a triumphant grin.

"That's right! Great Gram is 100 today!"

The dear lady we affectionately called "Gram" was born on April 1, 1903, in Winstead, Connecticut. Dorothy had weathered 90 New England winters, most of those spent in the two-story family home near Syracuse, New York, before moving to an assisted living facility in Richmond, VA to be near Liz and Pete. When her health declined, she had transitioned to a skilled nursing facility, and Liz had faithfully served as her caregiver throughout these past ten years.

A graduate of Vassar, Dorothy was a fiercely independent woman with a keen intellect and impeccable manners. An avid reader, her interests were diverse, ranging from antiques to birdwatching, from cooking to gardening.

Oh, what marvels she had witnessed in her 100 years of life! She had begun with horse-drawn carriages and wall-crank telephones and had lived to see cell phones, plane travel and even the space shuttle. Not only that, but she had gracefully weathered countless trials over the course of her years: the stock market crash of 1929, the Great Depression, two World Wars and countless others, the horrific scourge of polio that had afflicted her oldest son at the age of 16, and the untimely loss of her beloved husband at the age of 57. Through it all, she had dealt with every crisis with a steely resolve and a courtly sense of grace. In all the years I had known her, I never heard her complain about anything, accepting both the joys and sorrows of life with forbearance and determination. Watching her on this special birthday, I was struck by this testimony of faith and perseverance, a valuable life lesson for me as I faced my own trials.

Liz called us to attention, and the party began in earnest with the jingle of "Happy Birthday to you!" It was all smiles around the table as everyone joined in, thrilled to be gathered together to celebrate a century.

Just In Time

For six years, Eric had successfully telecommuted from home. It was such a blessing to have him working out of his home office throughout Jonathan's elementary school years. Yet, as Jonathan embarked upon middle school, Eric's work prospects rapidly deteriorated. The once thriving telecommunications industry suffered a near collapse, putting Eric's company in financial jeopardy. Eric was informed that his job functions were being outsourced to India, and within a few months, he was laid off.

While Eric had a broad skill set, most of his career had been spent in the telecommunications sector, and those jobs were quickly drying up. The available job prospects in our area were limited. For over six months, Eric searched in vain for employment. Thankfully, I was able to pick up more hours at the hospital to ease the financial strain, but the difficult job search took its toll on both of us.

While Eric had recently procured one prospect with a local company, the interview process seemed to move at a crawl. As time inched forward, we were both getting more and more frazzled with worry.

To make matters worse, the number of ride options available to me had gradually dwindled over the past year. My rides with my close friend Marianne had ended when she left the hospital to pursue her consulting business on a full-time basis. While I had been consistently riding with Susan D and Hope for a couple of years, I had just received the fabulous news that Hope was getting married. I was absolutely thrilled for my friend, but there was a downside. She was moving out of the area within two months. I certainly was delighted for Hope, yet perplexed as to how to manage my work commute.

I knew from past experience that having only one ride option would not be practical. I needed some flexibility to accommodate for vacation time and unexpected sick days. I wondered how I would make the rides work in the months to come.

For months, we had been praying for the right job opportunity, yet no such option had presented itself. It was a chance meeting at the hospital that began to turn the tide.

My co-worker had acquired a new computer, and a technician from the hospital's IT department came to install the equipment. In the course of conversation, I casually asked the technician, "Hey, you guys don't have any open positions down there, do you?"

I went on to explain my husband's predicament and his skill set. With an assurance that he would check out the job postings, the technician left our area. I had no inclination that I would ever hear anything further from him, but I lived to be surprised. Just a few days later, the technician returned with the news that there were indeed several openings. Better still, one of the positions might fit Eric's skill set, and he supplied me with the supervisor's name for follow-up.

I couldn't wait to get home and tell Eric. He was thrilled at the prospect, and we made a plan for me to take a copy of his resume directly to the supervisor in hopes of obtaining further details on the position.

The next morning, resume in hand, I marched down to the IT department, lifting up prayers with every step. Finding the supervisor's office, I knocked on the open door and introduced myself. Inquiring about the open position, I handed over the resume, asking, "Would it be possible for you to take a look at my husband's resume and see if his qualifications might fit the requirements of your open position?"

Mark smiled politely and invited me to take a seat. After taking a few minutes to scan the resume, he asked for more information on Eric's situation. Describing Eric's background as best I could, I explained that while we knew he needed to go through the human resources process, we simply wanted to clarify whether the job was a good fit for Eric's skill set. What I didn't say was that my ulterior motive was to enhance the chances that he would actually see Eric's resume given the huge volume of applications that flow through HR. Perhaps this personal contact might prompt a closer look at Eric's application.

Mark was most gracious and seemed genuinely interested. After some discussion, Mark requested that Eric submit an application, and then he would like to set up a phone interview. His interest made my heart skip a beat. I left the office with a promise to get Eric started on the HR application process.

There was a joyful bounce in my step as I made my way back to my office. This might be a real possibility. Could this be our long-awaited answer to prayer? If Eric could work at the hospital, it would solve our transportation issues.

"Oh Lord, please let this work out. If this is meant to be, Lord, please let this work out!"

True to his word, Mark called Eric within a few days. While the conversation was quite positive, it took two weeks to set up his interview.

On the day of the interview, I was bursting with excitement, all the while, praying feverishly. When Eric returned to my office with a big smile on his face, I was elated. The interview had gone well.

I thought we were home free, but alas, that's when the real waiting began. While I knew the wheels of HR turned slowly, I thought I would jump out of my skin as time slowly dragged on. I understood that other candidates had to be interviewed, and the results reviewed before a final decision could be made. Still, that made the waiting no less difficult. Weeks went by without a word.

One morning, I woke up mad. That's the best way I can describe it. I was just plain angry. I was worried, tired, and just plain sick of waiting.

For seven months, I had waited for God to work something out. Believing that God had a good plan for Eric, I had prayed fervently, while managing to remain encouraged. Painting a smile on my face, I had tried hard not to worry. Now, here we were, so close to what seemed like the perfect answer to our prayers, and nothing was happening. It was absolutely maddening.

Rising early to get a walk in before the day's activities began in earnest, I proceeded to the treadmill located in Eric's home office. Alone with my raging thoughts, I turned up the speed on the treadmill and began to pray. It was time to be honest with God. I was in no mood for subterfuge.

"Lord, I am so angry. I am so frustrated. I am at the end of my rope. Lord, I can't keep going on this way. We need an answer. We need a job. Lord, it's time to give us a job. Father, if this job at the hospital is supposed to work out, then please, let them call. Let it work out, please. We need You."

CHAPTER 13
The Box Comes Down

Perhaps it wasn't right to rant with God, but I decided that He knew my thoughts anyway. Besides, I had to get my feelings out. It was time to be honest. If I didn't, then surely I would explode.

That very afternoon, Eric got a call from his other prospect. After several months of virtually no word on the selection process, this other local company was offering Eric a good position. While we both should have been elated, our hearts actually sank. We suddenly realized that we had been putting all our hopes on the hospital job. Now finally, we had the long-awaited job offer, but it was not the one we wanted.

Eric negotiated 48 hours to review the offer. After some discussion, we decided that Eric should make a call directly to Mark at the hospital, just to confirm whether that door was actually closed before accepting this other offer.

Mark responded quickly to Eric's call. Realizing he was about to lose an excellent candidate due to the tediously slow HR process, Mark took action. The next day, Eric had an offer from the hospital. Our long wait was over!

Eric and I were positively ecstatic. It was like a dream come true. The prospect of having both of us working in the same place was simply amazing. My rides to work were solved. There was no more scheduling or stressing necessary. I could simply walk out my back door, get into the truck and go to work. No hassles, no planning, no worries. What a gift!

I could not help but smile when I remembered my morning rant with God. Perhaps God had appreciated my honest appeal after all. For surely, God had responded to my fervent plea with lightning speed. The waiting was over. God had answered our prayers.

Eric began his new job two days before Jonathan's 12th birthday. We had so much to celebrate. Interestingly, my friend's wedding took place two weeks later. With God's perfect planning, He had given me a permanent ride to work just in the nick of time. Isn't that just like God?

CHAPTER 14
Fellow Traveler

Hallway Chat

I had just finished teaching Sunday School. Descending the staircase, I headed toward the Sanctuary for our morning worship service. That's when I saw my good friend Kim F standing in the hallway. She and I have been very close friends for many years. Kim is a spiritual buddy, the kind of friend who can go deep with you, especially when you are struggling. She has always been very clued in when it came to my vision challenges, supporting me through some dark and difficult days.

When Kim looked up, she smiled and motioned for me to join her. I could tell she was excited about something. "Anita, you're not going to believe this. You know I have been doing these Bible studies on Wednesdays at another church, right? Well, we just started a new series. We watched the video this week, and the study is led by this woman who is blind. Anita, she has the same eye disease you do!"

I stared at her, dumbstruck, finding it hard to take in her words, my surprise so complete. Kim began to explain how the author of the study lost her vision in her teenage years due to Retinitis Pigmentosa. Her vision loss began suddenly and progressed quickly leaving her blind in her college years. Her Bible study "Walking By Faith"[3] describes her life journey and God's faithfulness through her battle with vision loss.

"Oh Anita, she is a beautiful woman, and the stories she tells...they remind me of you. She talks about things I have heard you talk about. You have just got to see this and read her book. Her name is Jennifer Rothschild."

---

[3] Rothschild, J. (2003). *Walking By Faith* Bible Study Video Series. LifeWay Press.

CHAPTER 14
Fellow Traveler

I felt a little shiver run up my spine, that warm glow that washes over you when you feel the presence of the Holy Spirit. I knew this was no random chance. I was supposed to hear about this author.

Excitement bubbled up within me as I listened to Kim recount some of Jennifer's amazing story. Thanking Kim for sharing this news with me, we parted with her promise to share more details as the study continued.

During the worship service, my mind returned again and again to thoughts of a devout Bible teacher who understood the struggles of vision loss. It is so rare to meet anyone with this diagnosis. How often had I felt like the only person in the world who knows such pain and loss? I knew that wasn't true, and yet, my heart often wallowed in a deep well of loneliness.

To think that another woman not only shares my struggles, but stands firmly on her faith; now that was an encouraging thought. I wanted to know her story and hear her insights.

As the weeks went by, Kim shared snippets of the video lessons with me. With each conversation, my heart lifted just a bit. This amazing and talented woman had lost most of her vision, and still, she enjoyed a full and active life as an author, speaker, wife and mother.

If Jennifer could overcome her struggles and live an abundant life, perhaps I could too. Perhaps God was showing me a victorious example of overcoming the hardships of blindness. The thought lightened my soul. Surely, it was something new to consider.

Life On The Truck

For four years, I had traveled all over the county teaching people about how to prevent heart disease. My partner Joan and I had taught countless classes at churches, schools, workplaces and community centers. Every Wednesday, our program offered blood pressure screenings at different locations in the community. I bet Joan and I checked 10,000 blood pressures in four-years' time, if not more! We ran large cholesterol screenings several times per year, counseling hundreds of people on how to eat healthy and lower their risk of heart disease.

I loved it! It was one of the most satisfying jobs I had ever had. Joan and I worked so well together. We made a great team, and we became close friends. Our program coordinator Kristen was fabulous to work for, keeping the stress low and the outcomes high. We were making a difference, improving the overall health of the community. The work suited me beautifully, playing to my strengths and unhampered by my visual limitations.

The program was funded by a four-year grant, and as the days of the funding grew short, my colleagues and I wondered what we would do next. To our great relief, the hospital administration was very impressed by our work in the community and wanted to continue the program. Our challenge was to find new funding.

To apply for another grant, we needed a new focus in our program, a new way to impact heart disease prevention. Our team put our heads together and began brainstorming. What if we had an easy way to move about the county checking cholesterol and blood pressures? We had found that people were more motivated for change when you shared their personal results with them. However, the equipment and resources to put together mass cholesterol screenings were cumbersome, and logistics limited the volume we could handle.

What if we had some kind of mobile screening vehicle housing all our equipment, making it easier to take the screening to worksites and busy community locations? That's how the idea of "The Truck" was born.

We applied for a federal grant and received funding for a mobile screening program. We accessed an aging ambulance, stripped and refurbished it with our equipment, and set up shop. "The Truck" had plenty of space for all the necessary equipment and enough seating for two patients to be screened at a time. We added an awning to the side of the vehicle and made an outdoor registration area. It worked like a charm!

CHAPTER 14
Fellow Traveler

There was just this little issue of driving. Staffed with two part-time nurses, there was not sufficient funding for a driver. Yes, the nurses had to learn to drive that big old ambulance! Obviously, I was not going to drive it, which meant I had to have several partners who could manage the driving responsibilities.

Our hospital had a critical care transport team that came to the rescue. Their fleet manager taught my colleagues how to manage that massive vehicle. We trained a total of four staff members to ensure we had coverage for our rotating schedules and vacation time. We even trained our secretary Brenda to drive that big old truck!

My job was navigation. I kept the directions handy, and the map within easy reach. My nurse friends maneuvered that truck into tight spots, and we regularly received strange looks when two women stepped out to set up. It was hard for some folks to imagine that female nurses could manage that heavy duty vehicle, but manage it we did.

Joan decided to scale back her hours for family issues, but continued to work several days per month with me. We were blessed to have Lisa, a registered dietitian, working with us occasionally to provide screening coverage. Her fountain of knowledge was a tremendous asset as we grew in our dietary counseling repertoire. However, I needed a steady partner to make things work. That's when Alisa stepped in. A new mother, the change in hours and stress levels were a perfect fit for this new season in Alisa's life.

Alisa was a master at wrangling that big old Truck into tight spaces. She could back it up like it was a little Honda. Her father was a truck driver, and we decided that her propensity for managing heavy duty vehicles must have been genetic.

We roamed around the community, meeting people of all backgrounds and age groups. We encountered patients with dangerously high blood pressures or blood sugars, sending more than a few straight to the emergency room. My colleagues and I became quick and confident performing the screenings and spent quality time counseling patients about what to do to achieve healthier lifestyles.

The program was a dramatic success. I could tell you story after story of people we found in crisis who acted on our advice and made healthy changes. More than once, we were greeted at a return location with the statement, "You saved my life." We met people in their own environment, established a quick rapport and helped them see that their current lifestyle was on a dangerous course.

I could not have been happier in my work. I had loved the classes and screenings of the first four years, but I loved this new avenue even more. The one-on-one, hands-on approach to teaching made the work even more meaningful and rewarding.

At first, I was nervous about how my visual limitations might impact this type of work. Could I handle the finger sticks, manage the screening equipment? At that point, I still had excellent visual acuity, although my central field was very small. Thankfully, I was still able to compensate for the missing portions of my visual field by moving my eyes up and down, back and forth, to take in the full picture of my surroundings. Like most things along the way, I can learn to manage them well once I figure them out. With just a little bit of practice, I was quickly ready for prime time. We set the truck up to support an easy flow of work tasks, and soon I was handling a busy caseload of patients with no problem. The counseling came easily. I think I was born to teach, and this was just a new format.

Working with Alisa was a dream. We were quite a pair, playing off each other's strengths, complimenting one another's skill sets.

Best of all, we became the best of friends. A strong, faithful Christian, Alisa set a positive example for me. She encouraged me when life wore me down. She helped me sort through my periodic angst over my eyes, offering a Christ-centered perspective on my struggles. I could talk to her about anything and feel better once I did. Her wise counsel shaped my thoughts and lifted my spirits.

CHAPTER 14
Fellow Traveler

Since I was further along on the parenting continuum, I could offer tips and advice as Alisa waded through the challenges of motherhood. We discussed everything from teething and toilet training to day care and doctor visits. I was glad that I could support her as she grew in her parenting role.

Between the wonderful work and the fabulous friendships, God had placed me in the perfect spot for that season of my life. I needed that support as I waded through the issues of vision loss and handled the normal challenges of parenting a teenager. "Life on the Truck" offered the perfect environment to grow professionally and spiritually.

Turning A Teenager

In June of 2004, we reached a family milestone. Jonathan was an official teenager. I could scarcely believe it.

His middle school years had been busy. His love of swimming had not abated. He continued his year-round competitive swimming as his primary sport and added tennis and band as extracurricular activities at school. He kept us hopping with swim meets, tennis matches and band concerts.

The youth group at church combined fun activities with good friendships, and he stayed active in community service projects. Jonathan still loved swimming on the summer league swim team, and I continued to serve as the swim team coordinator. If I wasn't at work, the two of us could be found poolside on hot summer days.

Getting him to swim practice still presented challenges since Eric and I were both working over 30 miles from home. Thankfully, I was able to work out carpool arrangements for some weekdays. On others, I hired one of my close friends to transport him to practice after school. Jonathan loved those trips with Donna because they often involved a stop for a milkshake along the way.

Like a typical teenager, he started sleeping late and getting interested in music. He had television shows that he followed closely. He procrastinated on his homework, and his mother had to stay after him on that.

However, little changed in our relationship. He and I remained close, chatting about everything. I kept expecting him to pull away from me, but he never did. Sure, we got on each other's nerves on occasion, but mostly we just enjoyed doing things together.

Jonathan loved hanging out with his dad. The two of them had been NASCAR fans since he was a little boy. They still followed the drivers closely and watched the races together. Eric would spring for race tickets once or twice a year, and they would have a blast. My father would often join them on these adventures, and the three of them shared wonderful times together. They even let Mom tag along sometimes. Our little family was still tight, and that meant the world to me.

Study Plan

Though months had gone by since Kim first mentioned Jennifer Rothschild's Bible Study, I had not forgotten the details Kim had shared about Jennifer's amazing story. I knew I needed to do that study. The idea hung in the back of my mind like a delicious fruit that I needed to pluck from the vine. I just had not done anything about it yet. It was time to correct that oversight.

As autumn approached, I tossed out an idea to Kim. "What would you think about doing a Women's Bible Study at our church and doing the Jennifer Rothschild study? Would you help me lead it?"

Kim was immediately sold on the idea. We decided that the fall was too busy to foster much participation, but perhaps January might be a good time. With excitement, we set our plan into motion.

CHAPTER 14
Fellow Traveler

Video Connection

On a cold Saturday morning in early January, Kim and I convened our small group series. Watching Jennifer Rothschild's "Walking By Faith"[4] videos felt like coming home. Here was someone who understood my struggles. Her stories could have been my own. I was glued to Jennifer's every word, and so was the rest of our group.

The video lessons told the story of her journey through blindness. My heart ached as she described how 15-year-old Jennifer had begun to notice her failing vision. She described the meeting with the ophthalmologists, and their diagnosis of Retinitis Pigmentosa. She recalled the silent car ride home with her parents as they all struggled to process this heartbreaking news. Oh, how I could relate. I could feel her anguish, totally comprehend her loss. I had sat in one of those exam chairs, and then ridden home in silence, the ache so deep I could not voice my pain.

Yet, that moment for Jennifer did not end in pain and silence. She came into her home from that desperate car ride and went straight to the piano, playing from memory for the first time. No sheet music to depend on now, her eyes no longer able to see the notes. What was the song she played? From the hand of God to Jennifer's young fingertips came the tune of the well-worn hymn, "It Is Well With My Soul."

Talk about a touching moment! I sat there stunned, overwhelmed by the sure hand of God's Grace in the face of that heartbreaking adversity. Of all the songs that might come to mind, here was a song that spoke volumes to Jennifer on that day long ago, and it spoke to me sitting there in our church library.

Jennifer went on to say that "It can be well with your soul, even when it is not well with your circumstance."[4] What powerful words. They were words of truth. When Jennifer closed the video session

---

[4] Rothschild, J. (2003). *Walking By Faith* Bible Study Video Series. LifeWay Press.

with her own rendition of "It Is Well With My Soul," a voice sequestered deep in the recesses of my soul joined her in that beautiful melody.

I had always loved that hymn. Long before I ever knew anything about my eye disease, that song became part of a daily ritual for me as I drove alone to the hospital. As I made my way down the road, I would bellow out the words of that hymn as well as several others. It seemed a good way to start my day. Over the years, the words of that powerful hymn had flowed back to me again and again.

"When peace like a river attendeth my way,
When sorrow like sea billows roll,
Whatever my lot, Thou hast caused me to say,
It is well, it is well with my soul."[5]

To hear this beautiful woman share the news of her heartbreaking loss followed by the melody of this ancient hymn, well, it was a God-moment. God was touching my heart as He had so many times before. He was sending me a message, a reminder that no matter what happens in this life, it can still be well with my soul.

As I worked through the study materials on my own, I took time to ponder Jennifer's experiences. I looked up scriptures and meditated on their meaning. I saw familiar passages in a new light. The scriptures comforted me, their insights offering a fresh perspective on my situation.

I remember looking again at Matthew 14:25-33 where Peter walks to Jesus on the water. Peter did the impossible because he trusted His Lord. As long as Peter kept his eyes fixed on Jesus, he did not sink. Yet, when he looked down at the waves tumbling beneath his feet, when he focused on the rough waters of his circumstances, the sea began to swallow him.

I had faced wave after wave of losses in this journey through blindness. When my eyes were fixed on Jesus, I could keep my head

---

[5] Spafford, Horatio and Bliss, Philip. "It is Well With My Soul". 1873.

above the raging waters. Yet, so often, I let my circumstances tug at my heels and pull my focus down to the peril of my problems. Reading this Bible story with fresh eyes, I caught a new insight. Like Peter, I can traverse the waves beneath my feet if I keep my eyes on the One who can calm the sea. The waves will still come, but with Jesus before me, I can walk on the churning waters.

There were funny moments too. I laughed as Jennifer recounted the day she mixed up her eyeliner and lipliner, appearing to her family with bright, red eyes and black lips. I loved that she wore makeup and dressed stylishly. As she told her strategies for applying makeup and selecting her clothes, I was encouraged. Blindness did not mean that I could not look my best. There are ways to accomplish my makeup routine, strategies I can employ to dress the way I want to dress.

I loved that Jennifer baked cookies and used tactile dots to manage in her kitchen. She was overcoming her limitations.

Listening to Jennifer's story, I felt hope. Until that point, I had looked at vision loss as only a battle to be fought, a war that must be won. I fought against the losses, resented the limitations. I had to be tough, to be brave all the time. Refusing to give into blindness, I believed I could beat this disgusting disease somehow. I was determined to lead a normal life.

Something about Jennifer's story softened my heart. Here was this woman who had lost all of her vision, and still, she was productive, full of joy, and firm in her faith. She had accepted her disease, choosing to rise above the losses, resolving to make the best of what life offered.

If Jennifer could do that, perhaps I could too. I still had so much more vision than she did, and yet, I often let the dread of eventual blindness eat at me. Perhaps it wouldn't be so bad after all. Maybe I could learn to live abundantly despite my failing vision.

Those musings brought to mind my epiphany of so many years before, as I listened to the speaker reflect on Romans 8:28. She had asserted, "Not in some things or in most things. But in all things,

God works for the good of those who love Him, who have been called according to His purpose" (Romans 8:28 *NIV*). I had asked myself a question on that church pew so long ago. "Cannot the God of the universe who is sovereign and in control take this very hard thing and work it for my good?"

God had worked good out of Jennifer's hard circumstances. Surely, He could do the same for me.

I cannot fully convey the depth of encouragement I received from that study. How can six sessions change your life? I don't know, but clearly, it did. Jennifer had said, "I cannot control my circumstances, but I can choose how I respond to my circumstances."[6] I could not stop my encroaching blindness, but I could choose how I respond.

I savored that thought like sweet honey, allowing it to trickle down the walls of my hurting heart, coating, soothing, opening its depths to new possibilities. Out of the dark recesses of my spirit rose a shiny glimmer of hope.

Headed for High School

For his 14th birthday, Jonathan had a special request. He wanted to do the Richard Petty Ride Along at the Charlotte Motor Speedway. The event offered a chance to ride in the passenger seat of a race car as it made high speed turns around the track. Jonathan's Dad was immediately sold on the idea, and Granddaddy bought in quickly. I decided that it sounded like fun and signed up for a ticket.

We were not disappointed by the experience. It was exhilarating! The rush of adrenaline when the race car maneuvered into the turns definitely kicked up the heart rate.

After our thrilling ride around the track, we paused for a photo opportunity. Standing between his father and grandfather, dressed in full racing gear, Jonathan looked like a boy no longer. He was

---

[6] Rothschild, J. (2003). *Walking By Faith* Bible Study Video Series. LifeWay Press.

growing up. Trying to hide the tears, I turned away. I did not want to spoil the mood, but I was having a "Mommy moment." Life was changing fast. My son was becoming a young man.

That summer brought lots of new opportunities for Jonathan. He was now old enough to be a teen volunteer at the hospital where Eric and I worked. He signed up for work in both the pharmacy and patient discharge area. He loved it. Not only was it a great experience, but it was fun to have him go to work with us.

On his first volunteer day, I had given him a stern motherly warning to pay attention and work hard. "Don't embarrass me now. I know people all over this hospital."

He had shrugged his shoulders and no doubt inwardly rolled his eyes. He didn't dare do that outwardly.

When he returned to my office at the end of the day, he greeted me with a note of amazement. "You weren't kidding. Everybody knows you!"

Jonathan quickly learned new skills as he helped the pharmacy technicians with a variety of supervised tasks. One day in the cafeteria, the lead pharmacy technician sought Eric out and shared what a wonderful job Jonathan was doing. "He is such a good worker!"

Of course, Eric and I glowed with pride. We got similar feedback from his supervisor at the YMCA where he worked as a lifeguard that summer. Although he only worked a few shifts a month, the learning opportunity and responsibility was an important stepping stone into the world of work. Eric and I felt it was important for him to learn what work was all about.

Of course, there was swim team that summer. In fact, it was one of the best summer seasons we ever had together as a team. Our coaches had done a phenomenal job of grooming the younger swimmers. Our older swimmers had perfected their skills and dramatically improved their times. Our team had always been small compared to others, but our swimmers were exceptional.

Best of all, the kids had grown up together, playing and having fun, acting more like a big family than just a team. For Jonathan, those kids were like siblings. All the parents were good friends as well, with both parents and kids spending hours hanging out around the pool. It was our summer home.

In late July, our team reached our pinnacle of achievement, winning the quality award at the county swim championships! The quality award measured points achieved relative to size and leveled our playing field against the much larger teams. Our team was ecstatic!

When the award was announced at the conclusion of the championship meet, no one was more thrilled than I. I had coordinated that swim and dive team since Jonathan was five years old. We were always the underdog due to our size, but finally we had claimed the long-sought title.

I cannot imagine how many hours I put into that team over the years. It truly was a part-time job, albeit unpaid, but that's really not accurate. I did get paid. My payment was the smiles on those children's faces when they won a race or posed for the team picture. That pool was where those kids felt safe and loved. It was, in a way, my ministry to those children and their families, my labor of love. It was a good thing, and I was so thankful that our family had been a part of it.

Later that summer, Jonathan traveled to the Grand Canyon with his grandfather Pete, his Uncle Steve and cousin Elizabeth. The four of them delighted in a rafting adventure down the Colorado river. He was gone for almost three weeks. It was a fabulous experience for him, but the house was awfully quiet without him. I knew that in a few short years, this was how it would be. He was about to begin high school, and the slow but necessary process of letting go was beginning.

CHAPTER 14
Fellow Traveler

Let It Go

Once again, I sat on a couch in Bob's office, waiting for him to arrive. It was a familiar spot, for I had made my way to his office many times. There were months, even years, between visits. As I grew more comfortable with my "new normal," I needed Bob less and less. Still, every now and then, I would find myself "sinking in sad" once again. I managed well when my yearly eye exams revealed little to no disease progression, but when the news was not good, I found I needed to talk things out.

No doubt about it, Bob had been a lifeline for me. While I was better at sharing my feelings with my family and close friends, I found Bob's balanced perspective particularly helpful. His gentle, probing questions helped me examine my responses more objectively, allowing me to regain my equilibrium and move forward.

The news from my recent eye exam had not been good. There was more disease progression, and once again, I was a mess.

Bob's smile was warm and genuine as he crossed the room to give me a quick hug of welcome. Seated in his swivel chair, he opened the discussion with a quiet question, and as usual, my latest saga tumbled out. He listened quietly, nodding with compassion, prodding with a gentle question here and there.

"I just feel so upset all the time, and I don't want to be this way. I keep thinking I will get over this, but I don't seem to."

His tone was soothing as he asked, "So do you ever let yourself feel sad?"

"I don't know. No, not really, I guess. I guess I worry that if I ever let myself cry, I would never stop."

"So what would it be like to let yourself be sad or angry for a bit, and then let it go? What would it be like to feel the way you feel for a little while, and then consciously choose to let it go?"

The question stopped me in my tracks. I had somehow never considered such a concept. I feared the sadness. I repressed the frustration. I didn't want others to see me that way. I felt out of control when those emotions took hold, and I did not like being out of control.

There was often a hidden battle raging underneath my well-ordered persona. I felt like I had to fight those emotions, lest they take over and destroy me. Here was Bob, giving me permission to feel the way I feel. I could quit fighting and allow myself to feel sad or be angry. The difference was that instead of drowning in those feelings, I could allow them to remain for a time, and then, release them. My feelings did not have to control me. Rather, I had the power to control them.

"Wouldn't that be better than burying them inside, than denying that the feelings are even there?" Bob's eyes were locked on mine as he asked that powerful question.

It made sense. His perspective had stunned me, and still, I knew he was right. The feelings would never leave me for long. The losses were destined to continue.

For so long, I had placed those emotions in that box on the shelf, and gone on with life. But the box couldn't stay on that shelf, because the losses kept coming. With every loss, the box came down, and it was harder and harder to put it away again.

It was time to try something new. I wondered aloud, "I don't know, but I need to do something different. I'd like to try. Perhaps I can feel the way I feel, and then let it go."

Looking back, that was an important moment in my journey. While this new approach offered a better strategy for dealing with my emotions, it took time for me to learn to employ it effectively. Gradually, however, I realized that I had the power to let my feelings go. I might have a bad day, but it did not mean that every subsequent day would be bad. I could choose to feel the way I feel, and then, when I am ready, release those emotions and move forward.

CHAPTER 14
Fellow Traveler

Untimely Ending

After winning the Quality Award at our summer league swimming championships the summer before, our swim team was nearly bursting with excitement. At our swim and dive team banquet, the owner of our swim club had announced plans for a brand-new pool, courtesy of the new developer who had purchased the property, planning to build fancy new condominiums on the site of the existing pool. The new pool would be fabulous, a new location with luxurious amenities.

Our club members were excited, but wondered if the pool could be built and ready by the next summer. The club manager brushed off such concerns with promises that all would be well.

By May of 2006, there was a hole in the ground where the old pool had resided, and no new pool to replace it. Our team joined forces with a club across town, the arrangement supposedly temporary.

As summer turned to fall, our swim team families were discouraged at the lack of progress. In the months that followed, the developer went bankrupt. Our pool was gone, and so was our swim team.

Looking back, I can still feel the heartbreak of that fateful day when we learned that our pool days were done. Those pool families had formed tight bonds as we raised our kids together in the warm summer sun. The pool had been mine and Jonathan's refuge, the place we could get to easily, the place we could spend time with friends. With a finger snap, it was all over.

To say that we mourned that loss is no understatement. I still miss those interactions, regret the loss of those tight bonds of friendship we once shared. But all good things must come to an end, and our summer swim team days were finished.

Women Of Faith

The phone rang. Kim F was on the line, her voice bubbling with excitement. "Anita, Jennifer Rothschild is speaking at Women of Faith, the women's conference we have talked about before. She's going to speak in Charlotte. We can hear her speak in person!"

I could hardly believe my ears. I had so loved Jennifer's Bible study series, so appreciated her perspective on the trials of life. Her words had offered so much comfort and encouragement, but I had never dreamed I would have the chance to hear her speak in person. I was elated.

Anticipating my reaction, Kim had already made plans to go. We bought our tickets and waited with anticipation for the October event.

Arriving at the Charlotte Coliseum, Kim and I were immediately engulfed in a sea of women. The hallways were flooded with ladies of all sizes, shapes and shades, all talking a mile a minute. It was overwhelming, and at the same time, exhilarating. To think that this many Christian women were gathered under one roof to praise, worship and grow, now that was amazing.

When Kim had ordered our tickets, she had explained about my vision issues, asking to be seated near a monitor. She knew the arena style seating might make it hard for me to see the speakers.

Tickets in hand, we followed the directions to our seats, descending slowly down the long flight of concrete steps, lest I stumble and fall. Those types of stairs are quite challenging for me. Following Kim down the stairs, I was surprised at how close we were to the arena floor. When she stopped at row four, I was jubilant. These were great seats.

Settling into our seats, we noted a monitor within easy viewing distance. Better still, the stage was a stone's throw away. I would definitely be able to follow the proceedings from this spot.

In a few minutes, we were joined by a large group of hearing-impaired ladies. Their interpreter stood directly below our section and began to gesture to the group using sign language. The scene was fascinating to watch, and my excitement grew as I observed the joy-filled signing of my hearing-limited neighbors.

As the music ramped up, Kim and I watched the speakers file into their seats in what we later learned was affectionately called, "The Porch." Their rocking chairs sat in an enclosed area beside the stage, allowing for easy access to the podium when it was time for their event. Kim and I were delighted because "The Porch" stood directly ahead of us. We could watch the speakers easily throughout the program.

The program began with praise and worship music, and we had no trouble getting into the music. The event host opened the day's proceedings, and soon, Kim and I were hanging on every word. One after another speaker took the stage, sharing their stories, each one touching both of our hearts in some meaningful way.

As the time drew near for Jennifer to speak, I could barely sit still in my seat. I had waited for months for this moment. I could not escape the idea that this event was significant, that I was supposed to be there to take in some new insight.

Jennifer's husband Phillip walked her onto the circular stage, leading her to a tall, round table before departing. Jennifer touched the table to get her bearings and smiled brightly at an audience that she could not see. She was a strikingly beautiful woman, immaculately dressed, her countenance radiating warmth and compassion. My heart hammered as she began to speak.

I cannot recall all the things she said. Several of her stories were repetitions from her video, but to hear her tell them in person was powerful. I sat there mesmerized, soaking in every word, completely captivated.

Emotions flooded my spirit. My soul soared with delight at a humorous antidote and sank in despair with the pain of her anguish. It felt like someone was singing my life story, like we were the only two people in that huge arena, and our struggles were linked.

I could have listened to Jennifer for hours, but soon, the session was over. The host reminded the audience that Jennifer would be signing books after the session at a set location on the concourse. Kim had noted this opportunity in the program book already. Since I had purchased a "Walking By Faith" CD as we browsed through the bookstore that morning, I planned to have Jennifer sign the CD cover.

As soon as the session concluded, Kim and I hightailed it to the book signing spot, taking our place in line. I could hardly contain my excitement. I could not believe that I was going to have a chance to speak to this woman who had helped me so much on my own journey through blindness.

As Kim and I edged closer, I was able to spot Jennifer and her husband standing on the opposite side of a long, high table. Phillip was speaking to each person and getting the items ready for her to sign. Jennifer was nestled closely beside him, and as the participants stepped up to speak to her, Phillip quietly conveyed each person's name.

When it was my turn, I smiled, extended my hand to Phillip and introduced myself.

"Hi. My name is Anita. I am so excited to meet Jennifer. I have RP too."

There are moments when time stands still. This was one of those moments. At my words, Phillip paused and looked intently into my eyes. It was a look of deep compassion, a sincere empathy conveyed through his moist eyes. He took my hand in his and covered it with his own as if to offer a little embrace. Turning to Jennifer, he said, "Jennifer, this is Anita and she has RP."

I watched as her beautiful features changed, her face taking on a look of profound tenderness that spoke volumes.

I could barely speak, so overcome with emotion at their responses to my disclosure. "Jennifer, it is so good to meet you. Your words have meant so much to me."

I could tell the tears were coming, felt the words catch in my throat. Phillip had taken my hand and placed it gently into

Jennifer's. As she took in the import of my words, Jennifer covered my hand with hers just as he had done, giving my hand a gentle squeeze. Nodding empathetically, she offered, "Keep on walking by faith, Anita. Keep on walking by faith."

We stood there with our hands locked together for a long moment before Jennifer pulled away to sign her name on the cover of my CD. With a word of thanks, I stepped away, tears leaking from the corners of my eyes. Kim shook Jennifer's hand as well, although I did not catch their words. I was too overcome by the power of that moment.

Kim and I walked up the hallway, finding a spot to pause and catch our breath. It had been an emotional experience for us both. The weight of that meeting was not lost on Kim either. Kim had walked this road with me, had listened to my stories for years, had offered support in my times of struggle. She had first learned of Jennifer's story and had known the comfort it would bring to my heart. The moment had touched her as deeply as it had me. We both needed some space to collect ourselves.

I am not one to be starstruck by celebrities. I don't think I have ever stood in line for another autograph, but this meeting was different. It was as if I was traveling alone on an isolated dirt road, my footsteps falling heavy from the burden I carried on my back. Suddenly, another traveler comes into view, dressed in my same apparel, speaking my own language. Nothing could keep me from running forward and grasping my fellow traveler's hand. I needed her company, wanted to feel her hand clasped in mine, if only for a moment. It was as if I knew that such a chance meeting would release the load I carried, changing everything about the rest of my journey.

I have never forgotten that moment. It stands clearly in the recesses of my memory. It was beyond powerful, another God-moment.

Jennifer's words echo in my mind to this day. That brief encounter touched my heart and fueled my hope. I knew what I had to do. "Keep on walking by faith, Anita. Keep on walking by faith."

CHAPTER 14
Fellow Traveler

CHAPTER 15
Rough Places Smooth

We Need Your Brain

"Life on the Truck" remained good. I was busy and productive. The mobile screening program was a tremendous success, touching countless lives and making a difference in the health of our community. I adored my co-workers and looked forward to going to work each day.

Still part-time, I was available for Jonathan and had plenty of time to pursue my volunteer work. With Eric working at the hospital, our stress levels were so much lower. There were no more worries about transportation to work. When my schedule required an early arrival or late departure to accommodate a screening appointment, Eric and I just altered our work times. The flexibility made life so much easier. Every day, I would get a call at 4 PM. Eric's voice would be on the other end of the line, "Ready?" I would reply "Yes!" and off we would go. No worries, no hassles.

Everything was going great until we got the notification. Our mobile screening program was being funded by a federal grant. We were achieving the desired outcomes, on track with all our goals, and still had one year left on our grant. Without any hint of warning, our program coordinator received notification that the grant funding would cease in three months. The federal administration had changed directions, and our type of grant was no longer funded.

My colleagues and I were crushed. It felt like the rug had been pulled out from under our feet. It was totally unexpected.

Worse still, the current economic environment was presenting new challenges for the hospital. While the hospital administration was still extremely positive about our work in the community, there was no option to receive full funding from the health system's operating budget. Without grant funding, our program was over.

CHAPTER 15
Rough Places Smooth

Just like that, I needed a new job. Fortunately, we had three months' notice, and the hospital had promised to find appropriate positions for each of our staff members. I began to hunt for other options.

During my years in the heart disease prevention program, I had maintained strong relationships with my former nursing colleagues. Periodically, I had picked up extra hours teaching EKG classes or consulting on other projects. The extra work had been a great help when Eric had been out of work several years earlier. Thankfully, I was still held in high regard within the organization. I just hoped that regard would translate into a good position.

That's how I ended up in Deb's office one afternoon. We had known each other for years, and she had been gracious to find those extra projects for me along the way. I was hoping that there might be a possibility of an opening in her department.

Deb supervised the Clinical Nurse Specialists (CNS) throughout the organization. Given my qualifications and previous experience as a CNS, I was hopeful that there might be an opportunity to return to that role. I knew there was a full-time position open, but I was not sure if this was the right fit for me.

While I loved the CNS role, I felt some trepidation about pursuing this option. The posted position was full-time. I had worked half time since Jonathan's birth. It had worked beautifully for our family, and I had savored the time at home with Jonathan. Even though he was now a teenager, I was grateful for the opportunity to be more available to him.

Could I manage the stress levels of this full-time position? The CNS role is very demanding. I knew that I had the talent and experience to perform the teaching, consulting and project work, but how would I juggle the job and my home life? I knew my work habits. If given a job, I will get it done. I will throw myself into it full force, determined to make things work. Yes, there are some Type A personality traits there. In my part-time positions, I had found a good balance between work and home. Could I do that if I worked full-time?

My part-time schedule offered considerable benefits for our family. I could take care of domestic duties and ease some of Eric's load. I thoroughly enjoyed my various volunteer efforts and appreciated the opportunity to give back in those endeavors. Going full-time would change all that.

My biggest reservation was my visual limitations. The role I performed prior to my eye disease diagnosis had included direct patient care, something I knew I could not do visually. My friends had shared that staffing was no longer a job requirement. Yet, I knew that part of the job was to consult on patient care issues. Staff might have questions on procedures or equipment. Could I see well enough to answer their questions? Could I do the job justice, given my visual limitations?

These were the thoughts that plagued me as I sat down at the round table in Deb's office. Opening the conversation, I shared my situation and asked about the open position. Deb explained that the position was a broader medical-surgical focus, rather than the pure cardiology focus that was my background. However, she was quite comfortable that we could tailor the role a bit to better fit my skill set.

I asked about the possibility of working part-time, but Deb was firm that she needed a full-time person. Well, that answered that question. I would have to make the leap to full-time if I wanted this job.

"Deb, you know about my eyes. I am nervous about whether I can do the job the way it needs to be done. I can't staff. There are some things I just can't do."

Deb looked at me intently and smiled gently. "Anita, I know all that. The role has no staffing requirements now. You are an excellent teacher, and you can do all the consulting and project work. You can do this."

CHAPTER 15
Rough Places Smooth

"I know, but I'm just worried that I can't do certain things. I don't know how long my vision will let me do the things I need to be able to do."

Nodding with empathy, Deb went on, "Anita, we need your brain, not your eyes. We need your insights and your knowledge. We can make the other stuff work. You can do the job. I have no doubts."

I left the office with a lot to consider. Deb had essentially offered me the job. Of course, I would have to go through an interview process, but I knew I had the position if I wanted it.

That was the real question. "Do I want this job?"

Prayerful Decision

In the weeks following my meeting in Deb's office, I spent a lot of time in prayer, asking God to show me the right path forward. "Lord, if this is not the right job for me, then show me, Lord. Make it clear what I should do."

Of course, Eric and I debated the pros and cons, discussing all my concerns. While going full-time had its drawbacks, the extra income would come in handy. Jonathan would be off to college in two years, and we must be ready to pay the tuition.

The timing was good in that Jonathan would be turning 16 in just a few weeks. Once he had his driver's license, that solved a myriad of hurdles for us. Still absorbed in year-round swimming, he had swim practice four afternoons per week. With his license, he would likely practice even more. On my days off, he didn't get home from practice until supper time. He was busy enough now that being home for him was less important than it used to be. He was growing up.

After my reassuring talk with Deb, I had followed up with other colleagues who had nothing but reassurance that the job was perfect for me. Still, I fretted, praying for a sign. Sometimes, it would just be nice to receive a handwritten note with a clear directive!

All my concerns had been addressed and still I waited. I kept watching the job postings, but there was nothing else available that suited my skill set. The end of the grant was drawing near. After a month of prayer, no other job had presented itself. I decided that the silence of the job board was my sign. I called Deb and told her that I wanted the job. I was going to be a CNS once again.

Wheels

Of all his birthdays, there had never been one so eagerly anticipated. Jonathan could not wait to turn 16, and he wasn't the only one. His parents were counting down the days. For our family, the idea of Jonathan driving was like a release from bondage. While other parents fear this moment, Eric and I were more than ready. So was Jonathan.

Eric had done an excellent job preparing Jonathan for this big day. When Jonathan turned 15 and received his learner's permit, Eric and my father started hunting for a small used truck with a manual transmission. They found a good deal on a 2004 Nissan Frontier and made the purchase. This meant that Jonathan could learn to drive on the vehicle that would eventually become his own. He had to master a clutch while he learned to navigate the highways. As part of the deal, Jonathan invested $1000 of his own money into the purchase. That commitment enhanced his desire to handle his driving responsibilities with care. It was a good plan and a valuable way to learn.

On the day of his 15th birthday, we were first in line at the driver's license bureau. I waited in our larger truck for him and his dad to go in and get the permit. When Jonathan returned with a wide grin on his face and a bounce in his step, I knew the permit was in his pocket.

We were headed to the beach that morning to celebrate the big occasion. To my surprise, Eric handed Jonathan the keys and directed him to the driver's seat. Eric was actually going to let Jonathan drive us to the beach. I'm not sure who was more surprised, Jonathan or me.

It was a smart move. While Jonathan had completed driver's education, and the two of them had done some practice driving together, that first official trip in the driver's seat was a big deal for all of us. In that one gesture, Eric had shown Jonathan that he had faith in his ability to master driving. Eric was quite particular with his truck. Handing over the truck keys was a vote of confidence and a huge responsibility. Jonathan rose to the challenge and did quite well.

Over the ensuing months, Eric surprised me with his level of patience, and Jonathan quickly mastered the mechanics of driving. Jonathan soon managed traffic with relative ease and became competent driving in all types of weather. He practiced on both trucks giving him more versatility in his skills.

My dad even joined in on the training regime, helping him master using the clutch smoothly. Dad had taught me to drive so many years before, and he was a good teacher. I must admit to a pang of sadness as I watched Jonathan and his grandaddy drive down the road. It brought back memories of my driving lessons. Oh, how I missed driving, even after all these years. So often, the loss of driving was just about the means of transportation to a given place, but there were moments when I mourned the loss of that independent feeling that surfaces when you climb behind the wheel. I missed the joy of driving. Now, my son was experiencing what I could not, and there was a little pang of regret as I watched them speed away.

As the days grew closer to Jonathan's milestone birthday, Eric and I were quite comfortable with Jonathan's driving skills. He was still not particularly social, so we were not concerned about joy riding with friends or foolish teenage stunts. To Jonathan, driving was a privilege, and he treated it as such. He had grown up enduring the trials of my transportation struggles. Like me, he had waited for rides, hoping they would show up. Like me, he had missed out on things he would have liked to have done because there was no way to get there. Jonathan never really verbalized this, but I knew by the way he talked about his license that he appreciated it as a precious gift to be handled with care. "Mama, when I get my license, I'll take you anywhere you want to go."

His 16th birthday fell on a Saturday, so he had to wait until Monday to go to the DMV office. First thing Monday morning, he was up and dressed without any parental prodding. Returning with his Dad several hours later, he was nestled behind the wheel with a grin so wide I thought it might stretch his face.

"Take your mama somewhere," his dad said with an equally wide grin. Jonathan had wheels!

That was a fun summer. Transportation problems solved, Jonathan increased his swim practice regimen and began working several days a week as a YMCA lifeguard. He continued his volunteer work at the hospital, riding into work with Eric and me, allowing for some good family time. On my days off, we would run errands or drive across town to the different pool we had joined. He adored getting a bacon, egg and cheese biscuit from Biscuitville, and I think he spent a fair portion of his wages on those biscuits. A Biscuitville stop became a regular part of our Sunday morning church routine.

As we rode around town, we would chat happily about one thing or another. He often talked more when I had him cornered in that tiny truck cab. I learned lots of things on those little jaunts. After taking me wherever I wanted to go, he would grin at me sheepishly from the driver's seat, "Mama, do we need a milkshake?"

That was code for a stop at Cook-Out for a tasty shake with Mom buying. I never minded. It was fun to have a little treat together, just the two of us. I could never do that with him growing up. We always went places with someone else, never just us two. Those little treats were tasty, but for me, the real treat was being out and about with my boy.

CHAPTER 15
Rough Places Smooth

One day, we were cruising down the road toward our house when a classic rock and roll song came on the radio station he preferred. I looked over and grinned at him. "Crank it up, J. That song's meant to be played loud."

He looked at me astonished. "Wow, Mom. You're cool!"

I wasn't always cool, but I was that day. He and I enjoyed our tunes together as we rolled down the road.

Having the ability to go where we needed to go was just a Godsend. It was like someone had freed us from an unjust incarceration. I think Jonathan enjoyed being able to do stuff for me. He knew the burden it had been for me not to drive. He was very sensitive to my needs. In small ways, he had always tried to take care of me. Now, he had a major way to do so. He had wheels!

Taking The Plunge

In my years as the volunteer swim team coordinator, I had overseen the dive team. While I had never been able to dive myself, I learned so much from working with the coach and watching the kids master new skills. It was magical to watch those divers flip and turn high in the air and then hit the water gracefully with barely a splash.

In August of 2007, it was time for me to take the plunge into full-time work. I knew there would be challenging flips and turns. I just hoped I could manage the move gracefully.

With barely two months of the new job under my belt, I was handed a huge organization-wide project. My orientation was over. It was time to hit the ground running.

Yes, it was stressful, but it was also invigorating. I loved being a CNS again, delighted in working with staff and teaching classes. It was the right job at the right time.

Jonathan was getting older and needed me less. He had his license, and our transportation struggles were solved. My life had been so interwoven with Jonathan's needs and interests. It was

hard to disentangle myself from all of his activities, but Jonathan needed to try his hand at more independence. Since I couldn't always keep myself from obsessing over his school work and decisions, it was better for me to be busy. And busy, I was.

Full-time work was an adjustment, but overall, the transition went smoothly. My hours matched Eric's, and I had a great deal of autonomy and flexibility. I was glad I had taken those bouncing steps off the board into new professional opportunities.

Down Under

In December of 2007, we made a memory destined to last a lifetime. My fabulous mother-in-law had surprised us two years earlier with a plan that had been long in the making. For years, Liz had been squirreling away money for a special family trip. At our Christmas gathering at Pipestem in 2005, Steve and his kids, Elizabeth and Ben, were gathered around the fire with the three of us. Liz chose this moment to reveal her big surprise. When she announced that she planned to take our entire family to Australia for her and Pete's 50th wedding anniversary, the six of us were absolutely dumbstruck. When she unveiled her plans for the two-and-a-half-week trip over the Christmas break, we were ecstatic!

For two years, Liz had been teasing us with trip details, but when we all landed in Atlanta from our various connecting flights, we knew this was really happening. We were headed to Australia!

The trip was beyond incredible! We saw kangaroos and koalas, swam with dolphins, and meandered down some of the most pristine beaches I had ever surveyed.

On Christmas Day, we sailed on the Great Barrier Reef, and most of the group donned snorkeling gear to take an underwater gander at all manner of sea creatures. Liz and I preferred a more passive activity, floating happily in our life jackets on a gently lapping sea.

On the Great Ocean Road, we sped along in the pouring rain as the sea rolled and tumbled in the distance. We even braved the depths of a "Down Under" jungle. Eric and I celebrated our 25th

CHAPTER 15
Rough Places Smooth

wedding anniversary strolling along the cliffs and shoreline of Kangaroo Island.

Perhaps the most precious part of the trip was the family time. Sharing a van seat with Elizabeth as we searched for wildlife was a priceless treasure. She and I got so tickled at all the cute little Aussie expressions of speech that she bought a small notebook to record the sayings. As our guides uttered some native quip, we would giggle and remark, "There's another one for the book!" She and I had grown even closer the past few years as she adjusted to her parents' divorce. Savoring the sights together afforded lots of girl time to talk and giggle, and our tight bond grew even tighter.

At eight years old, Ben was absolutely adorable on that trip. He was fascinated by every creature, every sight and every food option. We couldn't believe the dishes he was willing to try. I will always remember his newfound affection for hot tea. Ordering it on one of our first stops, the tea arrived on a fancy tray with all the fixings. He made the whole thing an experience as he added his cream and stirred in his sugar, ordering the treat every chance he could. I loved the day we spent at the Cairns Zoo as we both held a cuddly koala on our shoulders!

For the grand climax, our whole family watched the fireworks over Sydney Harbor on New Year's Eve. The fact that we viewed the festivities from a corner window on the 15th floor of a luxurious downtown hotel was my fault.

When Liz began planning the trip, she had asked Eric about navigating me in the dark through the crowded downtown streets. My night vision had declined significantly by this stage of the disease, and Eric expressed his hesitation on the idea. Liz had already been concerned about this issue. She and the travel agent searched for a better way to view the fireworks. That amazing hotel room was the outcome of their deliberations. Watching the fireworks over Sydney on New Year's Eve had been a lifelong dream for Liz. With her spouse of 50 years at her side, and her family gathered all around her, we made that dream come true.

For five years, Eric and I had stayed close to home for vacations, adjusting to a change in salary for Eric as well as keeping up with all of Jonathan's swim meets and such. Aside from a few short cruises, our trips had been local. On the Australia trip, I began to think again about traveling. The chance to see all those spectacular sights was so incredible.

The years were moving on, and my internal clock of retinal degeneration was still ticking. How much more time did I have to see all those spots on my bucket list? Perhaps now that my income had increased with my full-time hours, it was time to think about travel once again.

Miracle Worker

My vision was blurry. It was hard to focus. I sat in my office, staring at the computer, trying to wade my way through the sea of emails. It wasn't working well.

The double vision had been getting worse for a while now. I kept thinking I was just tired or stressed, and soon, my vision would clear up. In my gut, I knew better. The headaches were worsening, and I was exhausted from eye strain at the end of the day.

Finally, I made an appointment with my optometrist, Dr. Woodard. We went through the normal battery of tests. Thankfully, my overall visual acuity had not really changed.

The issue was the discrepancy in vision between the eyes. The disease had always been more pronounced in my left eye, causing the visual field loss to be more intense, and the visual acuity more limited. Since the right eye was less affected, the difference between the eyes was causing double vision. Dr. Woodard did not have an easy answer for the problem.

In my reading, I had learned the importance of seeing a low vision specialist when dealing with retinal degenerative diseases. Low vision specialists were experts at adjusting glasses and adding other visual aids to help maximize remaining vision. I brought the idea up to Dr. Woodard.

He considered the idea for a few moments and agreed. Going to a resource in his office, he identified two specialists within a reasonable distance from our home. I knew nothing about either, but looking at the information, I decided a female physician might be appealing.

That's how I came to know Dr. Whitaker. Of course, I had selected her off a simple paper list with a black and white photo, but God had planned for her consult long before I ever even considered the need for a low vision specialist. Without a doubt, Dr. Whitaker was a gift from God sent straight to me.

On the day of the appointment, Eric and I arrived at the eye clinic a bit early, certain there would be paperwork to complete. Walking through the double doors of the front entrance took me back in time. Fifteen years earlier, I had stepped through those same doors, wondering what this second opinion might yield. Later that day, I had walked back through those double doors burdened with the heavy weight of profound loss.

Oh, how much had changed in my life since that fateful day. I had learned to cope with what I was certain I could never do, making a life for myself, mastering a "new normal." I had not done it on my own merits or by some gritty tenacity. No, I had learned to walk this challenging road led by the Hand of God's grace.

Now here I was again in the same place, concerned about a new problem, unsure if this was the beginning of a more rapid deterioration of my vision. I had done so well for so long, far better than I ever thought possible on that day in 1993. Was this the beginning of further decline? The thought tugged at my heart. I forced those thoughts away. "Just see what the doctor says. Just wait and see."

The optical assistant called me into the exam room to measure my visual acuity and obtain my history. I did well on the eye chart which restored some of my waning confidence.

Before long, the doctor entered the room. She was a beautiful young woman with striking features and long blonde hair cascading down the back of her white lab coat. Her radiant smile projected warmth, her charming manner immediately putting me at ease. Shaking my hand in introduction, she crossed the tiny room and shook Eric's hand as well.

Seated in a rolling chair across from me, she queried me on what brought me to see her. As I shared my story, she prompted me with more questions, periodically turning to the computer to review some piece of information. She was very thorough, asking detailed questions about both my history and activities of daily living.

"It's just that lately things have been getting so much harder. I am having a really hard time seeing things on the computer. It's harder to see things across the room or even at a distance. It feels like I'm seeing double. I don't know if my eyes are just getting worse, but it's really getting tough."

Dr. Whitaker looked up, made eye contact and nodded. Matter-of-factly, she blurted out, "I can fix that."

I stared at her in amazement. Did I hear her correctly? "You can?"

"Oh yes. I can fix that with a prism. We can solve the double vision with a prism."

Explaining more about the prism, she described how this addition to my eyeglass lens would pull my eyes back to working together. Since my left eye had lost more visual function, it tended to wander slightly. This took it out of alignment with the right eye, leading to double vision. The prism would compensate for this disparity and help me see more clearly.

Pulling out a series of lenses, she held them in front of my eyes. Directing me to look at two large circles on the wall, she instructed me to tell her when I saw just one circle. As she tried different lenses, I stared at the two circles until suddenly, as if by magic, the two circles became one. We had found the right prism.

She then made me an unusual set of glasses that held these new lenses, a test pair that allowed me to walk around the hallways to see if I could tell a difference. I probably looked like "The

CHAPTER 15
Rough Places Smooth

Terminator" with those weird looking glasses on, but the lenses worked like a charm. I could see clearly. No double vision.

I could hardly believe that such a fix was possible. Writing up a very detailed prescription for new glasses, she instructed me to return in four months so we could see how things were working. Obviously, I could return sooner if I needed anything.

Before leaving, I spent time with her assistant reviewing some of the visual aid technology available for the computer. I was so surprised to see how helpful some of the tools could be. Armed with several handouts on various technology options, we made a plan to review these at home and discuss further options at the next appointment.

I walked out of the office full of joy. Earlier that morning, I was convinced that there would be no help for me. Two hours later, my world had been turned upside down, in a good way. There was hope, hope that I could continue working, hope that I could still travel and enjoy the sights of life. Dr. Whitaker was not simply a low vision specialist. She was a miracle worker.

Looking back, that was a pivotal moment in this long journey. I had entered that office discouraged and fearful. I had left it full of hope.

The wonderful thing was that the hope was not in vain. The prism worked. I could see normally, or at least as normally as I would ever be able to see. I could use the computer more easily and see things well at a distance. My eye strain lessened, and the stress headaches went away.

The prism made the lenses in my glasses quite thick and odd looking, making my eyes appear a bit larger than normal, but I shrugged and ignored the oddities. At least I could see clearly, and that was all that really mattered.

Returning every four to six months, Dr. Whitaker made frequent adjustments to the prism, each tweak allowing me to compensate for my declining vision. These adjustments necessitated one or two new sets of glasses per year. My vision insurance didn't quite cover all that, but we made it work. I bought two pairs of frames and alternated changing out the lenses as necessary.

The visual aids for the computer were another huge help. I bought a program for both my home and office computers. Finding the cursor on the screen when typing a document had become quite challenging. This computer software marked the cursor with a large red arrow and circle. The program had a variety of other options, but that one feature was worth every penny, saving both time and eye strain.

I cannot imagine what life would have been like without Dr. Whitaker. She made me functional, enabling me to get the most out of the vision I had left. Over time, we became friends. Being both health care professionals, we had a lot in common. I looked forward to seeing her at each visit. My faith in her amazing abilities was well placed. She really has been my miracle worker.

Dishes

I stepped off the elevator, headed for my office. Reaching my doorway, I stopped short and stared, a puzzled frown crossing my face. There was a Food Lion plastic grocery bag hanging from the handle of my office door. Racking my brain for a clue to the contents of the parcel, I wondered aloud, "What on earth is this?"

Lifting the package, I was even more perplexed by its weight. Something heavy was inside. "What in the world?"

Opening the door to my tiny office, I deposited the hefty parcel on my desk. Curiosity peaked, I rifled through the bag, searching for a note from the sender. Nothing, no note of any kind. All I could feel was something hard wrapped in thick canvas paper. "What is this? Who has sent this?"

Dumping the contents of the bag onto my desk, I noted that it was not just one package, but rather a series of smaller bundles wrapped securely in heavy packing paper. Searching my memory for any hint of what this little package was all about, I plucked one of the bundles from the pile and began unwrapping it. Inside the

Rough Places Smooth

paper was a plate, a clear glass plate. I held it in both hands, staring at it hard, willing it to tell me its story. It was just a plain glass plate, nothing special, nothing unique. "What is this? Who sent this?"

Confused, I grabbed another bundle, unwrapping it carefully. Another plate. The same kind of plate. I grasped another bundle. Another plate.

Moving quickly now, I reached for another package, this one a different size and shape from the others. A cup and saucer, clear glass just like the plates. "Dishes? What in the world? Who is sending me dishes?"

And then, I remembered. Like a flash, the memory popped into my head. I fell into my chair in a fit of laughter, a good belly laugh racking my entire frame.

It felt good to laugh. I had not been doing much of that lately.

In fact, the last few weeks had been tough. I had recently returned from my annual eye exam at NIH. Given the lack of treatment options, this annual battery of tests often dredged up my typically well concealed anguish. I had known for a long time that I was going blind, yet despite the years, the pain of that loss was never fully extinguished.

I had learned to set my grief aside, to put it in a box on the shelf of my mind, and go on with life. Still, every year, as the autumn leaves showcased their splendor, I was forced to face the fact that the day would come when I would no longer bear witness to that annual kaleidoscope of color. It should have been easier to accept by now, but it wasn't.

Once again, I had sat in that cold exam chair waiting for the doctor's report. My stomach tightened at the mere tone of her voice. I knew instantly. The news was not good. More changes. My eyes were getting worse.

This was nothing new. It had happened before, but this time, my response was different. Over the years as my eye disease progressed, there had been lots of sad times, weeks of feeling blue, sometimes a period of depression. Gradually, with time and support, the gloom would lift, and life would go on.

This time was different. This time, I was mad.

I did not recognize it at first. I tried to go on with life, perform my day-to-day tasks, get over myself. However, the level of frustration wouldn't go away. It kept bubbling up, blasting out even when I tried to hold it in.

One Saturday morning, I went outside to do some yard work. As I came around the corner, I glanced at the brick wall in the carport. In my mind, something clicked, and I stopped in my tracks. I felt paralyzed, rooted in place, unable to tear my eyes away from that tan brick wall.

A cascade of thoughts whirled around in my head. "This isn't fair. I am sick of this. I don't want this to get worse. Why does this have to happen?"

With my eyes locked on those bricks, I felt an almost irresistible urge to hurl something hard against the wall. I wanted to throw something, to hear it crash, to watch it shatter.

Out of nowhere, the thought came suddenly. "Dishes! I want to throw some dishes!"

That fueled my fantasy. My mind envisioned china plates in my hand, lifting them from a pile, holding them up, hurling them furiously against that hard brick wall.

I could see the plate hit the wall, the impact sending shards of glass flying everywhere. I fantasized about the ear-splitting crash as the dish slapped against the wall, hundreds of tiny pieces falling like rain drops to the concrete floor.

I stood there for a long time, pondering that scene in my mind, thinking that somehow this would make me feel better. "What is wrong with me? Why am I thinking this?"

I shook my head in bewilderment, but still, I did not move. My mind kept replaying the images. I actually contemplated going through with the idea. I could just step into the kitchen, open the cabinet, grab a plate, and let it rip.

CHAPTER 15
Rough Places Smooth

But then, reason took hold. No way! I couldn't break one of my dishes. All the same, I continued to stand there, visualizing that scene in my mind. It would feel so good just to throw that plate. I was furious. Tears of hot anger flooded my eyes. It was a moment of pure rage.

I'm not quite sure how long I stood there, but finally, I shook my head in disgust, muttering, "Well, this is not doing anybody any good." Shrugging my shoulders, I went back into the house and busied myself with household duties.

For the next couple of days, I replayed that moment in my head. "What was this all about? Why did I keep thinking about throwing those dishes?"

By this point in my journey, I knew the warning signs. Obviously, I was not doing well. It was time to talk this out.

Recognizing my need for counseling, I went to see my friend Bob as I had done so many times before. Sharing my story, he responded with a question. "What did it feel like when you looked at that brick wall?"

"I was angry. But I shouldn't be angry. That's not right. I feel guilty about it."

Bob looked me squarely in the eye and asked quietly, "Anita, why do you think that you shouldn't be angry?"

I thought for a long moment, "It's just not right. If God has put me in this place, I should accept it and not be angry. I just need to deal with it."

Bob held my gaze, but said nothing. After a long moment, I blurted out, "It's not OK to be angry. I can't be angry with God."

Then, Bob said something that I will never forget. "Why isn't it OK for you to be angry? Didn't Jesus get angry? He turned over the tables in the temple in a fit of rage. If it was OK for him to be mad, why can't you be?"

You could have heard a pin drop in that room. I stared at him for a long time. "I don't know. I've never thought about it that way."

A long pause transpired. "I'm going to have to think about this."

Rough Places Smooth

At work the next day, I couldn't get my mind off the matter. Needing the insights of an old friend, I caught up with Alisa, one of my faithful prayer warriors. Not only was she a great listener, but somehow, she always knew just the right thing to say.

I told Alisa the story. She took it all in, listening intently. As I finished my tale, I noted a little smile playing on her lips. With a hint of embarrassment, she murmured, "I'm sorry. I am thinking about you throwing dishes."

I met her eyes, watching her mouth stretch wider into a sheepish grin, hearing a little chuckle emerging from deep inside her frame. Observing this transformation of my friend's beautiful face, a little smile formed on my lips. Then suddenly, in perfect unison, we burst out laughing. Somehow, it all seemed a bit comical.

Through our girlish giggles, we began to make jokes. Alisa blurted out, "They should make a place where people can go and throw plates against the wall."

I laughed even harder. Then she said, "You could throw the plates and you wouldn't have to clean up the mess."

Another fit of laughter. "It's a new business concept. People would pay for this!" More spasms of laughter.

The laughter went on for a while. Gradually, our giggles subsided, and we sat staring at each other in silence, neither of us knowing what else to say.

Our lunch break was over, and she needed to leave. Gathering up her lunch trash, her kind eyes found mine. "I don't know if I helped?"

My smile answered her question, but I added words too. "Yes, you did. It felt good to laugh. I'll be OK."

With a wink and a little chuckle, Alisa offered, "Yeah, you will. I'll keep praying, and if we need to, we can always throw some dishes!"

I watched her go, feeling so much better after telling her my crazy story. The laughter had felt good. It was a release, like a valve being opened to blow off hot steam.

CHAPTER 15
Rough Places Smooth

A week had passed since that fit of laughter. Now, here I was sitting in my little office, looking at a pile of dishes. They had stickers on them from Goodwill. I knew exactly who had left me this gift. I could not help chuckling all over again. "What a friend. What a fine Christian friend!"

Suddenly, I was not so angry anymore.

By the way, I never did throw those dishes, but I still have them, just in case!

Rough Places Smooth

Several weeks had passed since my fit of laughter over the dishes. While my conversations with Bob and Alisa had certainly helped, I still found myself struggling. The anger had receded, but the sadness had not.

On a crisp October evening, I was standing at my kitchen sink doing the dishes as I stared out my window at a beautiful autumn sunset. At the edge of my yard, the old pine tree stood tall and proud, perfectly framed by a glowing skyline covered in shimmering strands of pink, orange and gold. Gazing at that glorious sunset, I thought to myself, "One of these days I won't be able to see this anymore." In that moment, I thought that my heart would break. Silently, I began to pray.

"Lord, I just can't do this anymore. I can't go on this way. I just can't stay in this pit any longer. I'm not strong enough, and I can't stand this anymore. Lord, I just have these hollow places inside of me that I can't fill up. Lord, you are going to have to fill up these hollow places because I can't do this anymore."

Trying to fight the tears that flooded my eyes, I finished the dishes. My husband and son were watching TV there in the kitchen, so I went back to my bedroom to find a quiet spot.

Earlier in the day, I had talked with my good friend Mary about how I was feeling. We talked about the anguish I could not seem to overcome. I described the overwhelming sense of sadness that I could not shake off. Mary listened intently to my concerns as she always does. She let my torrent of words and emotions wash over her as she considered what to say.

I had learned to trust her guidance and pay attention to her intuitive responses. The best of friends for over 17 years at that point, we had helped each other work through many crises along the way. We often remarked about how sometimes God chose to speak through our conversations. Both of us could recall times of trial or sorrow when we truly felt we received a divine message from something that was said in our heart-to-heart talks. I had learned to trust Mary's counsel as she had learned to trust mine.

I watched her closely as she considered her words. Sitting back in her chair, Mary looked at me and let out a long sigh. "Anita, I don't know. I know it's hard. Maybe, I guess. Maybe you need to read the book of Job."

With a shrug of my shoulders, I murmured, "Yeah, maybe so."

We shared a little smile as we continued our discussion. Long after Mary left my office, her reference to the Book of Job kept resurfacing in the jumbled mess that claimed my brain that afternoon.

As I sat down in my chair in the bedroom, Mary's words came to mind once more. I replayed our conversation, digesting her comments yet again. It had helped to talk things out with her, but the venting session had not absorbed my unrelenting anguish.

Suddenly, a rush of emotion overwhelmed me. I felt so alone, so miserable, so desperate. Tears welled in my eyes as I leaned my head back against the chair. "What am I going to do? I can't go on this way." Again, in my mind, I heard Mary say, "Maybe you need to read the book of Job."

"Why did she say that?" I shrugged my shoulders. "Well, maybe that would help."

Reaching for the basket beside my chair, I pulled out my Bible, intent on finding the Book of Job. As I unzipped my black cover, the Bible seemed to fall open in my hands. I paused to look down as I wondered where to locate the book of Job in the Old Testament.

CHAPTER 15
Rough Places Smooth

Staring back at me was a page from the book of Isaiah. Now, at the time, I had not read much of Isaiah. Looking down at the page, I was surprised to see that I had underlined several lines on the page. I was curious, because I did not recall ever being in this part of Isaiah before.

Focusing on the underlined verse, I began to read. The highlighted passage was Isaiah 42:16, and here is what it said:

"I will lead the blind by ways they have not known, along unfamiliar paths I will guide them; I will turn the darkness into light before them, and make the rough places smooth" (Isaiah 42:16a *NIV*).

I caught my breath in surprise. I was quite simply stunned. I sat there trembling, absolutely awestruck. Not five minutes earlier, I had stood at my kitchen window crying out to God, lamenting about the hollow places in my heart. Now, here I was, five minutes later, staring at a passage promising how God will make the rough places smooth.

In that moment, I knew beyond a shadow of a doubt, that God was speaking directly to me. He was using that passage to tell me that He would lead me on this journey through blindness, that He would be my Guide, that He would lead me through the darkness into the light.

Hands clasped tightly on the Bible in my lap, images flashed like lightning through my mind, revealing all the painful struggles we had endured since my devastating diagnosis. As I considered each of those very difficult challenges, I realized with absolute clarity that God had taken each of those hard things, those rough places, and made them smooth. Somehow, He had worked out all those hard things. He had solved all those problems that we thought were unsolvable. God had brought people to help us, supplying rides to everywhere we needed to go. He had worked it all out. He had orchestrated our circumstances in ways we could never have imagined in the beginning.

Rough Places Smooth

I saw it all so clearly. Sitting there with my Bible open in my hands, I was amazed at God's provision, blown away by His goodness to us. I felt God's presence with me, enveloping me in a blanket of love. There was no doubt, no fear. God was with me.

In that moment, I faced the reality of impending blindness. I thought to myself, "One day, I may lose all my vision, and if that happens, it will be OK. Because God will be with me. He will walk this hard road with me. He will supply all our needs. He will make the rough places smooth."

Staring out my bedroom window at the gathering dusk, I felt this unbelievable sense of peace envelop me. It was, in that moment, that I finally accepted the possibility that I may go completely blind someday. Yet, to my great surprise, the paralyzing fear and angst were gone. God's presence was in that room.

God had shown up with a divine message. He wanted me to see that His grace had been sufficient to get me through all the hurdles of the past. He wanted me to have faith that He would lead me through whatever lies ahead. I need not worry or fear. God will lead me. He will guide me. He will turn my darkness into light, and He will make my rough places smooth.

That was the turning point in my journey. Of all the stories I have shared, of all the God-moments I have witnessed, this was the most powerful moment of my life. I know with absolute certainty that God was in that room with me, and He was sending a clear message. That message changed the course of my journey.

Certainly, there have been difficult days since that October evening, but something changed inside me that night. God instilled a hope in me that has not been washed away by the waters of further adversity. Yes, there has been sadness. Certainly, there has been pain. Yet somehow, deep inside me, there is a certainty that it will all work out somehow. For if God loves me enough to send me such a direct message, if He cares that much about my anguish, then surely, somehow, some way, He will work out the challenges of my future. God can, and He will, make the rough places smooth.

CHAPTER 15
Rough Places Smooth

Cap And Gown

On a warm evening in June 2009, I took my seat on the bleachers overlooking the high school football field. In the distance, a sea of red caps and gowns billowed in the evening breeze. The graduates were lining up, and Jonathan was among them.

My eyes grew moist as I wondered just how we had gotten to this point. Where had the time gone? Just yesterday, I was chasing that toddler around the backyard, and now I was watching my tall, handsome son prepare to walk across the stage and receive his high school diploma.

From the time Jonathan had earned his driver's license, time seemed to shift into high gear. His junior year had been busy keeping up with his academic schedule while actively participating in both year-round and high school swim teams. There were weekly high school meets, and several year-round swim meets per month. Jonathan had made it to the high school state swimming championships for each of his four years of high school. Needless to say, it had been busy, but we loved every minute of cheering him on.

Jonathan had continued life guarding both in the summer and throughout the school year, adding in the hospital volunteer work too. He was actively involved in our church youth group, participating in community service and mission trips.

The previous summer, Jonathan and I had taken some road trips scoping out colleges. Looking primarily in North Carolina, we had narrowed down the choices for his college applications. He was interested in collegiate swimming, but wasn't quite fast enough for the big schools.

I thought we had the list paired down to four schools, but the list changed after our family vacation. Traveling up to see some friends in Ohio, we decided to take a route down through Virginia on our way home. All this looking at colleges made me nostalgic for my days at JMU. Both Eric and I had graduated from James Madison

University in Harrisonburg, Virginia. Just for fun, we decided to stop and show Jonathan our old stomping ground. Without any serious intentions, we did stop by the Admissions department to ask about a tour. Listening to their general overview of the school, Jonathan seemed bored and uninterested. When the talk was over, Jonathan asked, "Do we really need the tour? Can't you guys just take me around?"

Eric and I looked at each other and smiled. Well, of course we could, and so we set off on a tour of our old haunts. Jonathan seemed to enjoy hearing our college tales, but was not particularly excited.

As his senior year got rolling, it was time to start the application process. I asked him to rank the list of where he wanted to apply. To my shock, JMU was tops on the list. I was dumbfounded. Apparently, he was more interested than we had thought.

So much for keeping the college costs down. Our jaunt down memory lane was going to mean out-of-state tuition. If he could get in, that is.

But he did get in. When the letter came with the James Madison University seal in the upper left-hand corner, there was great joy in our house. He was going to be a "JMU Duke!"

His senior year had flown by. Much to my chagrin, there had been a battle with a bad case of "senioritis" in the Spring, but on that warm summer evening, all that was behind us.

All four grandparents were seated beside Eric and me, each full to the brim with joy at this landmark event. Tami was seated with the faculty on the stage, no doubt experiencing a mix of joy and relief. As his other mother, she had invested lots of time and energy into Jonathan's success, particularly during high school. She had gone above and beyond simple rides to school, even hauling him to early morning tutoring when he was struggling with math. Arriving at school in the early morning darkness, she had laughed and told him, "You know I love you to get here this early! You know how you can pay me back? Pass this class!" He had, and now, like me, Tami was enjoying the fruits of her labor.

CHAPTER 15
Rough Places Smooth

I tried to keep it together, but the tears were hard to hold back. I vacillated between jumping for joy and bawling my eyes out.

As I heard Jonathan's name called, watched him walk across the stage to claim that scroll of paper, my heart thumped with pride and joy. I gave thanks to God again and again.

"Lord, I thought I would never see this day. All those years ago, I thought my eyes would never make it this far. I prayed that you would let me see him walk across the stage and Lord, you have done it. O Lord, how You have blessed me. O Lord, thank You, thank You, thank You!"

I know other mothers were struggling in that stadium, the thought of letting go heavy on their minds. For me, there was a little of that, but mostly, I just felt exceedingly grateful. God had answered a prayer I had first lifted on a gorgeous November day, my recent eye disease diagnosis weighing heavily on my heart. God had heard my prayer, and now, 16 years later, He had answered with a resounding "Yes!" Dressed in that bright red cap and gown, I had been able to watch my precious son step across that stage and graduate from high school.

Grand Adventure

I heard the noon bells chime, my mouth stretching into a gleeful grin. Turning to my parents walking beside me, I pointed to the sky. "Look, it's Big Ben! And there's Parliament!" The smiles that spread over their upturned faces were priceless.

Just five days following high school graduation, Jonathan stood on the streets of London, eyes searching the city skyline. No senior beach week for him, Europe instead. However, lest you think him more spoiled than he is, the real reason for the trip was to celebrate my parent's 50th wedding anniversary. That the trip coincided with Jonathan's graduation was simply icing on the cake.

Mom and Dad had dreamed of a European visit my whole life. A history major, this trip had been on Dad's bucket list forever. The three of us had traveled all over the world courtesy of the US Army, but never Europe. With every duty request form, Dad had ranked Germany first on the list, but the Army in its infinite wisdom had sent us everywhere else.

As the time drew near for the 50th Anniversary, I made my dad a deal. If he would buy, I would plan. And plan the trip, I did. From London to Paris and then Munich, we saw it all. Staying in the three major cities, we took day trips to all manner of sites, touring battlefields and monuments, museums and castles. I think Dad's favorite part was the first-class train ride through the Chunnel, connecting London to Paris. Mom was fascinated with the Changing of the Guard at Buckingham Palace.

We were humbled by Normandy and the Somme, impressed by the Eiffel Tower. Treated to a private tour by a cousin who is a historian, we roamed the cobblestone streets of Munich.

The best part was being together, our little tight-knit family of five. We smiled and laughed and loved every minute of it.

Like a vivid dream, I can still recall every minute of that amazing trip. The memories are priceless. We still tell the stories, still smile about the "Aha" moments. It truly was our Grand Adventure!

Heart-To-Heart Talk

We sat in sand chairs watching the tide roll in. It was a blistering August day, the sun beating down on our sun-screened shoulders. We had come to the beach, just the two of us, Jonathan and his mom.

It was somewhat of a last hoorah, a celebration of his entrance into college in a few weeks, one last time to have him all to myself before he left me for this next season of his life. While the expressed purpose of the trip was to have some final fun hours together, I hoped I could use the time to share some motherly wisdom about his next big step.

CHAPTER 15
Rough Places Smooth

But there was also another reason for this trip that had weighed heavily on my mind throughout that summer. It was time to talk to my son about the threat of Retinitis Pigmentosa.

From the moment of my diagnosis, I had worried about the possibility that Jonathan might have inherited this eye disease from me. When pressed, the doctors had all reassured me that the risk was low, yet they would never say the risk was null. The physicians at NIH had offered to test Jonathan when he was a little boy, but Eric and I had decided to forego such testing.

Even if Jonathan had inherited RP, the reality was that with no surefire treatment options available, there was nothing we could do about it anyway. While Vitamin A therapy was an option to slow disease progression, it was not advisable to take this supplement in childhood.

Would I have wanted to know that I had this disease when I was growing up? Would I have wanted to carry that burden in my teenage years, particularly if there were no obvious symptoms? I had asked myself those questions, and the answer had come back a resounding "No!"

And so we had never discussed the possibility with Jonathan, deciding to wait until he was old enough to decide it for himself. Now, he was 18, and it was time for that discussion.

The waves tumbled and crashed against the sandy shore as I brought up this heavy subject with my beloved son. I gave it to him straight, sharing the information the doctors had shared with me. Finishing my remarks, I ended with, "J, it's up to you. If you want to be tested, we can set that up, but the decision is yours to make."

Jonathan had been quiet as I explained the information, staring out to the horizon, but actively listening the whole time. We settled into silence together as we stared out to sea.

After a few minutes, he said quietly, "I don't think I want to know, Mom. If I have it, then I'll deal with it later, but right now, I just don't want to know."

He went on to say that he had discussed the possibility of having RP with his best friend David. He and David had grown up together, introduced as babies in daycare and remaining buddies throughout their childhood and adolescence. David knew me well and understood the effects of this disease. Apparently, their discussions about these issues had led Jonathan to the conclusion that he would rather live his life fully as if he was unaffected by the disease. If later he developed symptoms, he would deal with it as I had. It was better not to know.

I couldn't blame him. That would have been the choice I would have made. Had I known I had RP in my teenage years, I would never have chosen a nursing career. From this vantage point, I knew what a terrible loss that would have been. Nursing had been my passion, and my career had been exceptional despite the disease. No, I wouldn't have wanted to know either.

It was a good heart-to-heart talk. I was glad we had brought the subject out into the open. It enabled me to disclose my concerns for my future, allowing us to discuss my visual decline more fully than we ever had before. He listened intently, making a few reassuring comments, and then he offered the phrase he had imparted so many times before, "It'll be OK, Mom. It'll work itself out."

I had come to the beach to share some wisdom with my college-bound son, and now, my grown-up son was imparting some words of wisdom to me.

CHAPTER 15
Rough Places Smooth

Part 6
Walking By Faith

JANUARY 2010 – DECEMBER 2021

Let us hold tightly without wavering to the hope we affirm,
for God can be trusted to keep his promise.

—Hebrews 10:23 *NLT*

Part 6
Walking By Faith

CHAPTER 16
A New Guide

Unbidden Question

It had been a routine visit with Dr. Whitaker, just another sizzling August day in the boiling hot summer of 2010. I sat quietly waiting in the exam chair, listening as she pounded away on her computer keys from across the tiny room. Our discussion had covered the typical questions, "What are you struggling with at the moment? Have you noticed any changes?" Responding to my answers, Dr. Whitaker had played with the prism in my glasses, making a slight adjustment. Nothing new really. We had done all this countless times before.

I don't know what made me think about the subject as I sat there waiting. Curiosity, I guess. Perhaps it was something I had read about that triggered the thought. I'm not sure, but the topic of orientation and mobility training appeared in my mind.

At the "Visions" conferences I had attended years ago, I had learned that starting mobility training early was important. The speakers had cautioned not to wait until it was mandated before exploring the techniques. Early adoption would make the training easier.

I had learned that mobility training assisted the visually impaired to navigate their surroundings and perform activities of daily living as independently as possible. Trained therapists employ a variety of techniques to support safe movement. Effective use of low vision aids to simplify routine tasks is also part of this training. The occupational therapist at the eye clinic had recommended a few of these aids, and I had even found the tactile dots helpful in highlighting the keys on my microwave screen.

The early adoption policy advocated by those long-ago speakers had made sense to me. As a nurse, I knew the value of early preparation so that when a tool or technique became a necessity, it was not a crisis, but rather, a smooth transition.

CHAPTER 16
A New Guide

I didn't really need any of that stuff yet, but sitting there in that exam chair, an unbidden question formed in my brain, a question I had not intended to ask. "So when do you think I need to consider getting mobility training? I mean when is something like that helpful?"

Her answer caught me off guard. Turning to look at me squarely in the eyes, she replied, "Now." Her tone was determined, very matter-of-fact. "You might want to consider looking into that now."

"Now?"

She nodded and forged ahead, offering more detail about the training process. "I think it's a good idea to get started on this now."

I looked at her quizzically, thinking to myself, "Do I really need this now? Surely not."

Handing me a business card, she instructed, "Give them a call and talk to them about it. I'll put a consult in for you."

Dr. Whitaker was calm, as if it was the most common thing in the world. I was not so calm. Without much comment, I exited her office, wondering just what in the world had I gotten myself into.

Coming Of Age

On an October afternoon in 2010, I received a call from Liz. "I have a question for you. What are you doing the last week of April?"

"April? I have no idea!"

"Do you think you could take some time off and hang out with your mother-in-law?"

I chuckled. "Well, sure. What'd you have in mind?"

"Could you manage Paris? I want to take Elizabeth to Paris for her graduation, and I want you to come with us!"

My heart nearly leapt out of my chest. "Really? Paris? A girls' trip? I'm in!"

A picture of my precious Elizabeth popped into my head, my girl, all grown up, a senior in high school. Where had the time gone? Just yesterday, she was smiling at me from her baby carrier, and now, she was a beautiful brunette with soft brown eyes and long straight hair that flowed well past her shoulders. Her gentle heart was reflected in the warmth of her bright smile. Gone were the days of American Girl dolls and Madeleine stories. Now, we were shopping for sweaters and earrings, and talking of prom dresses and college applications. My girl was growing up fast. She was coming of age.

"Oh, Liz! A girls' trip! Just the three of us! Paris? I can't wait!"

Just An Assessment

Upon returning from my August exam with Dr. Whitaker, I deposited the business card for the mobility training services on the kitchen counter and proceeded to ignore it. Still, the conversation kept replaying in my mind. I didn't think it was time for this yet. Maybe I could just put it off for a while, until later, when I really needed it.

But her words wouldn't go away. Finally, I made the mistake of asking Eric his thoughts on the matter. I had told him about the recommendation on the way home from the eye appointment, but he had not commented at the time, following his usual preference to think before speaking.

"I haven't done anything about the mobility training, but I don't really think I need that yet. Do you?"

His answer stunned me. "Yeah, I do. I think it's time."

"You do?"

"Yeah, I do. You are missing more these days. You're gonna get hurt."

I frowned, but didn't comment. The stubborn side of me was annoyed, thinking, "I'm not that bad yet. I don't need this yet."

More perplexed than ever, I stepped up my prayers. "Lord, am I really supposed to do this? Do I really need this now?" Despite my repeated prayers, no billboard answers appeared. Neither did I receive any peace on the matter.

CHAPTER 16
A New Guide

Mary had listened to the report of my eye appointment, allowing me to share my angst, but wisely remained neutral. "I guess it wouldn't hurt to call and talk to them," her tone supportive without pushing. Tami's reaction was much the same.

Finally, after a few more weeks of procrastination, I relented. I would call and get some information. No commitments. "I'll just check into it."

I had finally made the call, and somehow ended up with an appointment for a home assessment and evaluation. "It's just an assessment. Let's just see what he says."

The orientation and mobility coach arrived at my house on a sunny October afternoon. He was a kind, gentle man who approached this difficult topic with a great deal of care and concern. His approach calmed my frayed nerves, and Eric and I spent a long time answering questions about my lifestyle, and my activities of daily living. He reviewed a variety of mobility techniques, much of which we had already figured out on our own. He was pleased to learn how we had mastered walking in tandem together as well as our strategies for negotiating dark environments. He was impressed with how easily I functioned within my home and was glad I had chosen to use the tactile dots in key places. He made further helpful suggestions, and I promised to explore those. I was hoping that was the end of it, but it was not. "So I'd like to get you measured for your cane, and I'll get that ordered. It has to be the right height for you to use it effectively."

I swallowed hard and watched as he took the measurements. With a promise to call when he received the cane, he departed. Again, I thought, "What in the world have I gotten myself into?"

Tap Lessons

About two weeks later, the coach returned, white cane in hand. Out to the driveway, we went. He demonstrated the proper technique of the various skills and had me repeat each skill several times. Over and over, we practiced.

Surprised, I found the technique much harder to master than I would have thought. It looks like a simple "tap, tap, tap," but there is much more to it than that. The back-and-forth arm motion of tapping must be aligned with each footstep. The goal is to keep the cane out ahead of you while making wide sweeps from one side to the other. Like an antenna, the trick is to use the cane to sense upcoming obstacles so they can be avoided. It's an early warning system.

It was hard to get the rhythm, and I was not quite prepared for the difficulty of the skill, let alone the emotional baggage that came with it. My trainer was quite patient, instructing me to practice for a week or two, and he would return for more training.

The Cane

I stared long and hard, my eyes boring holes into the white aluminum cylinder. Leaning in the corner was a long metal rod adorned with a golf club handle, its four sections held together by a black bungee cord running the inside length of its hollow core. I scowled at it, wishing hard that I could snap my fingers, and it would disappear. But it wasn't going anywhere. It seemed that this white cane was here to stay.

It was just a simple piece of metal, but the visceral reaction it created within me was far from simple. The cane had a voice, and the voice was screaming, "BLIND!"

Inside my head, I was screaming back. "Stop! Go away!"

It can't be time for this, can it? Not me, not yet.

CHAPTER 16
A New Guide

Practice Makes Perfect

Although I knew I should practice, I kept avoiding it. As the days grew closer to my coach's return, I finally pulled the cane off the shelf where it had lain untouched.

It was a chilly early November evening, when I headed out to the driveway. I had grabbed the cane without a word to Eric and grudgingly stomped out the back door. It was quite dark which was actually not too bad of a test for the concept.

"Tap, tap, tap," up and down the driveway I went, trying to remember the coach's instructions, while attempting to silence my incessant grumble. "I don't need this. This is for later. I don't want to do this!"

Suddenly, out of the darkness, came a voice. "Hey Anita!"

Startled, thinking I was all alone out here in the dark, I jumped and turned around quickly, white cane swinging around with me. Paused at the edge of my driveway was my neighbor Jerry seated on his bicycle. Apparently, he had decided to take a spin around the neighborhood after dinner.

"Oh Anita, it's Jerry. I'm sorry. I didn't mean to startle you!" Pausing, he pointed toward the cane, "Anita, I didn't realize that you needed that."

I looked down at the cane and back up to his face. I tried to speak. The words wouldn't come, but the tears did, gushing out like someone turned on the faucet.

"Anita, I didn't mean to upset you. I'm sorry."

Trying to squelch the tears and find my voice, I muttered, "It's OK. It's not your fault. It's just that I'm learning to use this and I don't want to." My voice trailed off, but after a moment, I pulled myself together and explained more. We talked on for a bit before he took his leave, promising to pray for me and offering to help in any way he could.

I watched him ride off, upset and embarrassed at my outburst. The tears had come so quickly, signaling just how difficult this process was for me, perhaps even more than I had already realized.

I looked down at that white cane in my hand, and I saw defeat. That cane was a very visible reminder of what I did not want to happen. So long ago, I had laid down those car keys and learned to manage life without them, but I had held my ground on everything else. I had refused to give into disability. I was determined to overcome my limitations. I was determined to keep going, to be as capable and dependable as anyone else, to live a normal life, or at least, as normal as it could be.

I had succeeded. My compensation strategies worked. By moving my eyes rapidly back-and-forth, I could scan a scene and understand what was there. I became so adept at compensating for my visual field deficits that my disease was invisible to most people. Even those who knew about my vision loss forgot about it most of the time.

That white cane would not be invisible. The cane was a blaring announcement that I needed help, and that hurt my pride. It was announcing to the world that I was going blind, but worst of all, it was announcing it to me.

For so long, the disease had been like a train whistle in the distance. I could hear the train coming, but it was still a long way off. I could keep walking the rail without interruption, continue the difficult balancing act without risk. I still had time. I could still escape the threat of that slow-moving train. But suddenly, warning lights were flashing, alarm bells clanging. That white cane told me the train was coming, its massive locomotive barreling down the tracks, gaining speed, headed straight for me.

I had not forgotten God's promise of Isaiah 42:16. I had accepted that if total blindness comes, it will be OK because God will be with me. If that happens, God will make the rough places smooth.

If that happens. If blindness comes. "If," my focus had been on the "if." That white cane had changed the "if" to "when." This was no longer a possibility, a distant train whistle in the wee hours of the night. The train was coming, moving fast. I could see it, knew I needed to take action, to leap to safety. But I wasn't ready. I just wasn't ready yet.

"Lord, I can't do this. Help me. Make this rough place smooth."

The Pit

Have you ever stood on the edge of a pit and looked down? Consider this for a moment. Visualize a huge crater in the earth spreading out before you. You are standing on the edge, peering down. You search for the bottom of this hole in the earth, but you cannot find it. Although you might be intrigued by the size and depth of the giant hole stretched out before you, you know for sure that you don't want to fall in.

Shortly after my mobility coach left me holding that white cane, I started falling. The peaceful status quo I had maintained for quite some time vanished. Emotions I had avoided for such a long time came bubbling to the surface.

I found myself staring into the pit, a deep, dark pit of self-pity. Not only was I gazing down into it, I was losing my foothold. Slowly, inch by inch, I found myself sliding down into that great abyss.

I was not a stranger to the pit of despair. I had been there before. I knew what it was like to feel like you were flailing in a deep, dark well of emotion. You so want to drag yourself out of this dark place. You want to feel better again. Yet, try as you might, you just can't seem to break free.

My past battles with situational depression following an episode of visual decline had left me sad and even angry. But the emotion I had come to fear was self-pity. That is a dangerous emotion. Nothing good comes from it. It leads you into a pit in which escape is almost impossible.

When I looked at that white cane, I had a sinking feeling, as if I was being sucked down into that giant hole in the earth. I just couldn't wrap my mind around this. The further I fell, the more silent I became, saying little about it to my friends or family. For Anita, silence is never a good sign.

I had finished several sessions of training with my mobility coach. The sessions had gone well. The training was expensive so I was determined to learn what I was being taught, and managed to keep my emotions in check during the instruction. My coach suggested taking a break for a few weeks to allow me time to practice using the cane in a variety of settings. I could call him when I was ready, and he would return for further instruction.

He left, and I laid the cane on the shelf. It lay there untouched and unwanted. Finally, after several weeks, the guilt got to me. Perhaps I could just put it in my pocketbook, and if I needed it, I could pull it out. I even had Tami take me to TJ Maxx to buy a purse large enough to fit the cane inside.

For weeks, I carried that cane around in my purse, but I never pulled it out. It was just there, weighing me down, pulling me further and further down in that deep, dark pit.

The Ultimatum

Eric knew I was struggling. I think he has always known, even though I try to hide it. He seldom says much, but tries to lift my spirits with teasing or some other distraction. He must have been really worried this time, because he planned a trip to a mountain cottage. The thought of going somewhere for our wedding anniversary did lift my spirits. We had a wonderful trip, and that improved my mood through the holidays. The subject of the cane was not mentioned.

January rolled by with no progress on using the cane. It remained safely hidden in the bottom of my purse. I think Eric thought that I would eventually take action. He was waiting on me to do so, but by mid-February, seeing no progress, he decided I needed a push.

The April girls' trip to Paris was steadily drawing closer.

CHAPTER 16
A New Guide

Eric was happy for me to go on the trip, but he was very concerned about me going so far away without him to help me navigate the unfamiliar surroundings. He knew that my mother-in-law and niece would do their best to help me get around without falling or tripping, but no one was as good as he was at helping to guide me.

So one night, he sat me down to have a serious conversation. He told me that he wanted me to go on this trip, but that he was very concerned about me going without him. He said in his no-nonsense tone, "You can't go to Paris without me, unless you start using that cane."

He was very serious, explaining his concerns for my safety and his fears of me getting hurt. "I know it's hard. I know you don't want to use it. But if you want to go to Paris, you better start using that cane."

I guess I could have gotten angry with him. In truth, I appreciated his honesty. I knew I needed to quit skirting the issue and do something about it, but it was just so hard. Every time I looked at the cane, I felt nauseous. It symbolized what I didn't want to be. The disease was getting worse, and my whole being rebelled against that thought. Not yet, please not yet.

It was still my choice whether to use the cane or not, but I could not ignore the fact that Eric had recognized that I needed more help. He understood my limitations better than anyone. He was observing that I was struggling a bit more, missing things that could be hazardous for me. He recognized that it was time. Despite all my reservations, I knew that he was right.

It was time to stop the pity party and get on with it. I had my marching orders. I needed to accept where I was and make the best of it, just like I had done with all the other hard things.

Hesitation

The gauntlet had been thrown down, the challenge made, and yet I still struggled on how to move forward. Just figuring out how to use the cane was daunting enough. There was so much to remember. Mastering the technique was a real challenge. It was much more than just a little tapping.

However, people's reactions were what I feared the most. I dreaded the stares, the questions, the well-meaning comments that felt like knife wounds. I would have to tell the story, explain about the disease, admit that I needed help. Just the thought of it made my stomach clench up in knots.

In a way, it was like going back to the beginning. It reminded me of how I felt when I had to give up driving. That decision had rocked my world. This white cane was rocking it again.

Over the years, I had reclaimed a sense of normalcy, and now, I was losing that status quo. I had no illusions about this step. It would be difficult. I knew that all too well, because I had been here before. My time for procrastination was at its end. It was time to get started.

Trip To Baltimore

As luck would have it, I would be traveling to Baltimore for a nursing conference in early March. Several of my colleagues were going, but Eric was not. Other than the friends who were traveling with me, I would not know anyone there.

It occurred to me that this might be a good opportunity to try out the cane. Other than my colleagues who were all well aware of my eye disease, no one there would know that this was my first experience using the cane. It was like a free trial, no questions asked. I could see how it went, and perhaps that would help me with what to do about using the cane elsewhere.

CHAPTER 16
A New Guide

Mary was going on this trip with me. She and I had discussed my trepidations as well as Eric's ultimatum. When I shared my fledgling plan with her, she was immediately supportive.

Mary was driving as we headed for Baltimore, two other colleagues riding with us. As usual, the conversation flowed easily, but the knot in my stomach grew as I prepared to make my little speech.

I could feel Mary's quiet support as I brought up the subject, sharing the situation, the doctor's recommendations and my plan to try out the cane on this trip. My colleagues were quick to support the idea. Relieved, I took a deep breath to steady my nerves. I just hoped I could do it. "Lord, help me!"

I remember the tremendous anxiety I felt that first time I pulled the white cane out of my pocketbook. When we pulled up to the hotel entrance, I emerged from the vehicle, paused, and released the strap on the cane, allowing the cane to snap into place. The snapping sound rang in my ears, and I just knew the sound would stop traffic. It didn't.

Cane in hand, I inhaled deeply to steady myself. Determined, I lifted my head high and began tapping. No one seemed to pay much attention. No one but me, seemed uncomfortable. The bellman spotted the cane immediately and asked if I needed any assistance. I politely declined and moved through the double doors.

As I walked through the lobby and went through the registration process, I found the staff to be very solicitous and helpful. The other guests noticed the cane, but simply moved out of the way to allow me an ample path. Instead of feeling ostracized and alienated, I felt supported. While I was still anxious, I quickly realized that I was a lot more comfortable moving around the lobby than I normally was in new situations. To my great surprise, I felt confident, instead of disconcerted.

I made it through the lobby and took the elevator up to my hotel room. Closing the door behind me, I fell on the bed, letting out a deep sigh of relief. "Thank You, Lord!" I had survived. I had taken that first awkward step.

The remainder of the weekend went surprisingly well. While I did feel the stares as people watched me walking past, it was not as bad as I thought it would be. In fact, I was overwhelmed by how kind and helpful people were to me. Though the purpose of the cane was navigation, it also announced to people that I might need assistance. I was amazed by the graciousness of strangers who offered to assist me in the buffet line or to help me find the restroom. I no longer had to stare at the floor looking for trip hazards as I walked along. Instead, I could look around the room at eye level and allow the cane to find the trip hazards. I was amazed at how much easier that was on me.

Walking city streets was much less stressful. The cane helped me find the curbs and identify the changes in the height of pavement. I could walk faster. I felt so much more in control than I did walking solo in unfamiliar places. The anxiety that had plagued me about using the cane actually lessened the more I used it.

Perhaps the biggest surprise showed up in the dark. On our way back from dinner, I stepped out on the dark city street alone, able to walk comfortably down the sidewalk without clinging to someone's arm as I normally did. Mary was relieved, laughing with me as I stepped out in front of our little crowd to show off my newfound independence. She was pleased, but she still ran up beside me, just a little afraid I might fall into the Baltimore harbor.

No one was more surprised than I was about my reaction. I could tell almost immediately that it was helpful. I knew in my gut that I needed this device.

I returned home with a positive attitude about using the cane. There was so much to tell Eric about my experiences. I had overcome my initial fears, adjusting to people's reactions and being pleasantly surprised by their kindness.

Now I had a big decision to make. Now that I knew that the cane was helpful, how should I begin using it at work, in my social circles, at church, or in my neighborhood? "Lord, thank You for helping me through that. Now what do I do?"

Baby Steps

The Baltimore experience had been surprisingly positive, but pulling the cane out and surprising friends or neighbors made me very nervous.

I decided that telling people ahead of time might be the right approach. Instead of shocking people with the sight of me holding a white cane, perhaps it might be better to prepare my friends and colleagues in advance. This would make them more comfortable about the change, and as a result, I would be more comfortable.

Just as a toddler learns to walk with baby steps, I needed to take baby steps in learning to walk with the white cane.

My first step was to use the cane at church and around my home community. I met individually or in small groups with friends and neighbors. While those conversations were a little painful at first, the more I told the story, the more I grew comfortable with telling it.

I was amazed at the outpouring of support I received, and that made the transition easier. Everyone in my church or neighborhood was well aware of my eye disease, so many of them serving as chauffeurs at one time or another.

Tami was with me when I whipped out the cane for the first time at the shopping mall. I know she was watching me out of the corner of her eye, but she just kept on talking a mile a minute, choosing to treat this as the new normal. That bolstered my courage, and although it felt weird at first, the sense of protection and control the cane offered far outweighed the prickly discomfort of strangers' stares.

Using the cane at work, however, was quite another matter.

That would be a giant step, and I was scared to death about taking it. So many people at the hospital had no idea that I had an eye disease. It had been 18 years since my diagnosis, and I compensated so well for my visual field losses that even those that knew about it never gave it a second thought. While I couldn't drive, most people never noticed. I showed up at the hospital on time, and did my job well without any visible effects.

With a white cane in my hand, I would be very visible. There was no glossing over this. How would my colleagues react? Would I be treated differently? Would full-scale knowledge of my limitations impact my career?

This would not be telling a few friends. This would be telling everyone I came in contact with. The thought of all those conversations gave me heartburn. "How do I even go about this? What am I gonna say to all these people?"

Getting Some Guidance

It was clear I needed some advice on how to take this big step.

As I considered the need for guidance, Debbie came to mind. While she was the Vice President of Nursing, she was also a friend. We had known each other for many years, and I had always admired her kindness, generosity, and good judgment. Debbie had known about my vision issues from the very beginning, so this would not be a total surprise. Her executive leadership role would also be helpful in paving the way for this change. I scheduled an appointment with her and prepared myself for this conversation.

I was nervous as I took a seat at the table in Debbie's office. The lump in my throat felt like a boulder. Our greetings complete, I swallowed hard and began the conversation I had practiced in my head. Debbie listened intently, offering supportive comments that held the perfect degree of kindness and understanding.

"Debbie, I'm nervous about people's reactions. I don't know what to say or how to go about it. I'm most nervous about telling the nursing staff on my units. Most of my nurses have no idea that I even have an eye disease."

CHAPTER 16
A New Guide

As my explanations came to an end, Debbie acknowledged my concerns. While she understood my trepidation, she cautioned, "I think you will likely be surprised at how well the staff accepts your news. After all, they are health care workers and they are used to dealing with disabilities."

She pointed out that this would likely be harder on me than anyone else and wanted to make this as painless as possible. "Anita, everyone thinks so highly of you. This will not change that, and I think you will be surprised at the support you receive."

She understood my hesitancy about starting to use the cane, but she also felt some urgency about this. She was concerned about my safety. "Anita, if the cane is helpful to you and will keep you safe, I want you to start using it now. I am less concerned about people's reactions. My priority is your safety."

I was surprised by her passionate response. I understood the safety concerns, but I still felt paralyzed about taking this step and said as much.

Debbie looked me squarely in the eyes as she asked, "So Anita, if you were caring for a diabetic who was taking insulin, and he was not checking his blood sugars at home, what would you say to him?"

With a sheepish smile, I answered, "I would tell him to check his blood sugar."

She smiled as she leaned toward me, "Of course you would. You would want him to be safe, to manage his disease correctly. Why is this any different? If the cane will keep you safe, then you need to use it."

She had me there, and she knew it. Reluctantly, I agreed that she was right. Debbie pressed me for a date. "You need a deadline. That will keep you moving forward. What date can you commit to for beginning to use the cane?"

I squirmed in my seat, with a grimace for an answer. Debbie wasn't giving up. "How about April 15?"

I sighed heavily but agreed. "But how do I go about this?"

We talked at length about various approaches for sharing the information. Debbie suggested mapping out my message. "What do you want to share?" She emphasized that her concern was for my comfort level. I was not required to share anything. We were all well aware of the rules around protected health information. Reassuring her that I was not worried about privacy, I relayed that my concern was about how to share the information and not get emotional.

She encouraged me to prepare several levels of messages and to employ multiple strategies for reaching different groups. For close friends and colleagues, more detail could be shared individually. For other co-workers, I could share the information, but limit the detail. Perhaps I could share the message at a team meeting and reach more colleagues at once. An email might even work for a larger group that would be hard to reach at one time. For acquaintances, I could have a standard answer like, "I have an eye disease, and the cane prevents me from tripping and keeps me safe."

This approach made a lot of sense to me. It seemed doable. There were definitely people I wanted to tell individually, but there were other small groups that I could inform at one time. While the written email approach was less personal, I considered that it might be a good way to reach large groups of people for whom gathering them as a group might be hard to orchestrate.

I had a lot to consider as I left Debbie's office. I thanked her profusely for her time and her counsel. She had offered me the perfect blend of support and advice, while still pinning me down to a deadline. It had been the right decision to meet with her. It was the jump start I needed.

CHAPTER 16
A New Guide

The Notification Process

On the ride home, I shared Debbie's advice with Eric. Although I was still nervous, Debbie's suggestions made a lot of sense to me. I could feel a plan forming in my head.

Over the next few days, I mulled over the information, considering what I would say. I made a list of all the people I wanted to tell upfront. Recognizing that I would not catch everyone ahead of time, I accepted that there would be some surprise encounters.

The following Monday, I took a deep breath and prayed for courage. Squaring my shoulders, I got started, following the approach Debbie outlined. The first couple of conversations were tough, but as Debbie predicted, I got better at telling the story. The more I told it, the easier it got.

It took almost three weeks to address all the individuals and groups I wanted to reach. For the nursing staff on my departments, I shared my news at a staff meeting and then followed up with an email to ensure all the staff on different shifts would have a personal message from me.

I was unprepared for the outpouring of love and support I received as I shared my story. Of course, there were tears, but no one fell apart. Most just offered a hug, a hand squeeze, or a promise of prayer. Everyone thanked me for telling them personally, and like Debbie, they were anxious for me to start using the cane. They wanted me to be safe. Some had questions about the disease and my limitations. Most accepted my message with a nod of understanding and a question of "How can I help?"

It all went so much better than I could ever have imagined. The support I received bolstered my courage and steeled my resolve. It was time to start this thing.

On April 15, I emerged from the car in the parking deck. Eric was standing there watching me as I pulled out the cane. Releasing the strap, the cane snapped to attention. With Eric by my side, I stretched the cane out in front of me and began walking. As we entered the building, I held my head high. My stomach was in knots, but I was determined to persevere. I could feel a few stares, but no one stopped us. I made it to my office and flopped into my chair with a sigh of relief. I had done it.

Each time I extended the cane, it got a little easier. I won't deny that it took all the courage I could muster to walk on my nursing departments for the first time. Yet, the hospital walls did not collapse. No one fell apart. Mostly, I got kind smiles, warm hugs and little pats on the shoulder as I went about my work.

There were a few surprise encounters, and those were a little awkward. Still I forged ahead with my well-practiced message, and the reactions were kind and supportive.

It turned out that my worries were unfounded. Because of the love and support of everyone I came in contact with, the whole process of using the cane was so much easier than I had imagined. It still made me nervous. I still felt the stares of hospital visitors, but I got through it. Soon, it felt normal to have the cane in my hand.

Adopting the cane had taken courage that I didn't know I had. God was surely with me through the whole ordeal, equipping me with the strength I needed to cope with yet another hard thing. I had taken a big step, white cane in hand.

To Paris With A Cane

The gravel crunched under our feet as we walked up to the impressive granite wall. Leaning over the gray stone wall, I peered out, catching my breath in delight. Paris lay before me, the lush green space of the Champs-Élysées giving way to the skyline of ornate buildings that marked the exclusive shopping district. In the distance, the Eiffel Tower seemed to sparkle, as if sending us a note of welcome. I could hear the tinkle of wine glasses as the patrons lunched at the cafe on the nearby corner, their mingled conversations floating through the air. A gentle breeze ruffled my

CHAPTER 16
A New Guide

hair as I turned to smile at my companions, Liz and Elizabeth. "Girls, we have arrived! Paris awaits!"

As Elizabeth led us along the path in search of the River Seine, I tapped behind her with my white cane. I was getting much more proficient at using the cane to alert me to trip hazards. I had to admit that it really was helpful, even if I felt awkward using it. I still felt the stares of onlookers as I strolled down the sidewalk. I sensed the panic of young mothers as they dashed to pull their children out of my path, lest I hit the kids with my cane. I was getting used to those responses, even if they were a bit disconcerting. However, I was not at all prepared for how the French would treat me and my white cane.

I had noticed a difference at the airport. The French authorities immediately noticed my white cane and ushered us to the front of the customs line, instead of allowing me to weave back and forth with the rest of the arriving passengers. We moved through the process with ease, a far cry from the way TSA had handled my situation as we departed from the USA.

I noticed that other pedestrians quickly identified my cane and stepped out of the way. The crowds parted easily as I walked along. There was a certain deference for the white cane that I had never experienced in the United States. The French understood the meaning of a white cane and showed me a heightened level of courtesy.

The first real surprise came the next day when we decided to tour the Opera House. As the three of us entered the building, we made our way to the ticket counter with me tapping along behind Liz. As we approached the clerk, she made a gesture toward my cane. Liz began to pull out money for the tickets, but the clerk began waving her hands dismissively and saying something we could not understand.

Fortunately, Elizabeth had taken four years of French in high school and was quite adept at both speaking and understanding the language. Tugging on Liz's sleeve, Elizabeth explained, "She is saying that it's free. Aunt 'Nita is free."

I looked at her in surprise, "Why?"

"Because of your cane, there is no charge."

The conversation with the clerk continued as she asked Elizabeth if Liz was my guide. When Elizabeth replied yes, the clerk informed her that Liz would also be free. Elizabeth was to be charged a student rate.

Eyes wide with surprise, Elizabeth turned to us and attempted to explain the clerk's directions. We all looked at each other, absolutely mystified over the charges. Liz paid our paltry bill, and the three of us moved forward to wait for the tour.

We assumed that the mysterious treatment at the Opera House was specific to that venue. We had no idea what was coming.

On Easter Monday, we showed up at the Louvre early, hoping to snag a spot in line before the crowds arrived. It was just before 8 am when we crunched our way up the gravel path. Although the doors did not open until 9 am, we were dismayed to note that a significantly long line had already formed near the entrance. I was walking ahead of Liz and Elizabeth, tapping along with my cane and moving at my usual brisk walking pace. When I saw the line forming, I hurried up toward the queue, hoping to secure a place for us before the line got any longer. As I approached the line, I looked up to find a security guard headed straight toward me, waving her hands dramatically, her words a flurry of French. Elizabeth nudged me on the shoulder, "She is saying for you to come with her."

Confused, I stepped to follow the animated guide, wondering what I had done wrong. She pointed to Liz and Elizabeth, "With you?" Her accent was so thick, I had trouble understanding the simple words, finally nodding in recognition. "Yes, they are with me."

She pointed to them, "Come!" Turning back toward the museum entrance, she hurried off. Bewildered, the three of us looked at each other, and turned in unison to follow the guard.

CHAPTER 16
A New Guide

Pausing in front of the entrance door, she motioned for us to wait there. We complied, looking at each other, a bit dismayed. Was it the cane again? Abashed, I looked out at the long line of people waiting, while I stood first in line.

In disbelief over this special treatment, I stood there amazed. My amazement turned to joy when they let us inside ten minutes early, provided free passes to Liz and me, and then directed us to enter the museum. We were the first visitors to the Louvre on that holiday morning!

That was not the last of the star treatment. Everywhere we went that entire week was handled with that same care and courtesy. I never paid one ticket fee, and we never waited in any line. I was astounded!

From the outset, Liz had been relieved for me to be using the cane. No doubt Eric had shared his perspective on the matter, and she had long since concurred. At the airport, she had pushed me to show the cane so we could board the plane early, her intent to make things easier for me. That didn't feel so easy, but as I had done so often, I took a deep breath and did it. Liz was thankful for the cane, glad for a tool to keep me safe. It was a much harder transition for my sweet Elizabeth.

Like me, Elizabeth was still learning to adjust to the idea of the white cane. The first time she had seen me hold it in my hand was the evening before the trip began. While she wanted me to be safe, she hated that I needed it, that my eyes were now bad enough to require such assistance. She was uncomfortable with the attention the cane commanded. She did not like the stares of passersby. Perhaps some of that discomfort stemmed from the typical eighteen-year-old desire to blend in with the crowd, but it was more than that. She did not want me to feel like I was some kind of circus exhibit.

More than once, I caught her staring onlookers down with a "What are you looking at?" challenge. She would mutter under her breath, "Stop staring!" I tried to reassure her that it was OK. Most of the time I couldn't see them anyway, but it still bothered her.

However, by the time we bypassed the long lines at several museums and received free entry, Elizabeth started feeling better about things. By the end of the week, we were all joking about my privileged status, and they were letting me walk in front just to see what kind of reception I would receive. Liz would smile and say, "Show them the cane!" as if it was a magic wand. In a way, it was.

Not only was the cane my free pass, it kept me from injury on several occasions. While both Liz and Elizabeth watched out for me, they couldn't be vigilant every second. However, the cane could, and it saved me from several mishaps.

Thankfully, all three of us got used to the white cane. We all recognized its value in preventing me from falling. I felt much more independent. I could walk solo and not be afraid. Our special treatment allowed us to joke about it, and that helped me adapt to this new normal for me.

Sadly, our star treatment did not continue upon our arrival back in the US. The TSA in Atlanta took my cane away to scan it and left me standing alone with no assistance or direction as to where to go. Liz and Elizabeth ended up in a different line. The whole area was overcrowded and chaotic. Confused about where to go, I asked for directions. The agent just looked at me and pointed as if I could follow the gesture. It was both frustrating and disappointing after the wonderful treatment I had received in France.

Our whole trip to Paris was fantastic. It was the perfect girls' trip! We saw so much and thoroughly enjoyed this opportunity to celebrate our beloved Elizabeth's "Coming Of Age!"

Looking back, that trip was a turning point for me to adapt to using that white cane. I came home from Paris and moved forward without hesitation. I still get curious stares and mothers clutching their toddlers as I pass by, but I just smile and tap my way on down the street, thankful for this tool that keeps me safe.

CHAPTER 16
A New Guide

White Cane, White Flag

All those years ago, I had laid down the car keys, but it was a long time before I actually gave them up. I laid them down, but I didn't let them go. I hung on to the loss, regretting and resenting it, until finally with God's grace, I made my peace with that loss.

Interestingly, picking up that white cane had held the same dilemma for me. I fought so hard against it, unwilling to accept that it was time for this step. I hated it, resented its intrusion into my life. But when I finally let go of the loss this step symbolized, when I eventually accepted that this tool was essential, I once again found peace.

The cane became a friend, not my enemy. Instead of announcing my dependency, it opened the door to more independence. Instead of hating it, I welcomed its assistance.

I got over being uncomfortable with people's reactions, choosing to find humor in the rare inappropriate comments or questions I received. The kindness and support I continue to receive from others at the sight of that cane far outweigh any negative reactions.

I came to accept the white cane, just as I did the loss of driving. We cannot escape the hard things of this life, but rather, we must learn to endure them with grace and trust. For though we encounter suffering in this life, God can and He will work all things together for our good.

For me, finding peace was about surrendering to God my pain and my problems. I had to raise the white flag in order to move forward. I had to accept that I wasn't in control, and once I did, things got easier.

I have always viewed surrender as a sign of defeat. But as I walked with God down this hard road, I have come to see that surrender opens up a pathway to peace. When we give up fighting for a control we don't have anyway, when we open our hands and let our hard things go to God, we find that trust brings peace, and peace allows joy and hope to brighten the path ahead.

It Will All Work Out

More than a year had passed since our girls' trip to Paris. I had returned from that trip with new resolve. The cane had passed the test, proving its value. It had become a normal extension of my arm, as natural as wearing shoes.

Now, it was another waiting room moment, time for another eye check up with Dr. Whitaker. I was pounding away on my iPad, trying to answer work emails while I waited for the doctor.

That's when I saw the little family come in. The mother was conversing with one of the technicians in an adjacent office, while a blonde-headed little boy scampered around her feet. He darted up and down the small hallway as the young father tried in vain to catch him. He was touching everything and mumbling in that typical toddler language that no one else can quite grasp. Little bursts of glee would rise from his tiny frame as he located something new to explore. He was absolutely precious.

The mother finished her conversation, and the little family settled in the seats near me. The young couple was in their late 20s, still full of energy and enthusiasm. They needed it as they chased after the little boy who laid claim to their hearts.

That's when I noticed the older woman was with them, likely the child's grandmother. The mother picked up the child to entertain him on her lap, but he was having none of it. He wanted to move.

My work emails were calling me, but I could not help watching the little boy scamper to and fro. He would squirm down from his mother's lap and head down the short hallway. Dad would pop up and chase after him, retrieving him back to their little space, trying to corral him in the corner. But it didn't work. The little fellow was up and moving, intent on exploration. He never cried or screamed, but simply emitted a little squeal as Mom or Dad retrieved him from his wayward pursuits.

He was so cute. I could not help but smile. I remembered what it was like to keep a little boy occupied in a waiting room full of

CHAPTER 16
A New Guide

people. It's just impossible for them to sit still, no matter how hard you try. This little boy had a zest for life. You could tell he had good parents, for his countenance radiated the joy of being well loved.

While his mom and dad were getting a workout bobbing up and down to capture their delightful child, I began to wonder about the young boy. Did he have vision problems? We were in an eye clinic after all. The doctor was a low vision specialist. Was this sweet child going blind? The thought tugged at my heartstrings. "Please God, no!"

I did not have time to consider my thoughts further, because the office door opened, and Dr. Whitaker called my name. Crossing the room toward the open door, I smiled at the little family and said a quick hello to the toddler.

Finishing up my routine appointment, Dr. Whitaker asked me to wait while she printed some material for me to take home. Exiting her office to take my seat beside Eric, I found the family still keeping fort in their waiting room corner.

My curiosity got the best of me, and I made eye contact with the child's mother. "He sure is cute!"

The pretty young woman looked up and smiled brightly. "Oh, thank you. I hope he is not driving you crazy?"

"Oh no, he's fine. He's precious."

She beamed at this remark. Gaining courage, I took the opening to ask my hard question. "Is there something wrong with his vision?"

The young woman shook her head emphatically. "Oh no! It's me. I'm the one with the eye problems."

Feeling a touch of relief, I nodded. "Oh, I see. Me too."

Sensing a willingness to talk further, I plunged ahead. "Do you mind if I ask what kind of problem you have?"

Unperturbed by the invasive question, she went on to explain that she had Stargardt's disease, another type of retinal degenerative disease that attacks central vision first. She was 26 years old and had known about the disease for several years.

Unfortunately, she had lost vision rapidly over the past two years. Unable to work or drive, she was a stay-at-home mom.

Her husband stood quietly a little distance behind her, listening intently to the conversation. The woman introduced as her mother was also following our discussion closely.

"I'm Jessica, by the way."

"I'm Anita. I'm glad to meet you. I have something similar called RP."

She bobbed her head, familiar with the disease. I shared a bit of my history, explaining my nineteen-year sojourn with this disease. The conversation flowed easily as we discussed our limitations, lamenting over the loss of driving and the difficulties inherent in managing life without car keys.

She seemed surprised, but pleased, to find that I was still working. I talked about the vision software that made using the computer feasible and encouraged her to check it out. She explained her recent purchase of a tablet to help with reading since she no longer could see printed material. I empathized with that limitation, having lost that function as well.

I saw her glance down at my white cane, curious, but afraid to ask. Holding up the white cane, "I have only had this a little over a year. I didn't want to do it, but it has ended up being such a help. It keeps me safe and helps me be independent."

Her husband and mother followed this part of the conversation closely. Jessica asked a few questions about learning to use the cane, and I shared some details about mobility training.

Jessica mentioned the challenges of household chores. I pointed toward Eric and said, "This guy here does a lot to help me. He does a lot around the house now. I used to do most everything, but he has had to do more these days. He takes good care of me. He even cooks!"

Jessica smiled and looked at her husband. "He does a lot too. He helps me a lot." The gratitude in her eyes was apparent, but there was also that hint of sadness as if she wished it was different

CHAPTER 16
A New Guide

somehow. I felt her pain. I could relate to wishing things were different.

Jessica's sweet son twirled around under her feet. We both look down with a smile for his toddler antics. Jessica spoke softly as if she wanted only me to hear her words. "I just hope he doesn't have it."

Her voice quivered as she watched her son. "I just hope I can take care of him."

Her words hit me like a knife. My heart sank, filled with the weight of her tremendous loss and her fears for the future. I knew that heartache all too well.

Reaching out to touch her arm, I spoke softly, my voice pleading with heartfelt empathy, "It will all work out. I know where you're coming from, but it really will all work out. You can't imagine now that it will, but somehow, you will find that it all works out."

Eric stepped over beside me. He had been listening and watching too. He smiled at this lovely young lady and said with tenderness, "Hang in there. It really will all work out."

Those words seemed small compared to the chasm of questions without answers, to the fears and the struggles this young couple were destined to face. What could I say? How could I help her? Mere words seemed insignificant when compared to the chaos that impending blindness portends.

Yet, as I watched the faces of this pretty young woman and her handsome young man, I saw their expressions soften as if the strain that tugged at their souls lightened just a bit. They had heard my words, found comfort in my reassurance.

It was time to go. Work awaited for both Eric and me. Jessica and I exchanged a long look, our diseased eyes opening a window of connection for two strangers on a similar journey. I smiled softly, touched her arm lightly, and made my departure.

As we walked out of the clinic toward the car, I reached for Eric's hand. "They reminded me of us so long ago, didn't they?"

"Yeah, they did." His tone was gentle as he, like me, remembered.

Riding down the road, we discussed the encounter. It was like staring at a snapshot of a past life. It was our life 19 years before, a little boy, a devastating diagnosis, the demands of childrearing, the loss of driving, an uncertain future. Things had seemed so overwhelming, so impossible then.

Flash forward 19 years, and I could not help but give thanks for the life we have shared. I had enjoyed a successful career. We had raised a wonderful son, our pride and joy. We had weathered the insurmountable challenges of vision loss, learning to cope with the loss of driving and independence.

We had stayed together, even when this life-changing disease threatened to tear us apart.

Overwhelmed, I marveled at what God had done for me in these 19 years. It was like standing on a mountaintop gazing at your life story, surveying the patterns, seeing the joys and sorrows all so clearly. His handprint was on all of it.

I had asked so many times over the years "How are we going to do this?" I thought there was no answer for my question. But God had answered the question. He had worked it all out.

I wish we could have done more to help Jessica and her husband. It did not seem like enough. Still, I knew what such a meeting might have meant to me when I was newly diagnosed. To have someone with a similar eye disease who could share a positive perspective on the road ahead, that would have meant the world to me. If I had encountered someone back then who had walked in my shoes and was not only surviving, but really living a full life, oh, that would have meant so much.

It is my ardent hope that Jessica found some reassurance in our conversation that morning. I hope our words gave her encouragement, that our conversation made her struggle just a little bit easier.

Although I never encountered Jessica again, I prayed for her little family, for God's grace on the long hard road ahead. That chance meeting meant so much to me. It allowed me to offer comfort to a fellow sojourner on this difficult journey through blindness. So many people have helped me along the way, and in a small way, I was able to give back to Jessica a taste of the love and support so freely given to me.

The conversation reminded me anew of how God has supplied our every need as we traveled along our life path. His Hand of grace has been ever present no matter the obstacles that blocked our path. These thoughts fill me with hope, a confident hope that blind or not, the future is bright because God walks by my side. My words to Jessica were true. "It really will all work out."

CHAPTER 17
The Fork In The Road

Tired

Thanksgiving was just days away. My parents were coming to visit, and Jonathan would be home from school. I should have been excited, but I didn't have the energy. I was just exhausted.

It was all piling up, a whole host of burdens piling up one on top of the other, pushing me further and further down. The year 2013 had been a horrible year of hardship. The crack had started earlier, small at first, but growing steadily until the foundation finally gave way.

It started with a reorganization of Eric's department at the hospital. The new reporting structure was destined to fail as Eric found himself reporting to two individuals with whom he had serious past conflicts. He tried so hard to wipe the slate and start fresh, but they were not interested in working things out. Instead, they only ramped up the pressure. Over a two-year period, the stress kept building toward a breaking point, culminating in a serious depression that forced Eric to take a medical leave and eventually resign.

It had been one of the most painful periods of our shared life together, but little by little, we had managed to dig our way out, just as we had done after my eye disease diagnosis. Supported with help from a wonderful counselor and strengthened by the lessons learned through our past trials, we had clung together and found our way out of that dark black hole.

After nine months of heartbreaking adversity, God had answered our prayers by opening a new path for Eric. With the help of a close friend, Eric returned to independent consulting, opening his home office once again.

Right in the midst of Eric's struggles, my aunt Tina had been diagnosed with breast cancer. As my mother's identical twin, Tina and I had always shared a tight bond. I went with her to her initial appointments, serving as both an advocate and second set of ears. She had endured a grueling course of chemotherapy only to find metastasis to the brain. After seven months, my sweet aunt had succumbed to the disease, and we had laid her to rest just two weeks earlier in mid-November. My mother was heartbroken, and so was I.

As if those things were not enough to weigh me down, my work was not going well either. Six months earlier, I had sat in a meeting room full of colleagues listening to plans for a huge multi-hospital project. I was not particularly concerned. I knew I would have to participate in the project, but my plate was already full with another enormous system-wide program. With tons of deadlines looming for that program, there was no time left for anything else. This would have to be someone else's project. I just didn't have time for it.

Well, the joke was on me. Before I could bat an eye, I was tasked to lead the clinical portion of the project. I had no time for this, but I also had no choice.

At that initial meeting, the group had projected that the planning and implementation would take 18 months to two years. That might have been doable. Instead, the hospital administration deemed it an organizational priority and gave us eight months to get it done.

The budget process took over two months, leaving me six months to accomplish what should have taken two years to do. To say I was stressed does not cover the level of pressure I felt.

I threw myself into the project full force, doing my best to move things forward. My work was hampered by unnecessary delays, difficult people and challenging logistics. I felt like I was herding cats, unruly ones at that. My cries for help fell on deaf ears. I was just told to get it done.

I had even taken a week off to travel to Bermuda with Eric for his work. He had landed an excellent contract supporting the Bermuda health system. Thanks to the miracles of modern technology, Eric could sit in his home office and support the implementation of a new computer system on the other side of an ocean. The visit to Bermuda was for the go-live of his project.

I thought that a week of rest in the sunshine would restore my spirits and ready me for the challenges ahead, but I was wrong again. The stress was even worse when I returned.

You're There

Needless to say, I was a mental wreck when I walked through the double doors of the eye clinic three days before Thanksgiving. Spending countless hours staring at the computer screen, the eye strain was significant. I felt like my vision was worse, but I hoped a simple adjustment of the prism in my glasses would fix the problem.

I had known for years that my vision always seemed worse in periods of high stress. I can manage most tasks with relative ease when I am not rushed. However, when the pace ramps up, and I must move rapidly, I struggle. It's as if the stress of the faster pace causes my central vision to narrow further, making me miss more in my environment. I knock over drinks on the counter and run into furniture that has not been moved. I stumble over objects that I normally would catch and avoid.

All those things were happening again. These were warning signs, but I ignored them. I did not have time to slow down right now.

When Dr. Whitaker's assistant checked my visual acuity, we were both disconcerted at the change since my last visit. As I waited in Dr. Whitaker's exam chair for her to enter, I began to worry. When she arrived and reviewed my test data, I could tell she was worried too.

"Tell me what is going on with you. Your acuity is significantly worse. What's going on?"

My saga of stress and worry tumbled out. She listened without much comment, turning in her rolling chair to review my data in the computer. She began to check the prism in my glasses, trying new lenses to see if these might improve my waning vision.

I kept quiet while she moved back and forth, fiddling with the lenses, reviewing the computer information. Her back was to me as she studied her computer screen. I heard myself ask a question that I had not planned to ask. I really was not sure where the question came from, except that I was so tired and overwhelmed. Perhaps I had subconsciously started to wonder about the subject.

"As far as disability goes, where am I on that continuum? I mean at what point would I begin to qualify for disability?"

It was a moment I will never forget. Her beautiful long blonde hair went flying as Dr. Whitaker whirled around in her office chair, her movements so intense, they stirred the air in the tiny room. Her look was deadly serious as she locked her eyes on my surprised face.

With an emphatic tone in her voice that I had not heard before, she blurted out, "Oh, you're there!"

The words hung in the air for a long moment as we stared at each other. "Anita, you meet the criteria now. You've been there for a long time. In fact, I don't know how you are still working with what you are able to see at this point."

I was totally stunned. I had no words. The question had been asked out of curiosity with no conscious thought that disability was even a consideration at this point.

Dr. Whitaker went on. "Anita, I see you out there working away on your iPad in the waiting room, and I can't imagine how you are doing all that. I don't know how you are managing to work with the vision you have at this point. I really think it's time for you to consider going on disability."

I could only stare back at her, my mind reeling. All I could think was, "Disability? How can that be?"

Finding my voice, I said, "I can't quit now. I have this huge project to finish. It's a really big deal. No one else can do this. I am too far into it. I can't stop now."

She leaned back in her chair and looked at me, assessing her words carefully. Before she spoke, I blurted out, "Dr. Whitaker, I'm not ready to give up nursing. I'm not ready to quit yet."

She continued to watch me closely. I am certain my face was a canvas of swirling emotions.

"Anita, I know you love your job. I understand your passion for your profession, but I am thinking about you, about your future. I am not sure how much longer you can go on like this. It is taking a toll on your vision, and the stress has to be taking a toll on your overall health. I really want you to think about this."

I sat there just bewildered, trying to comprehend her words. Could I really be here? Am I really at the point of disability?

She soldiered on, "I want you to go back to NIH and have your visual fields done again. That will help me know better what is going on. And I'd like for you to research the disability process at work. Get the paperwork and see what the benefits are. I will see you again in April. You can finish this project and go to NIH. We will talk again in April about disability. That gives you some time to work on that."

Her words were more of a directive. Her tone did not broker further conversation. She was deadly serious and had said what she meant to say. I knew her well enough at this point not to argue. Besides, I was so overwhelmed that I was at a loss for words. "OK. I'll think about it. Thank you."

Uncertain if my wobbly knees could keep me upright, I stumbled out into the waiting room wondering what in the world had I gotten myself into.

On the way home, I gradually opened up to Eric, giving him the Reader's Digest version. He said very little. I knew he needed time to process. So did I.

Later that evening, I sat on the sofa across from my mother. Being a verbal processor, I was ready to tell someone the story. Dr. Whitaker's words were still rolling around in my brain.

As Mom listened quietly, I told the tale of my eye appointment. When I finished my tale, I looked at her expectantly. I figured she would discount the need for disability and agree with me that such a step was down the road a ways.

"Well, why don't you just quit? If you're that tired. If your eyes are getting worse, then why don't you just stop working?"

For the second time that day, I was stunned. I had expected my mother to be concerned about money and the need for me to keep working. Surely, she would think that this is all too drastic a step. Apparently, she was seeing what my doctor was seeing.

I heard myself say, "Well, it's something to think about. But not now. I'll think about it later."

Tiny Field

The holidays passed in a blur; my mind completely inundated with my monumental work project. Throughout January and February, I worked nights and weekends just trying to finish the lengthy to-do list for the project implementation. Things did not slow down with the go-live date in mid-February, but seemed to speed up. As the nursing units adjusted to the new process, I went in early and stayed late to check on staff and ensure patient safety.

In late February, about ten days after I finished the system implementation, Eric and I traveled to NIH for my scheduled appointment. The timing was not particularly good from a work perspective, but I had put off the appointment as long as I thought I should. Dr. Whitaker had strongly encouraged me to go, so I took the time off.

The stress between November and the end of February was horrendous. There were moments when I did not think I would survive it. I was physically and emotionally exhausted when I arrived in Bethesda, Maryland on a chilly winter's day.

From the very first test of the day, I knew my eyes were worse. I had more difficulty reading the eye chart. I struggled with the visual field test and knew I was not seeing the little white lights as I should. By the time I sat down for the ERG that requires those awful contact lenses and electrode wires, I was an emotional wreck. I kept trying to calm myself down, but it was not working.

I recall waiting for the finale of the day, the meeting with the doctor to review my results. I was sitting in the waiting room, headset on, trying to listen to praise and worship music to distract myself and relieve some of the building anxiety. My thoughts were swirling around, dancing inside my head at a frenzied pace. I could hear Dr. Whitaker saying. "Anita, you're there. I don't know how you are still working..."

"Lord, what's happening? Do you really want me to stop working? Is it really time for that? Lord, I know my eyes are worse. Oh, help me Lord, I don't know what to do."

My suspicions were confirmed as we met with the doctor in the tiny exam room. He was slow and deliberate in explaining the test results. "You have some significant changes in your vision since your last visit here. Ms. Sherer, you have a very tiny central field in both eyes. There is healthy tissue there, but its size is quite limited. I am concerned about this. The central field is critical for you to remain functional, and it is very tiny at this point."

Sharing Dr. Whitaker's concerns about my declining vision and the need for disability, I asked his opinion on whether I needed to take that step.

He held my gaze as he responded. "I cannot answer that question. That is for you to decide. I will only say that you have a very limited central field in both eyes. It is critical for you to maintain that for as long as possible."

I could read between the lines of his thoughtful and well selected words. I did not have much good vision left to work with, and I could not afford to ignore the warning signs. A hard question formed in my mind. "If I keep on going this way, where will I be?"

It's Time

The month of March was just as busy as all the preceding months. I continued to put out fires. Every day seemed to generate a new crisis, and I ran around on speed dial trying to make things work.

By the time I walked through the doors of the eye clinic in early April, I was just plain weary. Seated in the exam chair, I waited for Dr. Whitaker to make her entrance, wondering what she would have to say this time.

Our customary greetings completed, I handed Dr. Whitaker the information I had brought back from my NIH visit. She poured over the documents at length.

The optical assistant had checked my visual acuity when I first arrived. It had declined since my November visit, but worse still, it had deteriorated since my exam at NIH in February. This was not good, and I knew it.

Dr. Whitaker turned in her chair to face me. "So what have you done about disability?"

The question caught me off guard. That was not the opening statement I was expecting. I knew from my last visit that she wanted me to consider the disability option, but her manner now suggested that it was a mandate.

"Well, nothing really. I'm not sure I'm really ready to quit working. I still have a lot to do on this project."

She frowned; her brow furrowed in deep deliberation. There was a long moment before she spoke again. "Anita, I hear you. I understand your concerns about work, but your vision is worse. Your acuity has declined since November and even further since February. You can't go on this way."

She paused, searching for words. "I thought you were going to check into disability, get the paperwork and be ready to start the process." She paused looking for a reaction from me.

"Well, I have been thinking about it. I did ask some questions about the process. But Dr. Whitaker, I'm not ready yet. Maybe later, like August or September when I've got things in better shape."

"Anita, it's time. You need to start the process now. I am worried about you. You cannot continue the way you have been going. I know you love your profession. I get that. I really do, but, Anita, it's time. I know you can do the work, but you can't handle the pace anymore. It's too much. It's time to pursue disability."

I just sat there, staring at her, trying to comprehend her words. My mind was issuing objections, retorts, fighting against what she was saying, but deep down in my heart, I knew she was right. I had known she was right since our first conversation in November. I just hadn't wanted to admit it.

I was so tired, so weary. The burden of this tremendous decision bore down on me, my shoulders sagging under the weight. My eyes filled with tears I could not blink away as I blurted out, "Dr. Whitaker, I don't want to do this. I don't want to give this up."

"I know. I know, but Anita, it's time."

Whether I had made up my mind or not, it was clear that this good doctor had made up hers. This miracle worker who had kept me functional for so long, who had helped me battle against the onslaught of vision loss, she was raising the white flag.

I knew full well she did not make this decision lightly. She was giving her best advice, considering my future, my overall health and well-being. I knew I needed to listen to her, but my heart was screaming "NO!"

With compassion in her voice, she proceeded to explain the next steps. "We need to move forward on this. It's what is best for you. Get the paperwork and fax it to me. I will fill it out as soon as I receive it. You need to pick a date to stop work, and it needs to be soon. I will expect to hear from you in a week or so with your plan."

She was done, discussion time concluded, plan complete. There was nothing left to say. I stood and moved toward the door.

"Anita, it's going to be OK. You are doing the right thing for your future. It's going to work out."

I mumbled "Thank you." It was all I could utter at the moment, my mind cluttered with competing thoughts. One thought took hold. "How in the world was this ever going to work out?"

CHAPTER 17
The Fork In The Road

Any Regrets

I had heard the softly spoken question. It had hung in the air just waiting, stopping me in my tracks. I knew it held the answer I had been searching for from the moment she asked it.

It was a warm, sunny Saturday morning in April of 2014. I was sitting on the front porch, sipping my Diet Coke. It had been about ten days since my visit to Dr. Whitaker. I awakened with a heavy sense of foreboding bearing down on me. I had a decision to make, one of the biggest decisions of my life. Actually, if I was honest about it, Dr. Whitaker had already made the decision. I was just fighting following through on that decision.

My weary brain was doing laps, getting nowhere fast. "Disability. How can that be? I am only 53. I thought I would work another 10 years. How can I quit now? I'm not ready for this. I can't stop nursing. I love my work. There is so much to do still. Why does it have to be this way?"

Those thoughts were on continual rewind, but they were doing battle with these other thoughts. "I am so tired. I just can't do this anymore. I can't go on this way. I can do the work, but not the pace. It's too fast. They want too much from me. I can't keep up. I am just so tired."

For ten days, I had agonized over Dr. Whitaker's words. I had cried. I had fretted. Eric and I had talked at length about it. I had called Human Resources and asked about what was involved in the process. I even had a copy of the paperwork, but that's where I stopped. I couldn't make the next move. I was stuck.

For more than a week, I had not slept well. Falling asleep when my head hit the pillow, I would rest for a few hours, only to wake in the middle of the night. Like flying arrows, my thoughts would battle against each other as I perseverated over what to do. Dr. Whitaker was waiting for my answer, expecting the paperwork on her desk. I had to make a decision.

The rocker squeaked against the brick floor of my front porch as I stared across the road at the tree line, searching the sky, fervently wishing I could knock on heaven's doors and have God outline His master plan. "Call Mary." The thought came out of nowhere. An image of my tall, gracious best friend flowed into my mind. "Call Mary." The Voice said again.

Not knowing what else to do, I obeyed and pulled out my cell phone. Mary answered immediately as if she knew I would be calling.

Mary knew what I was facing. I had told the story after returning from my eye appointment. She had been praying.

"Mary, I don't know what to do. I've got to decide something and I don't know what to do. I'm not ready to quit, but maybe it's time. I don't know. Maybe I could just work on for a while, see how things go. Work's going to get better, and maybe I can work on for a while."

I repeated myself several times, round and round, verbally processing. Finally, I stopped. "Mary, what do you think?"

Mary had been listening quietly, allowing my rant to run its course. Now, she took a long moment to respond. "So let's just say that you keep working. Let's just say that things settle out and you keep on doing the same thing. But what if in two years, you lose your vision? Let's just say in two years, you lose all your vision, and when that happens, would you look back at this moment and have any regrets? Would you look back and regret not stopping work now?"

The words struck a blow deep inside me, like a steel dagger stabbing deep into my heart. My response was visceral, like a wail of mourning rising up, screaming out from the depths of my soul.

I knew the answer to that question. Beyond a shadow of a doubt, I knew the answer to that question.

In a quiet little voice, I said, "Yes."

There was a long silence on the line as we both contemplated that question and my clear answer. Then Mary spoke.

"Well, I think you have your answer."

CHAPTER 17
The Fork In The Road

"Yeah. Yeah, I think I do. I would regret it. I know I would."

Mary was sincere, her tone reflecting the seriousness of the situation. "I know it's hard. I know you don't want to leave now, but I am thinking about you, about Eric, about Jonathan. I am thinking about your future, your life beyond that hospital. I don't want you to have any regrets."

I did not respond immediately, the silence hung on the line as I stared at the morning sky. From the deep recesses of my soul, I felt a quickening, a moment of clarity. It was a feeling I had experienced before at other crossroads in my life. I had prayed a thousand prayers beseeching God to show me the right path. Suddenly, I knew that God was speaking. He was speaking through a question, "Would you have any regrets?"

I knew the answer. It was "Yes." Yes, I would regret it.

That was the decision point. I knew what I had to do.

A long moment passed without a word. Then softly, I whispered, "I guess it's time to retire."

Plan In Motion

In the weeks that followed, I put the plan in motion. I spoke first with my manager Debbie who could not have been more supportive. Her first concern was my welfare, and what she could do to make things easier for me. She agreed wholeheartedly that this decision was about my future. It was about my sight. If continuing to work would hasten the onset of further vision loss, I needed to quit immediately.

"I want what's best for you, Anita. I want what's best for your future."

As I shared my news with my co-workers, I found that they shared Debbie's sentiments. All my friends and colleagues wanted what was best for me. They may have been concerned about the work, but first and foremost, they were worried about me.

Breaking the news to my peers and staff was heart wrenching for me. I felt nauseous with every conversation. There were tears and hugs and promises to pray. The look of anguish on their faces reflected the pain that filled my soul.

The telling was the worst part, and when it was done, I felt a tremendous sense of relief. With every hug, every kind word, my confidence in my decision seemed to grow. I was doing the right thing. Now it was time to get it done.

I set the date for July 3, 2014 and completed the paperwork. The plan for retirement was in motion.

I'm Gonna Walk

I was seated at a round table in my friend Annette's office when I got the call. She was running late for our appointment. The Vice President of Nursing, Annette was not only a superior, she was a longtime close friend. My stomach was in knots, as it had been for each of these difficult discussions.

Once again, I had to tell another old friend that I was leaving, that my eyes were worse and that I was retiring on disability. Once again, I would watch the tears form in her eyes, feel the heartbreak in her hug. Once again, I would relive the heartache of this loss.

That's when the phone rang. It was Jonathan. "Mom, I think I'm gonna make it. I think I'm gonna walk."

For the past month, I had ridden a rollercoaster of emotions as I deliberated over the decision to retire, but that was not the only stressor in our lives at that point. We were also worried about Jonathan.

Jonathan had gone to James Madison University as planned. He embraced college life with gusto, taking up mountain biking and skiing while forming strong friendships, but his academic life had been marked by highs and lows. Like many, he struggled to find the right major. There had been a series of false starts, and both he and his parents had wondered if it would all work out.

CHAPTER 17
The Fork In The Road

Over the past five years, I had spent so many hours in prayer for him that I needed knee pads. Again and again, I would remind myself of the promise I received on the morning of his freshman move-in day.

While the guys packed the truck for our departure, I paused in my bedroom for a tearful prayer, my heart heavy with loss and worry. I heard the promise clearly, the little voice saying, "I got him."

As always, God's promises prevail, and Jonathan had weathered the storms. He was in his final semester, at least we sincerely hoped so.

There was this little problem with Spanish. A graduation requirement, Jonathan had to pass his final Spanish class. Not gifted in the art of languages, he had struggled immensely.

We had visited him a few weeks before with the intention of telling him the news of my retirement in person. He took the news well, his reaction a mix of concern and relief. He knew how hard I had been working and agreed that if it was affecting my vision, it was time to retire.

During our visit, Jonathan had been uncertain about his standing. The semester was coming down to the wire, and Jonathan was sweating it. In order to graduate, he needed a "C" in Spanish, but could he pull it off? More time on my knees, more ardent prayers. Between my eyes and my son, heaven was working overtime hearing the prayers on our behalf.

Now here was Jonathan on the other end of the phone, his voice nervous, but excited. "Mom, I think I'm gonna make it. I think I'm gonna walk."

My heart thundered inside my chest as I absorbed the meaning of his words. "What? Did you pass the exam? Are you going to graduate?"

"Yeah, I think so. The professor said he'd pass me. I talked to the registrar's office. If I can get all the signatures on the form tomorrow, they will let me walk on Saturday!"

My heart soared with joy. Graduation... dare I hope? "Oh, buddy! That's so awesome!"

I could hear him smiling, his grin so broad, it was audible! He was on his way to the bookstore to see if he could still get a cap and gown. He had been so uncertain of the outcome that he had refused to let us make any plans for graduation. We had no hotel reservations in a college town where rooms were always tight. Eric and I had been on pins and needles over this, not to mention the little issue of my impending retirement.

We made a plan that he would call me once he had the official approval complete. I would then find hotel rooms, and Jonathan would call his grandparents to invite them. Could we pull this off on such short notice? "J, if you're gonna walk, we will be there to watch you, even if we have to drive all night!"

I hung up the phone in time to see my friend Annette walk through the office door. Following a hug of greeting, I gave her both the good and bad news. We smiled, then cried and then, prayed. My rollercoaster ride continued.

On Thursday afternoon, I got the call of confirmation. The grandparents received their joyous call too. I found what was no doubt the last hotel rooms in the area, and on Friday afternoon, we hit the road for JMU!

On that sunny Saturday morning, dressed in his purple and gold robe, Jonathan stepped across yet another stage to claim his college diploma. Seated on a row with all four grandparents and Eric's brother Steve, Eric and I held our breath until they called his name, our whole row erupting in cheers of pure bliss. No one was more thrilled than Jonathan. His grin was a mile wide!

Seated on the same quad that I had processed across in my graduation robes 32 years before, I lifted up a heartfelt prayer of thanksgiving. God had answered all those motherly prayers, and Jonathan had succeeded. More than that, God's grace had been sufficient to allow me to not only see Jonathan's high school graduation, but his college one too. I could see his handsome face,

CHAPTER 17
The Fork In The Road

his bright smile. I had been there to witness this marvelous milestone. Yet another miracle from a good and gracious God!

Retired

On a hot July morning, I dressed carefully, donning a dressy jacket and blouse instead of my usual shirt and white lab coat. It was a big day. It was my last day.

Time had flown since my decision point in April. The notifications were complete. The paperwork was in order. Files had been cleaned out and turned over. Thirty-two years of books, memorabilia and picture frames had been packed. There was nothing left to do, but say goodbye.

My farewell reception was scheduled for 11 am. I sat in my little office and looked around. Could this really be the end?

Silently, I conversed with God, thanking Him for all the years, all the opportunities to serve. What a wonderful career. What a privilege it had been to be a nurse, to have cared for others, to have made a difference. I felt a little sad, but more than anything, I just felt grateful. God had given me a wonderful profession and a passion for the work I did. I loved nursing, had always been so proud to be a nurse. It had been an honor to help people, a blessing to be able to make things better.

Now it was over. My career was done, and my heart ached, crushed in a vice grip of loss. I would miss it all so much: the people, my colleagues, the satisfaction of making a difference in someone else's life.

But it was time to move on. No regrets, only good memories. I was doing the right thing. No time for second guessing the plan.

I pulled on my lab coat and made one more set of rounds on the nursing units, accepting tearful hugs and fond farewells. My heartstrings tugged as I walked away. I would miss my nurses.

Returning to my office, I changed into my dressy jacket and headed downstairs for the reception. With Eric by my side, I entered the large room adorned with a long table laden with food, punch and a bouquet of flowers. I smiled in surprise. Could this all be for me? Then I wondered, "Will anyone come?"

I need not have wondered about that, for soon the room was packed. Friends filled the space, all pausing to greet me with a hug, each sharing a kind word. Some brought cards, others delivered flowers. We shared stories and laughed at the memories. A few tears were shed, but mostly, it was hugs and smiles.

Colleagues from all over the hospital came. There were nurses, physicians, pharmacists, nursing assistants, and secretaries. I was so honored.

Old friends, long since retired, came back to wish me well. My mentor Marianne drove two hours just to say her well wishes.

My old friend and supervisor Lynn was there, and she had orchestrated a fabulous surprise. She had pulled together our original leadership team from the nursing unit I had worked on at the time of my diagnosis. Five of my original co-workers were there waiting for me, bright smiles on their faces. Barry had driven all the way from Kentucky! He was the manager who had hired me 26 years before, and he had returned to see me off. After the reception, we enjoyed a lovely lunch together. I grinned at my forever friends around the table and realized I had come full circle.

It was a joyful celebration, and I was deeply honored. What a lovely send-off! The presence of all those fabulous friends and colleagues made the leaving easier. I was just so grateful.

We loaded the truck with flowers and boxes, and I looked back one last time at the hospital that had been such an important part of my life for so long. It was over now. I was retired.

Adjusting

When Monday rolled around and I did not go to work, it seemed strange. Still, I didn't mind the extra sleep. I was exhausted.

CHAPTER 17
The Fork In The Road

It was good that it was summertime. There were lots of activities to distract me. At times, I felt a bit lost, but I refused to give into regret or self-pity. I just got busy instead.

Cleaning closets and catching up on household tasks filled a few weeks. I planted a few flowers and had fun watching them grow.

I traveled down to South Carolina to see my parents for a long weekend. It had been a long time since I had visited them alone, and the three of us had fun hanging out and attending the family reunion.

I returned home to greet our old Army buddies, Susan and Bill, who had traveled from their home in Portland, Oregon to check on us. Susan said it was to see the Great Smoky Mountains, but I knew better. She wanted to lay eyes on me and see that I was OK. Having retired several years previous, she shared words of wisdom about adjusting to retirement, and their visit bolstered my spirits.

Following graduation, Jonathan had headed back to Tennessee to work again as a river raft guide for the summer. Wanting to pull the whole family together to celebrate his graduation and my retirement, my dear Aunt Sandra rented a house in the NC mountains, and the entire Texas clan came out for a visit. It was a happy week of family togetherness, a treasured reminder of my family's love for me.

Perhaps the greatest blessing of that summer came once again in the form of Tami. She had retired from teaching in early June, her retirement long planned, while mine was not. Without prior planning, we found ourselves adjusting to this new season together. We shopped and lunched, gardened in our yards, and visited on my porch or her patio. We even ran away to the beach for a week. With her wheels readily available, I didn't feel trapped at home. Once again, Tami saved the day!

My newfound freedom afforded the opportunity for another trip to the beach with two of my favorite girls. Mere days away from starting her senior year at the University of Richmond, Elizabeth headed south to join Liz and me for some fabulous girl time at

Wrightsville Beach. It was three days of sun, fun, food, and family stories. Priceless!

I'm not sure if there was a secret plot hatched by my family and friends to keep me busy that summer, but obviously, they did. As summer crept into fall, I was feeling better. Perhaps this retirement thing would work out after all.

Soaring

Eric watched me closely all summer, a little worried that I would have a hard time adjusting. The summer was full of fun trips and visits, but how would it be when things quieted down in the fall?

That's when he came up with a plan, knowing just what I needed. He proposed a trip to New England in October to see the autumn leaves. It wasn't hard to sell that deal.

The trip was absolutely amazing, just the two of us, rolling down the road in his hot little silver Mustang. I was unprepared for the magnificence of Niagara Falls, mesmerized by the mists that rose over that rushing water. As we made our way from Niagara to Maine, I soaked up the scenic views, simply stunned by the beauty of the fall color. Along the way, we admired quaint little towns and strolled along historic streets.

On my 54th birthday, we took a harbor cruise along the waters of Bar Harbor, Maine. Our guide was a naturalist regaling us with local history and pointing out the native wildlife. As we sailed slowly by a rocky cliff, he pointed high on the cliff toward an eagle's nest. Eric spotted the nest and called out, "There it is!" His voice cracked with excitement.

I scanned the cliff, knowing full well my search was in vain. With my tiny central field, it is almost impossible for me to find specific objects like that, particularly at such a distance. I was resigned to the fact that I wouldn't be able to see it. I was just happy Eric could.

But as usual, Eric was determined to try. Stretching his arm out, pointing at the nest, he pulled me close so that I could visually track down his outstretched arm. "Look! Follow my arm. See it there, right on the edge of the cliff?"

I followed his instruction, obedient, but not really hopeful. My eyes traveled down the length of his arm, and suddenly, I gasped in amazement. "I see it! I see it!"

There, clinging to the edge of the rocky cliff face was the largest nest I had ever seen, and peeking out the top was the gleaming white head of a bald eagle. "Oh, I see it! I see It!"

Eric's joy was palpable. "You got it? You see it? Oh, awesome!"

My heart thumped with pure joy as I stared, transfixed on this amazing sight. Just when I thought the moment could not get any better, the eagle took off in flight. And I saw it! Because I was locked on the bird in its nesting position, I had been able to follow its movement. It was incredible!

The eagle soared high against the October blue sky, its huge wings pumping hard. I was holding my breath, completely fixated on this magnificent creature.

Then suddenly, the eagle switched course, turning back in the direction of the boat. Still locked on his wings, I watched him shift in the wind, rotating his body in midair. With the cliff as a backdrop and the sun's rays glistening on his shiny feathers, the eagle passed directly in front of me, its outstretched wings tilted toward me in a salute of sorts. I marveled at the sight, completely astounded.

"Oh Lord, thank You. Thank You for letting me see this. Oh, it's amazing!"

The guide said the eagle was showing off, but I knew that amazing sight was my birthday gift from God. It was a promise. God was telling me that it would all work out, that life ahead would be good, that I had done the right thing. God was at work, and I must look forward. No turning back, no second guessing. He would lead the way forward. The future was filled with possibilities. That beautiful eagle was my messenger, a beacon of hope soaring high against a brilliant blue October sky.

Opportunity Knocks

Returning home from that trip with new resolve, I determined to embrace this new season of my life. I would let go of the loss of my career and reach out for new opportunities.

There was no need to reach out, however, because the opportunities started knocking on my door. Always involved in church activities, I began to take on more responsibilities. I had taught an adult Sunday School class for over 20 years and had participated on the Praise Team for three years. While these activities continued, I joined other church committees and the women's walking group.

Having a passion for service activities, I began to consider if there was a community need that I could address. Was there a community service project that I could get passionate about?

The answer to that question came during a worship service one Sunday morning. A guest speaker was discussing the issue of childhood hunger. I felt a quickening of the Spirit, knowing full well that this was the issue I could get passionate about. "But Lord, what shall I do?"

The response came quickly. Our church had just initiated a partnership with a local elementary school. I was asked to join the steering committee for the project. One of our first priorities was to expand the food backpack program that my Sunday School class had been leading. Our class had served fifteen families weekly. Our steering committee set a new goal of serving fifty students. I volunteered to lead the project. My mission to address childhood hunger had begun.

One of the best parts of retirement was being able to enjoy the outdoors. I bought a glider for the front porch and began a morning breakfast ritual of greeting the sunrise, just rocking and reflecting. I bought a few plants to spruce up the porch, and soon, I was planting flowers everywhere. Gardening became yet another new passion.

CHAPTER 17
The Fork In The Road

Before I could bat an eye, life was busy and full, full of purpose and passion again. Opportunity had knocked, and doors had opened.

Places to Be

Lady Liberty towered above me; her arm outstretched in welcome. I stood at the deck rail of our river cruise boat mesmerized by one amazing sight after another. I had come to "The Big Apple" with my girlfriends excited to explore New York City for a long weekend.

Our tour guide was my dear friend Leigh who is an expert at navigating the city sights. She led Tami, Kim F and me up and down the bustling streets and subways. I tapped along behind them, now comfortable with the white cane I had once resisted so intensely. I couldn't have navigated New York without it, and as I traversed the ancient subway stairs and crowded intersections, I gave thanks for that white cane that offered me independence.

My friends took great care of me as they always have. They were determined to ensure I could see and do it all. We made quite a scene as I tapped behind my three girlfriends, getting some quizzical stares from strangers. We had a blast!

Perhaps the most poignant moment of the weekend was our visit to the 9/11 Memorial. Walking around those fountains, hearing the stories of the victims and survivors, brought back the memories of that tragic day and those terrifying hours on the streets of D.C. Seeing that memorial rise from the ashes of loss, a new tower stretching toward the sky, reminded me that faith, hope and love will always triumph.

It was a wonderful weekend of new sights and sounds, food and fun, and best of all, friendship. Check! Another item ticked off on that bucket list, the first of many trips to come! So much to look forward to: a summer road trip to Texas, a Sherer family reunion in Bermuda, and the long-awaited return to Scotland in 2016. That retinal clock was still ticking. No time to slow down. I had places to be, and things to see!

Launched

The car was packed. Jonathan had everything he owned in there. Clothes and camping supplies filled the back end of his white Subaru Outback, the storage carrier on top crammed with skis and rafting gear. His mountain bike was strapped to the tailgate.

At the gas station, our tan Ford F-150 was parked on one side of the bank of gas pumps while his loaded down Subaru occupied the other. We were going to fill up his car with gas one more time. Eric put his credit card in the pump and started the process. Grabbing the handle of the gas hose, Jonathan began pumping.

It was a beautiful September day, a gentle breeze blowing, the crisp feel of fall in the air. The cornflower blue sky glowed with the golden sunlight that comes with autumn in the Carolinas. It was a perfect day for traveling.

I stood there watching my tall, handsome son, taking in his soft brown eyes, short brown hair and that manly beard. As he pressed against the car fiddling with the gas nozzle, his white Hard Rock t-shirt revealed broad, strong shoulders, his body lean and muscular, the kind of physique you would expect from a ski instructor and rafting guide. My outdoorsman, my adventure seeker, my boy was all grown up.

Answering my gaze, he smiled at me, forging ahead with small talk, trying to keep the conversation light. He knows his mama. He knew it was hard on me to watch him go. As excited as he was about the new adventure ahead, I think it was hard for him to go, for him to leave us. Like me, he knew this was it.

He was headed back to Breckenridge, Colorado to pursue his second year as a Level 2 ski instructor. This year, he was setting off to find a place to live, something permanent with a year-long lease. He planned to stay there at least two years, acquiring more training and experience before moving on. There would be no coming back

CHAPTER 17
The Fork In The Road

to Tennessee as he did this past summer. He will stay in the West, finding a new river rafting challenge out there.

As I watched him chat with his father, I reminded myself yet again, "He is happy. He is doing what he loves, chasing his dreams. It is as it should be."

You raise them to be independent, and then they are. You have to smile and accept it, because that's the way it's supposed to be. I would not want anything less for him. I want him to be motivated, dreaming dreams and following his life path. Do I wish he was closer? Absolutely. But that is not his dream, and I wouldn't squelch his passions just to have him nearby.

Just yesterday, the nurse was handing me that tiny baby looking so small and fragile in that little white blanket. I had stared at that tightly wrapped bundle, thinking, "Wow! How in the world are we going to do this?" For all my fears, there was nothing I wanted more than to be his mother.

Images flooded my mind: the grinning toddler at the top of that big yellow slide, eyes shining with excitement; the fierce four-year-old poised on the starting blocks, ready to race, the boy in the bright blue coat and tan knit cap bouncing down the London streets; the wide grin of the young man behind the wheel, driver's license now in his pocket. I recalled the handshake with Mickey Mouse, the racing adventures in the Jeff Gordon jacket, our little story circle as we read Harry Potter out loud together.

Now, twenty-four short years later, we were sending him off. The time had passed so quickly. I remember it all. I loved every moment of the life we shared as our little family of three.

He must go, but the memories will not. They are locked safely inside my heart, forever to be treasured. Standing there on that gas station pavement, I gave thanks to God for the precious gift of my son, for the tremendous joy he brought to my life. I prayed as always for his protection and direction, that he would be the man God created him to be.

The gas pump clicked; the tank was full. It was time. He bent down just a little to grab my waist and hug me tight. "I love you, Mama." I had to stand on my tippy toes to reach my arms around his neck and pull him close. "Oh, I love you, buddy!" He squeezed me that much tighter before pulling away.

Then he reached for his daddy, one of those manly back slapping hugs, and yet, it lasted a little bit longer than usual, ending in a tight squeeze before they both pulled apart. There was love in those hugs from our now grown son.

Jonathan turned away then, circling the car, putting some distance between the emotion that bounced around the three of us. He was calling out, "Maybe we can meet for Thanksgiving in Texas with the family. Maybe that will work out." With a big grin and a long last look at each of us, he opened the car door and slid behind the wheel. As he cranked the car, we headed for the truck. We followed him out of the gas station, down the road and watched him take the entrance ramp to the highway.

He was launched.

An Unexpected Gift

From the moment I quit work, the messages began to pile up. "Anita, you must write a book." From family to friends, I heard the same message. My old friend Ricky even challenged me, "You need to tell your story."

I smiled appreciatively, but essentially ignored these urges. I guess I wasn't ready.

I did begin journaling some, sharing some stories with my close friends. With every story, Tami remarked, "Anita, when are you going to share this with more people?"

As with most of God's plans, they present themselves in surprising ways. When our pastor's wife asked if I would take on the task of sending weekly emails to our church walking group, I responded affirmatively. Why not? I had the time.

CHAPTER 17
The Fork In The Road

The email was intended to notify the group of walking times and locations. Words of motivation and encouragement should be added to keep the members moving. It sounded simple. "Oh, and you can add a spiritual focus too."

That's how it started, and my Monday Motivations were born. Sending out a weekly message on Monday morning, I began to dabble with stories and words of inspiration. I quoted relevant scriptures and added a prayer.

Soon, I was on a roll, finding inspiration in everything from flowers to childhood memories. I began to write with gusto, enjoying the time I spent on my keyboard. Receiving positive feedback from friends, my interest grew. Was God opening a new door for me?

Enthusiasm led to passion, and soon, I was joining a writer's club. I threw myself into writing stories, even poetry. No one was more surprised than me.

One night, I woke in the wee hours, my mind on high alert. Unable to fall back asleep, I lay there in the quiet, listening to Eric's steady breaths. It was then that I heard the quiet voice, soft yet clear. "You will write about the moments, all the moments that were hard and you triumphed because of Me. You will write about my promise."

The voice was so clear, the words so unexpected. There was no doubt about the promise. It was Isaiah 42:16.

Still, I confess that I paused, wondering, "Did I really hear that?" But I quickly dismissed those doubts. I knew the message was from God, and He was blessing this new season of my life with an unexpected gift. Suddenly, the title was there, in my mind, crystal clear. The book will be called, "Rough Places Smooth." It will be about the moments in my journey through blindness.

I had a new calling, a new passion, a clear purpose once more, and this purpose is to write.

Free

Another eye chart, another exam chair. It should have been a routine appointment with Dr. Whitaker. Perhaps an adjustment in my glasses. No big deal.

I rose on a hot August morning in 2016 ready to meet the day, looking forward to seeing my good doctor and friend. What started as a glorious day suddenly went south.

For the millionth time, I sat in the exam chair as the technician flashed up the eye chart. I covered my left eye and read the normal row with my right eye. No worries. Onto the next step.

My right eye covered, I glanced at the eye chart with my left eye, and panic gripped my gut. Acid rose in my throat as I stared at the screen. There were no letters, only blurry lines. What was there only a moment before had vanished. Even the large "E" at the top of the chart had somehow left the room.

I felt sick. I knew what this meant. So did the technician. I looked at her, fear rising in my chest. "I can't see anything. I can't make out a single letter."

The central field in my left eye was gone. My central vision in that eye was lost, with no hope of return. The left eye had always been worse than the right. From the moment I was diagnosed, the disease had been more aggressive in the left eye. Now, the disease had won the battle and laid claim to the last vestiges of its capital territory.

I had known this day would come. I knew that one day the tiny island of vision that was my left central field would be lost. The visual acuity in that eye had been fading in tiny increments over the past few years. I knew it was only a matter of time. I just didn't know when I woke up on that August morning that this would be that dreaded day.

As the technician quietly left the room, my shoulders sagged under the weight of this devastating discovery. Fear gripped my heart, yanking it from my chest, then hurling it full force into the depths of the sea.

CHAPTER 17
The Fork In The Road

My mind began to race, spinning faster and faster as the anxious thoughts swirled around inside my head. "I hate this. I hate this disease. I hate how it can steal my joy. I hate the anger, the sadness, the worry. I hate that I have to live all this all over again."

And then, I stopped. "Stop this. You knew this could happen, but God is still here. He is still in control. He is good and He loves you."

I took some deep breaths and began to quote scripture to myself.

"Never will I leave you; never will I forsake you" (Hebrews 13:5 *NIV*).

"The Lord is my shepherd; I shall not want... Yea, though I walk through the valley of the shadow of death, I will fear no evil: for thou art with me; thy rod and thy staff they comfort me" (Psalm 23:1,4 *KJV*).

"For I know the plans I have for you," declares the Lord, "plans to prosper you and not to harm you, plans to give you hope and a future" (Jeremiah 29:11 *NIV*).

"And we know that in all things God works for the good of those who love him, who have been called according to his purpose" (Romans 8:28 *NIV*). I thought to myself, "NOT in some things or in most things, but in ALL things."

"I have told you these things, so that in me you may have peace. In this world you will have trouble. But take heart! I have overcome the world" (John 16:33 *NIV*).

"For the Lord is good and his love endures forever; his faithfulness continues through all generations" (Psalm 100:5 *NIV*).

Then, I heard it. That little voice was speaking again. It was a verse I had not referenced in a long time. "Then you will know the truth, and the truth will set you free" (John 8:32 *NIV*).

I had not thought of this verse in many years, but it was part of the lyrics to a song I had sung in my high school choral group. The song flooded my mind, its melody taking over. "You shall know the truth and the truth shall set you free."

Why was I remembering this now? Truth, it's talking about truth. Truth that can set you free.

I had always considered that this verse was talking about the salvation of Jesus Christ, how knowing Him would save us and set us free, but suddenly, I recognized a whole new meaning. I thought of this verse in light of the verses I had been quoting to myself. Those verses are filled with hope and comfort. "They are true. That is truth and that truth can set me free. Free from doubts. Free from fear. Free from anxiety. Free from worry."

I heard the little voice again, "You shall know the truth, and the truth shall set you free."

My anxiety dissipated, replaced by a peace that began to seep slowly into the depths of my being, soothing this soul so weighed down by the burden of blindness. I inhaled deeply, letting go of my fear as I slowly released my breath. "I could live free."

By the time Dr. Whitaker came into the room, I was calm. She was concerned, sitting down directly in front of me, never turning to her computer, but simply choosing to sit there with me, absorbing the moment. In due time, she asked about how I was doing.

I heard myself say, "I'm OK. I knew this day would come. I've had a lot of years to learn to live with this disease. It's been a long time coming. I'll be OK."

The interesting thing was that I really was OK. It was not just words. I truly felt His peace in that moment and in the moments that came thereafter.

Later in the evening, I contacted my prayer warrior friends and shared my sad news followed by my exam chair revelation. My longtime riding buddy and forever friend Susan emailed me back, saying that her devotional that morning had covered Isaiah 43:2. She felt the words of that verse were meant for me. "When you pass through the waters, I will be with you; and when you pass through the rivers, they will not sweep over you. When you walk through the fire, you will not be burned; the flames will not set you ablaze" (Isaiah 43:2 *NIV*).

CHAPTER 17
The Fork In The Road

My heart skipped a beat as I read that verse. The theme of water reminded me of my long-ago divine message, "You will get through this one day at a time, one wave at a time."

This was another wave, another wave in a sea of circumstances that threaten to drown me, but then as well as now, I am not afloat in that water alone. My God is there with me. He will keep my head above the waves.

No matter the storm, no matter the size of the waves, I will not drown. For I am not alone. God is with me in that water. I need not fear. I need not worry. He will never leave me nor forsake me. He will work all things for my good. That is the truth and that truth sets me free.

Faith Beyond Sight

We cannot always see where the path is leading us, we just have to step out in faith. My "Monday Motivations" started as a weekly message to motivate our women's walking group. I took this on as a simple task to support my church family, never dreaming how it would grow.

After six months of writing these messages, I shared one of my messages with my aunt Sandra. She and Uncle Tom have always been my balcony people, faithful lifelong cheerleaders who have applauded my successes and supported me through the losses. Sandra's enthusiasm about my writing prompted me to share my messages with a larger circle of family and friends.

When God blesses something, it grows. God blessed my weekly offerings, and soon, the list of email recipients became so long that it was cumbersome to manage. At Eric's prompting, I explored a new way to spread my weekly messages through means of a blog. Now a graphic designer and art director, Tami's daughter Linsey used her talents for web design to help me create my blog site. Faith Beyond Sight, www.faithbeyondsight.com, was born in

February of 2018. The blog has been blessed with a growing list of followers reaching all over the globe.

In June of 2016, as we journeyed through a sermon series on the book of Job, my pastor asked me to deliver the sermon message and share my testimony. Both surprised and intimidated by the request, I agreed to pray on it. Reaching out to my father for his wise counsel, I shared my anxious deliberations. His response took me off guard. "Why wouldn't you? Why wouldn't you do it?"

Well, I couldn't think of a rebuttal for that challenge, so I nervously agreed. It was a powerful experience to share how God had made the rough places smooth.

A year later, I delivered another sermon message describing my "Alone In The Desert" experience. Since then, God has placed other speaking opportunities in my path, and I have been honored to share my story with the hope that it would bring God the glory.

Yes, when God blesses something, it grows. When God calls us to do something, we must step out in faith, even if we can't see the path in front of us or where it will all end. We must have faith beyond sight. "For we live by faith, not by sight" (2 Corinthians 5:7 *NIV*).

Moving On

Hands on the steering wheel, Eric turned toward me, his face alight with a brilliant smile. I reached for his hand and squeezed, "Day 10 of Anita and Eric's Epic Adventure!"

It was September of 2018, and we were on the road again. Eric grinned, his hazel eyes shining, "Isn't it cool we get to do this?"

It was cool, very cool. Our epic adventure took us 34 days and 7627.5 miles across eighteen states. Spending 157 hours and 6 minutes in the truck seat, we went as far north as the Upper Peninsula of Michigan and as far west as Boise, Idaho, where we joined up with Jonathan as he completed his summer job on the Payette River. We toured Yellowstone National Park with him, and

CHAPTER 17
The Fork In The Road

then joined our old Army friends Susan and Bill in the Grand Tetons. Yes, it was cool, truly an epic adventure!

After three good years consulting for the Bermuda hospital system, the contract ended, leaving Eric with a big decision. After searching for other contracts and only finding fast paced, high pressure options, Eric decided to join me in retirement. In truth, I think he was jealous at all the fun I was having.

The timing was good as our aging parents were beginning to need us more. After a series of serious health issues, Eric's father Pete had become more limited in his mobility. The house in Richmond was not set up for his restricted mobility, prompting a move for Liz and Pete to a beautiful retirement facility near us. With them close by, Liz and I have relished our girl time around town. The new living situation lifted Pete's sagging spirits and offered the care he needed as his health continued to decline. Nearly four years after their move, we lost Pete to a massive stroke. We were so thankful to have shared these last years with him, grateful that we could be by his side when he passed from this life.

My parents remain down on the farm, and my visits to the old home place remain precious. After fully recovering from two serious heart attacks in his mid-40's, my father was hit with heart failure at age 80, later followed by a Parkinson's diagnosis. He has adapted to both insults with his usual steely resolve, and I am so thankful that I can serve as his personal cardiology nurse. My mother developed severe degenerative arthritis that limited her for many years, but thanks to the miracles of modern medicine, her situation dramatically improved following bilateral knee replacements, the success no doubt aided by the excellent nursing care she received from her daughter.

I had thought my nursing career was over, but instead I just changed course, serving as nurse case manager and patient advocate for each of our beloved parents. It has been our honor to care for them as they have cared so beautifully for us.

Rough Places Smooth

Ever the vagabond, Jonathan left Colorado for the mountains of Montana, still pursuing his passion for ski instructing on those snowy slopes. Summertime finds him moving from river to river as a raft guide. His schedule offers lots of opportunity for travel, and he returns home several times a year for a much-welcomed visit. He has found a special young lady in Jocelyn, and we are excited about their future together. He is independent, enjoying life and pursuing his passions. He is, and always will be, my joy.

Elizabeth is a beautiful young woman with a passion for the environment. Her vocational pursuits have taken her to Washington, D.C. and now on to San Francisco, California. Last summer, the entire Sherer clan gathered to celebrate her marriage to Tom, their nuptials spoken on a sunny rooftop, the beautiful Blue Ridge Mountains their backdrop. She was an absolutely gorgeous bride, and her favorite Auntie could not have been more proud. Distance limits our visits, but our hearts are forever intertwined.

Ben is a handsome young man, all grown up, living in Arizona and loving it. Ben has turned his love of cycling into a career path, recently pursuing an exciting new opportunity in the bike manufacturing industry. Like Jonathan, he embraces both skiing and mountain biking, and the two cousins pursue these passions together every chance they get. The boys are often accompanied by Eric's brother Steve who still thrives on outdoing his son and nephew on such physical pursuits. They all have a great time together. Steve has found the love of his life, Dorothy, and we are thrilled to have her as part of our family.

My girlfriends remain a cherished part of my life, their cars finding their way to my driveway often. My faithful prayer warriors are but a text away. There are lunches and play days with Mary, and shopping and patio visits with Tami. Marianne drops in for lunch now and then, and I still keep up with my church buddies. I thank God for my girlfriends.

Travel plans continue. We are the proud owners of a 20-foot travel trailer, and we are mastering the art of camping. Who knows where you will find us next?

CHAPTER 17
The Fork In The Road

Life is moving on, and we are moving with it, exceedingly grateful for every blessing and every opportunity. The journey continues, and I plan to keep on walking by faith.

CHAPTER 18
Final Reflections On The Journey

Porch Perspective

Swirls of color dance on the horizon as pink and gold meet blue. Light filters through the branches of the distant tree line. The birds flutter amongst the tree limbs, calling out their morning greetings to one another, the cacophony of sound growing ever louder with each passing moment. A sudden burst of orange eclipses the distant tree tops, and the birds go wild with applause.

Bathed in the golden light of the dawn, I relish this daily ritual of witnessing the sunrise. From the glider on my front porch, I claim a front row seat for this display of God's splendor. It is one of the best perks of retirement.

Hot tea in hand, I rejoice in the majesty of the morning. I sip and savor, rock and reflect, thankful for this quiet time with God. The joyful sound of the birdsong never fails to bring a smile to my face. I treasure these porch moments, soaking in every sight, knowing full well how easily it can all slip away.

More than 28 years after my heart-wrenching diagnosis, that donut-shaped ring of mid-peripheral vision is now completely gone in both eyes, as is the central field in the left eye. Photos, television and printed material are all but lost to me now. Color differentiation is a bit challenging, and faces are harder to recognize. Still, a tiny island of central vision remains in the right eye, allowing me to make out the large text letters on my iPhone or iPad. Accessibility features allow me to use these devices effectively. Even more amazing is that the disease has thus far spared my far peripheral vision. This large outer ring of healthy vision allows me to see images at the top, bottom and side of my visual field by scanning my eyes back-and-forth, up and down. It is not normal clear vision, but it is vision nonetheless.

Therefore, by the grace of God, it is an extraordinary blessing to still be able to watch the sunrise. Since the outdoors is my favorite place to be, I am so grateful that I can still take in my surroundings, still see the hot pink bloom of my geranium or the towering pine that shades my front yard. The sky is still blue, the grass green, the flowers a kaleidoscope of color. These images are a bit fuzzy and distorted, but they are still there. For all this, I am so very thankful.

From March to November, I greet the day in my glider, sometimes wrapped in a coat and blanket, other times soaking up the early morning rays in shorts and a t-shirt. Rain or shine, I rock and reflect. And I remember. I remember it all.

I recall the agony of those early days: the terror, the heartache, the lost dreams, the sheer frustration. I can still see the young woman at the window, clutching those car keys, angry tears spilling down her face, asking yet again, "How in the world are we going to do this?"

I didn't have the answer then, but I know it now. God answered "How?" God showed up and showed me how. He answered how with His people, His provision and His presence.

He began with the love of my precious family. Our loving parents were so incredible, such beacons of light guiding us through those dark days. They have stood by us in the sorrows and celebrated with us in the sunshine. The love of my extended family has brought such comfort and support. From my aunts, uncles and cousins to Steve, Elizabeth and Ben, each have offered their own brand of blessings to my life.

God knew I would need a rock to cling to when the waves of adversity came, and so, He gave me Eric. He knew I would need a strong and faithful partner to face the trials of encroaching blindness. Eric has been that and more. He has been my traveling companion, my soul mate, my very best friend. He knows me better than anyone else, and loves me anyway. He has lived true to his marriage vows, loving me for better, for worse, for richer, for poorer, in sickness and in health. Together, we have experienced the beauty of a shared life. I am forever grateful. It is truly a precious gift to travel this road of life by his side.

The timing of my diagnosis was no accident. There was a reason that I did not learn of the disease until age 33, and that reason was Jonathan. God knew that I would need a reason to go on, and that little boy became my lifeline. He was my reason to rise up in the morning, my reason to keep going in those hard, dark days. With his insatiable curiosity, those soft, brown eyes, and that brilliant smile, he brought the joy back into my life. He gave me purpose. I had to be the mother he needed me to be. Through the sweet embrace of a little boy, love triumphed over tragedy.

God showed up with the people He put in our path. From the kindness of strangers to the faithfulness of friends, God sent us messengers of hope. They were the helping hands just when we needed it most. I remember it all: Fred's voice on the line, "Anita, if you let me help you, it will help me;" Susan's bright smile, "I would love to give you a ride;" the roar of Tami's Taxi in my driveway; the heart-to-heart talks with Mary; the friendly voices on the other end of the line; the text messages that came at just the right time; the love of our church family. There is no doubt. God used our friends to see us through. We couldn't have made it without them.

God showed up with His provision. He provided the rides. He supplied the jobs. He gave me an amazing nursing career despite the limitations of vision loss. I look back across the years simply awestruck. God worked it all together for my good (Romans 8:28).

Ultimately, God showed up with His presence. God never left me alone. I may have turned away in fear and anger, or doubt and despair, but God never let go. His outstretched hand of grace was always there.

I can recall the moment so clearly, the kind voice of the speaker who clutched my arm and shared a divine message. "You will get through this one day at a time, one wave at a time."

This journey through blindness has been all about the waves. There were times that I thought I might drown in a sea of sorrow, but even in my most desperate hours, God was still there. Over the years, the waves of adversity kept coming, pounding away at the sand beneath my feet, crashing, churning, throwing me off balance.

CHAPTER 18
Final Reflections On The Journey

So many times, the waves knocked me down, the riptide washing me out to sea. I was certain all was lost, that I couldn't go on, that this would be the end of me. Yet, right then and there, I would find His outstretched hand. God never left me alone in those raging waters. He was always there, even when I couldn't see Him, even when I couldn't feel His arms lifting me up above the tumbling waves.

God doesn't promise us a trouble-free life. In fact, quite the contrary. Jesus said in John 16:33, "In this world, you will have trouble." But He didn't stop there. Jesus went on to say, "But take heart, I have overcome the world" (John 16:33 *NIV*). The trouble will still come, but we never have to face it alone. As promised, He will never leave us nor forsake us (Hebrews 13:5).

God didn't save me from the struggle. He just saw me through it, one day at a time, one wave at a time.

Bearing My Cross

All those years ago, I had asked, "Why, Lord, why? Why would you let this happen?"

God didn't choose to answer that question. God's thoughts are not our thoughts, His ways are not our ways (Isaiah 55:8). There are some things on this side of heaven that we will never understand. We live in a fallen and sinful world where things go wrong, and bad things happen to good people. While we struggle to comprehend why God allows suffering, I have learned that God can take the hard things of this life and work them together for good.

Jeremiah 29:11 tells us, "For I know the plans I have for you," declares the Lord, "plans to prosper you and not to harm you, plans to give you hope and a future" (Jeremiah 29:11 *NIV*). While things did go wrong with my eyes, God still had a good plan for my life. He gave me a future and a hope.

All these years later, I am struck by a very different question. "Why not me?" Who am I to be above suffering? Who am I to be above carrying my cross?

Blindness has been my cross to bear. I still remember my late-night epiphany that came from the guiding words of Dr. Dobson's book. "This is your cross. Accept it. Carry it. God will give you the grace to deal with it."

It took a long time for me to really accept this cross. I tried to carry it in those early years. I did my best to deal with it, trudging on doggedly despite the inner misery that always threatened to pull me down. Now I know that I never carried that cross alone. Jesus bore it with me. He held it up when my arms were not strong enough. He walked those hard roads with me using each challenge to teach me, to remind me that nothing is impossible with God (Mark 10:27).

Back then, I saw blindness only as a curse, a battle to be fought. However, as the years have passed, I can now see the blessings it has brought into my life. I see the people God put in my path to shepherd me. I see the opportunities I might have missed without the limitations of this disease. I cherish the sights and sounds of life around me in a way I would not have done otherwise. I would have been too busy, too driven, too caught up in my own agenda. I would have missed the moments.

Blindness has forced me to rely on God instead of my own self-sufficiency. I have had to stand on my faith, because nothing else could have delivered me from the darkness of this loss. Blindness fueled my faith, built my character, taught me perseverance, and through these things, I found hope (Romans 5:3-4).

In the hands of God, beauty can come from brokenness.

Staircase

As you have read my story, you have no doubt wondered how I could have received such God inspired epiphanies and then so easily forgotten their truths. You have ridden the seesaw of my faith walk and no doubt wondered why I couldn't hang on to those messages of comfort and hope. Why did I so often take one step up and two steps back? I have wondered these things myself.

What I have come to understand is that grief is a process, not a one-and-done deal. Loss is loss, no matter the cause, and we must grieve it to get beyond it. Working through the stages of grief is essential for healing. Before I could find my way to peace and acceptance, I had to spend time in all the stages of grief, from denial to anger, from bargaining to depression.

Many forms of chronic disease manifest in cycles of progression and plateaus, and RP is no exception. My bouts with grief followed those cycles, remitting and resurging over time. For years, I tried to shove my grief aside and move past it, but grief must be dealt with before it can be gone.

Chronic disease doesn't have to be crippling. While the disease may remain, the wounds of the spirit can be healed if we allow ourselves to work through our grief. Reaching out for help in the form of counseling was one of the best choices I ever made. It was a critical step on the pathway to peace.

Perhaps for some, the journey of faith is a linear climb from the valley to the mountaintop. Once there, they stand unwaveringly clinging to their faith no matter what storms come their way.

For me, the journey of faith has been more of a staircase, a circular staircase that slowly rises and turns from one landing to another. One step at a time, I have climbed, a life lesson learned with each shaky step.

Sometimes, the stairs were angled toward seasons of joy where I basked in the goodness of life, enjoying the happy moments and praising God. With each blessing, joy lifted my heart and grew my faith.

But then the staircase turned in another direction, ever climbing, but now framed in steps of sorrow, of hardship, of loss. These were harder steps to climb, taking my breath, stealing my energy. Still, I kept climbing, my gaze turned upward, my hope driving me forward.

Just when I thought I could not go on, just when I thought I couldn't take one more step, I would reach a landing and find it laden with peace. I rested there, relishing the lessons learned, breathing a sigh of relief at having arrived.

But the journey wasn't done. The stairway continued. With the steps looming ahead, again I climbed, sometimes struggling in pain, sometimes bounding forward in joy.

At times, I felt so alone on those stairs, convinced that God had forgotten me. Yet, I kept going, one foot in front of the other, one difficult step at a time. To my surprise, my faith grew stronger with each determined step, and my time on the peaceful landings grew even longer, affording me a better view.

From this vantage point, I can see the staircase behind me, the steps outlined so clearly. Now I see what I could not then. I was never alone on that journey. For as I took each step, as I reached out to grab the railing, my grasping hand found the open hand of God. He took hold, and by His grace, moved me forward.

With steps of joy and sorrow, the staircase climbed, finding landings of peace, but ever moving upward in hope. I have come a long way, but I am still climbing, and I think, I will do so until I reach the door of eternity, stepping through safely into the open arms of my Lord. To Him, be all glory, honor, majesty and praise! Amen.

Miracles

The sun warmed our backs as we sat under the cherry red umbrella, its canopy flapping in the gusty breeze. Two old friends chatting at a picnic table on a warm summer afternoon. It was the usual catch-up conversation, sharing news of our families, our friends, of life events since we had last sat down together.

Both of us now retired, Susan and I had made these lunchtime chats a monthly practice. Our sandwiches were spread out before us, lying on thick white wrapping paper. The paper fluttered in the strong breeze causing us both to grab our drink cups and place them on the paper lest our lunch go airborne.

Picking up my sandwich, I watched Susan closely, her beautiful face lighting up as she told her story. The wind stirred the strands of her light brown hair, dark sunglasses shading her soft brown eyes. Her genteel Southern drawl was hard at work as she told the tale of her recent trip. I hung on every word, thrilled that she had enjoyed her travels.

Pulling in my driveway that morning, our animated chatter had begun the moment I opened the car door, just as it had all those years ago when I had opened her car door for that first ride to work. With biscuits, coffee and sweet tea, we had begun our journey of friendship. What had been forced out of necessity quickly morphed into sisterhood.

Over the years, Susan and I became kindred souls, both of us traveling long hard roads of sickness and loss. After her breast cancer treatment in 1996, Susan had embraced motherhood, delighting in her precious little boy. We had ridden together for several years thereafter before Susan transitioned to a new role that offered more opportunity for time at home with her son. Though our commutes together had ceased, our close friendship continued. In 2002, we were hit with the devastating news that her cancer had metastasized. Thus began a journey of over nineteen years of constant chemotherapy and multiple surgeries. Continuing to work despite the ongoing treatment, she had forged bravely on. However, as the intensity of the chemotherapy progressed, Susan had decided to retire in late 2013, a mere eight months before my own retirement.

Just as Susan had helped me adapt to my new normal of not driving all those years ago, she had been there to help me transition into my early and unplanned retirement. She understood the mix of emotions all too well.

Enjoying each other's company and needing each other's support, we began meeting monthly over sodas and sandwiches.

These outings quickly became much more than amiable girl chitchat. They were a safe space to share the hard stuff too.

So as we sat together, we talked of cancer, of the chemo and the side effects. We talked of blindness. In her gentle way, she never failed to ask, "And how are your eyes?"

Ours was a friendship like no other. Tied together by mutual experiences of tragedy and loss, we supported and encouraged each other in a deeper, more heartfelt way. She and I shared the heartaches and mourned the losses. We gave voice to our fears, allowing each other the freedom to share openly and honestly. We coveted each other's prayers, stating our specific prayer requests.

And so as we sat there together under that bright red umbrella on that warm afternoon, we discussed her latest scan results. With a heavy sigh, she voiced, "I'm still hoping for a miracle. I still pray for that."

Offering my own weighty sigh, I nodded, "And I am too. I still pray for a cure."

As we settled into a wistful silence. I was struck by a thought, a thought that just seemed to appear in my brain. "But maybe, we already have the miracle. Maybe the miracle is just living through all this, surviving, living well despite our circumstances. Maybe that's the miracle."

We are all broken in some way. We all struggle to survive the challenges of this life. Some of our struggles are more obvious, but no one escapes suffering. Everybody has something.

Hard things happen in this life. How we choose to handle them makes all the difference. When suffering strikes, we are faced with a choice. We can choose to take the deep dive into the pit of despair, or let the bitterness build up to a boiling point. We can let the brokenness define us, or we can forge on in faith.

"Now faith is the substance of things hoped for, the evidence of things not seen" (Hebrews 11:1 *NKJV*). Susan never let the brokenness define her. Anxiety may have nipped at her heels. Fear often woke her up in the wee hours, but she chose not to live there. Susan had faith in what she could not see, but what she knew to be

CHAPTER 18
Final Reflections On The Journey

true. Her faith didn't spare her from the suffering, nor did it stop the endless rounds of chemotherapy, but her incredible faith in Jesus Christ paved the way to an abundant life. In John 10, Jesus declared, "I have come that they may have life, and that they may have it more abundantly" (John 10:10b *NKJV*). Susan found the abundant life by choosing to live beyond her hard circumstances. She chose joy in the midst of sorrow. She knew peace despite her affliction. She clung unwaveringly to the hope she affirmed, knowing with all certainty that God can be trusted to keep His promises (Hebrews 10:23).

Like Susan, my faith saved me. It saved me from a life of bitterness. It plucked me from the pit of despair. Blindness may have broken my heart and radically altered my life, but I found healing by reaching out in faith. That choice made all the difference.

We desire healing, but in our own way, by our own definition. God desires healing for us too, but in His way. His definition of our healing is sometimes different, but it is still healing, nonetheless.

Susan never received her miraculous cure for cancer, but she did receive her healing. She was freed from the ravages of metastatic breast cancer on August 23, 2021, when she went to live forever with her Lord. No more tears or fears or suffering. She is free. She is home.

Maybe the miracle that God sometimes delivers is not the cure for cancer or the recovery of sight to the blind. Maybe the miracle is the ability to go on with life anyway. It is the courage to traverse the rough waters that lie ahead. It is the strength that you didn't know you had. It is the peace that you couldn't imagine ever knowing. It is the joy that comes even in the midst of suffering. It is the hope that is not lost when the sickness still remains.

I believe the miracle is learning to live abundantly despite the blindness, the cancer, the betrayal, the adversity, the affliction. No matter the source of our suffering, the miracle is finding hope beyond hurt, and life beyond loss.

Whatever hard things we must face in this life, we don't have to face them alone. God's outstretched hand of grace is ready and waiting for us to grasp, waiting for us to trust and believe.

Don't give up. Know that God does answer prayer; maybe not immediately, but eventually, and sometimes, even eternally, the answer revealed not in this life, but in the life to come. Whatever the timing, God hears your prayers. He feels your pain. He weeps with you, and He walks with you through whatever trial you are facing. He may not take it away, but He will see you through it.

God answered the prayer of that young woman on that gorgeous November day as she stood by the swing set. He heard that prayer I lifted as my little boy headed for that bright yellow slide. I had prayed that God would let me see him grow up, that I would know what he looked like as a young man. God honored that prayer. I saw Jonathan step across his graduation stage, not just once, but twice. While I cannot see his face clearly, I know what he looks like as a young man of 30.

God answered that prayer as He did so many others. God has worked it all out. He has been faithful to the promise of Romans 8:28, "And we know that in all things God works for the good of those who love him, who have been called according to his purpose" (Romans 8:28 *NIV*). And I must add as I always do, not in some things or in most things, but in all things.

My journey continues. There will be more rough places in the road ahead. Still, I know the joy of knowing Jesus. I do not walk this road alone. God will fulfill the promise He made to me on a long-ago October evening.

"I will lead the blind by ways they have not known, along unfamiliar paths I will guide them; I will turn the darkness into light before them, and make the rough places smooth" (Isaiah 42:16a *NIV*).

Whatever road you find yourself on, whatever hard thing stands in your path, I know that we have a good, loving, and gracious God who will meet you there when you call His Name. We can trust in His promises. God can, and He will, make the rough places smooth.

CHAPTER 18
Final Reflections On The Journey

About The Author

Anita Peden Sherer is a retired cardiology nurse with a passion for storytelling that spans the genres of memoir, poetry, children's stories, and faith-inspired devotions. She is an active member of the Burlington Writers Club, receiving top honors in their annual writing contests. On her blog site, www.faithbeyondsight.com, Anita shares samples of her writing, including her Monday Motivations, weekly faith-inspired messages of hope and encouragement.

During her 32 years of nursing practice, Anita served in critical care, telemetry, cardiac rehabilitation, and community wellness. As a Cardiology Clinical Nurse Specialist, she performed the roles of educator, consultant, project manager, and nurse researcher. Anita published journal, magazine, and newspaper articles, authored two books, and served as a contributor for several other nursing textbooks. Gifted in the art of speaking, she taught countless nursing and community health education classes and presented her research and other nursing content at the local, regional and national level.

Anita and her husband Eric live in Graham, North Carolina and will soon celebrate 40 years of marriage. They have one adult son Jonathan who lives in Bozeman, Montana. Since her retirement, Anita has embraced gardening and travel, including a recent foray into RV life. She is actively engaged in volunteer work at her church and the local elementary school. Anita continues her passion for public speaking by sharing her inspirational story with community organizations, churches, and women's groups.

About The Author

Follow the Author

Want to hear more from Anita?

Visit her blog, *Faith Beyond Sight* at
faithbeyondsight.com

Look for her ***Monday Motivations*** for faith-inspired
encouragement to kick-start your week!

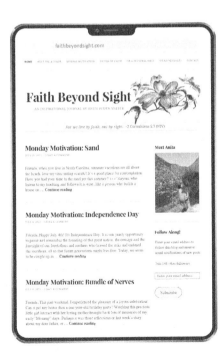

Become a subscriber to
her weekly ***Monday
Motivations*** and other
posts delivered directly
to your inbox.

HOW TO SUBSCRIBE

Find the 'Follow Along'
section on the home page,
click 'Subscribe' and enter
your email to receive new
post notifications.

Contact Anita by emailing hello@faithbeyondsight.com.

Follow the Author

Acknowledgements

Seven years have passed since the first time my fingers found the keyboard, seven years since I penned the first story in this collection. In my early post-retirement phase, the stories were about healing. Once again, my life had taken a sudden turn for which I was unprepared. Writing became an emotional outlet to offer some much needed perspective. Looking back over the years, I reminded myself of God's great faithfulness through all the hard things. The more I wrote, the more I became convinced that God had worked it all out before, and He would do so again, no matter the obstacles that lay ahead. The initial stories were written just for me, to remember, recall, to sort through it all. I had not planned to share my musings beyond the family, but God had other plans. Once again, He put people in my path to encourage me, to convince me that I could do this.

These stories would still be sequestered inside my computer without the unfailing support and endless encouragement of Tami Isley Northup. From the first story I shared, Tami posed the two questions she never stopped asking, "What are you going to do with these? When are you going to share these with more people?" She never gave up on the idea of a book, even when I had my doubts. She has been my developmental editor, grammar coach, proofreader, sounding board, and tireless promoter. Tami has lived these stories with me, and I couldn't have survived without her. She is, and always will be, my sister of the heart!

Likewise, Doug Northup has been instrumental in bringing this book to publication. When Tami shared my concerns and frustrations over the publishing process, Doug immediately volunteered to help, and what a tremendous help he has been. He brought his wealth of computer skills and extensive IT project management experience to the table. When he got on board, the project got going! It is by no means an overstatement to say that this book would still be locked away in my computer without Doug's energy and enthusiasm. My Northup House Publishing Team brought this book to press, and I am forever grateful! Tami and Doug, My heartfelt gratitude for a job well done!

I could not be more thrilled to have the astounding creativity, artistry, and design skills of Linsey Gray Puckett at Linsey Gray Creative on display in my book. Linsey's spectacular cover design and exquisite artwork simply left me awestruck! Linsey's artistic talents and web design skills are also showcased on my blog site, Faith Beyond Sight, which she cleverly designed for me several years ago. Not only did she make both my book and blog site look beautiful, but she also mentored me on the independent publishing process. Linsey, I am so incredibly proud and appreciative of your work. Thank you for being part of this project!

Special thanks to my good friend William Reinhart for the use of his beautiful photograph that graces my cover. Bill's amazing photographs of our joint travel adventures cover the walls of my home, and now, one of his signature photos covers my book! It is so incredibly special to have my long-time friends of 36 years as part of this project that is so dear to my heart. Thanks Bill and Susan!

To my fellow writers at the Burlington Writers Club, I extend my deep appreciation for their patient instruction, confidence-boosting enthusiasm, and wonderful critiques. Special thanks to Elizabeth Solazzo, Jan Sady, and Doris Caruso for their faithful mentorship throughout my writing and publishing journey. My sincere thanks goes to Mary Turner who provided developmental editing in the early stages of the book. Mary employed her creative playwright genius to help me re-organize my stories to produce the best effect and engage the reader. Thank you all!

To my reviewers, let me take a moment to sing your praises! You were incredible! You graciously donated your valuable time and energy to review and proofread my work, helping me catch those last-minute mistakes. You pointed out missing words, verb tense errors, inappropriate capitalizations, and spots for an extra comma or two. I quickly learned that I am hyphen-challenged, and clearly need some remedial work on their proper use! Thank you all for your thorough reviews and wonderful suggestions! A big bear hug of thanks goes out to: Becky Scarlett, Carolyn Stuart, Mary Welch, Kim Fulkerson, Chris Fulkerson, MJ Wilkerson, and Camilla Isley. Special thanks to Janice Shoffner and Susan Brink for their grammar coaching and English-teacher expertise.

I must mention my dear friend Susan Liles who lovingly read all my stories and never failed to murmur in her sweet, Southern drawl, "Oh, Anita, I just love this!" Susan was always my faithful cheerleader, continually urging me on, clapping enthusiastically as I met each milestone of the publishing process. She is not here to hold the finished book in her hands, but I know she is looking down from heaven with a broad smile on her radiant face, her whispered words reaching my ears, "Oh, Anita, I just love this!"

My loving family has supported me all my life in anything I chose to pursue, and my foray into creative writing has been no exception. They read my blog posts and brag on my stories. Their unfailing support means the world to me and has built my confidence as a writer. I want to especially thank my aunt Sandra and uncle Tom. From the very beginning of my writing journey, they began asking, "When are you gonna write a book?" They have always been "my balcony people," and I can hear them sending up their wild applause all the way from Texas!

Finally, I must thank all my friends and neighbors, my church family, my nursing colleagues, and especially, my girlfriends. This community of supportive people has seen me through the joys and struggles of life. There are so many more stories I could have written about all the good people who have touched my life, but the book would be too long, and you would have grown weary of reading! Words cannot adequately convey the depth of gratitude I feel for all of you. Thank you!

Thank you for reading! I hope that this book has been a source of encouragement for you as you face the countless losses inherent in this life. To those of you who are struggling with vision loss, I pray my words have bolstered your courage and renewed your hope. Sorrow may stay for a season, but joy is still within your reach, just waiting for you to grasp. As a wise woman once encouraged me, let

Acknowledgements

me encourage you. "Keep on walking by faith, keep on walking by faith!"

Blessings,
Anita

Made in the USA
Middletown, DE
30 April 2023

29751335R20235